Natural Language Processing

Natural Language Processing

Edited by:

Zoran Gacovski

ARCLER
PRESS

www.arclerpress.com

Natural Language Processing

Zoran Gacovski

Arcler Press
224 Shoreacres Road
Burlington, ON L7L 2H2
Canada
www.arclerpress.com
Email: orders@arclereducation.com

ISBN: 978-1-77407-776-4 (Hardcover)

DECLARATION

Some content or chapters in this book are open access copyright free published research work, which is published under Creative Commons License and are indicated with the citation. We are thankful to the publishers and authors of the content and chapters as without them this book wouldn't have been possible.

ABOUT THE EDITOR

Dr. Zoran Gacovski has earned his PhD degree at Faculty of Electrical engineering, Skopje. His research interests include Intelligent systems and Software engineering, fuzzy systems, graphical models (Petri, Neural and Bayesian networks), and IT security. He has published over 50 journal and conference papers, and he has been reviewer of renowned Journals. Currently, he is a professor in Computer Engineering at European University, Skopje, Macedonia.

TABLE OF CONTENTS

List of Contributors .... *xvii*

List of Abbreviations .... *xxii*

Preface .... *xxv*

Section 1 Natural Language Processing in IT and web systems

Chapter 1 Semantic Analysis of Natural Language Queries for an Object Oriented Database 3

Abstract 3

Introduction 4

Natural Language Database 6

Query Semantic Validation 10

Example Of Query's Validation 14

Experimental Results 15

Conclusions 15

References 16

Chapter 2 Communication Mediated through Natural Language Generation in Big Data Environments: The Case of Nomao 19

Abstract 19

Introduction 20

Research issues 21

Theoretical and methodological framework 28

Data, equipment and method 37

Results 39

Conclusions 44

References 45

Chapter 3 Web Semantic and Ontology 51

Abstract 51

What Do We Represent In An Ontology? 52
The Web Ontology Language Owl 53
Ontology Language Processors 58
Conclusion 60
References 61

Chapter 4 Towards Understanding Creative Language in Tweets 63
Abstract 63
Introduction 64
Task Description 65
Model Description 67
Experiments and Results 70
Results Analysis 73
Conclusions 75
Conflicts Of Interest 76
References 77

Section 2 Natural Language Processing in IT and Web Systems

Chapter 5 Resolving Topic-Focus Ambiguities in Natural Language 83
Introduction 83
Russell vs. Strawson On Definite Descriptions 86
Foundations of Til 89
Definite Descriptions: Strawsonian Or Russellian? 97
Topic-Focus Ambivalence In General 104
Conclusion 113
Acknowledgments 114
References 115

Chapter 6 Semantic Interoperability in E-Health for Improved Healthcare 117
Introduction 117
Semantic Electronic Medical Record (SEMR) System as SAAS Service Model 126
Conclusion 152
Acknowledgments 153
References 154

Chapter 7 **CCMF, Computational Context Modeling Framework – An Ontological Approach to Develop Context-Aware Web Applications... 159**
Introduction ... 159
Related Works ... 161
Case Studies ... 169
Conclusion and Future Work ... 179
References ... 181

Chapter 8 **Three Types of Episodic Associations for the Semantic/ Syntactic/Episodic Model of Language Prospective in Applications to the Statistical Translation ... 185**
Abstract ... 185
Introduction ... 186
The Brief Semantic/Syntactic/Episodic Model Of Language ... 187
Three Principles For Machine Translation Derived From The Semantic/Syntactic/Episodic Neurolinguistics ... 189
Behavioral Classification Of Living/Natural Words ... 190
Sentential/Paragraphic Categorization ... 193
Collection Of Frequent Word-Pairs ... 194
Word Episodic Symbolization For Computer Applications ... 194
Discussions ... 196
Conclusion ... 196
Highlights ... 197
Conflict Of Interest ... 197
Acknowledgments ... 197
References ... 198

Section 3 Mathematical Algorithms and Natural Language

Chapter 9 **Language and Mathematics: Bridging between Natural Language and Mathematical Language in Solving Problems in Mathematics ... 203**
Abstract ... 203
Natural Language And Mathematical Language ... 204
Differences Between Natural Language And Mathematical Language ... 205
Translating From Natural Language To Mathematical Language In Mathematical Word Problems ... 206
Towards Bridging Between Natural Language And Mathematical Language ... 211

Instruction Model For The Solution Of Mathematical Word Problems 213
Application Of The Teaching And Learning Model 219
Conclusion 225
References 227

Chapter 10 Spanish Language Grammatical Context—Acknowledging Specific Language Characteristics 231
Abstract 231
Introduction 232
Learning Language Retention 233
Grammar Patterns-Nouns Object/Thing/Place 234
Grammar Patterns-Singular/Plural-Nouns 236
Grammar Patterns-Definite And Indefinite Articles 236
Grammar Patterns-Adjectives 237
Adjectives-Outstanding-Note 238
Grammar Patterns-Agreement And Words-Order 238
Communication-Insights 239
Methodology-Schemes 242
Communicative Competence Approach 243
Objective Of The Research 244
Results And Discussion 244
Conclusion 245
Acknowledgements 246
Funding 246
Conflicts Of Interest 246
References 247
Additional Biography 247

Chapter 11 A Shallow Parsing Approach to Natural Language Queries of a Database 249
Abstract 249
Introduction 250
Football Events Data 251
Proposed Configuration 253
Conversion Steps 258
Training The Model 259

Evaluation 260
Conclusions 264
Appendix A 266
Appendix B 267
References 270

Chapter 12 A Comparative Study to Understanding about Poetics Based on Natural Language Processing 273
Abstract 273
Introduction 274
Materials And Method 275
Results 278
Discussion 280
Conclusion 282
References 283

Chapter 13 Computers And Language Learning 285
Abstract 286
Introduction 286
LISP 288
Recovering From Blind Alleys 292
Assessment 292
Conclusion 298
References 299

Section 4 Natural Language Processing in Mobile Computing

Chapter 14 Automatic Approach of Sentiment Lexicon Generation for Mobile Shopping Reviews 303
Abstract 303
Introduction 304
Related Work 306
Methods 309
Experiments 317
Conclusions 326
Data Availability 326
Conflicts Of Interest 326

Acknowledgments 326
References 327

Chapter 15 Using Sentence-Level Neural Network Models for Multiple-Choice Reading Comprehension Tasks........ 331
Abstract 331
Introduction 332
Chinese Reading Comprehension Datasets 334
Related Work 335
Sentence-Level Neural Network Reader 337
Experiments 339
Conclusion 344
Data Availability 345
Conflicts Of Interest 345
Acknowledgments 345
References 346

Chapter 16 A Bibliometric Review of Natural Language Processing Empowered Mobile Computing 349
Abstract 350
Introduction 350
Methods And Materials 353
Results 360
Discussions 376
Conclusions 380
Disclosure 380
Acknowledgments 380
References 381

Chapter 17 A Mobile-Based Question-Answering and Early Warning System for Assisting Diabetes Management 387
Abstract 387
Introduction 388
Related Work 390
Methods And Materials 393
Results 401

Conclusions.. 407
References.. 409

Chapter 18 Research on New English Mobile Teaching Mode under the Impact of Mobile Internet Age......... 415
Abstract.. 415
Introduction.. 416
Overview Of Mobile Learning.. 416
New English Teaching Mode Under The Background Of Mobile Internet.. 419
The Development Trend Of Mobile Learning In Future Education.......... 422
Conclusion.. 423
References.. 424

Index.. 427

LIST OF CONTRIBUTORS

Bentamar Hemerelain
Oran University, Wilaya of Oran, Algeria

Hafida Belbachir
University of Science and Technologie of Oran (USTO), Wilaya of Oran, Algeria

Jean-Sébastien Vayre
CERTOP (UMR-5044), University of Toulouse Jean Jaurès, Toulouse, France

Estelle Delpech
Human Factors, Airbus, Blagnac, France

Aude Dufresne
LRCM, University of Montréal, Montréal, Québec

Céline Lemercier
CLLE (UMR-5263), University of Toulouse Jean Jaurès, Toulouse, France

Elodie Marie Gontier
Professor of French and History, Paris, France

Linrui Zhang
Lymba Corporation, Richardson, TX, USA

Yisheng Zhou
Lymba Corporation, Richardson, TX, USA

Yang Yu
Lymba Corporation, Richardson, TX, USA

Dan Moldovan
Lymba Corporation, Richardson, TX, USA

Marie Duzi
VŠB-Technical University of Ostrava

Saman Iftikhar
School of Electrical Engineering and Computer Sciences National University of Sciences and Technology

Wajahat Ali Khan
School of Electrical Engineering and Computer Sciences National University of Sciences and Technology

Farooq Ahmad
School of Electrical Engineering and Computer Sciences National University of Sciences and Technology

Kiran Fatima
Department of Computer Sciences National University of Computer and Emerging Sciences, Pakistan

Luis Paulo Carvalho
UNIFACS-University of Salvador/IRT-InstitutoRecôncavo de Tecnologia

Paulo Caetano da Silva
UNIFACS-University of Salvador Brazil

Zi-JianCai
CaiFortune Consulting, Suzhou, China

Bat-Sheva Ilany
Beit-Berl College, Israel

Bruria Margolin
Levinsky College of Education, Israel

Joel Laffita Rivera
Faculty of Applied Communication (FAC), Multimedia University, Selangor, Malaysia

Richard Skeggs
College of Engineering, Design and Physical Sciences, Brunel University, London, UK

Stasha Lauria
College of Engineering, Design and Physical Sciences, Brunel University, London, UK

Lingyi Zhang
Wuxi No. 1 High School, Wuxi, China

Junhui Gao
American and European International Study Center, Wuxi, China

Junia Rocha
Department of Informatics, Federal Institute of Triangulo Mineiro, Patos de Minas, Brazil

Alexsandro Soares
Department of Computer Science, Federal University of Uberlandia, Uberlandia, Brazil

Mauro Honorato
Department of Informatics, Federal Institute of Sao Paulo, Barretos, Brazil

Luciano Lima
Department of Electrical Engineering, Federal University of Uberlandia, Uberlandia, Brazil

Nayara Costa
Department of Electrical Engineering, Federal University of Uberlandia, Uberlandia, Brazil

Elvio Moreira
Department of Education, Federal University of Uberlandia, Uberlandia, Brazil

Eduardo Costa
Department of Electrical Engineering, Federal University of Uberlandia, Uberlandia, Brazil

Jun Feng
College of Computer and Information, Hohai University, Nanjing 211100, China

Cheng Gong
College of Computer and Information, Hohai University, Nanjing 211100, China

Xiaodong Li
College of Computer and Information, Hohai University, Nanjing 211100, China

Raymond Y. K. Lau
Department of Information Systems, City University of Hong Kong, Hong Kong

Yuanlong Wang
School of Computer and Information Technology, Shanxi University, Taiyuan 030006, China

Ru Li
School of Computer and Information Technology, Shanxi University, Taiyuan 030006, China
Key Laboratory of Computation Intelligence and Chinese Information Processing of Ministry of Education, Shanxi University, Taiyuan 030006, China

Hu Zhang
School of Computer and Information Technology, Shanxi University, Taiyuan 030006, China

Hongyan Tan
School of Computer and Information Technology, Shanxi University, Taiyuan 030006, China

Qinghua Chai
School of Foreign Languages, Shanxi University, Taiyuan 030006, China

Xieling Chen
College of Economics, Jinan University, Guangzhou, China

Ruoyao Ding
School of Information Science and Technology, Guangdong University of Foreign Studies, Guangzhou, China

Kai Xu
School of Computer Science and Technology, Guangdong University of Technology, Guangzhou, China

Shan Wang
Department of Chinese Language and Literature, University of Macau, Macau SAR, China

Tianyong Hao
School of Computer, South China Normal University, Guangzhou, China

Yi Zhou
Zhongshan School of Medicine, Sun Yat-sen University, Guangzhou, China

Wenxiu Xie
School of Information Science and Technology, Guangdong University of Foreign Studies, Guangzhou, China

Ruoyao Ding
School of Information Science and Technology, Guangdong University of Foreign Studies, Guangzhou, China

Jun Yan
AI Lab, Yidu Cloud (Beijing) Technology Co. Ltd., Beijing, China

Yingying Qu
School of Business, Guangdong University of Foreign Studies, Guangzhou, China

Dan Xu
Faculty of International Studies, Henan Normal University, Xinxiang, China

LIST OF ABBREVIATIONS

BMI	Body Mass Index
CC	Coherence constraint
CR	Coherence rule
CSV	Comma separated value
CSV	Comma separated value
EMR	Electronic Medical Record
FAQs	Frequently Asked Questions
HMD	Hierarchical Message Description
HSSP	Health Services Specification Project
IDF	International Diabetes Federation
JTP	Java Theorem Prover
JVM	Java Virtual Machine
JVM	Java Virtual Machine
MC	Machine reading comprehension
NG	Nominal groups
NLGs	Natural Language Generation systems
NSP	Next Sentence Prediction
OI	Open innovation
OMG	Object Management Group
PHR-	Personal Health Record-
PMI	Point wise mutual information
POS	Part of Speech
RDB	Relational database
RIM	Reference Information Model
RMIM	Refined Message Information Model
SEO	Search Engine Optimization
SERP	Search Engine Results Page
SFM	Service Functional Models

SLA	Second Language Acquisition
SOA	Service Oriented Architecture
SQL	Structured Query Language
SVM	Support vector machine
TFIDF	Term frequency–inverse document frequency
TIL	Transparent Intensional Logic
TREC	Text Retrieval Conference
UMLS	Unified Medical Language System
W3C	World Wide Web Consortium
WHO	World Health Organization
WoS	Web of Science
WSMF	Web Service Modeling Framework
WSMO	Web Service Modeling Ontology

PREFACE

Natural language processing is a technology in its infancy, that triggers many of the artificial intelligence forms we are used to, and its application is expanding. Every day, people utter thousands of words that other people interpret to perform a multitude of activities. Basically, we're talking about the simplest communication, but we're all aware that words have a much deeper meaning. There is always a context that we draw from someone's speech, which means that we pay attention to body language, or what was repeated several times. Natural language processing does not focus on voice change, but draws conclusions according to the contextual patterns.

And this is where natural language processing shows its value. We will give one example to show how powerful it is - when used in a particular situation. When you enter text on your phone, which many of us do every day, you see word suggestions that appear based on what you are currently typing. It is an example of natural language processing in practice. It is such an insignificant procedure that we all take it for granted and for years, however, its significance is much greater. Let's put it all into the business world now.

A company tries to decide how to best advertise to its customers. They could use a Google search engine to find common search terms that the users enter when searching for one of their products. Natural language processing, in this case, allows for rapid aggregation of data into terms that are clearly related to the company's brand, as well as those that are not related. Using unusual terms can allow the company to advertise in a new way.

The first step in processing depends on the application of the system. Voice-based systems such as "Alexa" or "Google Assistant" must translate spoken words into text. This is mainly done with the help of Hidden Markov Models (HMM). HMMs use mathematical models to determine what has been said and to translate the words into text - that can be used by natural language processing systems. To put it simply, HMMs listen to sections of your speech that are 10 or 20 milliseconds long and look for phonemes (smallest units of speech) to compare them with previously recorded speech.

This is followed by an understanding of the language and the context. Each natural language processing system uses slightly different techniques, but in essence all are quite similar. Systems try to break down each word into word types (nouns, verbs, etc.). It happens through a series of coded grammar rules that rely on algorithms - that capture statistical machine learning to determine the context of what you said.

Unless we are considering speech recognition, the system skips the first step and immediately moves to word analysis using algorithms and grammar rules. The end result is the ability to categorize what has been said in many different ways. Depending on the main focus of natural language processing software, the results can be used in different ways.

This edition covers different topics from natural language processing, including natural language processing in IT / web systems, semantics in natural language processing, mathematical algorithms in natural language processing, and natural language in mobile systems.

Section 1 focuses on natural language processing in IT and web systems, describing semantic analysis of natural language queries for an object oriented database; communication mediated through natural language generation in big data environments; web semantic and ontology; and understanding creative language in tweets.

Section 2 focuses on semantics in natural language processing, describing resolving topic-focus ambiguities in natural language; semantic interoperability in e-health for improved healthcare; computational context modeling framework - an ontological approach to develop context-aware web applications; and three types of episodic associations for the semantic/syntactic/episodic model of language prospective in applications to the statistical translation.

Section 3 focuses on mathematical algorithms in natural language processing, describing bridging between natural language and mathematical language in solving problems in mathematics; Spanish language grammatical context—acknowledging specific language characteristics; shallow parsing approach to natural language queries of a database; comparative study to understanding about poetics based on natural language processing; computers and language learning.

Section 4 focuses on natural language in mobile systems, describing automatic approach of sentiment lexicon generation for mobile shopping reviews; sentence-level neural network models for multiple-choice reading comprehension tasks; bibliometric review of natural language processing empowered mobile computing; mobile-based question-answering and early warning system for assisting diabetes management; research on new English mobile teaching mode under the impact of mobile internet age.

SECTION 1
NATURAL LANGUAGE PROCESSING IN IT AND WEB SYSTEMS

CHAPTER

1

Semantic Analysis of Natural Language Queries for an Object Oriented Database

Bentamar Hemerelain[1], Hafida Belbachir[2]

[1]Oran University, Wilaya of Oran, Algeria;

[2]University of Science and Technologie of Oran (USTO), Wilaya of Oran, Algeria.

ABSTRACT

This paper presents the semantic analysis of queries written in natural language (French) and dedicated to the object oriented data bases. The studied queries include one or two nominal groups (NG) articulating around a verb. A NG consists of one or several keywords (application dependent

---

Citation: B. Hemerelain and H. Belbachir, "Semantic Analysis of Natural Language Queries for an Object Oriented Database," Journal of Software Engineering and Applications, Vol. 3 No. 11, 2010, pp. 1047-1053. doi: 10.4236/jsea.2010.311123.

noun or value). Simple semantic filters are defined for identifying these keywords which can be of semantic value: class, simple attribute, composed attribute, key value or not key value. Coherence rules and coherence constraints are introduced, to check the validity of the co-occurrence of two consecutive nouns in complex NG. If a query is constituted of a single NG, no further analysis is required. Otherwise, if a query covers two valid NG, it is a subject of studying the semantic coherence of the verb and both NG which are attached to it.

Keywords: Query, Nominal Group, Natural Language, Object Oriented Data Base, Semantic Validation

INTRODUCTION

On the earliest and most widely studied areas of natural language processing is the development of a Natural language interfaces to databases (NLIDB) [1-7]... A NLIDB allows users to input a query in a natural language such rather than in a formal query language and in conceptual terms particular to their understanding of the database application domain. In most works, the underlying database is assumed to be relational. In our work, we are interested in building a NLI for an object-oriented database (OODB). Unfortunately, the relational model and the object model are fundamentally different. Relational database (RDB) systems are based on twodimensional tables in which each item appears as a row. Relationships among the data are expressed by comparing the values stored in theses tables. The object model is based on the tight integration of code and data, flexible data types, hierarchical relationships among data types, and references [8].

This paper is concerned with the semantic validation of natural language query (NLQ) for an OODB. The natural language considered here is French.

A considerable amount of work has been published on the semantics of NLQ. Works, usually carried out by Computer Scientists, can be classified into two categories: 1) work based on established linguistic theories which are modified and/or extended such as [9-12]; 2) new ad hoc but efficient semantics that are not based on established linguistic theories. Examples are quoted by [2]. Some recent works are [13-15].

Our approach falls into category 2) and is designed on the principle of [13] who introduce the idea of semantically tractable (ST) questions. As their database is in the form of RDB, they define the ST questions as questions where the words correspond to relations (tables), attributes and values. The nature of the OODB introduces some new challenges, beyond these addresses for RDB. In this paper, we deal with the concept of class to model complex data, simple attributes, complex (composite) attributes with classes as their domains, and two special kinds of associations between classes: 1) inheritance which is the most powerful concept of object oriented. It is a mechanism of reusability: the news classes, known as sub-classes inherit attributes of the pre-existing classes, which are referred to as super classes; an inheritance relationship is created between the sub-class and the super-class. 2) reference: since a class C may have a complex attribute with domain C', a reference relationship can be established between C and C'.

Our center of interest is the analysis of NLQ consisting of one or two NGs articulating around a verb. At this step of analysis, we consider the NG constituted of one or several keywords and we ignore the DB independent words (article, relative pronoun,...). A keyword can be an application dependent noun or a value. The former matches a class name, a simple attribute name or a composite attribute name in an OODB.

In a NLQ, the verb is created by the DB administrator. It expresses the link which exists between a class and another class or between a class and one of its attributes. The application dependent nouns and the verbs with their semantic features are stored in a lexicon. This last includes inflection forms of nouns and conjugated forms of verbs. It is also augmented with relevant synonyms. This addition makes it possible to the user to write a query in various natural ways.

Heritage and reference relationships are added to lexicon allowing the safeguarding of the heritage and reference link of the OODB. These Heritage and reference relationships with the lexicon form the natural language database (NLDB).

The semantic analysis of a query first deals with identification of individual keywords in the NGs. It uses some simple semantic filters to determine their semantic value. If the NG is atomic and the single keyword identified, no further analysis is required. On the contrast, it is necessary to verify if the complex NG respects the conceptual constraints of the domain DB. The conceptual constraints mainly refer to inheritance and reference relationships and are function of the semantic value of the keywords and their combination in the NG. If the NLQ is constituted of a single NG, no supplementary treatment is necessary. If the NLQ covered two valid NGs, it is a subject of studying the semantic coherence of the verb and both NGs which are attached to him.

The paper is organized as follows: The Section 2 describes the lexicon and defines the inheritance and reference relationships in a NLDB. The Section 3 is divided into three parts. In the part 1, semantic filters are defined to identify keywords. With the introduction of the semantic coherence constraints of keywords, the part 2 discusses the process of NG's validation. Part 3 concerns the semantic coherence of the verb with its subject and its object. In Section 4, an example of illustration is treated to simulate the tools developed in preceding section. To understand this example and those that are quoted in the text; we give an extract of the database prototype which is used in our experimentation. The results of the experimentation are reported in Section 5. A conclusion is given in Section 6.

NATURAL LANGUAGE DATABASE

The natural language database (NLDB) is a translation of the object oriented database (OODB). The NLDB contains a lexicon and inheritance and reference relationships.

Lexicon

A natural language query consists of two parts: an interrogative particle and a phrase. A phrase is a succession of nominal and verbal groups. A nominal group (NG) in the natural language query (NLQ) consists of one or several meaningful words. The latter can be an application dependent noun, a verb or a value.

Definitions

Application dependent noun

The former matches a class name, a simple attribute or a composite attribute name in an OODB. Each application dependent noun is represented in the OODB as a variable whose name might be meaningful according to the naming conventions but not necessarily the same word in natural language (NL) (e.g. ENS, X). Thus, we generate, for each variable declared in an OODB, a word in NL (NW) (e.g. NW (ENS) →enseignant [teacher]; NW(X) →personne [person]).

Due to this, to each variable declared in the database, corresponds, a word family. It includes all of the inflection forms of the word (masculine singular (ms), masculine plural (mp), feminine singular (fs),…) (e.g. enseignant [teacher] →{enseignant (ms) [teacher], enseignants (mp) [teachers], enseignante (fs) [teacher], enseignantes (fp) [teachers]} and the set of its synonyms. (e.g. enseignant→ {maitre,…} [teacher → {schoolmaster,…}]).

Verb

The verb of the query expresses the link between two classes or a class and one of its attribute. Then, the verb is transitive. To each created verb, corresponds conjugate forms (3rd person of the singular (s), 3rd person of the plural (p)) (e.g. habiter [to live] → {habite (s) [lives], habitant (p) [live]} and the set of its synonyms (e.g. (habiter) → {résider, demeurer,...} [to live → {to reside, to dwell,…}]).

All the nouns and verbs usually depend heavily on the application. They constitute the lexicon. The initial set of synonyms is created with electronic dictionaries such that Wolf and Crisco and then proposed to expert individual who can modify it to reflect the specific senses of the DB application domain. The sibling relation that exists between the words of the same family permits the database requester to use any of them without affecting the meaning of the query. Thus, a family of words is represented by a single term called the stem which can be the first generated word in natural language.

Value

On the other hand, a value in the query is an instance of a simple attribute. It is identified via a dialogue with the database requester. If an attribute is designated by the DB administrator as key then its value is said to be key and non-key otherwise. A key value can specify a class. For example, in the query "what is the salary of Linda", Linda specifies the class "Employee" then it is a key value. However, in the query "what is the name of the module which has the coefficient 4", the value '4' is not key value because it specifies no class.

Description

Application dependent noun

Depending on the relation of the word to the database being handled, an application dependent noun is described, in the lexicon, by its stem and its semantic value which can be 'C' if it is about a class, 'SA' of a simple attribute or 'CA' of a composite attribute. In the description of a simple attribute, we add the stem of the class containing it and in the case of a composite attribute, the stem of the referenced class by the composite attribute. For example, the composite attribute 'matières' [matters] is described by its stem 'matière' [matter], its semantic value 'AC' and the stem of its referenced class ‘module’ [module].

Verb

A verb is described by its subject which is the class that contains it and its object which is either a declared attribute in the subject class or a referenced class by a composite attribute of the subject class. It is formally described by its stem, the stem of the subject entity and the stem of the object entity. For example, the verb ‘habiter’ [to live] is described by its stem ‘habiter’ [to live], the stem of the subject entity ‘personne’ [person] and the stem of the object entity ‘ville’ [town].

Inheritance Relationship

The inheritance relationship in the NLDB is an extension of the traditional inheritance relationship ‘HERITE’ in an OODB and is given by the relation Herite*. It allows handling the NLQ on a given class using the properties of the class itself or those of its super-classes and subclasses.

The extended inheritance relationship allows moving in both directions up and down the hierarchy of the classes. The direct inheritance relationship ‘herite’ is defined as follows:

Let CLASSE be classes stems of a NLDB.

herite: CLASSExCLASSE→{0,1}

(x,y) →herite (x,y)

{

herite (x, y): = 1 if NW^{-1} (x) HERITE NW^{-1} (y)/* NW(v) = x/‘v’ is a variable in the OODB and ‘x’ is the word corresponding in natural language */

herite (x, y):= 0 otherwise;

}

The relation Herite* is defined as follows:

Herite*: CLASSExCLASSE→{0,1}

(x,y) →Herite* (x,y)

{

Herite*: = 1

if (x = y) or (x ≠ y and (herite (x, y)

orherite (y, x))

or (x ≠ y and ∃ C1, C2,... Cn∈ CLASSE/
herite (x, C1)
and (∀i∈ [1, n–1] herite (Ci, Ci+1))
andherite (Cn, y)
or (x ≠ y and ∃ C1, C2,... et Cn∈ CLASSE/
herite (y, Cn) and (∀i∈ [1, n–1] herite (Ci+1, Ci)
andherite (C1, x))
Herite*: = 0 otherwise;
}

Reference Relationship

Let M1 be a class, M2 its composite attribute, M3 the referenced class and R1,2 a relation connecting M1 and M2.

The relation $R_{1,2}$ is also applicable between the class of definition M1 and the referenced class M3. It represents a direct reference link between these two classes. This relation is called the reference relationship in a NLDB. It is an extension of the traditional reference relationship in an OODB. It allows generating the verbs of the NLDB. We notice that the existence of a reference relationship, does not base itself on a criterion according to these links, but that it is random, thus the solutions in that case relaying on a linguistic analysis which indicates for all the roads of (direct) reference, the existence or the nonexistence of a verb of relation. They translate direct reference links between the classes. In that case, the existence of the verb can create a indirect reference link (e.g. travailler (chercheur, projet) [to work (searcher, project)] and appartenir (projet, laboratoire) [to belong (project, Laboratory)] ⇒travailler (chercheur, laboratoire) [to work (searcher, Laboratory)]).

NOTE. - The deducted relations can be calculated by combining the reference links and the links of inheritance (e.g. assurer (enseignant, module) [to ensure (teacher, module)] and Herite* (enseignant, personne) [Herite* (teacher, person)] ⇒ assurer (personne, module)).

Let Ref be an extension of the defined reference relationship previously. This relation is defined as follows:

Let 'ac' be a composite attribute.

Ref: CLASSExCLASSE→{0,1}

(x, y) → Ref (x, y)

{

Ref (x, y): = 1 if/* exists 'ac'/'x' is the class where 'ac' is defined or its sub or super-class and the class 'y' is the domain of 'ac' or a indirect reference link between the classes 'x' and 'y' */

Ref (x, y): = 0 else;

}

QUERY SEMANTIC VALIDATION

A NLQ consists of one or two NGs articulating around a verb. We consider a NG constituted by one or several keywords. A keyword is an application dependent noun or a value. So, the process of the validation of the query consists in:

- keyword's identification in the NG; In the case of a NG formed by an identified single keyword, no supplementary treatment is necessary since only one component is used: the NG is valid. If the NG is constituted by more than a keyword and that one of them is not identified, the NG is considered as erroneous. Should the opposite occur, it is necessary to carry out the NG's semantic validation.
- If the query is constituted by a valid NG, no furtheranalysis is required. If the query covered two valid NGs with an identified verb, it is a subject of studying the semantic coherence of the verb with its arguments.

Keyword's Identification

The first step of the analysis is to determine if a word of the query is a keyword. For this, we define a simple semantic filter denoted SF as the set of triplets {(*, *, ω)} associated with the semantic value ω. The first star in the triplet represents the lexical information while the second designates the syntactic information associated with the word.

For an application dependent noun, a semantic filter is defined by:

SF_N<ω> = {(*, Noun, ω)/ω∈ {C (class), SA (simple attribute), CA (composite attribute)}} where the star represents the word's stem.

For instance, to represent the word 'students' that matches the class 'Student'; we would have the semantic filter SF_N including the triplet (student, Noun, C).

Likewise, the semantic filter, for a value, has the same structure except that the category ω takes values from the set:

ω = {VK (Value_as_Key), VNK (Value_None_Key)} and the tagging information is the value in the first case, hence SFV = {(*, value, ω)}. For The number '4' in the NG "coefficient 4", we have the triplet (4, value, VNK).

From the query "what is the salary of the teacher Linda", salary $\in SF_N<SA>$, teacher $\in SF_N<C>$ and Linda $\in SF_V<VK>$ then all words are semantically correct.

The process of identification of a keyword 'mi' consists mainly in determining the corresponding simple semantic filter. It is defined by the following function: Function Ident (mi): boolean

{

ident: = 1 if\exist\ω∈{C, SA, CA, VK, VNK}/

(mi, *, *) $\in SF_N<\omega> \cup SF_V<\omega>$

ident:= 0 otherwise;

}

NG's Semantic Validation

In the case of a NG formed by several identified keywords, it is necessary to verify if the complex NG respects the conceptual constraints (semantic coherence constraints) of the domain database which amounts to associate semantic relations between every two consecutive keywords in the NG. These relations mainly refer to inheritance or reference relationships. They are based on the semantic values of the keywords and their combination in the NG.

For example, the NG 'salaire de l'enseignant' [salary of the teacher] is valid because the class 'enseignant' uses the attribute 'salaire' of its super class 'employé' [employee]. Thus, at the combination 'simple attributeclass' (SA-C), we must have an inheritance relationship between the class that contains the attribute (i.e. 'employé') and the specified class in the NG (i.e. 'enseignant'). Before giving the coherence constraints, we need to introduce some notations and notions:

- A part of a NG constituted by the succession of two keywords x and y is noted x – y.
- if (m, *, *) $\in FS_X$ (w)/w ∈ {SA, C, CA, VK, VNK} and x ∈ {N, V}, the keyword 'm' is respectively noted SA', C', CA', VK', VNK'.

- A class can be manipulated through its name, the name of the composite attribute which references it or a key value which is the value of its key attribute (e.g. 'module', 'matter' and 'Compilation' specify the same class 'module'). For that, 'class' will indicate these three information.
- In what follows we take:

X_i: = Classe (m_i) if m_i = C'

X_i: = Class-ref (m_i) if m_i = CA'

X_i: = Class (Attrib (m_i)) and

Y_i: = Attrib (m_i)

if $m_i \in$ {SA', VK', VNK'}

where Classe is a function which returns, for a class, thestem of this one and for a simple attribute that of the class where it is defined. Attrib gets, for a simple attribute or for a value, the stem of this attribute and Class-ref, for a composite attribute, the stem of its referenced class.

Semantic Coherence Constraints

The combination (COMB) of two keywords according to their semantic value is governed by a set of rules called coherence rules (CR). Based on the patterns of combination, we have formulated coherence constraints (CC) that express the semantic relation between these words.

CR_1: a class can be specified by either its super class or subclass. A class indicated by a key value cannot be specified by a class indicated by another key value. A key value can specify at most one class. The semantic relation is an inheritance relationship.

COMB1: $m_i \in$ {C', CA', VK'} and $m_{i+1} \in$ {C', CA', VK'}
/if m_i = VK' then $m_{i+1} \neq$ VK'
CC_1 ($m_i - m_{i+1}$): **Herite* (X_i, X_{i+1})**

CR_2: a simple attribute can be specified by its value. The attribute corresponding to the value must be identical to the specified attribute in the query and their class respective too.

COMB2: $m_i \in$ {SA'} and $m_{i+1} \in$ { VK', VNK'} or $m_i \in$ {VK', VNK'} and $m_{i+1} \in$ {SA'},
CC_2 ($m_i - m_{i+1}$): $\mathbf{Y_i = Y_{i+1}; X_i = X_{i+1}}$

CR_3: a simple attribute of a class can be used by its class, its super-classes or sub-classes. The semantic relation is an inheritance relationship.

COMB3: $m_i \in$ {C', CA', VK'} and $m_{i+1} \in$ {SA'} or $m_i \in$ {SA'} and $m_{i+1} \in$ {C', CA', VK'},
CC_3 ($m_i - m_{i+1}$): **Herite* (X_i, X_{i+1})**

CR_4: a class is associated with another class if there exits a reference link between these classes. The semantic relation is a reference relationship.

COMB4: $m_i \in$ {C', CA', VK'} and $m_{i+1} \in$ {C', CA', VK'},
CC_4 ($m_i - m_{i+1}$): **Ref (X_i, X_{i+1})**

Algorithm of NG Validation The operation of validation of a NG constituted by several identified keywords m_1-m_2-...-m_n consists in finding a pattern of the combination for every two consecutive words mi and mi+1 for i∈[1, n–1] and verifying the correspondent semantic relation CC_j ($m_i - m_{i+1}$).

The algorithm of validation is defined as follows:

```
{
i: = 1;
if i = n then
/ * NG ≡ 1 keyword */
if Ident (mi) then 'valid NG' else 'Erroneous NG'
else
/* NG ≡ several keywords */
while (i < n ∧ Ident (mi) ∧ Ident (mi+1) ∧∃ j ∈ [1,4]/
CCj (mi – mi+1)) do
i: = i + 1; end;
if i = n then 'valid NG' else 'Erroneous NG'
}
```

Semantic Coherence of the Verb with

Its Arguments In the lexicon, a verb is described with its real subject (RS) and its real object (RO). In a query, the subject of a verb is one of keywords of the subject NG which really carries out the action. It is noted (QS). The object is generally the first keyword of object NG which undergoes the action. It is noted (QO). A verb is compatible with its subject NG (QS) and its complement (QO) if:

- QS is identical to RS or it is its super or sub class because the subject is always a class;
  1) The object is a class, then QO must be identical to QS or be its super or sub class;
  2) The object is an attribute (or a value of an attribute) then the attribute QO must be identical to QS.

EXAMPLE OF QUERY'S VALIDATION

To understand the following example and the examples of illustration quoted in the text, we give an extract of a NLDB on the University of Oran, in French and its equivalent in English. The adopted syntax is the following one:

<class> ({<mother class>}, <attribute$_1$>, <attribute$_2$>,...
<attribute$_n$> , verb$_1$, verb$_2$,...)
Personne ({}, nom, ville, habiter)
Employé ({Personne}, salaire)
Enseignant ({Employé}, matière: Module)
Chercheur ({Enseignant}, projet: Projet)
Module ({}, nom, coefficient)
Projet ({}, laboratoire: laboratoire)
Laboratoire ({} ...)

Person ({}, name, town, to live)
Employee ({Person}, salary)
Teacher ({Employee}, matter: Module)
Searcher ({Teacher}, project: Project)
Module ({}, name, coefficient)
Project ({}, laboratory: laboratory)
Laboratory({}...)

Example: 'Donner le salaire des enseignants de Compilation qui habitent Oran'

[Give the salary of teachers of Compilation who live in Oran]

Verb = habiter;
NG1 = $m_1 - m_2 - m_3$ = noms – enseignants – Compilation;
$m_1 \in SF_N<SA>$, $m_2 \in SF_N<C>$, $m_3 \in SF_V<VK>$,
$m_1 - m_2 = COMB_3$;
CC_3 = Herite* (Classe (Attrib (nom)), Classe (enseignants))
= Hérite* (employée, enseignant): = true;
$m_2 - m_3 = COMB_4$ = Ref (Classe (enseignants), Classe (Attrib (Compilation))) = Ref (enseignant, module): = true;
NG2 = Oran; $m \in SF_V<VNK>$,

In the lexicon, we have: habiter (personne, ville) and in the query habiter (enseignant, Oran);

Herite* (personne, enseignant): = true, Attrib (Oran) = ville.

The keywords are identified, the CCj between them validated and the verb is coherent with its arguments, and then the query is valid.

EXPERIMENTAL RESULTS

To evaluate the performance of the system, we have tested our system on 120 significant queries collected from the students of computer department of university Oran. 7 queries were disregarded because they did not cover the BD application domain. Of the remaining queries, 102 queries were correctly analyzed (i.e. success rate 90, 26%). The errors were mainly due to unregistered keywords in the lexicon. Our lexicon contains nouns, verbs and their various synonyms that typically are used in a particular domain. Their semi-automatic generation involves inevitably false results. A better solution for the interface is the integration of a learning system to enrich the lexicon.

CONCLUSIONS

Our work proposes a method of query's validation for OODB. Define a query key information to be analyzed semantically: its structure from one part and its sense from another part, express the link which connects them and the method of handling them were the strong problems which we tried to solve. There is not dependency between our system and the DB application domain. When changing one DB to another, the only change occurs at the lexicon. Nevertheless, the study present limits relating to selected requests model (a request includes only one subject, only one complement and only one verb). These limits carried out knowingly, into a qualitative aim, make that, the developed tools remain incomplete but can be wide to more complex queries. Also note that, the presented information is necessary in NLDB, to treat the second aspect of the semantics which is the translation of the NLQ to formal language query such as OQL [16].

REFERENCES

1. A.Copestake and K. S. Jones, "Natural Language Interfaces to Databases," The Knowledge Engineering Review, Vol. 5, No. 4, 1989, pp. 225-249.
2. I. Androutsopoulos, G. Ritchie and P. Thanisch, "Natural Language Interfaces to Databases – An Introduction," Journal of Language Engineering, Vol. 1, No. 1, 1995, pp. 29-81.
3. J. Chae and S. Lee, "Natural Language Query Processing in Korean Interface for Object-Oriented Databases," Proceedings of First International Workshop on Applications of Natural Language to Databases (NLDB'95), Versailles, 1995, pp.81-94.
4. P. Reis, J. Matias and N. Mamede, "Edite – A Natural Language Interface to Databases: A New Dimension for an Old Approach," Proceedings of the Fourth International Conference on Information and Communication Technology in Tourism (ENTER'97), Edinburgh, 1997.
5. Y. Chandra and R. Mihalcea, "Natural Language Interfaces to Databases," Thesis (M. S.), University of North Texas, Denton, 2006.
6. M. Owda, Z. Bandar and K. Crockett, "ConversationBased Natural Language Interface to Relational Databases," International Conference on Web Intelligence/IAT Workshops, 2007, pp. 363-367.
7. M. Minock, P. Olofsson and A. N. Aslund, "Towards Building Robust Natural Language Interfaces to Databases," Proceedings of the 13th International Conference on Natural Language and Information Systems, Berlin, 2008, pp 187-198.
8. J. Robie and D. Bartels, "A Comparison between Relational and Object Oriented Databases for Object Oriented Application Development," POET Software Corporation 800-950-8845, 1994.
9. J. Clifford and D. S. Warren, "Formal Semantics for Time in Databases," ACM Transactions on Database Systems, Vol. 8, No. 2, June 1983, pp. 215-254.
10. R. A. Frost and P. Boulos, "An Efficient Compositional Semantics for Natural Language Database Queries with Arbitrarily-Nested Quantification and Negation," Lecture Notes in Computer Science, Vol. 2338, 2002, pp. 252-267.
11. H. D. Lee and J. C. Park, "Interpretation of Natural Language Queries for Relational Database Access with Combinatory Categorial

Grammar," International Journal of Computer Processing of Oriental Languages, Vol. 15, No. 3, 2002, pp. 281-304.

12. R. A. Frost and R. J. Fortier, "An Efficient Denotational Semantics for Natural Language Database Queries," Natural Language Processing and Information Systems, Vol. 4592, 2007, pp. 12-24.
13. A. M. Popescu, O. Etzioni and H. Kautz, "Towards a Theory of Natural Language Interfaces to Databases," Proceedings of the 8th International Conference on Intelligent User Interfaces, Miami, 2003, pp. 149-157.
14. J. Little, M. Ga, T. Ozyer and R. Alhajj, "Query Builder: A Natural Language Interface for Structured Databases," Lecture Notes in Computer Science, Vol. 3280, 2004, pp. 470-479.
15. V. Boonjing and C. Hsu, "A New Feasible Natural Language Query Method," International Journal on AI Tools, Vol. 15, No. 2, 2006, pp. 323-330.
16. G. G. R. Cattel, "ODMG-93 Standard des Bases de DonnéesObjet,"Addison-Wesley, Boston, 1995.

CHAPTER 2

Communication Mediated through Natural Language Generation in Big Data Environments: The Case of Nomao

Jean-Sébastien Vayre[1], Estelle Delpech[2], Aude Dufresne[3], Céline Lemercier[4]

[1]CERTOP (UMR-5044), University of Toulouse Jean Jaurès, Toulouse, France

[2]Human Factors, Airbus, Blagnac, France

[3]LRCM, University of Montréal, Montréal, Québec

[4]CLLE (UMR-5263), University of Toulouse Jean Jaurès, Toulouse, France

ABSTRACT

Along with the development of big data, various Natural Language Generation systems (NLGs) have recently been developed by different

Citation: Vayre, J. ,Delpech, E. , Dufresne, A. and Lemercier, C. (2017), "Communication Mediated through Natural Language Generation in Big Data Environments: The Case of Nomao". *Journal of Computer and Communications*, **5**, 125-148. doi: 10.4236/jcc.2017.56008.

companies. The aim of this paper is to propose a better understanding of how these systems are designed and used. We propose to study in details one of them which is the NLGs developed by the company Nomao. First, we show the development of this NLGs underlies strong economic stakes since the business model of Nomao partly depends on it. Then, thanks to an eye movement analysis conducted with 28 participants, we show that the texts generated by Nomao's NLGs contain syntactic and semantic structures that are easy to read but lack socio-semantic coherence which would improve their understanding. From a scientific perspective, our research results highlight the importance of socio-semantic coherence in text-based communication produced by NLGs.

Keywords: Big Data, Natural Language Generation, Socio-Semantic Coherence, Cognitive Load, Reading, Eye Tracking

INTRODUCTION

Capitalism as we know it today is often referred to as cognitive based [1] . Thus knowledge about information management and mass communication brings considerable advantages to the actors in different spheres of our society. Consequently, Natural Language Generation (NLG) is a hot topic in today's big data movement. Indeed, NLG is a way to facilitate access to big data by transforming it into a human-readable and semantically adequate form. Once in the form of a text, big data have an improved socio-economic value.

For instance, NLG is increasingly used in the field of data-journalism [2] , i.e. the case of "robot journalists" like Quakebot for the Los Angeles Times, Wordsmith for the Associated Press, Quill for the US business magazine Forbes or Data 2 Content for the French newspaper Le Monde. In addition, some companies like Yseop in France offer decision support systems that are based on NLG and automatically generate customized reports for their customers.

Thus, in the light of these recent developments in the field of mass communication, it seemed appropriate to research how texts can be automatically generated and how these texts are read and understood by end-users. To serve this goal, we propose in this paper to study the case of the Natural Language Generation system (NLGs) developed by the company Nomao.

Nomao has edited since 2007 an online directory that lists local businesses in France. This directory exists in the form of a mobile and a web application. Nomao's NLGs plays a major role in the production of the text content of this directory. Indeed, the role of the NLGs is to transform the raw data collected by Nomao about businesses into human readable texts. This paper addresses several innovative issues in the field of humanities: how does Nomao's NLGs work? What are the socio-economic stakes that have guided its development? How do end-users read and understand the texts generated by the system?

In the first section, we describe the functioning of Nomao's NLGs and identify related economic stakes. We show that Nomao's NLGs is powerful. Yet, it has never been evaluated from a user perspective (Section 1). Therefore, we propose in Section 2 a theoretical and methodological framework for evaluating the quality of Nomao's texts from a user perspective. In Section 3, we describe the experimental setup, which was deployed to conduct this evaluation. In Section 4, we show that while Nomao's texts contain easy-to-read syntactic and semantic structures, they still lack socio-semantic coherence which could improve their understanding. We conclude this paper by underlying the fact that, from a scientific perspective, our research results underline the importance of socio- semantic coherence in text-based communication produced by NLGs.

RESEARCH ISSUES

As stated above, Nomao's NLGs is of primary importance in the functioning of Nomao's application. Nomao's NLGs selects, combines and regenerates in the form of a text the data about local businesses that have been previously collected by Nomao. Thus, Nomao's NLGs generates a large part of the textual content that is present in Nomao's directory. Therefore, Nomao's NLGs plays a major role between users and business owners since it implements and release, through a short descriptive text, the representation of the businesses listed in Nomao's directory (cf. Table 2; Text 1).

To better understand the socio-cognitive and technical issue that underlies the evaluation of Nomao's NLGs, we propose to describe its functioning and the business model that influenced its design. Then we present the performance indicators that were used to evaluate the system so far and we will see that these indicators say nothing, from the user perspective, about the quality of the texts produced by this NLGs.

Nomao's Natural Language Generation System (NLGs)

As shown in Figure 1, Nomao's NLGs has been designed in accordance with the typical stages of NLGs [3] . These stages are: macro-planning (content selection followed by document structuring); micro-planning (syntactic planning, lexicalization, aggregation, referring expression generation) and surface realization (morphological adaptation, formatting).

Macro-planning is carried out in two sub-steps. First, content selection consists in selecting pieces of information that are to be conveyed to the end-user and which are relevant with regard to the communicative goals of the text. Second, document structuring consists in organizing the informational entities and establishing the rhetorical structure of the text. This first stage deals with the content of the text.

The goal of micro-planning is to determine how the informational entities selected and organized during macro-planning stage will be expressed in natural language. This second stage is carried out in four sub-steps: syntactic planning, lexicalization, aggregation and the generation of referential expressions. The second stage deals with the form of text.

Surface realization consists in operations that will transform the raw text outputted by microplanninng into the final text. This stage includes several sub- steps: morphological adjustment (eg, generation of inflected forms through gender/number or verb/subject agreements), typographical adjustment (spaces, punctuation) and formatting (bold, caps, underline). This last stage provides the final form of the text.

Macro-Planning

The first sub-step of macro-planning retrieves pieces of information about the businesses that are listed in Nomao's directory. To do this, the NLGs queries dedicated databases.

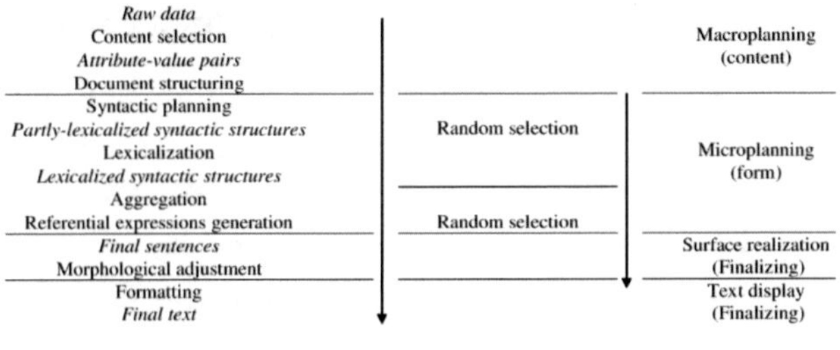

Figure 1. Nomao's NLGs processing.

More precisely, the NLGs was set up by its designers so that it selects the following pieces of information: business identifier (e.g., “22370”), name (e.g., “Chai Saint Sauveur”), street name/number (e.g., “30 rue Bernard Mule”), city (e.g., “Toulouse”), nearby metro stations (e.g., “François Verdier”), nearby businesses (e.g., “category: eating, distance: 50m, name: Afro Resto”; “category: eating, distance 100m, name: Patricia Général Alimentation”), category (e.g., “eating<=”” french=”” cuisine=”” south=”” west”),=”” tags=”” (e.g.,=”” “eating,=”” average=”” price,=”” reservation,=”” with=”” terrace,=”” wine=”” bar”)=”” and=”” terms=”” “terrace,=”” bar,=”” beautiful=”” decor,=”” cb=”” visa=”” mastercard”).=”” these=”” data=”” items=”” correspond=”” to=”” the=”” informational=”” entities=”” that=”” will=”” eventually=”” constitute=”” content=”” be=”” delivered=”” end-users.<=””>

The second sub-step of macro-planning consists in building the rhetorical structure of the text. Nomao NLGs’ designers have identified five types of paragraphs that structure the final text. These paragraphs are:

- the title paragraph which is composed of the name of the business and the name of the city where it is located;
- the introductory paragraph that contains informational units describing the type of business and its location;
- the main paragraph which provides the user with various information about the business (e.g., the atmosphere, accepted payment methods, served dishes and drinks, etc.);
- a paragraph that describes subway stations in the vicinity of the business;
- an “opinion” paragraph that contains informational units about the business e-reputation.

Micro-Planning

As exposed above, the micro-planning stage begins with a syntactic planning sub-step. The NLGs selects a syntactic pattern for each of the informational units selected during macro-planning.

This selection is made randomly among a set of patterns that are predefined and correspond to a specific informational entity. As shown in the example below, each pattern contains information about the syntactic relations underlying the organization of the various elements composing each statement.

It is worth noticing that some of the syntactic patterns can be nested into each other. For example, the pattern dedicated to the payment methods (cf. Figure 2) will be merged with the "ACCEPTED_PAYMENTS" pattern of Figure 3.

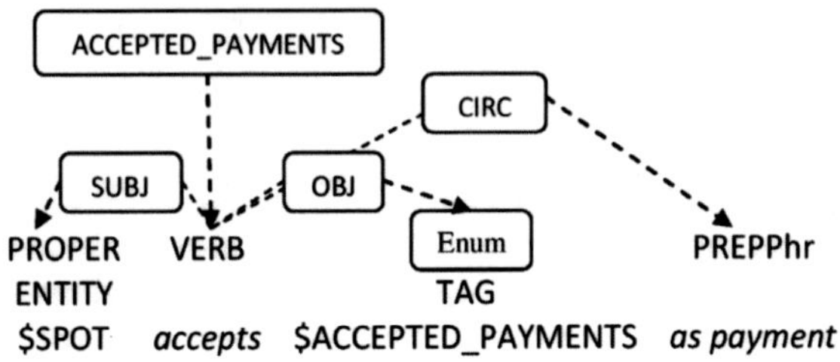

Figure 2. Example 1 syntactic pattern.

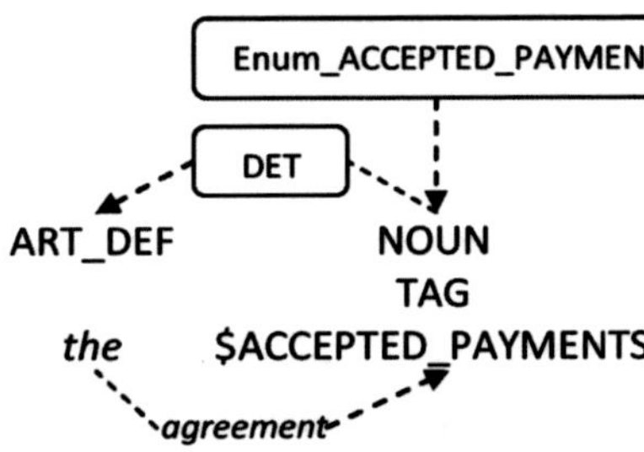

Figure 3. Example 2 syntactic pattern.

The lexicalization sub-step consists in inserting values in place of the variables contained in the syntactic patterns selected during the syntactic planning step. For example, the variables called "$SPOT" and "$ACCEPTED_PAYMENT" (cf. Figure 2) will be respectively replaced by their corresponding values: "restaurant" or "Chai Saint Sauveur" will replace $SPOT and "Credit Card" or "VISA" will replace $ACCEPTED_PAYMENTS.

In addition, morphosyntactic labels like "VERB" and "PREPPhr" will be replaced by corresponding natural language expressions randomly selected from a set of synonyms. The sets of synonyms have been previously defined by an expert linguist during the development of the NLGs. The synonyms were manually collected using the dictionary of the Research Center on Inter-languages Meaning in Context (CRISCO). For example, the verb "enjoy" in the statement "you will enjoy the draught beers of this bar" may be replaced by verbs like "appreciate" or "love".

Each of the values that replace the variables come with morphosyntactic features specifying gender and number (eg, "restaurant, masc: sing," "atmosphere, fem: sing", etc.) in order to carry out grammatical agreement during the morphological adjustment step. As shown below, these morphosyntactic features will be used to generate the inflected form of the articles that agree with these nouns.

As illustrated in Figure 4, the goal of the aggregation step is to avoid generating a cumbersome text by merging repetitive structures (e.g., sentences with identical subjects and verbs).

The referential expressions generation step has a similar goal: it avoids cumbersomeness and redundancy by eliminating the repetition of identical subjects. It replaces repetitive noun phrases by corresponding personal pronouns or referential expressions. For example, the sequence of sentences "Chai Saint Sauveur is a restaurant [...]. Chai Saint Sauveur specializes in [...]. Chai Saint Sauveur offers dishes [...]" becomes: "Chai Saint Sauveur is a restaurant [...]. It specializes in [...]. This restaurant offers [...]."

The referential expressions that replace the initial noun phrase ("Chai Saint-Sauveur") are chosen at random in a set of referential expressions that are semantically adequate to replace the initial noun phrase (e.g., "this restaurant", "this business", "this establishment").

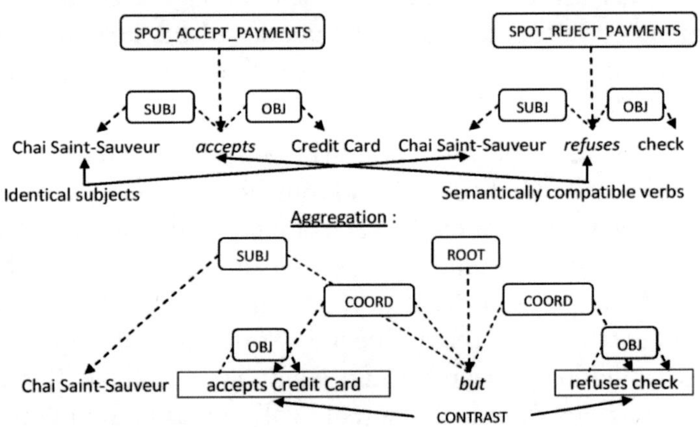

Figure 4. Aggregation example.

Surface Realization

The output of the micro-planning stage is a sequence of lemmas (non-inflected words) which should be morphologically adjusted.

Thus, the role of the surface realization stage is to apply agreement rules and perform surface operations like elisions and crasis so as to generate final word forms. For example, the French sentence "ce bar vous propose de faire une pause autour de un bon bière" becomes "ce bar vous propose de faire une pause autourd'une bonne bière" (where "un" has become "une"—article-noun agreement— and "de" has become "d'"—elision).Typographical adjustments apply classical typographic rules like uppercasing the first letter of each sentence and adding spaces between words. The final text is then ready to be displayed to end-users in the form of a short written description (cf. Table 3; Text 1) located in the web page of the corresponding business in Nomao's online directory.

Design and Evaluation of Nomao's NLGs

Nomao developed these NLGs in order to ensure the sustainability of its business model which consists in putting end-users in contact with businesses through premium rate telephone numbers. The company has not built any user community. Typical end-users land on Nomao's website after having entered a local search query on a general-purpose web search engine (e.g., "restaurant in toulouse" "restaurant Chai saint sauveurtoulouse"). It is thus obvious that the content of Nomao's online directory needs to be optimized so that search engines will reference it well and suggest Nomao's directory at the top of their search results. Good Search Engine Optimization (SEO) largely depends on the size and on the quality of the textual content that is inside a webpage: the better the content, the higher the ranking in the Search Engine Results Page (SERP).

Referring to the work of Cardon [4] , NLG is an interesting manner to efficiently produce textual content and thus obtain a better control of SERP ranking. However, this content must contain variations in expression for at least two reasons: first, end-users should not perceive that the contents of Nomao's directory have been machine-generated; otherwise this might hinder its acceptability by them. Second, Nomao's directory should not be regarded as malicious by search engines and be "blacklisted", especially by major search engines for which content quality is of high importance.

Thus, random lexical choices that are part of Nomao's NLGs ensure a certain variety of content as we can note with the two business descriptions below:

- V1 translation: "The best information about the "Mulligans" pub in Toulouse... Have a break in the pub "Mulligans" located 42 Rue Des Saules in the pleasant city of Toulouse. This establishment proposes various beers. The nearest metro station to this pub is Saint-Michel Marcel Langer. Near this pub you will find other places like De Danu or the Rosanna bar." (In french: "Le meilleur des infossur le pub "Mulligans" à Toulouse... Détendez-vous le temps d'une pause dans le pub "Mulligans" localisé 42 Rue Des Saulesdansl'agréableville de Toulouse. Différentesvariétés de bièresvousserontproposéesdanscetétablissement. La station de métro la plus près de ce pub estMétro Saint-Michel Marcel Langer. Dans les environs de ce pub vouspourreztrouver le lieu de divertissement De Danu ou encore le bar Rosanna.")

- V2 translation: "Do you know the pub "Mulligans" in Toulouse? Relax at the pub "Mulligans" situated at 42 Rue Des Saules in the beautiful city of Toulouse. The beer menu offers different varieties of beers to enjoy alone or with friends. The nearest subway station is Metro Saint-Michel Marcel Langer. Feel free to check for other places nearby, like the De Danu pub or Rosanna bar." (In french: "Connaissez-vous le pub "Mulligans" à Toulouse ?Détendez- vous le temps d'une pause dans le pub "Mulligans" localisé 42 Rue Des Saulesdans la jolieville de Toulouse. La carte de ce pub propose différentesvariétés de bières à apprécier en solitaire ou entre amis. L'arrêt de métro le plus près de ce pub estMétro Saint-Michel Marcel Langer. N'hésitez pas à repérer les autrespossibilités aux alentours. Le lieu de divertissement De Danuou le bar Rosanna se trouventprès de ce pub.")

Text variety is quantitatively monitored by Nomao with the Dice coefficient which measures similarity between two text samples. This coefficient is between 0 and 1. The closest to 1, the highest the similarity between the two text samples. More specifically, the Dice coefficient between a text sample X and a text sample Y is defined as twice the intersection between x and y divided by the sum of x and y; and where x is the set of open-class words uni-bi- and tri-grams in text sample X and y is the set of open word uni-bi- and tri-grams in text sample Y. An open-class word is either a verb, a participle, a noun, an adjective or an adjective-derived adverb. An n-gram is a sequence of n words. Dice coefficient formula:

$$s = 2|x \cup y| / (|x| + |y|) \quad (1)$$

For example, the texts X = "The restaurant is located in the beautiful city of Toulouse" and Y = "This restaurant is in the city of Toulouse" are respectively composed of 5 {restaurant, located, beautiful, city, Toulouse} and 3 {restaurant, city, Toulouse} open-class words. Their respective uni-bi- and tri-grams sets are: x = {restaurant, located, beautiful, city, Toulouse, restaurant located, located beautiful, beautiful city, city Toulouse, restaurant located beautiful, located beautiful city, beautiful city Toulouse} and y = {restaurant, city, Toulouse, restaurant city, city Toulouse, restaurant city Toulouse}. The intersection of the sets x and y is therefore the set x inter y = {restaurant, city, Toulouse, city Toulouse}. Therefore, the Dice coefficient corresponding to this example is as follows:

$$s = (2 \times 4)/(12 + 6) = 0.44 \qquad (2)$$

BenedictePierrejean [5] evaluated 5000 text snippets generated by Nomao's NLGs and found rather satisfactory results: 0.13 on average.

Although this indicator makes it possible to account for the diversity of Nomao's NLGs, it gives no information on how end-users read them and how they understand them.

THEORETICAL AND METHODOLOGICAL FRAMEWORK

In the previous section, we described the functioning of Nomao's NLGs. We have seen that this functioning is divided into three steps serve to ensure the coherence of macrostructure, microstructure and surface generated texts. We also stressed that this functioning covers a part of randomness which aims to improve the variety of content of the texts produced by Nomao's NLGs. We have said that the quality of this variety is important for Nomao insofar as:

- it should improve Nomao in the SERP ranking;
- it should ensure that Nomao's users do not perceive that the contents available on this site are produced by a machine.

We added that the quality of the texts produced by Nomao's NGLs have so far been a quantitative evaluation based essentially on a measure of similarity (i.e., the Dice coefficient). Finally, we pointed that, if the quality of the texts produced by Nomao's NLGs appears satisfactory from the point of view of their objective variety (cf. the Dice coefficient). We know nothing of their quality from the point of view of the subjects who read them[1].

Also, this third section aims at defining a theoretical and methodological framework for evaluating, from user point of view, the quality of texts generated by Nomao's NLGs.

To achieve this goal, we will first show that cognitive load theory is adequate for identifying the linguistic complexity of text from the user perspective. We then will present different methods—qualified as "on-line" and "off-line"— which are generally used to evaluate:

- cognitive and emotional load involved in reading activities;
- levels of understanding of textual documents.

Finally, we will present the assumptions and variables that we have used to evaluate, from the user perspective, the quality of texts generated by Nomao's NLGs.

Cognitive Load Theory

The cognitive load theory is often used to evaluate reading activities whether they are linear or non-linear [6] [7] . According to Sweller [8] , there are three types of cognitive load.

Extrinsic load is related to the volume of information conveyed by the media and the manner in which this information is presented to the reader. It refers both to the content (i.e., the number of information items) and to the form (i.e., information formatting) of a particular text. As such, it is possible to have the extrinsic load level vary by manipulating either the quantity or the quality of the information. Intrinsic load is directly related to the task. The only way to reduce it is to delete some of the task's elements. This load varies depending on the user's expertise level. Finally, essential load depends on the ease of integration of the information in Long Term Memory (LTM). This load enables the user to acquire new knowledge.

Thus, regardless of the intrinsic characteristics of the reader, a text may create a more or less important extrinsic load depending on the way it is written. Consequently, depending on its syntactic and semantic structure, a text may increase or decrease the intrinsic and essential loads that are necessary for its understanding.

More specifically, understanding in the course of reading implies that the reader will internally build different levels of text representation through the repetition of a number of construction and integration cycles [9] . During the construction stage, the reader uses various text meaning production rules so as to organize components of the text into an association network that forms an intelligible text base. The integration phase consists in strengthening the construction process by selecting items that appear to the reader as the most relevant and by inhibiting those that seem the least appropriate.

Thus, the way a reader understands a text depends on his prior knowledge of the words that make up the text, on their graphic form, on their meaning but also on the grammatical and syntactic forms that structure the text. In other words, the understanding of a text by a reader depends on its linguistic complexity that is on the difficulties that a reader will experience while decoding the message conveyed by the text and inferring the significations that are associated with it [10] .

From the reader perspective, a text with a strong linguistic complexity requires expensive processing in the Working Memory (WM). Because it involves a higher activation of the WM, increasing the linguistic complexity of a text may result in reducing the resources that the reader can allocate for storing information in LTM and thus hinder the understanding of the text [8] [11] [12] [13] .

Two types of methods are generally used to evaluate both subjectively and objectively the cognitive load: on-line methods (e.g., eye movement recording) and off-line methods (e.g., survey that evaluate mental and emotional load and recall task techniques).

On-Line Methods: Eye Movement Recording

Eye movement recording is a good method to observe reading activities since it makes it possible to objectively measure the cognitive load involved during the processing of a text. Therefore, eye movement recording is a good way to evaluate the linguistic complexity of a text from reader perspective. Indeed, measuring the amount of cognitive load involved in a reading task is a way to evaluate the difficulties that the reader can meet as he reads the text. Therefore, it is an adequate way to measure the level of linguistic complexity from the reader's point of view (cf. Table 1).

Past works on eye movement analysis in reading situations generally show that eye movements are composed of a sequence of saccades and fixations that form three sequences which can in turn be associated with two different states [14] [15] [16] :

- at state n, the reader changes the focus of his attention from the word he was fixing (sequence 1) and moves his attention to a new word to be fixed (i.e., saccade stage during which no information is processed; sequence 2);
- at state n + 1, the reader focuses his attention on the new word

to be fixed (i.e., fixation stage during which information is processed; sequence 3).

Many research works on reading activities show that the more a word is simple, the more its recognition can be achieved peripherally during the fixation stage [17] [18] . In this way, the short time span between the preparation of the saccade before state n + 1 (see sequence 1 to state n) and its implementation (see sequence 2 of the state n) may be sufficient to allow the reader to understand the word corresponding to n + 1 (see attachment sequence 3). Therefore, during this short time pan, the saccade can be reprogrammed: the reader ignores the old n + 1 fixation state that was previously programmed during the state n and reprograms the saccade to move to a new n + 1 state. Thus, based on the work of O'Regan [17] and Rayner [18] , it is possible to say that the more a text is made of simple words, the larger are the saccades. Plus, the saccades would also tend to be more numerous (we shall see below that theoretically the simpler a text, themore fixations will occur; thus increasing the number of saccades) and to be longer in time (because the saccades would be larger[2]).

Table 1. Linguistic complexity indicators.

	Low linguistic complexity	High linguistic complexity
Number of saccades	High	Low
Duration of saccades	Long	Short
Amplitude of saccades	Great	Small
Number of fixations	High	Low
Fixation time	Short	Long

Equally, many research works in the field of air traffic control show that air traffic controllers perform a high number of saccades when they examine a complex situation (see the phenomenon of "attentional tunneling"; [19] [20] [21] [22]). Furthermore, Stein [23] found that the duration of saccades tends to decrease if the situation examined by the air traffic controller is more complex. Still, this last observation is has come under debate [24] . Consequently, a text showing strong linguistic complexity should lead the reader to realize fewer saccades and theses saccades should be of short duration.

Furthermore, it has been clearly demonstrated in research about air traffic control and reading, that an increase in the complexity of an air control situation or of a text tends to decrease the amplitude of the saccades performed by the controller or the reader [23] [25] [26] [27] . In other words, in reference to O'Regan [17] and Rayner [18] , in sequence of complex words a reader cannot recognize as well words in a peripheral manner. Thus, the reader cannot ignore and reprogram fixation steps; he cannot perform ample saccades as well.

We can conclude from these various research results that the linguistic complexity of a text, because it involves a greater cognitive load for the reader, can be objectively observed by checking the number of saccades, their duration and amplitude.

As far as fixations are concerned, research in air traffic control show that they are less frequent when the situation is less complex [23] [28] . Similarly, a text with a strong linguistic complexity should lead the reader to perform fewer fixations.

Concerning the duration of the fixations, it should be noted that:

- frequent and common words are subject to shorter fixation periods [29] [30] [31] [32] [33] ;
- the words which can be easily predicted from their context are also subject to shorter fixation periods [34] [35] [36] [37] [38] ;
- the words that are less predictable are subject to longer fixation periods [37] [39] [40] [41] ;
- abstract and/or ambiguous syntactic forms can generate longer fixation periods [42] [43] .

In short, these studies results show that if the linguistic complexity of a text increase (which implies a greater cognitive load for the reader), it can be objectively observed through a lower number of fixations and an increase in their duration.

Off-Line Methods: Emotional and Cognitive Load Questionnaires, Recall Tasks

As explained above, the study of eye movement is an interesting method to objectively observe the level of cognitive load involved in a reading task. However, analysis of eye movement does not give information on how well or how much this cognitive load is subjectively perceived by the user.

This is why eye movement recording is often completed with a cognitive load evaluation questionnaire. Gerjets, Scheiter and Catrambone [44] propose a shorter version of the NASA-TLX questionnaire, which evaluates the three aspects of cognitive load [8] and the stress of the user:

- the level of mental activity required to read the document (this aspect evaluates the requirements of the task; see the intrinsic load);
- the level of mental work required to understand the information displayed in the document (this aspect evaluates the effort involved in achieving the task; see the essential load);
- the effort required to navigate inside the document(i.e., to find and retrieve relevant information; this aspect evaluations navigation demands; cf. extrinsic load);
- the level of stress experienced during the reading task.

This version of the NASA-TLX questionnaire, which is designed to evaluate subjective cognitive load involved in reading hypertext documents, is well suited for evaluating the cognitive load involved in reading linear texts.

In addition, some studies highlight that the emotional load, whether positive or negative, has effects on cognition [45] . Correspondingly, Raufaste, Mariné and Eyrolle [46] show that positive emotions often allow decision-takers to perform more complex and effective cognitive processing. Conversely, negative emotions always tend to alter and degrade decision-takers' cognitive processing. Further- more, in reference to the work of Isen [47] , it seems that negative emotions tend to lead to attentional focus, which, by encouraging deep processing, consumes a lot of resources. In contrast, positive emotions tend to lead to some attentional aperture and improve synthesis ability (the ability to integrate knowledge and the information disclosed and to infer relationships among disparate ideas to build a solution).

Thus, increasing the linguistic complexity of a text may reduce the resources that the reader allocates for storing the information in LTM by increasing the workload of the WM [11] [12] [13] . However, this complexity may also have the effect of improving the emotional load involved in the reading. In this way, by inducing positive emotions in the mind of the reader, a difficult text may ultimately have the effect of enabling the reader to perform more cognitively complex and effective processing [46] . Thereby increasing the complexity of the text may, to some extent, facilitate its understanding and memorization by encouraging attentional aperture and improving the reader synthesis ability [47] . Thus, measuring the emotional load involved in reading seems to be an adequate manner to better understand the role of the linguistic complexity of a text on its understanding. More precisely, in the case of the understanding and memorization of a text describing a business (BDT—Business Describing Text), aspects such as reader confidence (which is one Plutchik's [48] eight fundamental emotions) and reader interest (related to anticipation; also part of Plutchik's [48] fundamental emotions) should be taken into account. Confidence and interest are indeed two important dimensions in processes like information dissemination and appropriation on the market [49] [50] [51] [52] .

Finally, to objectively determine whether the increase of linguistic complexity of a text rather has negative or positive effects on its understanding, recall tasks and response time measurements are generally used [53] [54] . These two types of measurement are carried out by asking the reader questions about the form and the content of the text and by monitoring the time spent in answering these questions. Although this measure is subject to debate [55] , pupil diameter measurement during the response time can help to indicate the level of cognitive load involved during the processing and the elaboration of the answer: the larger the diameter, the higher the cognitive load.

Assumptions and Variables

As explained below, the experimentation consisted in asking participants to read the two texts below: Text 1 (T1) entitled "Angelina" was generated by Nomao's NLGs (i.e., a machine-generated text) and Text 2 (T2) entitled "Chez Janou" was written by humans.

Texts 1 and 2 have approximately the same number of characters (c) and words (w)—respectively 813 c and 159 w versus 767 c and 150 w. In addition, the number of characters per word (c/w) is identical in the two texts (cf. Table 2). From a quantitative viewpoint, texts 1 and 2 are of similar complexity.

Nonetheless, if one looks at the syntactic structure, text 1 is less complex than text 2. Text 1 has 11 sentences (s) whereas text 2 has 8 sentences. Its average number of words per sentence (w/s) is lower than text 2 (14.45 w/s for T1 against 18.75 w/s for T2). In addition, text 1 contains 5 commas (v) and 4 coordinating conjunctions "and" (cc_{et}) whereas text 2 has 10 v and 8 cc_{et}. The average number of commas per sentence (v/s) and the average number of cc_{et} per sentence (cc_{et}/s) are strongly higher in text 2 (0.45 v/s and 0.36 cc_{et}/s in T1 versus 1.25 v/s and 1 cc_{et}/s for T2).

Table 2. Quantitative evaluation of text 1 (T1) and text 2 (T2) complexity.

	T1	T2
Number of characters (c)*	813	767
Word Count (w)	159	150
Average number of characters per word (c/w)	5.11	5.11
Number of sentences (s)	11	8
Average number of words per sentence (w/s)	14.45	18.75
Number of commas (v)	5	10
Average number of commas per sentence (v/s)	0.45	1.25
Number of coordinating conjunctions "et" (cc_{et})	4	8
Average number of cc_{et} per sentence (cc_{et}/s)	0.36	1

**Not including spaces.*

From a qualitative viewpoint, text 1 also appears less complex than text 2. Quantitatively, text 1 is usually composed of short sentences. Contrary to text 2, text 1 does not have any subject noun phrase. It does not have any long or detailed adverbial phrases either.

Moreover, unlike text 1, text 2 has a socio-semantic coherence that enriches its macrostructure on the semantic level. In reference to socio-cognitive approaches in human and social sciences [56] , the socio-semantic coherence of a text can be defined as the organized set of socially shared representations that are conveyed by the text and that should enable the reader to construct a stereotypical mental picture of its referent. Text 2 is structured around various social representations that are culturally associated with a particular region of southern France: Provence. More precisely, the socio-semantic coherence is built from the following groups of words: "very good bistro from the Marseille planet"; "Marcel Pagnol" (name of a local author); "the Provence cuisine is tasty and generous"; "atmosphere is both thrilling and friendly"; "the owner is very kind and the service is courteous"; "charming terrace where you can chill down with friends and enjoy a Pastis" (Pastis is a local drink); "to eat without breaking the bank"; "dishes from Provence"). Conversely, given the functioning of Nomao's NLGs, text 1 does not include any socio-semantic coherence. It does not convey any socially shared represen- tations thus allowing readers to build a stereotyped mental image of its referent. Indeed, it is mainly composed of pieces of factual and practical information written with simple syntactic and semantic structures.

Therefore, from both a quantitative and qualitative viewpoint, text 1 displays less complex syntactic and semantic structures than text 2. However, text 2 is stylistically more elaborated than text 1 and it offers stereotypical representations of its referent in the sense that it refers to a set of socially shared representations that are culturally associated with the south-east region of France (Provence). Also, the socio-semantic coherence of text 2 is likely to produce positive emotional charges in the reader in terms of both confidence and interest. Text 2 is thus likely to foster text's understanding and macrostructure's memorization.

Referring to the work we have presented above, we therefore make the following two general assumptions (gA):

- gA_1: reading a text generated by Nomao's NLGs (i.e., the text 1 "Angelina") involves—both subjectively and objectively—a lower cognitive load than the text written by humans (i.e., text 2 "Chez Janou");
- gA_2: because it involves a higher positive emotional charge, the text written by humans is likely to foster a better understanding than the text generated by Nomao's NLGs.

Also, we propose to operationalize gA_1 and gA_2 with the four specific assumptions (sA) presented below:

- sA_1: reading a text generated by Nomao's NLGs objectively involves less cognitive load than reading a text written by humans;
- sA_2: reading a text generated by Nomao's NLGs subjectively involves a lesser cognitive load than reading the text written by humans;
- sA_3: reading a text generated by Nomao's NLGs subjectively involves a lesser positive emotional charge than reading a text written by humans;
- sA_4: a text generated by Nomao's NLGs is less understandable than a text written by humans.

DATA, EQUIPMENT AND METHOD

In this section, we describe the data, equipment and method that we used to test the hypothesis presented above.

To do this, we first describe the main characteristics of the sample population, then the experimental equipment and data processing techniques that we used in our experiments. Finally, we present the experimentation we designed and whose goal is to evaluate the performance of Nomao's NLGs from the users point of view.

Population Sample

Our experiment was conducted with 28 students from the University of Montreal. These students were not paid. 7 of them are male (60.7%) and 11 are female (39.3%). The average age is 24 with a standard deviation of 5.8. The median age is 23.

Equipment and Data Processing Software

For eye-movement recording, we used a Tobii TX 300 screen, and we set the sample rate to 60 Hz (i.e., a sample is released every 17 milliseconds). The maximum angle between two fixations was set to 0.5 degrees. For data recording, we used the Tobii 3.2 software. For data processing, we used the Excel and SPSS software.

Given that each participant was exposed to two experimental situations (i.e., the text 1 "Angelina" and the text 2 "Chez Janou"), we performed within-subject.

The advantage of within-subjects ANOVA compared to between-subjects ANOVA is that it avoids measuring effects that are due to the characteristics of the population samples. Its disadvantage is that the measured performance may be contaminated by the order in which the tasks are performed. To avoid this, we defined two groups of 14 students (G1 and G2) who made each experimen- tation in a different order.

In addition, we used the Friedman test for all ordinal data available (see the cognitive and emotional questionnaires). The Friedman test is an alternative to the within-subject ANOVA in the case of ordinal data: it is a non-parametric test developed to perform one-factor within-subject experiments.

Experimentation

Our experiment consists in presenting texts 1 and 2 to each participant for a period of 90 seconds (cf. Table 3).

After each text display, a series of eight closed questions on key informational units of each text are asked to each participant. Once these recall tasks have beenperformed, the participants answer an emotional load evaluation questionnaire (2 items: interest and confidence levels on a 1-to-9 Likert scale; see section 3.3) and a cognitive load evaluation survey (4 items: intrinsic, essential, extrinsic loads and stress levels on a 1-to-100 Likert scale; see section 3.3). At the end of the each experiment, we asked different open questions to the participants so as to make them verbalize the perceptions they had of each text.

Table 3. Overview of machine-generated text (T1) and human-written text (T2).

Text 1 (T1): "Angelina"	Text 2 (T2): "Chez Janou"
Translation: "Angelina" is a restaurant located in the 1st district of Paris. It is specialized in French cuisine. There, you will taste seafood and salads. This restaurant includes a café and proposes take-away food. Angelina accepts credit card as mean of payment. If you wish to go there by public transportation, the metro station "Tuileries" is 20m away and the metro station "Pyramides" is 600 m away. Your opinion about Angelina: twenty-three reviews refer to the service, 3 are positive versus 20. The way in which the restaurant was decorated pleased 3 guests ("refined decoration", "aspettoelegante" and "beginning charm"). No negative comment about the breakfast was found. On a total of 7, 3 internauts liked the prices. The desserts were favorably mentioned in 3 reviews ("great hot chocolate", "delicious chocolate", "best hot chocolate").	Translation: Come discover Chez Janou nearthe place des Vosges in the 4th district of Pairs. A very good bistro from the Marseille planet which has been decorated for Marcel Pagnol's fans and where the Provence cuisine is tasty and generous. The atmosphere is both thrilling and friendly. The owner is very kind and the service is courteous. Reservation is mandatory in this very busy place. Not far away from the Marais neighbourhood, the restaurant Chez Janou has an ideal location and has a charming terrace where you can chill down with friends and enjoy a Pastis or else... At lunch time, a 14.50?menu will allow you to eat without breaking the bank, and with à la carte service, you will discover various dishes from Provence with little more than 30 ?.. Cold ratatouille, anchoïade and tapenade, Saint-Nectaire toasts, Provence stuffed vegetables, grilled bass with pesto, spelt and scallops risotto...

In french: "Angelina" estunrestaurantsitué à Paris dans le 1er arrondissement. Il estspécialisédans la cuisine française. Vouspourrez y déguster des fruits de mer et des salades. Ce restaurant dispose d'un café et propose des plats à emporter. Angelina accepte la carte de créditcommemoyen de paiement. Si jamaisvouschoisissez de vous y rendre en transports en commun, vouspourrezsortir à la station MétroTuileries qui estsituée à 20 mètresou à la station MétroPyramides qui estsituée à 600 mètres. Votre opinion sur Angelina: vingt-troisavisévoquent les prestations, troissontpositifscontrevingt. La manièredontaétédécoré le restaurant a séduit 3 hôtes ("décor raffiné", "aspettoelegante" et "charme du début"). Pas de commentairenégatifrelevésur le petit-déjeuner. Sur 7, 3 internautesontapprécié le prix. Les desserts ontétémentionnésfavorablementdanstroisavis ("super chocolatchaud", "chocolatdélicieux" et "meilleurchocolatchaud").	In french: Venezdécouvrir Chez Janouprès de la place des Vosges dans le 4ème arrondissement de Paris. Un très bon bistrot de la planète Marseille spécialementdécoré pour les fans de Marcel Pagnoloù la cuisine provençale y estsavoureuse et généreuse. Ambiance à la foisélectrisante et sympathique. Le propriétaireestbiengentil et le service estcourtois. La réservationest indispensable dansce lieu trèsfréquenté. À deux pas du Marais, le restaurant Chez Janoujouit d'un emplacement idéal et possèdeuneterrassepleine de charme, oùil fait bon se poser entre amis pour un Pastisouautre... À midi, uneformule à 14.50?permet de se restaurer sans se ruiner, et à la carte, un peu plus de 30? pourdécouvrirdifférents plats aux saveursprovençales... Assiette de ratatouille froide, anchoïade et tapenade, Toastades de saint-nectaire, Farcisprovençaux, Bar grillé au pistou, Risotto d'épeautre et ses Saint-Jacques...

Recall that both 14 students groups G1 and G2 carried out the experiments in a different order to avoid contamination effects that are usually associated with within-subject experiments. Thus, G1 started with text 1 and G2 started with text 2.

RESULTS

In this section, we present the results of the experimentation. Recall that, in general, these results are intended to test specific hypotheses sA1, sA2, sA3 and sA4 in order to allow the testing of general hypotheses gA1 and gA2 that we outlined in Section 3.4. So, the following subsections describe the effect of the text on eye behavior, the effect of the text on subjective cognitive and emotional loads, the effect of the text on understanding. The final subsection discusses all the results.

Text Effect on Eye Behavior

As illustrated in Table 4, from eye-movement analysis viewpoint, it appears that reading the text generated by Nomao's NLGs (i.e., the text 1 "Angelina") involves an objective cognitive load significantly lower than reading the text written by humans (i.e., text 2 "Chez Janou").

Indeed, although the difference between the numbers of saccades that participants present when reading texts 1 and 2 is not significant ($p > 0.05$), the average length of the saccades is significantly longer when reading text 1 than for text 2 (37.47 milliseconds (ms) for T1 against 35.86 ms for T2; $F(1,27) = 11.526$; $p < 0.01$).

Moreover, our results also show that the average vertical amplitude of the saccades is almost significantly higher ($p = 0.058$) during the reading of text 1 than during the reading of text 2 (47.70 pixels for T1 versus 42.73 pixels for T2).

In addition, although the difference between the numbers of fixations that participants perform during the reading of texts 1 and 2 is not significant ($p > 0.05$), the average duration of fixations is significantly shorter when reading text 1 that for text 2 (196.55 milliseconds for T1 versus 205.57 ms for T2; $F(1,27) = 11.951$, $p < 0.01$).

Text Effect on Subjective Cognitive and Emotional Loads

If reading text 1 implies a lesser objective cognitive load than reading text 2, it appears that from a subjective viewpoint, our participants do not perceive this difference (cf. Table 5).

Table 4. Evaluation of eye behavior for text 1 (T1) and text 2 (T2).

	T1	T2	Significance
Number of saccades	417.61 s*	405.46 s	F(1,27) = 3.162, p = 0.870
Average duration of saccades	37.47 ms*	35.86 ms	F(1,27) = 11,526; p = 0.002
Number of fixations	352.43 f*	347.04 f	F(1,27) = 1.780, p = 0.193
Average duration of fixations	196.55 ms	205.57 ms	F(1,27) = 11,951; p = 0.002
Average saccades vertical amplitude	47.70 px*	42.73 px	F(1,27) = 3.922, p = 0.058
Average saccades horizontal amplitude	22.84 px	19.86 px	F(1,27) = 2.279, p = 0.143

*Unit: saccade (s); millisecond (ms); fixation (f); pixel (px).

Table 5. Evaluation of subjective cognitive and emotional loads for text 1 (T1) and text 2 (T2).

	T1	T2	Significance
Cognitive load	1.54 r*	1.46 r	$x^2(1) = 0.143$, $p = 0.705$
Intrinsic load	1.46 r	1.54 r	$x^2(1) = 0.182$, $p = 0.670$
Essential load	1.54 r	1.46 r	$x^2(1) = 0.167$, $p = 0.683$
Extrinsic load	1.59 r	1.41 r	$x^2(1) = 1.087$, $p = 0.297$
Stress	1.52 r	1.48 r	$x^2(1) = 0.053$, $p = 0.819$
Emotional	1.32 r	1.68 r	$x^2(1) = 5.000$, $p = 0.025$
Interest	1.3 r	1.7 r	$x^2(1) = 6.368$, $p = 0.012$
Confidence	1.38 r	1.63 r	$x^2(1) = 2.882$, $p = 0.090$

*Unit: rank (r).

Our results actually show no statistical significance ($p > 0.05$) in how the par- ticipants evaluated the cognitive loads involved in reading texts 1 and 2 and in their different dimensions (i.e., intrinsic, essential, extrinsic loads and stress; see Section 3.3).

In contrast, our results show that participants experienced an emotional load significantly less positive when reading text 1 that for text 2 (rank 1.32 in the case of T1 versus rank 1.68 for T2; $x^2(1) = 5.000$; $p < 0.05$).

More precisely, it appears that interest in text 1 is significantly lower than for text 2 (rank 1.3 in the case of Q1 versus rank 1.7 in the case of T2; $x^2(1) = 6.368$; $p < 0.05$). Furthermore, although this result is not significant ($p = 0.090$), participants also seem to give a confidence level lower than the text 1 text 2 (rank 1.38 in the case of T1 against rank 1.63 in the case of T2).

Text Effect on Understanding

Finally, as shown in Table 6, it seems that participants find it easier to understand text 2 that text 1.

Although the results for recall tasks are very similar (8.01/10 for T1 versus 7.81/10 for T2; $F(1,27) = 0.279$; $p > 0.05$), the results concerning average response time and average pupil diameter show statistically significant differences.

As illustrated in Table 7, it should be noted that the questions about the text 1 have an average of 93.62 characters per question (c/q) and 20.62 words per question (w/q) versus 105.37 c/q and 23.75 w/q for the questions about text 2.

Although the questions about text 1 have fewer characters and words than the questions about text 2, participants significantly take longer time to read and answer the questions about text 1 (6.140 ms in the case against T1 versus 4.940 ms in the case of T2; $F(1,27) = 16.742$, $p < 0.001$). Moreover, the average pupil diameter of participants is significantly larger during the answering of questions about text 1 than for text 2 (3.094 millimeters for T1 versus 3.057 mm for T2; $F(1,27) = 6.320$; $p < 0.05$), which also suggests difficulty.

Table 6. Evaluation of recall tasks performance, average response time and average pupil diameter for text 1 (T1) and text 2 (T2).

	T1	T2	Significance
Recall task	8.01/10*	7.81/10	F(1,27) = 0.279, p = 0.602
Average response time	6140 ms	4940 ms	F(1,27) = 16,742; p = 0.000
Average pupil diameter	3.094 mm*	3.057 mm	F(1,27) = 6.230, p = 0.019

*Unit: score of 10 (/10); millimeter (mm).

Table 7. Quantitative evaluation of the complexity of the questions about text 1 (q T1) and text 2 (q T2).

	q T1	q T2
Number of characters (c)	749	843
Word Count (w)	165	190
Number of questions (q)	8	8
Average number of characters per question (c/q)	93.62	105.37
Average number of words per question (w/q)	20.62	23.75

Discussion

Under sA_1, we found that the text generated by Nomao's NLGs (i.e., the text 1 "Angelina") objectively involves a less important cognitive load than the text written by humans (i.e., Text 2 "Chez Janou").

However, our results do not confirm sA_2 since we did not find significant differences between the level of subjective cognitive load involved in the reading of text 1 (machine-generated text) and the level of subjective cognitive load involved in the reading of text 2 (written by humans).

sA_3 is validated since our results show that reading text 1 (machine-generated) subjectively implies a significantly less positive emotional charge than reading text 2 (written by humans).Our results also confirm sA_4: we have found that participants significantly better understand the human-written text than the machine-generated text. Note however that this difference is not visible in the recall tasks scores, only the response time and pupillary diameters back up this assumption.On a general level, it appears that Nomao's NLGs fulfills its function since, during the questions-verbalization stage done at the end of each experiment, all participants stated that the machine-generated text was correctly written that it seemed to be written by competent humans. Thus, we can claim that the micro-planning stages are properly carried out by Nomao's NLGs since the syntactic and semantic structures of text 1 objectively posed no reading difficulties to the participants.Experiments also show that participants do not subjectively perceive a lower cognitive load while reading the machine-generated text (which refutes sA_2). This might be due to the fact that text 1 is not structured around a set of socially shared representations as in the case of text 2 which is written by humans; these socially shared representations generally produce positive emotions in the reader and thus facilitate the general understanding of the text.Indeed, the machine-generated text is composed of a sequence of practical and factual information presented in the form of simple syntactic and semantic structures that are partly organized at random. Moreover, although it is subject to some kind of organization during macro-planning, the macrostructure of the machine-generated text does not have any particular socio-semantic coherence like in human-written texts. Thus it seems that this lack of socio-semantic coherence in the machine-generated text explains why the participants experienced a more positive emotional charge and a better understanding when they read the human-written text.From a scientific perspective, our results highlight the importance of socio-semantic coherence in text-based communication produced by NLGs. This is worth noticing since socio-semantic coherence is generally not considered in the modeling of reading activities in cognitive science research. For example, Gernsbacher [57] explains that the matching processes allowing readers to build a mental representation of a text depend on the text's referential, temporal, spatial, structural and causal coherence which all differ from socio-semantic coherence. Yet, it is this latter form of coherence that is lacking in the texts generated by Nomao's NLGs.Finally, we wish to underline that our results are exploratory and should therefore be extended over a larger amount of text and a larger population sample in order to control the level of replicability as well as the mediating effect that may be produced by individual variables that we did not consider here. It is possible that the dual task paradigm [58] could better explain the effect of the text on the cognitive and emotional loads involved in the reading task and in the understanding of the text.

CONCLUSIONS

In short, the case study that we proposed in this paper is interesting for two main reasons.

The first is that it emphasizes that the objective indices for measuring the quality of content generated by NGLs such as the Dice coefficient are not sufficient. Our article allows to point out the need to evaluate this quality from the point of view of users who read these contents in order to truly identify and understand the communicative performance of an automatically generated text. We then showed how on-line (i.e., eye tracking) and off-line (i.e., questionnaire) measurements on cognitive and emotional charge can be used to perform this type of evaluation.The second reason is that the case study we have proposed highlights the role of socio-semantic coherence in textual communication. Our work thus points to a dimension of textual communication that is, to our knowledge, not sufficiently considered in the field of NLG. Our results show that for a text to be understood and memorized, it must not only make it easy to read, that is to say coherent from the point of view of its macrostructure, microstructure and surface. Our study shows that for a text to succeed in transmitting easily the "communicative intention" [10] of which it carries, it is also necessary that the representations that it conveys be endowed with socially shared meanings. Also, it seems to us that in the era of big data, one of the main challenges of NLG might be to seek new artificial intelligence technology to automate the production of this socio- semantic coherence.

Conflict of Interest

The authors declare that there is no conflict of interest regarding the publication of this manuscript

REFERENCES

1. MoulierBoutang, Y. (2012) Cognitive Capitalism. Polity Press, Cambridge.
2. Parasie, S. and Dagiral, E. (2013) Data-Driven Journalism and the Public Good: “Computer-Assisted Reporters” and “Programming-Journalists” in Chicago. New Media & Society, 15, 853-871. https://doi.org/10.1177/1461444812463345
3. Mitkov, R. (2003) The Oxford Handbook of Computational Linguistics. Oxford University Press, Oxford.
4. Cardon, D. (2013) In the Mind of Page Rank. A Study of Google’s Algorithm. Réseaux, 1, 63-95.
5. Pierrejean, B. (2013) Amélioration d’un système de générationautomatique de texte pour les commerceslocaux. Master Thesis, University Toulouse Jean Jaurès, Toulouse.
6. Amadieu, F., Tricot, A. and Mariné, C. (2009) Prior Knowledge from Learning in a Non-Linear Electronic Document: Disorientation and Coherence of the Reading Sequences. Computer in Human Behavior, 25, 381-388.
7. Amadieu, F., Tricot, A. and Mariné, C. (2010) Interaction between Prior Knowledge and Concept-Map Structure on Hypertext Comprehension, Coherence of Reading Orders and Disorientation. Interacting with Computers, 22, 88-97. https://doi.org/10.1016/j.intcom.2009.07.001
8. Sweller, J. (1988) Cognitive Load during Problem Solving: Effects on Learning. Cognitive Science, 12, 257-285. https://doi.org/10.1207/s15516709cog1202_4
9. Kintsch, W. (1988) The Role of Knowledge in Discourse Comprehension: A Constructive-Integration Model. Psychological Review, 95, 163-182. https://doi.org/10.1037/0033-295X.95.2.163
10. Sperber, D. and Wilson, D. (1986) Relevance. Communication and Cognition. Blackwell, Oxford.
11. Gaonac’h, P. and Larigauderie, D. (2000) Mémoireetfonctionnementcognitif: La mémoire de travail. Armand Colin, Paris.
12. Just, M.A. and Carpenter, P.A. (1992) A Capacity Theory of Comprehension: Individual Differences in Working Memory. Psychological Review, 99, 122-149. https://doi.org/10.1037/0033-295X.99.1.122

13. Oakhill, J.V. Cain, K. and Yuill, N. (1998) Individual Differences in Children's Understanding Skill: Toward an Integrated Model. In: Hulme, C. and Joshi, R.M., Eds., Reading and Spelling: Development and Disorders, Erlbaum, Mahwah, 343- 367.
14. Fisher, B. (1986) The Role of Care in Visually Guided Eye Movements in Monkey and Man. Psychological Research, 48, 251-257. https://doi.org/10.1007/BF00309089
15. Fisher, B. and Breitmeyer, B. (1987) Mechanisms of Visual Attention Revealed by Saccadic Eye Movements. Neuropsychologia, 25, 73-83.
16. Morrison, R.E. (1984) Manipulation of Stimulus Onset Delay in Reading: Evidence for Parallel Programming of Saccades.. Journal of Experimental Psychology: Human Perception and Performance, 10, 667-682. https://doi.org/10.1037/0096-1523.10.5.667
17. O'Regan, J.K. (1975) Constraints on Eye Movements in Reading. Unpublished Doctoral Thesis, University of Cambridge, Cambridge.
18. Rayner, K. (1979) Eye Guidance in Reading: Fixation Locations within Words. Perception, 8, 21-30. https://doi.org/10.1068/p080021
19. Cabon, P., Farbos, B. and Mollard, R. (2000) Gaze Analysis and Psychophysiological Parameters: A Tool for the Design and the Evaluation of Man-Machine Interfaces. Technical Report No. 2000-015, EUROCONTROL Experimental Center, France.
20. Endsley, M.R. and Rodgers, M.D. (1998) Distribution of Attention Situation Awareness, Workload and in a Passive Air Traffic Control Task: Implications for Operational Errors and Automation. Air Traffic Control Quarterly, 6, 21-44.
21. Tole, J.R., Stephens, A.T., Harris, R.L. and Ephrath, A.R. (1982) Visual Scanning Behavior and Mental Workload in Aircraft Pilots. Aviation, Space, and Environmental Medicine, 53, 54-61.
22. Willems, B., Allen, R.C. and Stein, E.S. (1999) Air Traffic Control Specialist Visual Scanning II: Task Load, Visual Noise, and Intrusions into Controlled Airspace. Technical Report No. DOT/FAA/CT-TN99/23, William Hughes FAA Technical Center, Atlantic City.
23. Stein, E.S. (1992) Air Traffic Control Visual Scanning. Technical Report. No. DOT/ FAA/CT-TN92/16, William Hughes FAA Technical Center, Atlantic City.
24. Willems, B. and Truitt, T.R. (1999) Implications of Reduced Involvement in Road Traffic Air Control. Technical Report No. DOT/

FAA/CT-TN99/22, William Hughes FAA Technical Center, Atlantic City.

25. Ahlstrom, U. and Friedman-Berg, F.J. (2006) Using Eye Movement Activity as a Correlate of Cognitive Workload. International Journal of Industrial Ergonomics, 36, 623-636.
26. Pavlidis, G.T. (1983) The "Dyslexia Syndrome" Objective and Its Diagnosis by Erratic Eye Movements. In: Rayner, K., Ed., Eye Movements in Reading: Perceptual and Language Processes, Academic Press, New York.
27. Rayner, K. (1978) Eye Movements in Reading and Information Processing. Psychological Bulletin, 85, 618-660. https://doi.org/10.1037/0033-2909.85.3.618
28. Togami, H. (1984) Affects on Visual Search Performance of Individual Differences in Fixation Time and Number of Fixations. Ergonomics, 27, 789-799. https://doi.org/10.1080/00140138408963552
29. Chaffin, R. Morris, R.K. and Seely, R.E. (2001) Learning New Word Meanings from Context: A Study of Eye Movements. Journal of Experimental Psychology: Learning, Memory and Cognition, 27, 225-235. https://doi.org/10.1037/0278-7393.27.1.225
30. Inhoff, A.W. and Rayner, K. (1986) Parafoveal Word Processing during Eye Fixations in Reading: Effects of Word Frequency. Perception & Psychophysics, 40, 431- 439. https://doi.org/10.3758/BF03208203
31. Juhasz, B.J. and Rayner, K. (2003) Investigating the Effects of a Set of Intercorrelated Variables on Eye Fixation Durations in Reading. Journal of Experimental Psychology: Learning, Memory and Cognition, 29, 1312-1318. https://doi.org/10.1037/0278-7393.29.6.1312
32. Rayner, K. and Duffy, S. (1986) Lexical Complexity and Fixation Times in Reading: Effects of Word Frequency, Verb Complexity, and lexical Ambiguity. Memory & Cognition, 14, 191-201. https://doi.org/10.3758/BF03197692
33. Williams, R.S. and Morris, R.K. (2004) Eye Movements, Word Familiarity, and Vocabulary Acquisition. European Journal of Cognitive Psychology, 16, 312-339. https://doi.org/10.1080/09541440340000196
34. Ehrlich, S.F. and Rayner, K. (1981) Contextual Effects on Word Perception and Eye Movements during Reading. Journal of Verbal Learning and Verbal Behavior, 20, 641-655.
35. Balota, D.A., Pollatsek, A. and Rayner, K. (1985) The Interaction of

Contextual Constraints and Parafoveal Visual Information in Reading. Cognitive Psychology, 17, 364-388.

36. Rayner, K. and Well, A.D. (1996) Effects of Contextual Constraint on Eye Movements in Reading: A Further Examination. Psychonomic Bulletin & Review, 3, 504-509. https://doi.org/10.3758/BF03214555
37. Rayner, K., Warren, T., Juhasz, B.J. and Liversedge, S.P. (2004) The Effect of Plausibility on Eye Movements in Reading. Journal of Experimental Psychology: Learning, Memory and Cognition, 30, 1290-1301. https://doi.org/10.1037/0278-7393.30.6.1290
38. Ashby, J. Rayner, K. and Clifton, C.J. (2005) Eye Movements of Highly Skilled and Average Readers: Differential Effects of Frequency and Predictability. The Quarterly Journal of Experimental Psychology Section A, 58, 1065-1086. https://doi.org/10.1080/02724980443000476
39. Murray, W.S. and Rowan, M. (1998) Early, Mandatory, Pragmatic Processing. Journal of Psycholinguistic Research, 27, 1-22. https://doi.org/10.1023/A:1023233406227
40. Ni, W.J. (1996) Sidestepping Garden Paths: Assessing the Contributions of Syntax, Semantics and Plausibility in Resolving Ambiguities. Language and Cognitive Promcesses, 11, 283-334. https://doi.org/10.1080/016909696387196
41. Ni, W., Fodor, J.D., Crain, S. and Shankweiler, D. (1998) Anomaly Detection: Eye Movement Patterns. Journal of Psycholinguistic Research, 27, 515-539. https://doi.org/10.1023/A:1024996828734
42. Rayner, K., Carlson, M. and Frazier, L. (1983) The Interaction of Syntax and Semantics during Sentence Processing: Eye Movements in the Analysis of Semantically Biased Sentences. Journal of Verbal Learning and Verbal Behavior, 22, 358-374.
43. Clifton, C. (2003) We Eye-Tracking Using Data to Evaluate-Theories of On-Line Sentence Processing: The Case of Reduced Relative Clauses. 12th European Conference on Eye Movements, Dundee, Scotland.
44. Gerjets, P., Scheiter, K. and Catrambone, R. (2004) Designing Instructional Examples to Reduce Intrinsic Cognitive Load: Molar versus Modular Presentation of Solution Procedures. Instructional Science, 32, 33-58. https://doi.org/10.1023/B:TRUC.0000021809.10236.71
45. Damasio, A.R. (1995) L'Erreur de Descartes: La raison des émotions. Odile Jacob, Paris, 293.
46. Raufaste, E., Eyrolle, H. and Mariné, C. (1998) Pertinence Generation

in Radiological Diagnosis: Spreading Activation and the Nature of Expertise. Cognitive Science, 22, 517-546. https://doi.org/10.1207/s15516709cog2204_4

47. Isen, A.M. (1993) Positive and Affect Decision Making. In: Lewis, J. and Haviland, M., Eds., Handbook of Emotions, Guilford Press, New York.
48. Plutchik, R. (1980) Emotion: A Psychoevolutionary Synthesis. Harper & Row, New York.
49. Hirschman, A. (1977) The Passions and the Interests: Political Arguments for Capitalism before Its Triumph. Princeton University Press, Princeton.
50. Yalch, R.F. and Yoshida, S. (1983) Consumer Use of Information and Confidence in Making Judgements about a New Food Store: An Attribution Theory Analysis. Advances in Consumer Research, 10, 40-44.
51. Pieniak, Z., Verbeke, W., Vermeir, I., Bruns, K. and Olsen, S.O. (2007) Consumer Interest in Fish Information and Labelling. Journal of International Food & Agribusiness Marketing, 19, 117-141. https://doi.org/10.1300/J047v19n02_07
52. Swedberg, R. (2010) The Structure of Confidence and the Collapse of Lehman Brothers. Research in the Sociology of Organizations, 30A, 71-114.
53. Dee-Lucas, A. and Larkin, J.H. (1995) Learning from Electronic Texts: Effects of Interactive Overviews for Information Access. Cognition & Instruction, 13, 431- 468.
54. Kellman, P.J. and Massey, C.M. (2013) Perceptual Learning, Cognition and Expertise. Psychology of Learning and Motivation, 58, 117-165.
55. Chen, S. and Epps, J. (2013) Automatic Classification of Eye Activity for Cognitive Load Measurement with Emotion Interference. Computer Methods and Programs in Biomedicine, 110, 111-124. https://doi.org/10.1016/j.cmpb.2012.10.021
56. Wassilew, A.Z. (2014) A Social-Cognitive Approach to Semantic Analysis and Categorization Processes. Online Journal of Applied Knowledge Management, 2, 172- 181.
57. Gernsbacher, M.A. (1996) Coherence during Mapping Cues Understanding. In: Costermans, J. and Fayol, M., Eds., Processing Interclausal Relationships in the Production and Comprehension of

Text, Erlbaum, Hillsdale.

58. Kellogg, R.T. (1987) Effects of Topic Knowledge on the Allocation of Processing Time and Cognitive Effort to Writing Processes. Memory & Cognition, 15, 256-266. https://doi.org/10.3758/BF03197724

CHAPTER 3

Web Semantic and Ontology

Elodie Marie Gontier

Professor of French and History, Paris, France

ABSTRACT

Ontologies have become a popular research topic in many communities. In fact, ontology is a main component of this research; therefore, the definition, structure and the main operations and applications of ontology are provided. Web content consists mainly of distributed hypertext and hypermedia, and is accessed via a combination of keyword based search and link navigation. Hence, the ontology can provide a common vocabulary, and a grammar for

Citation: Gontier, E. (2015), "Web Semantic and Ontology". Advances in Internet of Things, 5, 15-20. doi: 10.4236/ait.2015.52003.

publishing data, and can supply a semantic description of data which can be used to preserve the ontologies and keep them ready for inference. This paper provides basic concepts of semantic web, and defines the structure and the main applications of ontology.

Keywords: Ontology, Semantic Web, Language OWL

WHAT DO WE REPRESENT IN AN ONTOLOGY?

In the context of Semantic Web, ontologies describe domain theories for the explicit representation of the semantics of the data. In other words, ontology should be seen as a right answer to provide a formal conceptualization. Indeed, ontology must translate an explicit consensus and develop a certain level of division. It has two essential aspects to allow the operation of the resources of web by various applications or software agents. The ontologies serve then:

1) For the vocabulary, the structuring and the operation of metadatas;
2) As representation pivot for the integration of springs of heterogeneous data;
3) To describe the web departments, and generally, everywhere it is going to be necessary to press software modules on semantic representations requiring certain consensus.

Ontology (def. 1): all the objects recognized as existing in the domain. To build an ontology, it is also to decide on the way of being and to exist objects. To continue towards a definition of ontology, it seems to us essential to remind that the works on the ontologies are developed in an IT context that is the case, for instance, for Engineering of knowledge, Artificial intelligence or, more specifically here, the context of Semantics Web where the final goal is to specify an IT artefact. In this context, the ontology becomes then a model of the existing objects which makes a reference to it through concepts of the domain.

The developments are a free performance of the reasons adduced for the works of Guarino and Giaretta [1] . They aim at progressing towards a definition reporting an evolutionary process of construction.

Ontology (def. 2): an ontology involves or includes a certain worldview compared with a given domain. This sight is often conceived as a set of concept—e.g. entities, attributes, and process—their definitions and their interrelations. We call it a “conceptualization”. An ontology can take various forms, but it will include inevitably a vocabulary of terms and specification of their meaning. So, it is a specification partially reporting a conceptualization. This second definition proposes another point of view compared with the first one, coherent with her but more precise, in terms of specification and compared with web operation.

Ontology is good at conceptualization, like said Thomas Gruber "it's an explicit specification of concep- tualization":

1) Afterward,it must be used in an IT artefact, but we have to specify it more later. Ontology will also have to be a logical theory for which we shall specify the manipulated vocabulary;
2) Finally, the conceptualization is sometimes specified in a very precise way. That's why a logical theory cannot always report it in an exact way: she can accept the interpretative wealth of the domain conceptualized in an ontology and make it thus only partially. This gap between the conceptualization and the formal specification is described by Guarino as the ontological commitment which the designer has to accept in the passage of the one to the other one.

The ontology is a theory on the representation of the knowledge. As indicated in 2000, the ontology "defines the kinds of things that exist in the application domain". It is by this theory that it unifies in the domain of the computing. The ontology "is a formal, explicit specification of a shared conceptualization" (Gruber, 1993). For the IT specialist of semantic web, the ontology is a consensual model, because the conceptualization is shared and brings then to build a linguistic specification with the vocabulary RDF/RDFS and the language OWL. In the semiotic perspective, conceptualization according to Gruber relates to the domain of the speech because it is the abstraction. The domain of the speech takes place of the referent. In semiotics, we shall say that the ontology symbolizes the conceptualization, the terms, the notions and the relations which are conceptualized.

THE WEB ONTOLOGY LANGUAGE OWL

The rapid evolution of semantic web ontology languages was enabled by learning from the experiences in developing existing knowledge representation formalisms and database conceptual models, and by inheriting and extending some of their useful features. In particular, the semantic web significantly improves visibility and extensibility aspects of knowledge sharing in comparison with the previous approaches [2] . Its URI-based vocabulary and XML-based grammar are key enablers to web scale knowledge management and sharing.

One of the strong results of semantic web on the ontologies is the normalization of their expression. This point, essential if we want that the ontologies can be shared, exactly seems to find a solution in the context of semantic web: the definition of the language OWL (Web Ontologies Language) at various levels of complexity (capacity of complexity of the descriptions versus calculability) is the best example.

Although already recognisable as an ontology language, the capabilities of RDF are rather limited: they do not, for example, include the ability to describe cardinality constraints (such as Hogwarts Students having at most one pet), a feature found in most conceptual modelling languages, or to describe even a simple conjunction of classes.

The need for a more expressive ontology language was widely recognised within the nascent semantic web research community, and resulted in several proposals for "web ontology languages", including SHOE, OIL and DAML + OIL. The architecture of the web depends on agreed standards and, recognising that an ontology language standard would be a prerequisite for the development of the semantic web, the World Wide Web Consortium (W3C) set up a standardisation working group to develop a standard for a web ontology language. The result of this activity was the OWL ontology language standard [3] . OWL exploited the earlier work on OIL and DAML + OIL, and also tightened the integration of these languages with RDF. The integration of OWL with RDF includes the provision of a RDF based syntax. This has the advantage of making OWL ontologies directly accessible to web based applications, but the syntax is rather verbose and not easy to read. For example, the description of the above mentioned class of Student Wizards would be written in RDF/XML as:

<owl:intersectionof<></owl:intersectionof<>

rdf:parseType="Collection">

In the remainder of this paper, I will instead use an informal \human readable" syntax based on the one used in the Protege 4 ontology development tool [4] . A key feature of OWL is its basis in Description Logics (DLs), a family of logic-based knowledge representation formalisms that are descendants of Semantic Networks and KLONE, but that have a formal semantics based on rstorder logic [5] . These formalisms all adopt an object-oriented model, similar to the one used by Plato and Aristotle, in which the domain is described in terms of individuals, concepts (called classes in RDF), and roles (called properties in RDF). Individuals, e.g., "Hedwig", are the basic elements of the domain; concepts, e.g., "Owl", describe sets of individuals having similar characteristics; and roles, e.g., "hasPet", describe relationships between pairs of individuals, such as "HarryPotterhasPet Hedwig".

In order to avoid confusion, I will keep to the already introduced RDF terminology and from now on refer to these basic language components as individuals, classes and properties. As well as atomic class names such as Wizard and Owl, DLs also allow for class descriptions to be composed from atomic classes and properties. A given DL is characterised by the set of constructors provided for building class descriptions. OWL is based on a very expressive DL called SHOIN (D) a sort of acronym derived from the various features of the language [6] . The class constructors available in OWL include the Booleans and, or and not, which in OWL are called intersectionOf, unionOf and complement Of, as well as restricted forms of existential and universal quantication, which in OWL are called, respectively, "some Values From" and "all Values From" restrictions. OWL also allows for properties to be declared to be transitive| if has Ancestor is a transitive property, then Enoch has Ancestor Cain and Cain has Ancestor Eve implies that Enoch has Ancestor Eve. The S in SHOIN (D) stands for this basic set of features.

In OWL, some values from restrictions are used to describe classes whose instances are related, via a given property, to instances of some other class. For example, Wizard and hasPet some Owl describes those Wizards having pet Owls. Note that such a description is itself a class, the instances of which are just those individuals that satisfy the description; in this case, those individuals that are instances of Wizard and that are related via the hasPet property to an individual that is an instance of Owl. If an individual is asserted to be a member of this class, then we know that they must have a pet Owl, although we may not be able to identify the Owl in question, i.e., some values from restrictions specify the existence of a relationship. In contrast, all values from restrictions constrain the possible objects of a given property and are typically used as a kind of localised range restriction.

For example, we might want to state that Hogwarts students can have only Owls, Cats or Toads as pets without placing a global range restriction on the hasPet property (because other kinds of pet may be possible in general). We can do this in OWL as follows:

Wizard and hasPet some Owl

describes those Wizards having pet Owls. Note that such a description is itself a class, the instances of which are just those individuals that satisfy the description; in this case, those individuals that are instances of Wizard and that are related via the hasPet property to an individual that is an instance of Owl. If an individual is asserted to be a member of this class, then we know that they must have a pet Owl, although we may not be able to identify the Owl in question, i.e., some values from restrictions specify the existence of a relationship. In contrast, all values from restrictions constrain the possible objects of a given property and are typically used as a kind of localised range restriction. For example, we might want to state that Hogwarts students can have only Owls, Cats or Toads as pets without placing a global range restriction on the has Pet property (because other kinds of pet may be possible in general). We can do this in OWL as follows:

Class: HogwartsStudent

SubClassOf: hasPet only (Owl or Cat or Toad)

In addition to the above mentioned features, OWL also allows for property hierarchies (the H in SHOIN (D)), extensionally denied classes using the one of constructor (O), inverse properties using the inverse of property constructor (I), cardinality restrictions using the minCardinality, maxCardinality and cardinality constructors (N), and the use of XML Schema datatypes and values (D) [7] . For example, we could additionally state that the instances of Hogwarts House are exactly Gryndor, Slytherin, Ravenclaw and Huepu, that Hogwarts students have an email address (which is a string) and at most one pet, that isPetOf is the inverse of hasPet and that a Phoenix can only be the pet of a Wizard:

Class: HogwartsHouse

EquivalentTo: {Gryffindor, Slytherin

Ravenclaw, Hufflepuff}

Class: HogwartsStudent

SubClassOf: hasEmail some string

SubClassOf: hasPet max 1

ObjectProperty: hasPet

Inverses: isPetOf

Class: Phoenix

SubClassOf: isPetOf only Wizard

An OWL ontology consists of a set of axioms. As in RDF, subClassOf and subPropertyOf axioms can be used to dene a hierarchy of classes and properties. In OWL, an equivalent Class axiom can also be used as an abbreviation for a symmetrical pair of subClassOf axioms. An equivalentClass axiom can be thought of as an "if and only if" condition: given the axiom C equivalentClass D, then an individual is an instance of C if and only if it is an instance of D. Combining subClassOf and equivalentClass axioms with class descriptions allows for easy extension of the vocabulary by introducing new names as abbreviations for descriptions. For example, the following axiom:

Class: HogwartsStudent

EquivalentTo: Student and attendsSchool

value Hogwarts

introduces the class name HogwartsStudent, and asserts that its instances are just those Students that attend Hogwarts. Axioms can also be used to state that a set of classes is disjoint, and to describe additional characteristics of properties: as well as being Transitive, a property can be Symmetric, Functional or Inverse Functional. For example, the axioms:

DisjointClasses: Owl Cat Toad

Property: isPetOf

Characteristics: Functional

state that Owl, Cat and Toad are disjoint (i.e., that they have no instances in common), and that isPetOf is Functional (i.e., pets can have at most one owner). The above mentioned axioms describe constraints on the structure of the domain, and play a similar role to the conceptual schema in a database setting; in DLs such a set of axioms is called a TBox (Terminology Box). OWL also allows for axioms asserting facts about some concrete situation, similar to data in a database setting; in DLs such a set of axioms is called an ABox (Assertion Box). These might, for example, include the facts:

Individual: HarryPotter

Types: HogwartsStudent

Individual: Fawkes

Types: Phoenix

Facts: isPetOf Dumbledore

Basic facts (i.e., those using only atomic classes) correspond directly to RDF triples|the above facts, for example, correspond to the following triples:

HarryPotterrdf:type, HogwartsStudent

Fawkes rdf:type Phoenix

Fawkes isPetOf Dumbledore

The term ontology is often used to refer just to a conceptual schema or TBox, but in OWL an ontology can consist of a mixture of both TBox and ABox axioms; in DLs, this combination is known as a Knowledge Base. Description Logics are fully edged logics and so have a formal semantics. DLs can, in fact, be seen as decidable subsets of rst-order logic, with individuals being equivalent to constants, concepts to unary predicates and roles to binary predicates. As well as giving a precise and unambiguous meaning to descriptions of the domain, this also allows for the development of reasoning algorithms that can provide correct answers to arbitrarily complex queries about the domain. An important aspect of DL research has been the design of such algorithms, and their implementation in (highly optimised) reasoning systems that can be used by applications to help them "understand" the knowledge captured in a DL based ontology.

ONTOLOGY LANGUAGE PROCESSORS

As we can see, ontologies are like taxonomies but with more semantic relationships between concepts and attributes; they also contain strict rules used to represent concepts and relationships. An ontology is a hierarchically structured set of terms for describing a domain that can be used as a skeletal foundation for a knowledge base. According to this definition, the same ontology can be used for building several knowledge bases.

Indeed, an ontology construct conveys descriptive semantics, and its actionable semantics is enforced by inference. Hence, effective tools, such as parsers, validators, and inference engines, are needed to fulfill the inferenceablity objective:

1. OWLJessKB is the descendent of DAMLJessKB and is based on the Jess Rete inference engine [7] .
2. Java Theorem Prover (JTP) developed at Stanford university [8] supports both forward and backward chaining inference using RDF/RDFS and OWL semantics.
3. Jena (http://jena.sourceforge.net/), developed at HP Labs at Bristol, is a popular open-source project. It provides sound and almost complete (except for blank node types) inference support for RDFS. Current version of Jena also partially supports OWL inference and allows users to create customized rule engines [9]

4. F-OWL developed at UMBC, is an inference engine which is based on Flora-218 [10] .
5. FaCT ++ uses the established FaCT algorithms, but with a different internal architecture. Additionally, FaCT ++ is implementated using C ++ in order to create a more efficient software tool, and to maximise portability [11] .
6. Racer (https://www.ifis.uni-luebeck.de/index.php?id=385) is a description logic based reasoner. It supports inference over RDFS/DAML/OWL ontologies through rules explicitly specified by the user [12] .
7. Pellet (http://www.w3.org/2004/04/13-swdd/SwoopDevDay04.pdf), developed at the University of Maryland, is a "hybrid" DL reasoner that can deal both TBox reasoning as well as non-empty ABox reasoning [13] . It is used as the underlying OWL reasoner for SWOOP ontology editor [14] and provides in-depth ontology consis- tency analysis.
8. TRIPLE developed by Sintek and Decker into Proceedings of the 1st International Semantic Web Con- ference [15] , is a Horn Logic based reasoning engine (and a language) and uses many features from F-logic. Unlike F-logic, it does not have fixed semantics for classes and objects. This reasoner can be used by translating the Description Logics based OWL into a language (named TRIPLE) handled by the reasoner. Extensions of Description Logics that cannot be handled by Horn logic can be supported by incorporating other reasoners, such as FaCT, to create a hybrid reasoning system.
9. SweetRules (http://sweetrules.projects.semwebcentral.org/) is a rule toolkit for RuleML. RuleML is a highly expressive language based on courteous logic programs, and provides additional built-in semantics to OWL, including prioritized conflict handling and procedural attachments. The SweetRules engine also provides semantics preserving translation between a various other rule languages and ontologies (implicit axioms).

The semantics conveyed by ontologies can be as simple as a database schema or as complex as the back- ground knowledge in a knowledge base. By using ontologies in the semantic web, users can leverage the ad- vantages of the following two features:

1) Data are published using common vocabulary and grammar;
2) The semantic description of data is preserved in ontologies and ready for inference.

Ontology transformation [16] is the process used to develop a new ontology to cope with new requirements made by an existing one for a new purpose, by using a transformation function t. In this operation, many changes are possible, including changes in the semantics of the ontology and changes in the representation formalism. Ontology Translation is the function of translating the representation formalism of an ontology while keeping the same semantic. In other words, it is the process of change or modification of the structure of an ontology in order to make it suitable for purposes other than the original one.

There are two types of translation. The first is translation from one formal language to another, for example from RDFS to OWL, called syntactic translation. The second is translation of vocabularies, called semantic translation [17] . The translation problem arises when two Web-based agents attempt to exchange information, describing it using different ontologies. The goal of an ontology is to achieve a common and shared knowledge that can be transmitted between people and between application systems. Thus, ontologies play an important role in achieving interoperability across organizations and on the semantic web, because they aim to capture domain knowledge and their role is to create semantics explicitly in a generic way, providing the basis for agreement within a domain. Thus, ontologies have become a popular research topic in many communities. In fact, ontology is a main component of this research; therefore, the definition, structure and the main operations and applications of ontology are provided.

CONCLUSION

Elodie Marie Gontier Ontologies play an important role in achieving interoperability across organizations and on the semantic web, because they aim to capture domain knowledge and their role is to create semantics explicitly in a generic way, providing the basis for agreement within a domain. In other words, the current web is transformed from being machine-readable to machine-understandable. So, ontology is a key technique with which to annotate semantics and provide a common, comprehensible foundation for resources on the semantic web.

REFERENCES

1. Guarino, N. and Giaretta, P. (1995) Ontologies and Knowledge Bases. In: Towards Very Large Knowledge Bases, IOS Press, Amsterdam, 1-2.
2. Web Ontology Language (OWL) Offers Additional Knowledge Base Oriented Ontology Constructs and Axioms. http://www.w3.org/2002/Talks/04-sweb/slide12-0.html
3. Ian Horrocks, Ontologies and the Semantic Web, Oxford University Computing Laboratory. http://protege.stanford.edu/
4. Baader, F., Calvanese, D., McGuinness, D., Nardi, D. and Patel-Schneider, P.F., Eds. (2003) The Description Logic Handbook: Theory, Implementation and Applications. Cambridge University Press, Cambridge.
5. Horrocks, I. and Sattler, U. (2007) A Tableau Decision Procedure for SHOIQ. Journal of Automated Reasoning, 39, 249-276.
6. Joseph, K. and William, R. (2003) DAMLJessKB: A Tool for Reasoning with the Semantic Web. IEEE Intelligent Systems, 18, 74-77.
7. Joseph, K. And William, R. (2003) DAMLJessKB: A Tool for Reasoning with the Semantic Web. IEEE Intelligent Systems, 18, 74-77.
8. Richard, F., Jessica, J. and Gleb, F. (2003) JTP: A System Architecture and Component Library for Hybrid Reasoning. Stanford University, Stanford.
9. Carroll, J.J, Ian, D., Chris, D., Dave, R., Andy, S. and Kevin, W. (2004) Jena: Implementing the Semantic Web Recommendations. Proceedings of the 13th International World Wide Web Conference on Alternate Track Papers & Posters, 2004, 74-83. ISBN:1-58113-912-8.
10. Zou, Y.Y., Finin, T. and Chen, H. (2004) F-OWL: An Inference Engine for the Semantic Web. Formal Approaches to Agent-Based Systems. Vol. 3228 of Lecture Notes in Computer Science. Springer-Verlag, Berlin. Proceedings of the Third International Workshop (FAABS), 16-18 April 2004.
11. Dmitry, T. and Ian, H. (2003) Implementing New Reasoner with Datatypes Support. Wonder Web: Ontology In- frastructure for the Semantic Web Deliverable.
12. Ian, H. (1998) TheFaCT System. Automated Reasoning with Analytic Tableaux and Related Methods. International Conference Tableaux-98, Springer Verlag, Berlin, 307-312.

13. Evren, S. and Bijan, P. (2004) Pellet: An OWL DL Reasoner. In: Description Logics, CEUR-WS.org, 9.
14. Aditya, K., Bijan, P. and James, H. (2005) A Tool for Working with Web Ontologies. International Journal on Semantic Web and Information Systems, 1, 4.
15. Michael, S. and Stefan, D. (2002) TRIPLE—A Query, Inference, and Transformation Language for the Semantic Web. Proceedings of the 1st International Semantic Web Conference (ISWC-02), Springer-Verlag, Berlin, 364-378.
16. Chalupsky, H. (2000) OntoMorph: A Translation System for Symbolic Knowledge. Proceedings of KR, Morgan Kaufmann Publishers, San Francisco, 471-482.

CHAPTER 4

Towards Understanding Creative Language in Tweets

Linrui Zhang, Yisheng Zhou, Yang Yu, Dan Moldovan

Lymba Corporation, Richardson, TX, USA

ABSTRACT

Extracting fine-grained information from social media is traditionally a challenging task, since the language used in social media messages is usually informal, with creative genre-specific terminology and expression. How to handle such a challenge so as to automatically understand the opinions that people are communicating has become a hot subject of research. In this paper, we aim to show that leveraging the pre-learned knowledge can help

Citation: Zhang, L. , Zhou, Y. , Yu, Y. and Moldovan, D. (2019), "Towards Understanding Creative Language in Tweets". Journal of Software Engineering and Applications, 12, 447-459. doi: 10.4236/jsea.2019.1211028.

neural network models understand the creative language in Tweets. In order to address this idea, we present a transfer learning model based on BERT. We fine-turned the pre-trained BERT model and applied the customized model to two downstream tasks described in SemEval-2018: Irony Detection task and Emoji Prediction task of Tweets. Our model could achieve an F-score of 38.52 (ranked 1/49) in Emoji Prediction task and 67.52 (ranked 2/43) and 51.35 (ranked 1/31) in Irony Detection subtask A and subtask B. The experimental results validate the effectiveness of our idea.

Keywords:- Natural Language Processing, Deep Learning, Transfer Learning

INTRODUCTION

The social media messages have been commonly used to share thoughts and opinions about the surrounding world and have become a new form of communication [1]. Unfortunately, understanding social media messages is not straightforward. The language used in these messages is very informal, with creative vocabularies and expressions, such as creative spellings, #hashtags and emojis, making it more challenging to understand than traditional text, such as newswire [2]. For example, the tweet "Monday mornings are my fave :) # not" is an irony with negative sentiment, but it may be considered as a positive one with traditional sentiment analysis model [3]. With the resurgence of Deep Learning, the recent study of social media understanding mainly focuses on using neural network models. For instance, [4] proposed a connected LSTM model for Tweet Irony Detection. [5] predictedEmojis from Tweets using RNNs with attention. [6] constructed a model with various neural network models, including DeepMoji [7], Skip-Thought [8], etc. to infer the effectual state of a person from the tweets. Even though neural network models can offer reasonably efficient computation, as well as better modeling of sequence, they also suffer from several issues. One major problem is that the training process of these models is purely data-driven, i.e. the knowledge they gained is entirely from the corresponding training data. Such training mechanism may work well for traditional text genres with formal sentences; however, it usually achieves an unsatisfiable performance with informal text, such as social media data. In addition, preparing substantial high-quality training data set also requires a lot of manual effort.

Transfer Learning is a machine learning strategy that stores knowledge gained in solving some upstream tasks and then applies the stored knowledge to solving some new but related downstream tasks [9]. It can be used to solve the above-mentioned issues in neural network models since 1) the transfer learning brings extra knowledge to the target tasks, which may be used to handle the social media messages and 2) the extra knowledge gained from the upstream tasks do not rely on the training data of the target tasks, which can reduce the human effort in preparing the corresponding training set. To validate this idea, we proposed a transfer learning-based model and tested it with two Twitter messages understanding tasks provided by SemEval 2018. We aim to evaluate whether leveraging the pre-learned knowledge can help neural network models understand the creative language in Tweets.

In literature, there are various works focusing on social media Analysis. From SemEval-2013 [10] sentiment analysis in Twitter to SemEval-2018 [11] affect Twitter, social media analysis has been a continuous hot topic in SemEval competition. However, the approaches proposed in these competitions are either rule-based or feature-based (traditional machine learning-based) [12], which usually require considerable manual efforts to develop. Some recent models though leveraged some naïve deep learning technologies, still cannot reach a satisfactory performance [13]. In this paper, we proposed a transfer learning-based system, which requires very limited human effect, but can achieve a state-of-the-art performance. The primary contributions of our paper are as follows:

- We demonstrate the effectiveness of transfer learning model in understanding creative language in Tweets.
- Our model advances the state of the art models in Irony Detection task and Emoji Prediction task in Tweets described in SemEval 2018, exceeding the top performer at Emoji Prediction task by 2.53% in F-score and surpassing the 2-ranked and 1-ranked performer at Irony Detection subtask A and subtask B by 0.7% and 0.3% respectively.
- We perform an ablation study to analyze the factors that affect the performance of our transfer learning model and compare our model with other state-of-the-art learning models in literature on the given tasks.

TASK DESCRIPTION

In this section, we discuss the two selected tasks and introduce the related works.

Task 1: Emoji Prediction

Emojis are graphic symbols that represent ideas or concepts used in electronic messages and web pages [14]. Currently, they are largely adopted by almost any social media service and instant messaging platforms. However, understanding the meanings of emojis is not straightforward, i.e. people sometimes have multiple interpretations of emojis beyond the designer's intent or the physical object they evoke [15]. For instance, 🙏 intends to mean pray, but it is mis-used as high five in many occasions. A misunderstanding of emojis can reverse the meaning of sentences and mislead people. Therefore, effectively predicting emojis is an important step towards understanding text content, especially for the emoji-enriched social media messages, e.g. Twitter. SemEval-2018 Task 2 [16] introduced an Emoji Predication Task.

Given a text message including an emoji, the goal is to predict that emoji based exclusively on the textual content of that message. Specifically, the messages are selected from Twitter data and assume that only one emoji occurs inside each tweet. Figure 1 illustrates an example of a tweet message with an emoji at the end.

Task 2: Irony Detection in Tweets

Irony Detection of Tweets is a challenging task. Previous works, either rule-based systems or supervised machine learning systems, mainly focused on exploiting lexical features from text [17] [18]. This makes the machine has difficulty in assessing the semantic meanings of ironic text and only interprets the text in its literal sense. For example, the sentiment of the tweet Love these cold winter mornings 🙂 best feeling everrrrr! has a high chance to be classified as positive by tradition irony detection systems, since a positive feeling can be inferred from the word love, best feeling and 🙂. However, for human readers, it is obvious that the author does not enjoy the cold winter at all.

SemEval-2018 Task 3 presented a task on Irony Detection in Tweets. Given a tweet, the task aims to determine whether the tweet is ironic (Subtask A) and which type of irony is expressed (Subtask B). Specifically, Subtask A is a binary classification task that requires the submitted systems to predict whether a given tweet is ironic or not. Examples (1) and (2) illustrate an ironic and non-ironic tweet.

National Siblings Day #WeAreFamily #HappyNationalSiblings Day #SisterLikeUs @ TimeSquare… 😘

Figure 1. Example of a tweet with an emoji at the end.

1) Ironic. Yay for another work at 4 am 😐

2) Non-ironic. On my lunch break so sleepy 😴

Subtask B describes a multiclass irony classification task to define whether a tweet contains a specific type of irony. Examples (3) to (6) provide an explanation of each irony class, associated with one example. For more details about how each kind of irony is defined, please refer to the original paper.

3) Verbal irony by means of a polarity contrast. This category applies to instances containing an evaluative expression whose polarity is inverted between the literal and the intended evaluation.

Example: I love waking up at 8 am on a Saturday morning after going to bed at midnight.

4) Other verbal irony. This category contains instances that show no polarity contrast between the literal and the intended evolution, but are nevertheless ironic.

Example: @someuserYeah keeping cricket clean, that's what he wants #Sarcasm

5) Situational irony. This category contains instances that describe situations that fail to meet some expectations.

Example: As if I need more water in my pasture.

6) Non-ironic. This category contains instances that are not ironic.

Example: On my lunch break so sleepy 😴.

MODEL DESCRIPTION

Currently, almost all popular transfer learning-based NLP models follow a pre-training and fine-tuning strategy. The model is pre-trained unsupervisely over different upstream tasks and then is customized to solve related downstream tasks by fine-tuning the model parameters with the training data provided by the downstream tasks. Typical transfer-learning based NLP models include: GPT [19], BERT [20] or XLNet [21]. BERT is currently the most popular model in NLP community. It takes the advantage of bi-directional training and can outperform the performance of GPT and meanwhile the BERT based model needs less computational power than XLNet. In this case, we decided to build our system based on BERT.

We selected the pre-trained BERT model designed for sequence classification (a.k.a Bert for Sequence Classification) and fine-tuned the model parameters using the labeled data of the target tasks. The main structure of our model is illustrated in Figure 2 and the detailed implementation is introduced in the following sections.

Input Preprocessing

Since there is a large variation of vocabulary used in Tweets, such as creative spellings, URLs, #hashtags, etc., we have to normalize the inputs before sending them to the system. We utilized the ekphrasis tool [22] as the Twitter processor.

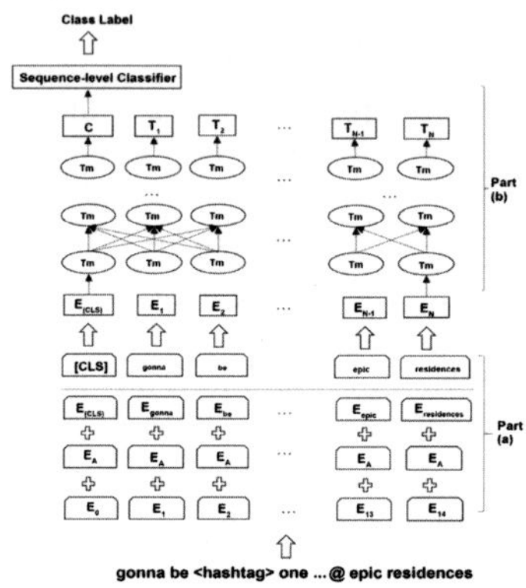

Figure 2. The main structure of our system.

It can perform tokenization, word normalization, word segmentation and spell correction for Twitter. There are several benefits of using the preprocessed tweets as inputs. For example, ekphrasis can recognize URLs (e.g. https://t.co/10PEnv2pz5) and substitute them with labels (). This can significantly reduce the vocabulary size of the system without losing too much information. Table 1 gives an example of a tweet processed by ekphrasis tool.

Pre-Training Step

To make the paper self-contained, we first briefly introduce the pre-training step of BERT. More details about the model structure and the pre-training step could be found in the original paper.

BERT is pre-trained with two unsupervised upstream tasks: Masked LM and Next Sentence Prediction (NSP). In the Masked LM task, the system randomly masked out 15% of the tokens in each sequence and used the rest of the content to predict the masked tokens. This allows the model to learn a deep bidirectional representation of a sequence. In the NSP task, the system is trained to predicate if a sentence B is directly following another sentence A from a corpus. This allows the model to learn the relationship between the two sentences.

Fine-Tuning Step

The fine-tuning step aims to fine-tune the parameters of the per-trained modelin order to customize the model for our new tasks. The details of the Fine-tuning step are discussed in this section.

Table 1. An example of a tweet processed by ekphrasis tool.

Original	Gonna be #oneepicsummer 3 Days|May 7th 2016 https://t.co/10PEnv2pz5 @Epic Residences
Processed	Gonna be one epic summer days @ epic residences

Structure

The structure of our model is illustrated in Figure 2. It contains two components: (a) sequence representation and (b) sequence classification.

The aim of part (a) is to process the tweets into the format that can be accepted by BERT. The BERT input embeddings are the concatenation of three different kinds of embeddings: 1) Token Embeddings (e.g. E_{gonna}), 2) Segmentation Embeddings (e.g. E_A) and 3) Position Embeddings (e.g. E_1). The token embeddings are initialized with the pre-learned word embeddings during the pre-training step. The segmentation embeddings indicate whether the input sentence belongs to the first or the second sentence in the pre-training step. The position embeddings describe the positions of the tokens in the input sentences.

After the input sequences are formed into BERT input format, they are passed through the sequence classification component (part b). We specifically selected the pre-trained Bert for Sequence Classification Model as the sequence classifier.

Bert for Sequence Classification is a fine-tuning model that includes Bert Model and a sequence-level classifier on top of the Bert Model. The parameters of the Bert Model are initialized with the same parameters from the pre-training step and the parameters of the sequence-level classifier are waited to be trained in the fine-tuning step.

Training

During the fine-tuning step, the pre-processed Twitter messages are feed into the system to generate the probability of the candidate class labels. We used back propagation and Adam optimizer to train the system. Since both downstream tasks are classification problems, we select cross-entropy loss as the object function, which is calculated as follows:

$$Loss = -\sum_{i=1}^{n} \sum_{j=1}^{m} y_i^j \log p_i^j \qquad (1)$$

where, y is a binary indicator (0 or 1) indicating whether a class label is correctly classified. P is the predicted probability of the correctly classified label. n is the number of training examples and i [1, n] is the index number of the training examples. m is the total number of the class labels and j [1, m] is the index number of the class labels.

Hyperparameter

The only new parameters introduced during fine-tuning step are the number_ of_labels in the output layer. We set it to be the same as the number of class labels of the corresponding tasks. The rest of the hyperparameters are set as default values in BERT. Table 2 shows the hyperparameters used for fine-tuning.

EXPERIMENTS AND RESULTS

Emoji Prediction Task

Corpus

For the Emoji Prediction Task, we used the corpus provided by SemEval-2018. It collected roughly 550 K tweets (500 K for training and 50 K for testing) that include one of the twenty emojis that occur most frequently in the Twitter data. The relative frequency percentage of each emoji in the train and test set is shown in Table 3. From the table, we could observe that the corpus is not balanced. In order to handle this imbalanced issue, we selected macro-averaged F1-measure as the evaluation matrix of our system.

Experimental Results

Table 4 illustrates the performance of our model compared with the top performers in SemEval-2018 Task 2. The macro-averaged precision recall and F-score are presented.

We selected the top 1 performer Tubingen-Oslo [23], top 2 performer NTUA-SLP top 4 performer EmoNLP [24], top 6 performer UMDuluth-

CS8761 [25] and the top 7 performer BASELINE system as the comparison system.

From the results, we can observe that our model can achieve state-of-the-art performance, exceeding the top performer Tubingen-Oslo (using SVM) by 2.53% in F-score, as well as the top neural network-based model NTUA-SLP (using RNNs) and the BASELINE model by 3.16% and 7.54%.

Effectiveness of Fine-Tuning Set Size

A key factor in the pretrain-finetune model is the size of the fine-tuning data. In this case, we present the F-score of our system against the training set size in Figure 3.

Table 2. Hyperparameters for fine-tuning.

Hyperparameter	Value
Max_sequ_length	128
Train_batch_size	32
Learning_rate	2e-5
Num_training_epochs	3
Number_of_labels (Emoji PredictionTask)	20
Number_of_labels (Irony Detection Task A)	2
Number_of_labels (Irony Detection Task B)	4
Pre-trained BERT model	Bert-base-uncased
Optimizer	BERT Adam
Lower case	True

Table 3. The distribution of the emoji labels.

#	Emoji	Train	Test	#	Emoji	Train	Test
1	❤️	22.4%	21.6%	11	📷	3.2%	2.9%
2	😍	10.3%	9.7%	12	🇺🇸	3.0%	3.9%
3	😂	10.2%	9.1%	13	☀️	2.9%	2.5%
4	💕	5.5%	5.2%	14	💜	2.6%	2.2%
5	🔥	4.9%	7.4%	15	😉	2.7%	2.6%
6	😊	4.7%	3.2%	16	💯	2.7%	2.5%
7	😎	4.3%	4.0%	17	😁	2.6%	2.3%
8	✨	3.6%	5.5%	18	🎄	2.6%	3.1%
9	💙	3.4%	3.1%	19	📸	2.6%	4.8%
10	😘	3.2%	2.4%	20	😜	2.6%	2.0%

Table 4. Comparison of the participating systems with our system by precision, recall and F-score (in percentage) in the test set of SemEval-2018 task 2.

Team	Precision	Recall	F-score
Ours	**40.64%**	**41.76%**	**38.52%**
Tübingen-Oslo	36.55%	36.22%	35.99%
NTUA-SLP	34.53%	38.00%	35.36%
EmoNLP	39.43%	33.70%	33.67%
UMDuluth-CS8761	39.90%	31.37%	31.83%
Baseline	30.34%	33.00%	30.98%

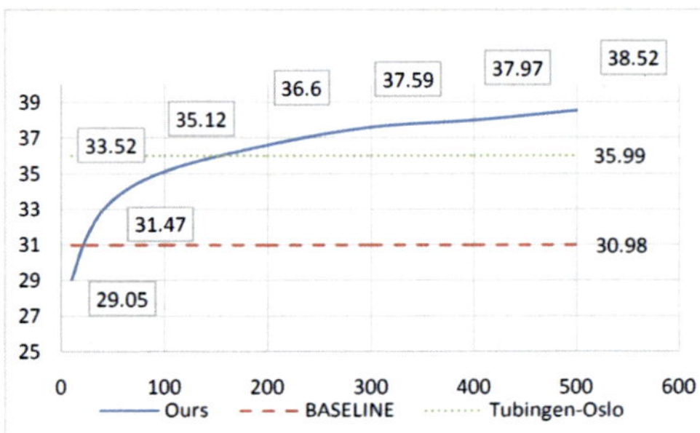

Figure 3. Learning curve of our model against the training set (×1000 instances). Horizontal axis indicate the size of the fine-tuning data and the vertial axis indicates the system performance in F_1 score.

From Figure 3, we can observe that the performance curve of our model is increasing with the increasing size of the fine-tuning set. Our model can surpass the BASELINE model and the top performer when the fine-tuning set size reaches to around 20 K and 200 K. Intuitively speaking, this indicates that our model is gradually customized to adapt to the target task.

Irony Detection Task

Corpus

SemEval-2018 Task 3 presents the task on irony detection. It contains two subtasks: subtask A determines whether a tweet is ironic or not and subtask B determines the irony types of the tweet. For both tasks, a training corpus of 3834 tweets, as well as a test set of 784 tweets, is provided. Subtask A is a binary classification problem, so we used regular F-score that only reports results for the class specified by positive label. Subtask B is a multi-label classification problem and has the same corpus imbalance issue with emoji predication task, so we used macro-averaged F-score as the evaluation matric. The distribution of the different irony types of Subtask B experimental corpus is presented in Table 5.

Experimental Results

Table 6 demonstrates the experimental results of our model compared with other participants. The top three performers THU_NGN, NTUA-SLP [26] and WLV [27] on Subtask A and UCDCC [28], NTUA-SLP and THU_NGN on Subtask B are selected as the comparison models.

From the results, we can observe that our model can obtain competitive to state-of-the-art result on Subtask A and state-of-the-art results on Subtask B.

Effectiveness of Training Epochs

Unlike the previous emoji prediction task that contains as large as 500 K training samples, the iron detection task only contains roughly 4 K training samples. This implies that the learning model is more likely to overfit the data. In order to illustrate the influence of overfitting, we show the system performance against the training epochs in Figure 4. From the table, we can observe that the overfitting appears after three training epochs.

RESULTS ANALYSIS

From the experimental results, we can have the following observations:

- Our model can achieve state-of-the-art performance on Emoji Predication task and Irony Detection subtask B described in SemEval-2018. The reason is that the pre-learned knowledge from BERT provides a high starting point for the downstream tasks to begin with. By leveraging these pre-trained knowledges, the system can better understand the semantic meanings of the input data.

Table 5. Distribution of the different irony categories in the corpus.

Class labels	# of instances
Verbal irony by means of a polarity contrast	1728

Other types of verbal irony	267
Situational irony	401
Non-ironic	604

Table 6. Comparison of the participating systems with our system by precision, recall and F-score in the test set of SemEval-2018 task 3.

Task	Team	Precision	Recall	F-score
A	Our	0.604	0.765	0.675
	THU_NGN	0.630	0.801	0.705
	NTUA-SLP	0.654	0.691	0.672
	WLV	0.532	0.836	0.650
B	Our	0.529	0.527	0.514
	UCDCC	0.577	0.504	0.507
	NTUA-SLP	0.496	0.512	0.496
	THU_NGN	0.486	0.541	0.495

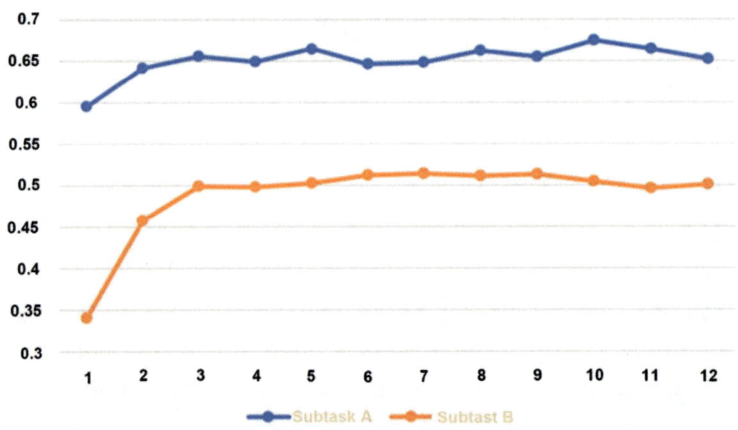

Figure 4. Performance curve of our model against the training epochs. Horizontal axis indicate the training epochs and the vertial axis indicates the system performance in F_1 score.

- The performance improvement is more obvious in Emoji Predication task than Irony Detection task. This indicates that fine-tuning set size is a very important factor in transfer learning. In Emoji Prediction task, we note that only after the system is fine-tune with 200 k samples, can it surpass the performance the state-of-the-art model. On the contrary, in the Irony detection task, we only have 4 k fine-tuning data. The system will overfit on the data before it can surpass the best performer in literature. From Figure 4, we can notice that the overfitting appears when the training epoch research to 3. As a result, our model can only rank 2nd place in Irony Detection subtask A and only beyond the best model by 0.7% on subtask B.

- Except from the pre-learned knowledge, the complex structure of BERT also contributes to the superior performance of the transfer learning model. Compared with the LSTM-based model, BERT contains 12 to 24 layers of transformer [29]. The multiple transformer layers enable BERT to learn a more complicated representation of the input sentences. This makes it easier for the classification layer to classify the input instances in the high dimensional space.
- The complex structure of BERT also leads to several issues. The first issue is the overfitting problem we have discussed earlier that we need more training data to fine-tune the system. The second issue is the time complexity. According to our experiment, the speed of the fine-tuning procedure is 100 examples/second on one NVIDIA Titan RTX GPU, which is much slower than the LSTM-based models

CONCLUSIONS

In this paper, we implemented a transfer learning based system with BERT and applied it to two social media understanding tasks, the Emoji Predication task and the Irony Detection task. Experimental results have shown that leveraging the pre-learned knowledge can significantly increase the ability of neural network model in understanding the creative language used in social media messages.

We also analyzed the features that have an effect on the transfer learning-based model and concluded that the quality of the model is highly dependent on the size of the fine-tuning set.

There are several avenues of future work. The primary work should be the optimization of the fine-tuning set. We will crawl more data, specifically focusing on social media genre, from online resources in order to improve the quality and gain the quantity of the fine-tuning data. Besides, we plan to integrate linguistic features into the system so as to leverage the lexical and syntactic information to improve the system performance. In addition, reducing the training and predicting time of the model so that our research can be more suitable for industrial applications, is another desirable improvement.

CONFLICTS OF INTEREST

The authors declare no conflicts of interest regarding the publication of this paper.

REFERENCES

1. Rosenthal, S., Farra, N. and Nakov, P. (2017) SemEval-2017 Task 4: Sentiment Analysis in Twitter. Proceedings of the 11th International Workshop on Semantic Evaluation (SemEval-2017), Vancouver, Canada, August 2017, 502-518. https://doi.org/10.18653/v1/S17-2088
2. Nakov, P., Ritter, A., Rosenthal, S., Sebastiani, F. and Stoyanov, V. (2016) SemEval-2016 Task 4: Sentiment Analysis in Twitter. Proceedings of the 10th International Workshop on Semantic Evaluation (Semeval-2016), San Diego, CA, June 2016, 1-18. https://doi.org/10.18653/v1/S16-1001
3. Van Hee, C., Lefever, E. and Hoste, V. (2018) Semeval-2018 Task 3: Irony Detection in English Tweets. Proceedings of The 12th International Workshop on Semantic Evaluation, New Orleans, LA, June 2018, 39-50. https://doi.org/10.18653/v1/S18-1005
4. Wu, C., Wu, F., Wu, S., Liu, J., Yuan, Z. and Huang, Y. (2018) THU_NGN at Semeval-2018 Task 3: Tweet Irony Detection with Densely Connected LSTM and Multi-Task Learning. Proceedings of The 12th International Workshop on Semantic Evaluation, New Orleans, LA, June 2018, 51-56. https://doi.org/10.18653/v1/S18-1006
5. Baziotis, C., Nikolaos, A., Kolovou, A., Paraskevopoulos, G., Ellinas, N. and Potamianos, A. (2018) NTUA-SLP at SemEval-2018 Task 2: Predicting Emojis Using RNNs with Context-Aware Attention. Proceedings of The 12th International Workshop on Semantic Evaluation, New Orleans, LA, June 2018, 438-444. https://doi.org/10.18653/v1/s18-1069
6. Paetzold, G. (2018) UTFPR at IEST 2018: Exploring Character-to-Word Composition for Emotion Analysis. Proceedings of the 9th Workshop on Computational Approaches to Subjectivity, Sentiment and Social Media Analysis, Brussels, Belgium, October 2018, 176-181. https://doi.org/10.18653/v1/W18-6224
7. Felbo, B., Mislove, A., Søgaard, A., Rahwan, I. and Lehmann, S. (2017) Using Millions of Emoji Occurrences to Learn Any-Domain Representations for Detecting Sentiment, Emotion and Sarcasm. Proceedings of the 2017 Conference on Empirical Methods in Natural Language Processing, Copenhagen, Denmark, September 2017, 1615-1625. https://doi.org/10.18653/v1/D17-1169
8. Kiros, R., Zhu, Y., Salakhutdinov, R.R., Zemel, R., Urtasun, R.,

Torralba, A. and Fidler, S. (2015) Skip-Thought Vectors. In: Advances in Neural Information Processing Systems, 3294-3302.

9. West, J., Ventura, D. and Warnick, S. (2007) Spring Research Presentation: A Theoretical Foundation for Inductive Transfer. Brigham Young University, College of Physical and Mathematical Sciences, 32.
10. Whlson, T., Kozareva, Z., Nakov, P., Rosenthal, S., Stoyanov, V. and Ritter, A. (2013) SemEval-2013 Task 2: Sentiment Analysis in Twitter. Proceedings of the International Workshop on Semantic Evaluation, Atlanta, GA.
11. Mohammad, S., Bravo-Marquez, F., Salameh, M. and Kiritchenko, S. (2018) Semeval-2018 Task 1: Affect in Tweets. Proceedings of the 12th International Workshop on Semantic Evaluation, New Orleans, LA, June 2018, 1-17. https://doi.org/10.18653/v1/S18-1001
12. Zhu, X., Kiritchenko, S. and Mohammand, S. (2014) Nrc-Canada-2014: Recent Improvements in the Sentiment Analysis of Tweets. Proceedings of the 8th International Workshop on Semantic Evaluation, Dublin, Ireland, August 2014, 443-447. https://doi.org/10.3115/v1/S14-2077
13. Tang, D., Wei, F., Qin, B., Liu, T. and Zhou, M. (2014) Coooolll: A Deep Learning System for Twitter Sentiment Classification. Proceedings of the 8th International Workshop on Semantic Evaluation, Dublin, Ireland, August 2014, 208-212. https://doi.org/10.3115/v1/S14-2033
14. Cappallo, S., Mensink, T. and Snoek, C.G. (2015) Image2emoji: Zero-Shot Emoji Prediction for Visual Media. Proceedings of the 23rd ACM International Conference on Multimedia, Brisbane, Australia, 26-30 October 2015, 1311-1314. https://doi.org/10.1145/2733373.2806335
15. Barbieri, F., Ballesteros, M. and Saggion, H. (2017) Are Emojis Predictable? Proceedings of the 15th Conference of the European Chapter of the Association for Computational Linguistics, 2, 105-111. https://doi.org/10.18653/v1/E17-2017
16. Barbieri, F., Camacho-Collados, J., Ronzano, F., Anke, L.E., Ballesteros, M., Basile, V., Saggion, H., et al. (2018) SemEval 2018 Task 2: Multilingual Emoji Prediction. Proceedings of The 12th International Workshop on Semantic Evaluation, New Or-leans, LA, June 2018, 24-33. https://doi.org/10.18653/v1/S18-1003
17. Bouazizi, M. and Ohtsuki, T.O. (2016) A Pattern-Based Approach for Sarcasm Detection on Twitter. IEEE Access, 4, 5477-5488. https://doi.org/10.1109/ACCESS.2016.2594194

18. Van Hee, C., Lefever, E. and Hoste, V. (2016) Exploring the Realization of Irony in Twitter Data. Proceedings of the Tenth International Conference on Language Resources and Evaluation (LREC 2016), 1794-1799.
19. Radford, A., Narasimhan, K., Salimans, T. and Sutskever, I. (2018) Improving Language Understanding with Unsupervised Learning. Technical Report, OpenAI.
20. Devlin, J., Chang, M.W., Lee, K. and Toutanova, K. (2019) BERT: Pre-Training of Deep Bidirectional Transformers for Language Understanding. Proceedings of the 2019 Conference of the North American Chapter of the Association for Computational Linguistics: Human Language Technologies, 1, 4171-4186.
21. Yang, Z., Dai, Z., Yang, Y., Carbonell, J., Salakhutdinov, R. and Le, Q.V. (2019) XLNet: Generalized Autoregressive Pretraining for Language Understanding. arXiv preprint arXiv:1906.08237.
22. Baziotis, C., Pelekis, N. and Doulkeridis, C. (2017) Datastories at Semeval-2017 Task 4: Deep LSTM with Attention for Message-Level and Topic-Based Sentiment Analysis. Proceedings of the 11th International Workshop on Semantic Evaluation (SemEval-2017), Vancouver, Canada, August 2017, 747-754. https://doi.org/10.18653/v1/S17-2126
23. Çöltekin, Ç. and Rama, T. (2018) Tübingen-Oslo at SemEval-2018 Task 2: SVMs Perform Better than RNNs in Emoji Prediction. Proceedings of The 12th International Workshop on Semantic Evaluation, New Orleans, LA, June 2018, 34-38. https://doi.org/10.18653/v1/S18-1004
24. Liu, M. (2018) EmoNLP at SemEval-2018 Task 2: English Emoji Prediction with Gradient Boosting Regression Tree Method and Bidirectional LSTM. Proceedings of The 12th International Workshop on Semantic Evaluation, New Orleans, LA, June 2018, 390-394. https://doi.org/10.18653/v1/S18-1059
25. Beaulieu, J. and Owusu, D.A. (2018) UMDuluth-CS8761 at SemEval-2018 Task 2: Emojis: Too Many Choices? Proceedings of The 12th International Workshop on Semantic Evaluation, New Orleans, LA, June 2018, 400-404. https://doi.org/10.18653/v1/S18-1061
26. Baziotis, C., Nikolaos, A., Papalampidi, P., Kolovou, A., Paraskevopoulos, G., Ellinas, N. and Potamianos, A. (2018) NTUA-SLP at SemEval-2018 Task 3: Tracking Ironic Tweets Using Ensembles of Word and Character Level Attentive RNNs. Proceedings of The 12th

International Workshop on Semantic Evaluation, New Orleans, LA, June 2018, 613-621. https://doi.org/10.18653/v1/S18-1100

27. Rohanian, O., Taslimipoor, S., Evans, R. and Mitkov, R. (2018) WLV at SemEval-2018 Task 3: Dissecting Tweets in Search of Irony. Proceedings of The 12th International Workshop on Semantic Evaluation, New Orleans, LA, June 2018, 553-559. https://doi.org/10.18653/v1/S18-1090
28. Ghosh, A. and Veale, T. (2018) IronyMagnet at SemEval-2018 Task 3: A Siamese Network for Irony Detection in Social Media. Proceedings of The 12th International Workshop on Semantic Evaluation, New Orleans, LA, June 2018, 570-575. https://doi.org/10.18653/v1/S18-1093
29. Vaswani, A., Shazeer, N., Parmar, N., Uszkoreit, J., Jones, L., Gomez, A.N., Polosukhin, I., et al. (2017) Attention Is All You Need. 31st Conference on Neural Information Processing Systems (NIPS 2017), Long Beach, CA, 5998-6008.

SECTION 2
NATURAL LANGUAGE PROCESSING IN IT AND WEB SYSTEMS

CHAPTER

5

Resolving Topic-Focus Ambiguities in Natural Language

Marie Duzi

VŠB-Technical University of Ostrava

INTRODUCTION

Natural language has features that are not found in logically perfect artificial languages. One such feature is redundancy, where two or more terms/expressions share exactly the same semantic and logical (but perhaps not pragmatic or rhetoric) properties. Another feature is its converse, namely ambiguity, where one term/expression has more than one meaning. A logical analysis of such a piece of natural language will typically translate each of its

Citation: Marie Duží (April 25th 2012). "Resolving Topic-Focus Ambiguities in Natural Language", Semantics in Action - Applications and Scenarios, Muhammad Tanvir Afzal, IntechOpen, DOI: 10.5772/36481.

unambiguous meanings into logically perfect notation. Frege'sBegriffsschrift was the first major attempt in modern logic to create such a notation (though he primarily intended it for mathematical language). 1 There are various origins and various manifestations of ambiguity, not least cases bearing on quantifier scopes, like "Every boy dances with one girl". Another sort of example is "John loves his wife, and so does Peter", which is ambiguous between Peter loving John's wife and Peter loving his own wife, because it is ambiguous which property 'so' picks up. 2 A third, and perhaps less-noticed, sort of ambiguity is pivoted on whether the topic or the focus of a sentence is highlighted. For instance, "John only introduced Bill to Sue", to use Hajičová's example, 3 lends itself to two different kinds of construal: "John did not introduce other people to Sue except for Bill" and "The only person Bill was introduced to by John was Sue". There are two sentences whose semantics, logical properties and consequences only partially overlap. A similar phenomenon also crops up in the case of propositional attitudes and their less-attended 'cousins' of notional attitudes like seeking and finding, calculating and proving.

In this chapter I will deal in particular with ambiguities in natural language exemplifying the difference between topic and focus articulation within a sentence. This difference is closely related to the disambiguation stemming from supposition de dicto and de re with which a particular expression is used. I will show that whereas articulating the topic of a sentence activates a presupposition, articulating the focus frequently yields merely entailment. Based on an analysis of topic-focus articulation, I propose a solution to the almost hundred-year old dispute over Strawsonian vs. Russellian definite descriptions. 4 The point of departure isthat sentences of the form "The F is a G" are ambiguous. Their ambiguity is, in my view, not rooted in a shift of meaning of the definite description 'the F'. Rather, the ambiguity stems from different topic-focus articulations of such sentences. Russell and Strawson took themselves to be at loggerheads; whereas, in fact, they spoke at cross purposes. The received view still tends to be that there is room for at most one of the two positions, since they are deemed incompatible. And they are, of course, incompatible – if they must explain the same set of data. But they should not, in my view. One theory is excellent at explaining one set of data, but poor at explaining the data that the other theory is excellent at explaining; and vice versa. My novel contribution advances the research into definite descriptions by pointing out how progress has been hampered by a false dilemma and how to move beyond that dilemma. The point is this. If 'the F' is the topic phrase then this description occurs with de re supposition and Strawson's analysis appears to be what is wanted. On this reading the sentence presupposes the existence of the descriptum of 'the F'. The other option is 'G' occurring as topic and 'the F' as focus. This reading corresponds to Donnellan's attributive use of 'the F' and the description occurs with de dicto supposition. On this reading the Russellian analysis gets the truth-conditions of the sentence right. The existence of a unique F is merely entailed.

Ancillary to my analysis is a general analytic schema of sentences coming with a presupposition. This analysis makes use of a definition of the 'if-then-else' connective known from programming languages. A broadly accepted view of the semantic nature of this connective is that it is a so-called non-strict function that does not comply with the principle of compositionality. However, the semantic nature of the connective is contested among computer scientists. I will show — and this is also a novel contribution of mine — that there is no cogent reason for embracing a non-strict definition and context-dependent meaning, provided a higher-order logic making it possible to operate on hyperintensions is applied. The framework of Tichý's Transparent Intensional Logic (TIL) possesses sufficient expressive power, and will figure as background theory throughout my exposition. 5

Tichý's TIL was developed simultaneously with Montague's Intensional Logic, IL. 6 The technical tools of disambiguation will be familiar from IL, with two exceptions. One is that we λ-bind separate variables w, w_1, …,w_n ranging over possible worlds and t, t_1, …, t_n ranging over times. This dual binding is tantamount to explicit intensionalization and temporalization. The other exception is that functional application is the logic both of extensionalization of intensions (functions from possible worlds) and of predication. 7 Application is symbolized by square brackets, '[…]'. Intensions are extensionalized by applying them to worlds and times, as in [[Intension w] t], abbreviated by subscripted terms for world and time variables: Intensionwt is the extension of the generic intension Intension at ⟨w, t⟩. Thus, for instance, the extensionalization of a property yields a set (possibly an empty one), and the extensionalization of a proposition yields a truth-value (or no value at all). A general objection to Montague's IL is that it fails to accommodate hyperintensionality, as indeed any formal logic interpreted set-theoretically is bound to unless a domain of primitive hyperintensions is added to the frame. Any theory of natural-language analysis needs a hyperintensional (preferably procedural) semantics in order to crack the hard nutsof natural language semantics. In global terms, without procedural semantics TIL is an anticontextualist (i.e., transparent), explicitly intensional modification of IL. With procedural semantics, TIL rises above the model-theoretic paradigm and joins instead the paradigm of hyperintensional logic and structured meanings.

The structure of this chapter is as follows. In Section 2 I briefly summarise the history of the dispute between Russell and Strawson (as well as their proponents and opponents) on the semantic character of sentences containing definite descriptions. Section 3 is an introduction to TIL. In paragraph 3.1 I introduce the semantic foundations of TIL and in 3.2 its logical foundations. Sections 4 and 5 contain the main results of this study. In Section 4 I propose a solution to the dispute over Strawsonian vs. Russellian definite descriptions. Paragraph 4.1 is an introduction to the problem of ambiguities stemming from different topic-focus articulation and a solution based on this distinction is proposed in paragraph 4.2. Section 5 generalizes the method of topic-focus disambiguation to sentences containing not only definite descriptions but also general terms occurring with different suppositions. To this end I make use of the strict analysis of the if-then-else function that is defined in paragraph 5.1. The method is then illustrated by analysing some more examples in paragraph 5.2. Finally, Section 6 summarizes the results.

RUSSELL VS. STRAWSON ON DEFINITE DESCRIPTIONS

There is a substantial difference between proper names and definite descriptions. This distinction is of crucial importance due to their vastly different logical behaviour. Independently of any particular theory of proper names, it should be granted that a proper proper name (as opposed to a definite description grammatically masquerading as a proper name) is a rigid designator of a numerically particular individual. On the other hand, a definite description like, for instance, 'the Mayor of Dunedin', 'the King of France', 'the highest mountain on Earth', etc., offers an empirical criterion that enables us to establish which individual, if any, satisfies the criterion in a particular state of affairs. The contemporary discussion of the distinction between names and descriptions was triggered by Russell (1905). Russell's key idea is the proposal that a sentence like

(1) "The F is a G", containing a definite description 'the F' is understood to have, in the final analysis, the logical form

(1′) $\exists x\,(Fx \wedge \forall y\,(Fy \supset x=y) \wedge Gx)$, rather than the logical form $G(\iota x\, Fx)$.

Though Russell's quantificational theory remains to this day a strong rival of referential theories, it has received its fair share of criticism. First, Russell's translation of simple sentences like "The F is a G" into the molecular form "There is at least one F and at most one thing is an F and that thing is a G" is rather enigmatic, because Russell disregards the standard constraint that there must be a fair amount of structural similarity between analysandum and analysans. Second, Russell proposed the elimination of Peano's descriptive operator 'ι' understood as 'the only', and deprived definite descriptions of their self-contained meaning. Third, Russell simply got the truth-conditions wrong in important cases of using descriptions when there is no such thing as the unique F. This criticism was launched by Strawson who in (1950) objected that Russell's theory predicts the wrong truthconditions for sentences like 'The present King of France is bald'. According to Russell'sanalysis, this sentence is false, but according to Strawson, this outcome does not conform to our intuitions about its truth or falsity. In Strawson's view, the sentence can be neither true nor false whenever there is no King of France. Obviously, in such a state of affairs the sentence is not true. However, if it were false then its negation, "The King of France is not bald", would be true, which entails that there is a unique King of France, contrary to the assumption that there is none. Strawson held that sentences like these not only entail the existence of the present King of France, but also presuppose his existence. If 'the present King of France' fails to refer, then the presupposition is false and the sentence fails to have a determinate truth value. 8

Russell (1957) in response to Strawson's criticism argued that, despite Strawson's protests, the sentence was in fact false:

Suppose, for example, that in some country there was a law that no person could hold public office if he considered it false that the Ruler of the Universe is wise. I think an avowed atheist who took advantage of Mr. Strawson's doctrine to say that he did not hold this proposition false would be regarded as a somewhat shifty character. (Russell, 1957)

Donnellan (1966) observed that there is a sense in which Strawson and Russell are both right (and both wrong) about the proper analysis of definite descriptions, because definite descriptions can be used in two different ways. On a so-called attributive use, a sentence of the form 'The F is a G' is used to express a proposition equivalent to 'Whatever is uniquely F is a G'. Alternatively, on a referential use, a sentence of the form 'The F is a G' is used to pick out a specific individual, a, and to say of a that a is a G. Donnellan suggested that Russell's quantificational account of definite descriptions might capture attributive uses, but that it does not work for referential uses. Ludlow in (2007) interprets Donnellan as arguing that in some cases descriptions are Russellian and in other cases they are Strawsonian.

Kripke (1977) responded to Donnellan by arguing that the Russellian account of definite descriptions could, by itself, account for both referential and attributive uses, and that the difference between the two cases could be entirely a matter of pragmatics, because there is an important distinction between what one literally says by an utterance and what one intends to communicate by that utterance. Neale (1990) supported Russell's view by collecting a number of previously observed cases in which intuitions about truth conditions clearly do not support Strawson's view. On the other hand, a number of linguists have recently come to Strawson'sdefence on this matter. For a detailed survey of the arguments supporting Strawson's view and also arguments supporting Russell's, see (Ludlow, 2007). Here it might suffice to say that Strawson's concerns have not delivered a knock-out blow to Russell's theory of descriptions, and so this topic remains very much alive. Recently, von Fintel in (2004) argues that every sentence containing a definite description 'the F' comes with the existential presupposition that there be a unique F. For instance, he argues against the standpoint that the sentence "Last week, my friend went for a drive with the king of France" is false. He claims that this sentence presupposes that there be a king of France and that in the technical sense the sentence has no truth-value.

In this chapter I am not going to take into account Kripke's pragmatic factors like the intentions of a speaker. In other words, I am not going to take into account what a speaker might have meant by his/her utterance, for this is irrelevant to a logical semantic theory. So I am disregarding Donnellan's troublesome notion of having somebody in mind. Instead, I will propose a literal semantic analysis of sentences of the form "The F is a G". What I want to show is this. First, definite descriptions are not deprived of a self-contained meaning and they denote one and the same entity in any context. Thus they are never Russellian. Second, Russell's insight that a definite description 'the F' does not denote a definite individual is spot-on. Rather, according to TIL, 'the F' denotes a condition to be contingently satisfied by the individual (if any) that happens to be the F. I will explicate such conditions in terms of possible-world intensions, viz. as individual roles or offices to be occupied by at most one individual per world/time pair. Third, I am going to show that Donnellan was right that sentences of the form "The F is a G" are ambiguous. However, their ambiguity does not concern a shift of meaning of the definite description 'the F'. Rather, the ambiguity concerns different topic-focus articulations of these sentences. There are two options. The description 'the F' may occur in the topic of a sentence and property G (the focus) is predicated of the topic. This case corresponds to Donnellan's referential use; using medieval terminology I will say that 'the F' occurs with de re supposition. The other option is 'G' occurring as topic and 'the F' as focus. This reading corresponds to Donnellan's attributive use of 'the F' and the description occurs with de dicto supposition. Consequently, such sentences are ambiguous between their de dicto and de re readings. On their de re reading they presuppose the existence of a unique F. Thus Strawson's analysis appears to be adequate for de re cases. On their de dicto reading they have the truth-conditions as specified by the Russellian analysis. They do not presuppose, but only entail, the existence of a unique F. However, the Russellian analysis, though being equivalent to the one I am going to propose, is not an adequate literal analysis of de dicto readings.

I am going to bring out the semantic nature of the topic-focus difference by means of a logical analysis. As a result, I will furnish sentences differing only in their topic-focus articulation with different structured meanings producing different possible-world propositions. 9 Moreover, the proposed solution of the problem of definite descriptions generalizes to any sentences differing in their topic-focus articulation. Thus I am going to introduce a general analytic schema of sentences that come with a presupposition. Since our logic is a hyperintensional logic of partial functions, I am able to analyse sentences with presuppositions in a natural way. It means that I furnish them with hyperpropositions, viz. procedures that produce partial possible-world propositions, which occasionally yield truthvalue gaps. 10

FOUNDATIONS OF TIL

TIL is an overarching semantic theory for all sorts of discourse, whether colloquial, scientific, mathematical or logical. The theory is a procedural (as opposed to denotational) one, according to which sense is an abstract, extra-linguistic procedure detailing what operations to apply to what procedural constituents to arrive at the product (if any) of theprocedure. Such procedures are rigorously defined as TIL constructions. The semantics is tailored to the hardest case, as constituted by hyperintensional contexts, and generalized from there to simpler intensional and extensional contexts. This entirely anti-contextual and compositional semantics is, to the best of my knowledge, the only one that deals with all kinds of context in a uniform way. Thus we can characterize TIL as an extensional logic of hyperintensions. 11 The sense of an empirical sentence is an algorithmically structured construction of the proposition denoted by the sentence. The denoted proposition is a flat, or unstructured, mapping with domain in a logical space of possible worlds. Our motive for working 'top-down' has to do with anti-contextualism: any given unambiguous term or expression (even one involving indexicals or anaphoric pronouns) expresses the same construction as its sense whatever sort of context the term or expression is embedded within. And the meaning of an expression determines the respective denoted entity (if any), but not vice versa. The denoted entities are (possibly 0-ary) functions understood as settheoretical mappings. Thus we strictly distinguish between a procedure (construction) and its product (here, a constructed function), and between a function and its value. What makes TIL suitable for the job of disambiguation is the fact that the theory construes the semantic properties of the sense and denotation relations as remaining invariant across different sorts of linguistic contexts. 12 Thus logical analysis disambiguates ambiguous expressions in such a way that an ambiguous expression is furnished with more than one context-invariant meaning that is TIL construction. However, logical analysis cannot dictate which disambiguation is the intended one. It falls to pragmatics to select the intended one.

Semantic foundations of TIL

The context-invariant semantics of TIL is obtained by universalizing Frege'sreferenceshifting semantics custom-made for 'indirect' contexts. 13 The upshot is that it becomes trivially true that all contexts are transparent, in the sense that pairs of terms that are codenoting outside an indirect context remain co-denoting inside an indirect context and vice versa. In particular, definite descriptions that only contingently describe the same individual never qualify as co-denoting. 14 Our term for the extra-semantic, factual relation of contingently describing the same entity is 'reference', whereas 'denotation' stands for the intra-semantic, pre-factual relation between two words that pick out the same entity at the same world/time-pairs.

The syntax of TIL is Church's (higher-order) typed λ-calculus, but with the all-important difference that the syntax has been assigned a procedural (as opposed to denotational) semantics. Thus, abstraction transforms into the molecular procedure of forming a function, application into the molecular procedure of applying a function to an argument, and variables into atomic procedures for arriving at their values. Furthermore, TIL constructions represent our interpretation of Frege's notion of Sinn (with the exception that constructions are not truth-bearers; instead some present either truth-values or truth conditions) and are kindred to Church's notion of concept. Constructions are linguisticsenses as well as modes of presentation of objects and are our hyperintensions. While the Frege-Church connection makes it obvious that constructions are not formulae, it is crucial to emphasize that constructions are not functions(-in-extension), either. They might be explicated as Church's 'functions-in-intension', but we do not use the term 'function-in-intension', because Church did no define it (he only characterized functionsin-intension as rules for presenting functions-in-extension). Rather, technically speaking, some constructions are modes of presentation of functions, including 0-place functions such as individuals and truth-values, and the rest are modes of presentation of other constructions. Thus, with constructions of constructions, constructions of functions, functions, and functional values in our stratified ontology, we need to keep track of the traffic between multiple logical strata. The ramified type hierarchy does just that. What is important about this traffic is, first of all, that constructions may themselves figure as functional arguments or values.

Thus we consequently need constructions of one order higher in order to present those being arguments or values of functions. With both hyperintensions and possible-world intensions in its ontology, TIL has no trouble assigning either hyperintensions or intensions to variables as their values. However, the technical challenge of operating on constructions requires two (occasionally three) interrelated, non-standard devices. The first is Trivialization, which is an atomic construction, whose only constituent part is itself. The second is the function Sub (for 'substitution'). (The third is the function Tr (for 'Trivialization'), which takes an object to its Trivialization.) We say that Trivialization is used to mention other constructions.[15] The point of mentioning a construction is to make it, rather than what it presents, a functional argument. Hence for a construction to be mentioned is for it to be Trivialized; in this way the context is raised up to a hyperintensional level.

Our neo-Fregean semantic schema, which applies to all contexts, is this triangulation:

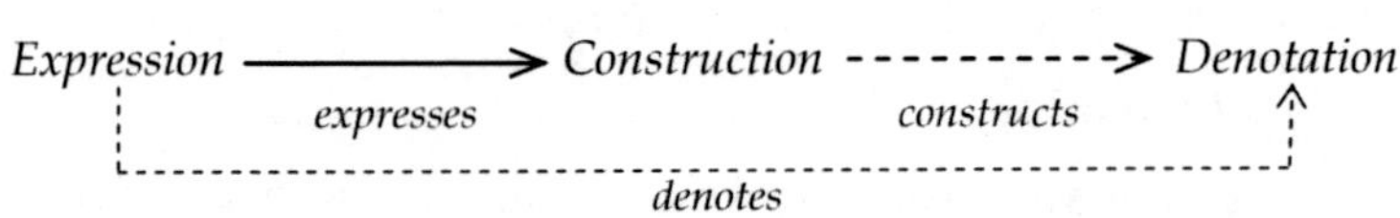

Figure 1. TIL semantic schema.

The most important relation in this schema is between an expression and its meaning, i.e., a construction. Once constructions have been defined, we can logically examine them; we can investigate a priori what (if anything) a construction constructs and what is entailed by it. Thus meanings/ constructions are semantically primary, denotations secondary, because an expression denotes an object (if any) via its meaning that is a construction expressed by the expression. Once a construction is explicitly given as a result of logical analysis, the entity (if any) it constructs is already implicitly given. As a limiting case, the logical analysis may reveal that the construction fails to construct anything by being improper.

Logical Foundations of TIL

In this section we set out the definitions of first-order types (regimented by a simple type theory), constructions, and higher-order types (regimented by a ramified type hierarchy), which taken together form the nucleus of TIL, accompanied by some auxiliary definitions. The type of first-order object includes all objects that are not constructions. Therefore, it includes not only the standard objects of individuals, truth-values, sets, etc., but also functions defined on possible worlds (i.e., the intensions germane to possible-world semantics). Sets, for their part, are always characteristic functions and insofar extensional entities. But the domain of a set may be typed over higher-order objects, in which case the relevant set is itself a higher-order object. Similarly for other functions, including relations, with domain or range in constructions. That is, whenever constructions are involved, we find ourselves in the ramified type hierarchy. 16 The definition of the ramified hierarchy of types decomposes into three parts: firstly, simple types of order 1; secondly, constructions of order n; thirdly, types of order n + 1.

Definition 1 (types of order 1). Let B be a base, where a base is a collection of pair-wise disjoint, non-empty sets. Then:

i. Every member of B is an elementary type of order 1 over B.

ii. Let $\alpha, \beta_1, \ldots, \beta_m$ $(m > 0)$ be types of order 1 over B. Then the collection $(\alpha\ \beta_1 \ldots \beta_m)$ of all m-ary partial mappings from $\beta_1 \times \ldots \times \beta_m$ into ˩ is a functional type of order 1 over B.

Nothing is a type of order 1 over B unless it so follows from (i) and (ii).

Definition 2 (construction) i. The Variable x is a construction that constructs an object X of the respective type dependently on a valuation v; x v-constructs X.

ii. Trivialization: Where X is an object whatsoever (an extension, an intension or a construction), 0X is the construction Trivialization. It constructs X without any change.

iii. The Composition $[X\ Y_1 \ldots Y_m]$ is the following construction. If X v-constructs a function f of a type$(\alpha\beta_1 \ldots \beta_m)$, and $Y_1, \ldots, Y_m$ v-construct entities $B_1, \ldots, B_m$ of types$\beta_1 \ldots \beta_m$, respectively, then the Composition $[X\ Y_1 \ldots Y_m]$ v-constructs the value (an entity, if any, of type ˩) of f on the tuple-argument $\langle B_1, \ldots, B_m \rangle$. Otherwise the Composition $[X\ Y_1 \ldots Y_m]$ does not v-construct anything and so is v-improper.

iv. The Closure $[\lambda x_1 \ldots x_m\ Y]$ is the following construction. Let x_1, $x_2, \ldots, x_m$ be pair-wise distinct variables v-constructing entities of types $\beta_1 \ldots \beta_m$and Y a construction vconstructing an ˩ -entity. Then $[\lambda x_1 \ldots xm_Y]$ is the construction λ-Closure (or Closure). It vconstructs the following function f of the type $(\alpha\beta_1 \ldots \beta_m)$. Let $v(B_1/x_1, \ldots, B_m/x_m)$ be a valuation identical with v at least up to assigning objects $B_1/\beta_1, \ldots, B_m/\beta_m$ to variables $x_1, \ldots, x_m$. If Y is $v(B_1/x_1, \ldots, B_m/x_m)$-improper (see iii), then f is undefined on the argument $\langle B_1, \ldots, B_m \rangle$. Otherwise the value of f on $\langle B_1, \ldots, B_m \rangle$ is the α-entity $v(B_1/x_1, \ldots, B_m/x_m)$-constructed by Y.

v. The Single Execution ^1X is the construction that either v-constructs the entity vconstructed by X or, if X v-constructs nothing, is v-improper (yielding nothing relative to v).

vi. The Double Execution ^2X is the following construction. Where X is any entity, the Double Execution ^2X is v-improper (yielding nothing relative to v) if X is not itself a construction, or if X does not v-construct a construction, or if X v-constructs a v-improper construction. Otherwise, let X v-construct a construction Y and Y v-construct an entity Z: then 2X v-constructs Z.

Nothing is a construction, unless it so follows from (i) through (vi).

Definition 3 (ramified hierarchy of types).

T1 (types of order 1). See Definition 1.

Cn (constructions of order n)

i. Let x be a variable ranging over a type of order n. Then x is a construction of order n over B.

ii. Let X be a member of a type of order n. Then ^0X, ^1X, ^2X are constructions of order n over B.

iii. Let X, X_1,..., X_m (m > 0) be constructions of order n over B. Then [X X_1... X_m] is a construction of order n over B.

iv. Let x_1,...x_m, X (m > 0) be constructions of order n over B. Then [λx1...xm X] is a construction of order n over B.

v. Nothing is a construction of order n over B unless it so follows from Cn (i)-(iv).

T_{n+1} (types of order n + 1). Let *n be the collection of all constructions of order n over B. Then

i. *n and every type of order n are types of order n + 1.

ii. If 0 < m and α, β_1,...,β_m are types of order n + 1 over B, then ($\alpha\beta_1$ ... β_m) (see T_1 ii)) is a type of order n + 1 over B.

Nothing is a type of order n + 1 over B unless it so follows from T_{n+1} (i) and (ii).

Remark. For the purposes of natural-language analysis, we are currently assuming the following base of ground types, which is part of the ontological commitments of TIL:

ο: the set of truth-values {T, F};

ι: the set of individuals (the universe of discourse);

τ: the set of real numbers (doubling as discrete times);

ω: the set of logically possible worlds (the logical space).

Empirical languages incorporate an element of contingency, because they denote empirical conditions that may or may not be satisfied at some world/time pair of evaluation. Nonempirical languages (in particular the language of mathematics) have no need for an additional category of expressions for empirical conditions. We model these empirical conditions as possible-world intensions. They are entities of type (β_ω): mappings from possible worlds to an arbitrary type β. The type β is frequently the type of the chronology of α-objects, i.e., a mapping of type (ατ). Thus α-intensions are frequently functions of type ((ατ)ω), abbreviated as '$\alpha_{\tau\omega}$'. Extensional entities are entities of a type α where α≠ (β_ω) for any type β. Examples of frequently used intensions are: propositions of type $o_{\tau\omega}$, properties of individuals of type $(o\iota)_{\tau\omega}$, binary relations-in-intension between individuals of type $(o\iota\iota)_{\tau\omega}$, individualoffices/roles of type $\iota_{\tau\omega}$. Our explicit intensionalization and temporalization enables us to encode constructions of possible-world intensions, by means of terms for possible-world variables and times, directly in the logical syntax. Where variable w ranges over possible worlds (type ω) and t over times (type τ), the following logical form essentially characterizes the logical syntax of any empirical language: $\lambda w \lambda t$ [...w....t...]. Where α is the type of the object vconstructed by [...w....t...], by abstracting over the values of variables w and t we construct a function from worlds to a partial function from times to α, that is a function of type $((\alpha\tau)\omega)$, or '$\alpha_{\tau\omega}$' for short.

Logical objects like truth-functions and quantifiers are extensional: $\wedge$ (conjunction), $\vee$ (disjunction) and $\supset$ (implication) of type (ooo), and $\neg$ (negation) of type (oo). The quantifiers $\forall^{\alpha}$, $\exists^{\alpha}$ are type-theoretically polymorphous functions of type $(o(o\alpha))$, for an arbitrary type α, defined as follows. The universal quantifier $\forall^{\alpha}$ is a function that associates a class A of α- elements with T if A contains all elements of the type α, otherwise with F. The existential quantifier $\exists^{\alpha}$ is a function that associates a class A of α-elements with T if A is a non-empty class, otherwise with F. Another kind of partial polymorphic function we need is the Singularizer I^{α} of type $(\alpha(o\alpha))$. A singularizer is a function that associates a singleton S with the only member of S, and is otherwise (i.e. if S is an empty set or a multi-element set) undefined.

Below all type indications will be provided outside the formulae in order not to clutter the notation. Furthermore, 'X/α' means that an object X is (a member) of type α. '$X \rightarrow_{v} \alpha$' means that the type of the object v-constructed by X is α. We write '$X \rightarrow \alpha$' if what is vconstructed does not depend on a valuation v. This holds throughout: $w \rightarrow_{v} \omega$ and $t \rightarrow v\ \tau$. If $C \rightarrow_{v} \alpha_{\tau\omega}$ then the frequently used Composition [[C w] t], which is the intensional descent (a.k.a. extensionalization) of the α-intension v-constructed by C, will be encoded as 'C_{wt}'. When using constructions of truth-functions, we often omit Trivialisation and use infix notation to conform to standard notation in the interest of better readability. Also when using constructions of identities of α-entities, $=_{\alpha}/(o\alpha\alpha)$, we omit Trivialization, the type subscript, and use infix notion when no confusion can arise. For instance, instead of

'$[{}^{0}\!\supset [{}^{0}\!=_{\iota}\ a\ b]\ [{}^{0}\!=_{((o\tau)\omega)} \lambda w \lambda t\ [P_{wt}\ a]\ \lambda w \lambda t\ [P_{wt}\ b]]]$'

where $=_{\iota}/(o\iota\iota)$ is the identity of individuals and $=_{((o\tau)\omega)}/(oo_{\tau\omega}o_{\tau\omega})$ the identity of propositions; a, b constructing objects of type ι, P objects of type $(o\iota)_{\tau\omega}$, we write

'$[[a = b] \supset [\lambda w \lambda t\ [P_{wt}\ a] = \lambda w \lambda t\ [P_{wt} b]]]$'

We invariably furnish expressions with procedural structured meanings, which are explicated as TIL constructions. The analysis of an unambiguous sentence thus consists in discovering the logical construction encoded by a given sentence. The TIL method of analysis consists of three steps:

1. Type-theoretical analysis, i.e., assigning types to the objects that receive mention in the analysed sentence.
2. Type-theoretical synthesis, i.e., combining the constructions of the objects ad (1) in order to construct the proposition of type $o_{\tau\omega}$ denoted by the whole sentence.
3. Type-theoretical checking, i.e. checking whether the proposed analysans is typetheoretically coherent.

To illustrate the method, we analyse the notorious sentence "The King of France is bald" in the Strawsonian way. The sentence talks about the office of the King of France (topic) ascribing to the individual (if any) that occupies this office the property of being bald (focus). Thus it is presupposed that the King of France exist, i.e., that the office be occupied. If it is not, then the proposition denoted by the sentence has no truth-value. 17 This fact has to be revealed by our analysis. Here is how.

Ad (1) King_of/$(\iota\iota)_{\tau\omega}$: an empirical function that dependently on ⟨w, t⟩-pairs assigns to one individual (a country) another individual (its king); France/ι; King_of_France/$\iota_{\tau\omega}$; Bald/$(o\iota)_{\tau\omega}$.

Ad (2) and (3). For the sake of simplicity, I will demonstrate the steps (2) and (3) simultaneously. In the second step we combine the constructions of the objects ad (1) in order to construct the proposition (of type $o_{\tau\omega}$) denoted by the whole sentence. Since we intend to arrive at the literal analysis of the sentence, the objects denoted by the semantically simple expressions are constructed by their Trivialisations: ^{0}King_of, ^{0}France, ^{0}Bald. In order to construct the office King_of_France, we have to combine ^{0}King_of and ^{0}France. The function King_of must be extensionalised first via the Composition $^0\text{King\_of}_{wt} \rightarrow v\ (\iota\iota)$, and the result is then applied to France; we get $[^0\text{King\_of}_{wt}\ ^0\text{France}] \rightarrow v\ \iota$. Abstracting over the values of w and t we obtain the Closure that constructs the office: $\lambda w \lambda t\ [^0\text{King\_of}_{wt}\ ^0\text{France}] \rightarrow \iota_{\tau\omega}$. But the property of being bald cannot be ascribed to an individual office. Rather, it is ascribed to the individual (if any) occupying the office. Thus the office has to be subjected to intensional descent first: $\lambda w \lambda t\ [_0\text{King\_of}_{wt}$ $0\text{France}]_{wt \rightarrow v\iota}$. The property itself has to be extensionalised as well: $^0\text{Bald}_{wt}$. By Composing these two constructions, we obtain either a truth-value (T or F) or nothing, according as the King of France is, or is not, bald, or does not exist, respectively. Finally, by abstracting over the values of the variables w and t, we construct the proposition:

$$\lambda w \lambda t\ [^0Bald_{wt}\ \lambda w \lambda t\ [^0King\_of_{wt}\ ^0France]_{wt}]$$

Gloss. In any world (λw) at any time (λt) do this. First, find out who is the King of France: [0King_of$_{wt}$ ^{0}France]. If there is none, then terminate with a truth-value gap because the Composition [^{0}King_of$_{wt}$ ^{0}France] is v-improper. Otherwise, check whether the so obtained individual has the property of being bald: [^{0}Bald$_{wt}$ [^{0}King_of$_{wt}$ ^{0}France]]. If he is, then T, otherwise F. So much for the method of analysis and the semantic schema of the logic of TIL.

DEFINITE DESCRIPTIONS: STRAWSONIAN OR RUSSELLIAN?

Now I am going to propose a solution to the Strawson-Russell standoff. In other words, I am going to analyse the phenomena of presupposition and entailment connected with using definite descriptions with supposition de dicto or de re, and I will show how the topic-focus distinction determines which of the two cases applies.

Topic-Focus Ambiguity

When used in a communicative act, a sentence communicates something (the focus F) about something (the topic T). Thus the schematic structure of a sentence is F(T). The topic T of a sentence S is often associated with a presupposition P of S such that P is entailed both by S and non-S. On the other hand, the clause in the focus usually occasions a mere entailment of some P by S. To give an example, consider the sentence "Our defeat was caused by John". 18 There are two possible readings of this sentence. Taken one way, the sentence is about our defeat, conveying the snippet of information that it was caused by John. In such a situation the sentence is associated with the presupposition that we were defeated. Indeed, the negated form of the sentence, "Our defeat was not caused by John", also implies that we were defeated. Thus 'our defeat' is the topic and 'was caused by John' the focus clause. Taken the other way, the sentence is about the topic John, ascribing to him the property that he caused our defeat (focus). Now the scenario of truly asserting the negated sentence can be, for instance, the following. Though it is true that John has a reputation for being rather a bad player, Paul was in excellent shape and so we won. Or, another scenario is thinkable. We were defeated, only not because of John but because the whole team performed badly. Hence, our being defeated is not presupposed by this reading, it is only entailed.

Schematically, if $\models$ is the relation of entailment, then the logical difference between a mere entailment and a presupposition is this:

P is a *presupposition* of *S*: $(S \models P)$ and $(non\text{-}S \models P)$

Corollary: If *P* is not true, then *neither S nor non-S* is true. Hence, *S* has no truth-value.

P is only *entailed* by *S*: $(S \models P)$ and neither $(non\text{-}S \models P)$ nor $(non\text{-}S \models non\text{-}P)$

Corollary: If *S* is not true, then we cannot deduce anything about the truth-value of *P*.

More precisely, the entailment relation obtains between hyperpropositions P, S; i.e., the meaning of P is analytically entailed or presupposed by the meaning of S. Thus $\models/((o^{*}n^{*}n)$ is defined as follows. Let C^S, C^P be constructions assigned to sentences S, P, respectively, as their meanings. Then S entails P ($C^S \models C^P$) iff the following holds: 19

$$\forall w \forall t\ [[{}^0True_{wt}\ C^S] \supset [{}^0True_{wt}\ C^P]]$$

Since we work with properly partial functions, we need to apply the propositional property $True/(oo_{\tau\omega})_{\tau\omega}$, which returns T for those ⟨w, t⟩-pairs at which the argument proposition is true, and F in all the remaining cases. There are two other propositional properties: False and Undef, both of type $(oo_{\tau\omega})_{\tau\omega}$. The three properties are defined as follows. Let P be a propositional construction ($P/^{*}n \rightarrow o_{\tau\omega}$). Then

$[{}^0True_{wt}\ P]$ *v*-constructs the truth-value **T** iff P_{wt} *v*-constructs **T**, otherwise **F**.
$[{}^0False_{wt}\ P]$ *v*-constructs the truth-value **T** iff $[\neg P_{wt}]$ *v*-constructs **T**, otherwise **F**.
$[{}^0Undef_{wt}\ P]$ *v*-constructs the truth-value **T** iff

$[\neg[{}^0True_{wt}\ P] \wedge \neg[{}^0False_{wt}\ P]]$ *v*-constructs **T**, otherwise **F**.

Thus we have:

$$\neg[{}^0Undef_{wt}\ P] = [[{}^0True_{wt}\ P] \vee [{}^0False_{wt}\ P]]$$

$$\neg[{}^0True_{wt}\ P] = [[{}^0False_{wt}\ P] \vee [{}^0Undef_{wt}\ P]]$$

$$\neg[{}^0False_{wt}\ P] = [[{}^0True_{wt}\ P] \vee [{}^0Undef_{wt}\ P]]$$

Hence, though we work with truth-value gaps, we do not work with a third truth-value, and our logic is in this weak sense bivalent.

The King of France revisited

Above we analysed the sentence "The King of France is bald" on its perhaps most natural reading as predicating the property of being bald (the focus) of the individual (if any) that is the present King of France (the topic). Yet there is another, albeit less natural reading of the sentence. Imagine that the sentence is uttered in a situation when we are talking about baldness, and somebody asks "Who is bald?" The answer might be "Well, among those who are bald there is the present King of France". If you got such an answer, you would most probably protest, "This cannot be true, for there is no King of France now". On such a reading the sentence is about baldness (topic) claiming that this property is instantiated, among others, by the King of France (focus). Since there are no rigorous grammatical rules in English to distinguish between the two variants, the input of our logical analysis is the result of a linguistic analysis, where the topic and focus of a sentence are made explicit. 20 In this chapter I will mark the topic clause in italics. The two readings of the above sentence are: (S) "The King of France is bald" (Strawsonian) and (R) "The King of France is bald" (Russellian). The analysis of (S) is as above:

$$\lambda w \lambda t\ [{}^0 Bald_{wt}\ \lambda w \lambda t\ [{}^0 King\_of_{wt}\ {}^0 France]_{wt}]$$

The meaning of 'the King of France', viz. $\lambda w \lambda t\ [\ {}^0 King\_of_{wt} {}^0 France]$, occurs in (S) with de re supposition, because the object of predication is the unique value in a ⟨w, t⟩-pair of evaluation of the office rather than the office itself. 21 The following two de re principles are satisfied: the principle of existential presupposition and the principle of substitution of coreferential expressions. Thus the following arguments are valid (though not sound):

The King of France is/is not bald

The King of France exists

The King of France is bald

The King of France is Louis XVI

Louis XVI is bald

Here are the proofs.

(a) existential presupposition:

First, existence is here a property of an individual office rather than of some non-existing individual (whatever it might mean for an individual not to exist). Thus we have $Exist/(o\iota_{\tau\omega})_{\tau\omega}$. To prove the validity of the first argument, we define $Exist/(o\iota_{\tau\omega})_{\tau\omega}$ as the property of an office's being occupied at a given world/time pair:

$${}^0 Exist =_{of} \lambda w \lambda t\ \lambda c\ [{}^0\exists \lambda x\ [x =_i c_{wt}]],$$
$$\text{i.e. } [{}^0 Exist_{wt}\ c] =_o [{}^0\exists \lambda x\ [x =_i c_{wt}]]$$

Types: $\exists/(o(o\iota))$: the class of non-empty classes of individuals; $c \rightarrow_v \iota_{\tau\omega}$; $x \rightarrow_v \iota$; $=_o/(ooo)$: the identity of truth-values; $=_{of}/(o(o\iota_{\tau\omega})_{\tau\omega}(o\iota_{\tau\omega})_{\tau\omega})$: the identity of properties of individual offices; $=_i/(o\iota\iota)$: the identity of individuals, x

$\rightarrow_v \iota$. Now let Louis/ι, Empty/(ο(οι)) the singleton containing the empty set of individuals, and Improper/$(o*_1)_{\tau\omega}$ the property of constructions of being v-improper at a given ⟨w, t⟩-pair, the other types as above. Then at any ⟨w, t⟩-pair the following proof steps are truth-preserving:

1)	$(\neg)[{}^0Bald_{wt}\ \lambda w \lambda t\ [{}^0King\_of_{wt}\ {}^0France]_{wt}]$	∅
2)	$\neg[{}^0Improper_{wt}\ {}^0[\lambda w \lambda t\ [{}^0King\_of_{wt}\ {}^0France]_{wt}]]$	by Def. 2, iii)
3)	$\neg[{}^0Empty\ \lambda x\ [x =_i [\lambda w \lambda t\ [{}^0King\_of_{wt}\ {}^0France]]_{wt}]]$	from (2) by Def. 2, iv)
4)	$[{}^0\exists \lambda x\ [x =_i [\lambda w \lambda t\ [{}^0King\_of_{wt}\ {}^0France]]_{wt}]]$	EG
7)	$[{}^0Exist_{wt}\ [\lambda w \lambda t\ [{}^0King\_of_{wt}\ {}^0France]]]$	by def. of *Exist*.

(b) *substitution*:

1)	$[{}^0Bald_{wt}\ \lambda w \lambda t\ [{}^0King\_of_{wt}\ {}^0France]_{wt}]$	∅
2)	$[{}^0Louis =_i \lambda w \lambda t\ [{}^0King\_of_{wt}\ {}^0France]_{wt}]$	∅
3)	$[{}^0Bald_{wt}\ {}^0Louis]$	substitution of identicals

As explained above, the sentence (R) is not associated with the presupposition that the present King of France exist, because 'the King of France' occurs now in the focus clause. The truth-conditions of the Russellian "The King of France is bald" are these:

- True, if among those who are bald there is the King of France
- False, if among those who are bald there is no King of France (either because the present King of France does not exist or because the King of France is not bald).

Thus the two readings (S) and (R) have different truth-conditions, and they are not equivalent, albeit they are co-entailing. The reason is this. Trivially, a valid argument is truth-preserving from premises to conclusion. However, due to partiality, the entailment relation may fail to be falsity-preserving from conclusion to premises. As a consequence, if A, B are constructions of propositions such that A ⊨ B and B ⊨ A, then A, B are not necessarily equivalent in the sense of constructing the same proposition. The propositions they construct may not be identical, though the propositions take the truth-value T at exactly the same world/times, because they may differ in such a way that at some ⟨w, t⟩-pair(s) one takes the value F while the other isundefined. The pair of meanings of (S) and (R) is an example of such co-entailing, yet nonequivalent hyperpropositions. If the value of the proposition constructed by the meaning of (S) is T then so is the value of the proposition constructed by the meaning of (R), and vice versa. But, for instance, in the actual world now the proposition constructed by (S) has no truth-value whereas the proposition constructed by (R) takes value F.

Now I am going to analyse (R). Russell argued for his theory in (1905, p. 3):

The evidence for the above theory is derived from the difficulties which seem unavoidable if we regard denoting phrases as standing for genuine constituents of the propositions in whose verbal expressions they occur. Of the possible theories which admit such constituents the simplest is that of Meinong. This theory regards any grammatically correct denoting phrase as standing for an object. Thus 'the present King of France', 'the round square', etc., are supposed to be genuine objects. It is admitted that such objects do not subsist, but nevertheless they are supposed to be objects. This is in itself a difficult view; but the chief objection is that such objects, admittedly, are apt to infringe the law of contradiction. It is contended, for example, that the existent present King of France exists, and also does not exist; that the round square is round, and also not round, etc. But this is intolerable; and if any theory can be found to avoid this result, it is surely to be preferred.

We have such a theory at hand, viz. TIL. Moreover, TIL makes it possible to avoid the other objections against Russell's analysis as well. Russellian rephrasing of the sentence "The King of France is bald" is this: "There is a unique individual such that he is the King of France and he is bald". This sentence expresses the construction

(*R**) $\lambda w\lambda t\ [^0\exists\lambda x\ [x =_i [\lambda w\lambda t\ [^0King\_of_{wt}\,^0France]_{wt}] \wedge [^0Bald_{wt}\ x]]]$.[22]

TIL analysis of the 'Russellian rephrasing' does not deprive 'the King of France' of its meaning. The meaning is invariably, in all contexts, the Closure $\lambda w\lambda t\ [_0King\_of_{wt}\ 0France]$. Thus the second objection to the Russellian analysis is not pertinent here. Moreover, even the third objection is irrelevant, because in (R*) $\lambda w\lambda t\ [^0King\_of^{wt0}France]$ occurs intensionally unlike in the analysis of (S) where it occurs extensionally. 23 The existential quantifier ∃ applies to sets of individuals rather than a particular individual. The proposition constructed by (R*) is true if the set of individuals who are bald contains the individual who occupies the office of King of France, otherwise it is simply false. The truth conditions specified by (R*) are Russellian. Thus we might be content with (R*) as an adequate analysis of the Russellian reading (R). Yet we should not be. The reason is this. Russell's analysis has another defect; it does not comply with Carnap's principle of subject-matter, which states, roughly, that only those entities that receive mention in a sentence can become constituents of its meaning. 24 Inother words, (R*) is not the literal analysis of the sentence "The King of France is bald"., because existence and conjunction do not receive mention in the sentence. Russell did avoid the intolerable result that the King of France both does and does not exist, but the price he paid is too high, because his rephrasing of the sentence is too loose a reformulation of it. TIL, as a hyperintensional, typed partial λ-calculus, is in a much better position to solve the problem.

From the logical point of view, the two readings differ in the way their respective negated form is obtained. Whereas the Stawsonian negated form is "The King of France is not bald", which obviously lacks a truth-value if the King of France does not exist, the Russellian negated form is "It is not true that the King of France is bald", which is true at those ⟨w, t⟩- pairs where the office is not occupied. Thus in the Strawsonian case the property of not being bald is ascribed to the individual, if any, that occupies the royal office. The meaning of 'the King of France' occurs with de re supposition, as we have seen above. On the other hand, in the Russellian case the property of not being true is ascribed to the whole proposition that the King is bald, and thus (the same meaning of) the description 'the King of France' occurs with de dicto supposition. Hence we simply ascribe the property of being or not being true to the whole proposition. To this end we apply the propositional property True/$(oo_{\tau\omega})\tau_{\omega}$ defined above. Now the analysis of the sentence (R) is this construction:

(*R'*) $\lambda w \lambda t\ [{}^0True_{wt}\ \lambda w \lambda t\ [{}^0Bald_{wt}\ \lambda w \lambda t\ [{}^0King\_of_{wt}\ {}^0France]_{wt}]]$

Neither (*R'*) nor its negation

(*R'*_neg) $\lambda w \lambda t\ \neg[{}^0True_{wt}\ \lambda w \lambda t\ [{}^0Bald_{wt}\ \lambda w \lambda t\ [{}^0King\_of_{wt}\ {}^0France]_{wt}]]$

entail that the King of France exists, which is just as it should be. (R'_neg) constructs the proposition non-P that takes the truth-value T if the proposition that the King of France is bald takes the value F (because the King of France is not bald) or is undefined (because the King of France does not exist).

Consider now another group of sample sentences:

(1) "The King of France visited London yesterday."

(1') "The King of France did not visit London yesterday."

The sentences (1) and (1') talk about the (actual and current) King of France (the topic), ascribing to him the property of (not) having visited London yesterday (the focus). Thus both sentences share the presupposition that the King of France actually exist now. If this presupposition fails to be satisfied, then neither of the propositions expressed by (1) and (1') has a truth-value. The situation is different in the case of sentences (2) and (2'):

(2) "London was visited by the King of France yesterday."

(2') "London was not visited by the King of France yesterday."

Now the property (the focus) of having been visited by the King of France yesterday is predicated of London (the topic). The existence of the King of France (now) is presupposed neither by (2) nor by (2'). The sentences can be read as "Among the visitors of London yesterday was (not) the King of France". The existence of the King of France yesterday is onlyentailed by (2) and not presupposed. 25 Our analyses respect these conditions. Let Yesterday/$((o\tau)_\tau)$ be the function that associates a given time t with the time interval that is yesterday with respect to t; Visit/$(o\iota\iota)_{\tau\omega}$; King_of/$(\iota\iota)_{\tau\omega}$; France/ι; $\exists^\tau/(o(o\tau))$: the existential quantifier that assigns to a given set of times the truth-value T if the set is non-empty, otherwise F. In what follows I will use an abbreviated notation without Trivialisation, writing '$\exists^x A$' instead of '$[{}^0\exists^\tau \lambda x\, A]$', when no confusion can arise. The analyses of sentences (1), (1') come down to

(1*) $\lambda w \lambda t\, [\lambda x\, \exists t' [[[{}^0Yesterday\ t]\ t'] \wedge [{}^0Visit_{wt'}\ x\ {}^0London]]\ \lambda w \lambda t\, [{}^0King\_of_{wt}\ {}^0France]_{wt}]$

(1'*) $\lambda w \lambda t\, [\lambda x\, [\exists t' [[[{}^0Yesterday\ t]\ t'] \wedge \neg [\ {}^0Visit_{wt}'\ x\, {}^0London]]\ \lambda w \lambda t\, [{}^0King\_of_{wt}\ {}^0France]_{wt}]$

At such a ⟨w, t⟩-pair at which the King of France does not exist neither of the propositions constructed by (1*) and (1'*) has a truth-value, because the extensionalization of the office yields no individual, the Composition $\lambda w \lambda t [{}^0King\_of_{wt}\ {}^0France]_{wt}$ being v-improper. We have the Strawsonian case, the meaning of 'King of France' occurring with de re supposition, and the King's existence being presupposed. On the other hand, the sentences (2), (2') express

$$\lambda w \lambda t\, \exists t' [[[{}^0Yesterday\ t]\ t'] \wedge [{}^0Visit_{wt'}\ \lambda w \lambda t\, [{}^0King\_of_{wt}\ {}^0France]_{wt'}\ {}^0London]]$$
$$\lambda w \lambda t\, \exists t' [[[{}^0Yesterday\ t]\ t'] \wedge \neg [{}^0Visit_{wt'}\ \lambda w \lambda t\, [{}^0King\_of_{wt}\ {}^0France]_{wt'}\ {}^0London]]$$

At such a ⟨w, t⟩-pair at which the proposition constructed by (2*) is true, the Composition $\exists^{t'}[[[0Yesterday\ t]t'] \wedge \lambda w \lambda t\, [{}^0King\_of_{wt}\ {}^0France]_{wt}'$ 0London]] v-constructs T. This means that the second conjunct v-constructs T as well and the Composition $\lambda w \lambda t\, [\ {}^0King\_of_{wt}\ {}^0France]_{wt}'$ is not v-improper. Thus the King of France existed at some time t' belonging to yesterday. On the other hand, if the King of France did not exist at any time yesterday, then the Composition $\lambda w \lambda t\, [\ {}^0King\_of_{wt}\ {}^0France]_{wt}'$ is v-improper for any t' belonging to yesterday and the time interval v-constructed by $\lambda t' [[[$ 0Yesterday t] t'] $\wedge$ [${}^0Visit_{wt}'$ $\lambda w \lambda t$ [${}^0King\_of_{wt}\ {}^0France]_{wt}'$ ^{0}London]], as well as by $\lambda t' [[[\ {}^0Yesterday\ t]\ t'] \wedge \neg [\ {}^0Visit_{wt}'\ \lambda w \lambda t\, [\ {}^0King\_of_{wt}\ {}^0France]_{wt}'$ ^{0}London]], is empty. The existential quantifier takes this interval to F. This is as it should be, because (2*) only implies the existence of the King of

France yesterday but does not presuppose it. We have the Russellian case. The meaning of the definite description 'the King of France' occurs with de dicto supposition in (2) and (2'). 26

TOPIC-FOCUS AMBIVALENCE IN GENERAL

Up until now we have utilised the singularity of definite descriptions like 'the King of France' that denote functions of type $\iota_{\tau\omega}$. If the King of France does not exist in some particular world W at some particular time T, the office is not occupied and the function does not have a value at ⟨W, T⟩. Due to the partiality of the office constructed by λwλt [^{0}King_of$_{wt}$ ^{0}France] and the principle of compositionality, the respective analyses construct purely partial propositions associated with some presupposition, as desired. Now I am going to generalize the topic-focus phenomenon to sentences containing general terms.

To get started, let us analyseStrawson's example

(3) "All John's children are asleep."

(3') "All John's children are not asleep." According to Strawson both (1) and (1') entail 27

(4) John has children.

In other words, (4) is a presupposition of (3) and (3'). If each of John's children is asleep, then (3) is true and (3') false. If each of John's children is not asleep, then (3) is false and (3') is true. However, if John has no children, then (3) and (3') are neither true nor false. Note that applying a classical regimentation of (3) in the language of the first-order predicate logic (FOL), we get

$$\text{“}\forall x\ [JC(x) \supset S(x)]\text{”}$$

This formula is true under every interpretation assigning an empty set of individuals to the predicate JC ('is a child of John's'). In other words, FOL does not make it possible to render the truth-conditions of a sentence equipped with a presupposition, because FOL is a logic of total functions. We need to apply a richer logical system in order to express the instruction how to evaluate the truth-conditions of (3) in the way described above. By reformulating the above specification of the truth-conditions of (3) in a rather technical jargon of English, we get

"If John has children then check whether all his children are asleep, else fail to produce a truth-value."

We now analyse the particular constituents of this instruction. As always, we start with assigning types to the objects that receive mention in the sentence: Child_of$((o\iota)\iota)_{\tau\omega}$: an empirical function that dependently on states-of-affairs assigns to an individual a set of individuals, its children; John/ι; Sleep/$(o\iota)_{\tau\omega}$; ∃/(o(oι)); All/((o(oι))(oι)): a restricted general quantifier that assigns to a given set the set of all its supersets.

The presupposition that John have children receives the analysis

$\lambda w \lambda t\ [\,^{0}\exists \lambda x\ [[\,^{0}Child\_of_{wt}\,^{0}John]\ x]]$.

Now the literal analysis of the sentence "All John's children are asleep" on its neutral reading (that is, without existential presupposition), is best obtained by using the restricted quantifier All, because using a general quantifier ∀ would involve implication that does not receive mention in the sentence. Composing the quantifier with the set of John's children at the world/time pair of evaluation, $[\,^{0}All\ [\,^{0}Child\_of_{wt}\,^{0}John]]$, we obtain the set of all supersets of John's children in w at t. The sentence claims that the population of those who are asleep, 0Sleepwt, is one such superset:

$$\lambda w \lambda t\ [[^{0}All\ [^{0}Child\_of_{wt}\ ^{0}John]]\ ^{0}Sleep_{wt}]$$

The schematic analysis of sentence (3) on its topic-like reading that comes with the presupposition that John have children translates into this procedure:

(3^s) $\lambda w \lambda t$ [If $[^{0}\exists \lambda x\ [[^{0}Child\_of_{wt}\,^{0}John]\ x]]$ then $[[^{0}All\ [^{0}Child\_of_{wt}\,^{0}John]]\ ^{0}Sleep_{wt}]$ else Fail.

To finish the analysis, we must define the if-then-else function. This I am going to do in the next paragraph.

The if-then-else function

In a programming language the if-then-else conditional forces a program to perform different actions depending on whether the specified condition evaluates true or else false. This is always achieved by selectively altering the control flow based on the specified condition. For this reason, an analysis in terms of material implication, ⊃, or even 'exclusive or' as known from propositional logic, is not adequate. The reason is this. Since propositional logic is strictly compositional, both the 'then clause' and the 'else clause' are always evaluated. For instance, it might seem that the instruction expressed by "The only number n such that if 5 = 5 then n equals 1, else n equals the result of 1 divided by 0" would receive the analysis

$[^0\mathrm{I}^\tau\ \lambda n\ [[[^05{=}^05] \supset [n{=}^01]] \wedge [\neg[^05{=}^05] \supset [n{=}[^0Div\ ^01\ ^00]]]]]$

Types: $\mathrm{I}^\tau/(\tau(o\tau))$; $n \rightarrow_v \tau$; $0, 1, 5/\tau$; $Div/(\tau\tau\tau)$: the division function.

But the output of the above procedure should be the number 1 because the else clause is never executed. However, due to the strict principle of compositionality that TIL observes, the above analysis fails to produce anything, the construction being improper. For, the Composition [^{0}Div^{0}1 ^{0}0] does not produce anything: it is improper because the division function takes no value at the argument ⟨1, 0⟩. Thus [n = [^{0}Div^{0}1 ^{0}0]] is v-improper for any valuation v, because the identity relation = does not receive a second argument, and so any other Composition containing the improper Composition [^{0}Div ^{0}1 ^{0}0] as a constituent also comes out v-improper. The underlying principle is that partiality is being strictly propagated up. This is the reason why the if-then-else connective is often said to denote a non-strict function not complying with the principle of compositionality. However, as I wish to argue, there is no cogent reason to settle for non-compositionality. I suggest applying a mechanism known in computer science as lazy evaluation. As we have seen, the procedural semantics of TIL operates smoothly even at the hyperintensional level of constructions. Thus it enables us to specify a definition of if-then-else that meets the compositionality constraint. The analysis of

"If P then C, else D"

reveals a procedure that decomposes into two phases. First, on the basis of the condition P, select one of C, D as the procedure to be executed. Second, execute the selected procedure. The first phase, viz. selection, is realized by the Composition

$$[^0\mathrm{I}^*\ \lambda c\ [[P \supset [c = {}^0C]] \wedge [\neg P \supset [c = {}^0D]]]]$$

Types: P →v o (the condition of the choice between the execution of C or of D); C, D/$*_n$; variable $c \rightarrow_v *_n$; $\mathrm{I}^*/(*_n(o*_n))$: the singularizer.

The Composition [[P ⊃ [c=^{0}C]] ∧ [¬P ⊃ [c=^{0}D]]] v-constructs T in two cases. If P v-constructs T then the variable c receives as its value the construction C, and if P v-constructs F then the variable c receives the construction D as its value. In either case the set v-constructed byλc [[P ⊃ [c=^{0}C]] ∧ [¬P ⊃ [c=^{0}D]]] is a singleton whose element is a construction. Applying I * to this set returns as its value the only member of the set, i.e. either C or D. 28

Second, the chosen construction c is executed. To execute it we apply Double Execution; see Def. 2, vi). As a result, the schematic analysis of "If P then C, else D" turns out to be

$$(*) \qquad {}^{2}[{}^{0}\mathrm{I}^{*}\ \lambda c\ [[P \supset [c = {}^{0}C]] \wedge [\neg P \supset [c = {}^{0}D]]]]$$

Note that the evaluation of the first phase does not involve the execution of either of C or D. In this phase these constructions figure only as arguments of other functions. In other words, we operate at hyperintensional level. The second phase of execution turns the level down to intensional or extensional one. Thus we define:

Definition 4 (If-then-else, if-then-else-fail). Let $p/^{*}n \rightarrow v\ o$; c, d_1, $d_2/*_{n+1} \rightarrow {}^{*}n$; ${}^{2}c$, ${}^{2}d_1$, ${}^{2}d_2 \rightarrow v_{\alpha}$. Then the polymorphic functions if-then-else and if-then-else-fail of types $(\alpha o^{*}{}_{n}{}^{*}{}_{n})$, $(\alpha o^{*}n)$, respectively, are defined as follows:

$${}^{0}\mathit{If\text{-}then\text{-}else} = \lambda p\ d_1\ d_2\ {}^{2}[{}^{0}\mathrm{I}^{*}\ \lambda c\ [[p \supset [c = d_1]] \wedge [\neg p \supset [c = d_2]]]]$$

$${}^{0}\mathit{If\text{-}then\text{-}else\text{-}fail} = \lambda p\ d_1\ {}^{2}[{}^{0}\mathrm{I}^{*}\ \lambda c\ [[p \supset [c = d_1]] \wedge [\neg p \supset {}^{0}\mathbf{F}]]]$$

Now we are ready to specify a general analytic schema of an (empirical) sentence S associated with a presupposition P. In a technical jargon of English the evaluation instruction can be formulated as follows:

At any ⟨w, t⟩-pair do this:

ifP_{wt} is true then evaluate S_{wt}, else Fail (to produce a truth-value).

Let $P/*_{n} \rightarrow o_{\tau\omega}$ be a construction of a presupposition, $S/*_{n} \rightarrow o_{\tau\omega}$ the meaning of the sentence S and $c/*_{n+1} \rightarrow_{v} *_{n}$ a variable. Then the corresponding TIL construction is this:

$$\lambda w \lambda t\ [{}^{0}\mathit{If\text{-}then\text{-}else\text{-}fail}\ P_{wt}\ {}^{0}S_{wt}] =$$

$$\lambda w \lambda t\ {}^{2}[{}^{0}\mathrm{I}^{*}\lambda c\ [[P_{wt} \supset [c = {}^{0}S_{wt}]] \wedge [\neg P_{wt} \supset {}^{0}\mathbf{F}]]]$$

The evaluation of S for any ⟨w, t⟩-pair depends on whether the presupposition P is true at ⟨w, t⟩. If true, the singleton v-constructed by λc […] contains as the only construction to be executed ${}^{0}S_{wt}$ that is afterwards double executed. The first execution produces S_{wt} and the second execution produces a truth-value. If $\neg P_{wt}$ v-constructs T, then the second conjunct becomes the Composition [${}^{0}T \supset {}^{0}F$] and thus we get λc 0F. The v-constructed set is empty. Hence, [I*λc 0F] is v-improper, and the Double Execution fails to produce a truth-value.

Now we can finish the analysis of Strason's example (3). First, make a choice between executing the Composition [[^{0}All [${}^{0}\mathrm{Child_of}_{wt}{}^{0}$John]]

${}^{0}Sleep_{wt}$] and a v-improper construction that fails to produce a truth-value. If the Composition [${}^{0}\exists\lambda x$ [[${}^{0}Child\_of_{wt}\,{}^{0}John$] x]] vconstructs T then the former, else the latter. The choice itself is realized by this Composition:

$$[{}^{0}I^{*}\lambda c\ [[\exists x\ [[{}^{0}Child\_of_{wt}\,{}^{0}John]\ x] \supset [c={}^{0}[[{}^{0}All\ [{}^{0}Child\_of_{wt}\,{}^{0}John]]\ {}^{0}Sleep_{wt}]]] \\ \wedge [\neg\exists x\ [[{}^{0}Child\_of_{wt}\,{}^{0}John]\ x] \supset {}^{0}\mathbf{F}]]]$$

Second, execute the chosen construction. To this end we apply Double Execution:

$$^{2}[{}^{0}I^{*}\lambda c\ [[\exists x\ [[{}^{0}Child\_of_{wt}\,{}^{0}John]\ x] \supset [c={}^{0}[[{}^{0}All\ [{}^{0}Child\_of_{wt}\,{}^{0}John]]\ {}^{0}Sleep_{wt}]]] \\ \wedge [\neg\exists x\ [[{}^{0}Child\_of_{wt}\,{}^{0}John]\ x] \supset {}^{0}\mathbf{F}]]]$$

The evaluation of this construction for any ⟨w, t⟩ depends on whether the presupposition condition $\exists x\ [[{}^{0}Child\_of_{wt}\,{}^{0}John]\ x]$ is true at ⟨w, t⟩:

a. $\exists x\ [[{}^{0}Child\_of_{wt}\,{}^{0}John]\ x] \rightarrow_{v} \mathbf{T}$.

Then $\lambda c\ [{}^{0}\mathbf{T} \supset [c={}^{0}[[{}^{0}All\ [{}^{0}Child\_of_{wt}\,{}^{0}John]]\ {}^{0}Sleep_{wt}] \wedge [{}^{0}\mathbf{F} \supset {}^{0}\mathbf{F}]]$ v-constructs this singleton: $\{{}^{0}[[{}^{0}All\ [{}^{0}Child\_of_{wt}\,{}^{0}John]]\ {}^{0}Sleep_{wt}]\}$. Hence the value of I^{*} is its only member and we have:

$^{2}[{}^{0}I^{*}\ \lambda c\ [{}^{0}\mathbf{T} \supset [c={}^{0}[[{}^{0}All\ [{}^{0}Child\_of_{wt}\,{}^{0}John]]\ {}^{0}Sleep_{wt}] \wedge [{}^{0}\mathbf{F} \supset {}^{0}\mathbf{F}]] =$

$^{20}[[{}^{0}All\ [{}^{0}Child\_of_{wt}\,{}^{0}John]]\ {}^{0}Sleep_{wt}] = [[{}^{0}All\ [{}^{0}Child\_of_{wt}\,{}^{0}John]]\ {}^{0}Sleep_{wt}]$.

b. $\exists x\ [[{}^{0}Child\_of_{wt}\,{}^{0}John]\ x] \rightarrow_{v} \mathbf{F}$.

Then $\lambda c\ [{}^{0}\mathbf{F} \supset [c={}^{0}[[{}^{0}All\ [{}^{0}Child\_of_{wt}\,{}^{0}John]]\ {}^{0}Sleep_{wt}] \wedge [{}^{0}\mathbf{T} \supset {}^{0}\mathbf{F}]] = \lambda c\ {}^{0}\mathbf{F}$. The v-constructed set is *empty*, function I^{*} being undefined at such set. Hence, $^{2}[{}^{0}I^{*}\lambda c\ {}^{0}\mathbf{F}]$ is v-improper, *fails*.

Finally, we must abstract over the values of w and t in order to construct a proposition of type οτω denoted by the sentence. The resulting analysis of (3) is this:

(3*) $$\lambda w\lambda t\ ^{2}[{}^{0}I^{*}\lambda c\ [\exists x\ [[{}^{0}Child\_of_{wt}\,{}^{0}John]\ x] \supset [c={}^{0}[[{}^{0}All\ [{}^{0}Child\_of_{wt}\,{}^{0}John]]\ {}^{0}Sleep_{wt}] \\ \wedge [\neg\exists x\ [[{}^{0}Child\_of_{wt}\,{}^{0}John]\ x] \supset {}^{0}\mathbf{F}]]]$$

In the interest of better readability I will in the remainder use a more standard notation. Hence instead of either "$\lambda w\lambda t\ [{}^{0}$If-then-else-fail $P_{wt}\ 0S_{wt}$]" or "$\lambda w\lambda t\ 2[0I^{*}\lambda c\ [[P_{wt} \supset [c = 0S_{wt}]] \wedge [\neg P_{wt} \supset {}^{0}F]]]$" I will simply write "$\lambda w\lambda t$ [If P_{wt} then S_{wt} else Fail]".

Additional examples

Consider now another pair of sentences differing only in terms of topic-focus articulation:

(4) "The global financial and economic crisis was caused by the Bank of America."

(5) "The Bank of America caused the global financial and economic crisis."

While (4) not only entails but also presupposes that there be a global financial and economic crisis, the truth-conditions of (5) are different, as our analysis clarifies. First, (4) as well as

(4') "The global financial and economic crisis was not caused by Bank of America"

are about the global crisis, and that there is such a crisis is not only entailed but also presupposed by both sentences. The instruction encoded by (4) formulated in logician's English is this: "If there is a global crisis then return T or F according as the crisis was caused by the Bank of America, else fail (to produce a truth-value)"

Since every TIL analysis is fully compositional, we first need to analyse the particular constituents of this instruction, and then combine these constituents into the construction expressed by the sentence.

As always, we start with assigning types to the objects that receive mention in the sentence. Simplifying a bit, let the objects be: Crisis/$o_{\tau\omega}$: theproposition that there is a global financial and economic crisis; Cause/$(o\iota o_{\tau\omega})_{\tau\omega}$: the relationin-intension between an individual and a proposition which has been caused to be true by the individual; Bank_of_America/$\iota\tau\omega$: the individual office occupiable by a corporation belonging to the American financial institutions.

A schematic analysis of (4) comes down to this procedure:

$$\lambda w\lambda t\ [\text{If } {}^0Crisis_{wt} \text{ then } [{}^0True_{wt}\ \lambda w\lambda t\ [{}^0Cause_{wt}\ {}^0Bank\_of\_America_{wt}\ {}^0Crisis]] \text{ else Fail}]$$

Here we are again using the propositional property True in the then-clause, because this clause occurs in the focus of the sentence, and thus with de dicto supposition. The existence of the Bank of America is not presupposed.

The truth-conditions of the other reading with 'Bank of America' as topic are different. Now the sentence (5) is about the Bank of America (topic), ascribing to this corporation the property that it caused the crisis (focus).

Thus the scenario of truly asserting that (5) is not true can be, for instance, this. Though it is true that the Bank of America played a major role in risky investments in China, the President of USA played a positive role in enhancing financial-market transparency and passed new laws that prevented a global crisis from arising. Or, a less optimistic scenario is thinkable.

The global financial and economic crisis is not due to the Bank of America's bad investments but because in the era of globalisation the market economy is unpredictable, hence uncontrollable. Hence, that there is a crisis is not presupposed by (5), and its analysis is this Closure:

$$\lambda w\lambda t\ [\text{If } [{}^0Exist_{wt}\ {}^0Bank\_of\_America] \text{ then } [{}^0True_{wt}\ \lambda w\lambda t\ [{}^0Cause_{wt}\ {}^0Bank\_of\_America_{wt}\ {}^0Crisis]] \text{ else Fail}]$$

Note that (5) presupposes the existence of the Bank of America, while the existence of the crisis is not presupposed. Yet, if (5) is true, then the existence of the crisis can be validly inferred. To capture such truth-conditions, we need to refine the analysis. A plausible explication of this phenomenon is this: x is a cause of a proposition p iff p is true and if it is so then x affected p so as to become true. Schematically,

$$\lambda w \lambda t\ [{}^0Cause_{wt}\, x\, p] = \lambda w \lambda t\ [p_{wt} \wedge [p_{wt} \supset [{}^0Affect_{wt}\, x\, p]]]$$

Types: $Cause, Affect/(o\alpha o_{\tau\omega})_{\tau\omega}$; $x \rightarrow \alpha$, α: any type; $p \rightarrow o_{\tau\omega}$.

If x is not a cause of p, then either p is not true or p is true but x did not affect p so as to become true: $\lambda w \lambda t\ \neg[{}^0Cause_{wt}\, x\, p] = \lambda w \lambda t\ [\neg p_{wt} \vee [p_{wt} \wedge \neg[{}^0Affect_{wt}\, x\, p]]]$ .29 By applying such an explication to our sentence, the construction corresponding to the 'then clause', viz. λwλt [0Causewt 0Bank_of_ Americawt 0Crisis], is refined to:

$$\lambda w \lambda t\ [{}^0Crisis_{wt} \wedge [{}^0Crisis_{wt} \supset [{}^0Affect_{wt}\, {}^0Bank\_of\_America_{wt}\, {}^0Crisis]]]$$

This Closure entails that there is a crisis, which is the desired (logical, though not economic) outcome.

The topic-focus ambiguity also crops up in the case of propositional and notional attitudes, as noted in the Introduction.30 Imagine one is referring to the tragedy in Dallas, November22, 1963, by "The police were seeking the murderer of JFK, but never found him". The sentence is again ambiguous due to a difference in topic-focus articulation, as evidenced by (6) and (7):

(6) The police were seeking the murderer of JFK, but never found him.

(7) The police were seeking the murderer of JFK, but never found him.

The existence of the murderer of JFK is not presupposed by (6), unlike (7). The sentence (6) can be true in such states-of-affairs where JFK was not murdered, unlike (7). The latter can be reformulated in a less ambiguous way as "The murderer of JFK was looked for by the police, but was never found". This sentence expresses the construction

$$\lambda w \lambda t\ [\text{If } [{}^0Exist_{wt}\, \lambda w \lambda t\ [{}^0Murderer\_of_{wt}\, {}^0JFK] \text{ then}$$
$$[[{}^0Seek_{wt}\, {}^0Police\, \lambda w \lambda t\ [{}^0Murderer\_of_{wt}\, {}^0JFK]] \wedge \neg[{}^0Find_{wt}\, {}^0Police\, \lambda w \lambda t\ [{}^0Murderer\_of_{wt}\, {}^0JFK]]]$$
$$\text{else } Fail.$$

Types: Seek, Find/$(o\iota\iota_{\tau\omega})_{\tau\omega}$: the relation-in-intension between an individual and an individual office (the seeker wants to find out who is the holder of the office); Police/ι; Murderer_of/$(\iota\iota)_{\tau\omega}$; JFK/ι.31

On the other hand, the analysis of (6) comes down to this construction:

$$\lambda w\lambda t\ [[{}^0Seek_{wt}\ {}^0Police\ [\lambda w\lambda t\ [{}^0Murderer\_of_{wt}\ {}^0JFK]]] \wedge \neg[{}^0Find_{wt}\ {}^0Police\ [\lambda w\lambda t\ [{}^0Murderer\_of_{wt}\ {}^0JFK]]]].$$

If the police did not find the murderer then either the murderer did not exist or the murderer did exist; only the search was not successful. However, if the foregoing search was successful, then it is true that police found the murderer and the murderer exists. Hence, a successful search, i.e. finding after a foregoing search, merely entails that the murderer exists and the following argument is valid:

$$\frac{\lambda w\lambda t\ [{}^0Find_{wt}\ {}^0Police\ [\lambda w\lambda t\ [{}^0Murderer\_of_{wt}\ {}^0JFK]]]}{\lambda w\lambda t\ [{}^0Exist_{wt}\ [\lambda w\lambda t\ [{}^0Murderer\_of_{wt}\ {}^0JFK]]]}$$

In order to logically reproduce this entailment, we explicate finding after a foregoing search in a manner similar to causing ($x \rightarrow_v \iota$; $c \rightarrow_v \iota_{\tau\omega}$; $Success\_Search/(o\iota\iota_{\tau\omega})_{\tau\omega}$):

$$\lambda w\lambda t\ [{}^0Find_{wt}\ x\ c] = \lambda w\lambda t\ [[{}^0Exist_{wt}\ c] \wedge [[{}^0Exist_{wt}\ c] \supset [{}^0Success\_Search_{wt}\ x\ c]]];$$
$$\lambda w\lambda t\ \neg[{}^0Find_{wt}\ x\ c] = \lambda w\lambda t\ [\neg[{}^0Exist_{wt}\ c] \vee [[{}^0Exist_{wt}\ c] \wedge \neg[{}^0Success\_Search_{wt}\ x\ c]]].$$

Thus the analysis of such an explication of the sentence "The police found the murderer of JFK" is this Closure:

$$\lambda w\lambda t\ [[{}^0Exist_{wt}\ \lambda w\lambda t\ [{}^0Murderer\_of_{wt}\ {}^0JFK]] \wedge [[{}^0Exist_{wt}\ \lambda w\lambda t\ [{}^0Murderer\_of_{wt}\ {}^0JFK]] \supset [{}^0Success\_Search_{wt}\ {}^0Police\ \lambda w\lambda t\ [{}^0Murderer\_of_{wt}\ {}^0JFK]]]]$$

From this analysis one can validly infer that the murderer exists and that the search was successful, just as we ought to be able to. And if the so constructed proposition is not true,then the murderer does not exist or the murder does exist, only the search did not meet with success. The next example I am going to analyse is again due to (Hajičová, 2008):

(8) "John only introduced Bill to Sue."

(9) "John only introduced Bill to Sue."

Leaving aside the possible disambiguation "John introduced only Bill to Sue" vs. "John introduced Bill only to Sue", (8) can be truly affirmed only in a situation where John did not introduce other people to Sue than Bill. This is not the case of (9). This sentence can be true in a situation where John introduced other people to Sue, but the only person Bill was introduced to by John was Sue. Hence the presuppositions of (8) and (9) are constructed by these Closures:

Presupposition of (8): $\lambda w \lambda t\ [\forall x\ [[^0 Int\_to_{wt}\ ^0 John\ x\ ^0 Sue] \supset [x = {}^0 Bill]]]$
Presupposition of (9): $\lambda w \lambda t\ [\forall y\ [[^0 Int\_to_{wt}\ ^0 John\ ^0 Bill\ y] \supset [y = {}^0 Sue]]]$

The construction C that is to be executed in case a relevant presupposition is true is here the Closure $\lambda w \lambda t\ [^0 Int\_to_{wt}\ ^0 John\ ^0 Bill\ ^0 Sue]$. *Types*: $Int\_to/(o\iota\iota\iota)_{\tau\omega}$. Types: Int_to/$(o\iota\iota\iota)_{\tau\omega}$: a relation-in-intension between the individual who does the introducing, another individual who is introduced, and yet another individual to whom the second individual was introduced; John, Sue, Bill/ι.

The resulting analyses are

(8*) $\lambda w \lambda t$ [If $\forall x\ [[^0 Int\_to_{wt}\ ^0 John\ x\ ^0 Sue] \supset [x = {}^0 Bill]]$ then $[^0 Int\_to_{wt}\ ^0 John\ ^0 Bill\ ^0 Sue]$ else fail];

(9*) $\lambda w \lambda t$ [If $\forall y\ [[^0 Int\_to_{wt}\ ^0 John\ ^0 Bill\ y] \supset [y = {}^0 Sue]]$ then $[^0 Int\_to_{wt}\ ^0 John\ ^0 Bill\ ^0 Sue]$ else fail].

Using technical jargon, the truth-conditions constructed by the construction (8*) are, "If the only person that was introduced by John to Sue is Bill, then it is true that John introduced only Bill to Sue, otherwise there is no truth-value". Similarly for (9*).

For the last example, consider the sentence "All students of VSB-TU Ostrava who signed up for the Logic course in the winter term of 2011 passed the final exam." There are again two readings matching two possible scenarios.

Scenario 1: We are talking about the students of VSB-Technical University Ostrava, and somebody then asks, "What about the students of VSB-TU Ostrava who signed up for the Logic course in the winter term of 2011 – how did they do?". The answer is, "They did well, they all passed the final exam". In this case the topic of the sentence is the students enrolled in the Logic course. Thus the sentence comes with the presupposition that there should be students of VSB-TU Ostrava having signed up for Logic in the winter term of 2011. If this presupposition is not satisfied (for instance, because the course runs only in the summer term) then the sentence is neither true nor false, leaving a truth-value gap. For the negated sentence cannot be true, either: "Some students of VSB-TU Ostrava who signed up for Logic in the winter term of 2011 didnot pass the final exam". Moreover, the positive sentence merely entails (and so does not presuppose) that the final exam has taken place. This is so because the sentence can be false for either of two reasons: Either some of the students did not succeed, or none of the students succeeded because the exam has yet to take place.

Scenario 2: The topic is the final exam. Somebody asks, "What about the final exam in Logic, what are the results?" One possible answer is, "All students passed". Now the sentence presupposes that the final exam have already taken place. If it has not then the sentence is neither true nor false, because the negated sentence ("The final exam has not been passed by all students ...") cannot be true, either. In this situation the (positive) sentence does not presuppose, but only entails, that some students signed up for the course.

The logical machinery of TIL, thanks not least to the application of Definition 4, makes it easy to properly distinguish between those two non-equivalent readings. In the situation corresponding to the first scenario the meaning of the sentence is this Closure:

$$\lambda w\lambda t\ [\text{If } [{}^0\exists\ [{}^0Students\_enrolled\_in_{wt}\ {}^0Logic] \\ \text{then } [[{}^0All\ [{}^0Students\_enrolled\_in_{wt}\ {}^0Logic]]\ [{}^0Passed_{wt}\ {}^0Exam] \\ \text{else } Fail]$$

The second scenario receives this Closure as analysis:

$$\lambda w\lambda t\ [\text{If } Exam_{wt} \text{ than } [[{}^0All\ [{}^0Students\_enrolled\_in_{wt}\ {}^0Logic]]\ [{}^0Passed_{wt}\ {}^0Exam] \\ \text{else } Fail]$$

Types: $\exists/(o(o\iota))$: the existential quantifier; Students_enrolled_in/$((o\iota)\iota)_{\tau\omega}$: an attribute (i.e. empirical function) that dependently on a given state-of-affairs assigns to an individual a set of individuals; Logic/ι (for the sake of simplicity); All/$((o(o\iota))(o\iota))$: a restricted quantifier, which is a function assigning to a set S of individuals the set of all supersets of S; Passed/$((o\iota)o_{\tau\omega})_{\tau\omega}$: a function that dependently on a given state-of-affairs associates a proposition (in this case an event) with the set of individuals (who are the successful actors of the event); Exam/$o_{\tau\omega}$: the proposition that the final exam takes place.[32]

CONCLUSION

In this chapter I brought out the semantic, as opposed to pragmatic, character of the ambivalence stemming from topic-focus articulation. The procedural semantics of TIL provided rigorous analyses such that sentences differing only in their topic-focus articulation were assigned different constructions producing different propositions (truthconditions) and having different consequences. I showed that a definite description occurring in the topic of a sentence with de re supposition corresponds to the Strawsonian analysis of definite descriptions, while a definite description occurring in the focus with de dicto supposition corresponds to the Russellian analysis. While the clause standing in topicposition triggers a presupposition, a focus clause usually entails rather than presupposes another proposition. Thus both opponents and proponents of Russell's quantificational analysis of definite descriptions are partly right and partly wrong. Moreover, the proposed analysis of the Russellian reading does not deprive definite descriptions of their meaning. Just the opposite; 'the F' receives a context-invariant meaning. What is dependent on context is the way this (one and the same) meaning is used. Thus I also demonstrated that Donnellan-style referential and attributive uses of an occurrence of 'the F' do not bring about a shift of meaning of 'the F'. Instead, one and the same context-invariant meaning is a constituent of different procedures that behave in different ways. The proposed analysis of topic-focus ambivalence was then generalized to sentences containing not only singular clauses like 'the F' but also general clauses like 'John's children', 'all students' in the topic or focus of a sentence. As a result, I proposed a general analytic schema for sentences equipped with a presupposition. This analysis makes use of the definition of the if-then-else function that complies with the desirable principle of compositionality. This is also my novel contribution to the old problem of the semantic character of the specification of the if-then-else function. I demonstrated the method by analysing several examples including notional attitudes like seeking and finding. The moral to be drawn from my contribution is this. Logical analysis disambiguates ambiguous expressions, but cannot dictate which disambiguation is the intended one (leaving room for pragmatics here). Yet, our fine-grained method of analysis contributes to language disambiguation by making its hidden features explicit and logically tractable. In case there are more senses of a sentence we furnish the sentence with different TIL logical forms. Having a formal, fine-grained encoding of linguistic senses at our disposal, we are in a position to automatically infer the relevant consequences.

ACKNOWLEDGMENTS

This research was funded by Grant Agency of the Czech Republic Project 401/10/0792 Temporal Aspects of Knowledge and Information. Versions of this study were read by the author as an invited talk at the University of Western Australia, Perth, Australia, March 4th, 2011. Portions of this chapter elaborate substantially on points made in (Duží, 2009a, 2009b). I am indebted to Bjørn Jespersen for valuable comments that improved the quality of this study.

REFERENCES

1. Carnap, R. (1947). Meaning and Necessity, Chicago: Chicago University Press.
2. Donnellan, K. S., (1966). Reference and definite descriptions, Philosophical Review, vol. 77, 281-304.
3. Duží, M. (2003). Notional Attitudes (On wishing, seeking and finding). Organon F, vol. X, No. 3, pp. 237-260, ISSN 1335-0668
4. Duží, M. (2004). Intensional Logic and the Irreducible Contrast between de dicto and de re. ProFil, vol. 5, No. 1, pp. 1-34, ISSN 1212-9097 Duží, M. (2009a). Strawsonian vs. Russellian definite descriptions. Organon F, vol. XVI, No. 4, pp. 587-614, ISSN 1335-0668
5. Duží, M. (2009b). Topic-focus articulation from the semantic point of view. In: Computational Linguistics and Intelligent Text Processing, A. Gelbukh (Ed.), Berlin, Heidelberg: Springer-Verlag LNCS, vol. 5449, 220-232.
6. Duží, M. (2010). The paradox of inference and the non-triviality of analytic information. Journal of Philosophical Logic, vol. 39, No. 5, pp. 473-510. ISSN 0022-3611
7. Duží, M & Jespersen, B. (forthcoming). 'Transparent quantification into hyperpropositional contexts de re', LogiqueetAnalyse.
8. Duží, M. & Jespersen, B. (submitted). An argument against unrestricted beta-reduction.
9. Duží, M., Jespersen, B. &Materna, P. (2010a): Procedural Semantics for Hyperintensional Logic; Foundations and Applications of Transparent Intensional Logic. Berlin: Springer, series Logic, Epistemology, and the Unity of Science, vol. 17, 2010, ISBN 978-90-481-8811- 6, 550 pp.
10. Duží, M., Jespersen, B. &Materna, P. (2010b). The logos of semantic structure. In: Philosophy of Language and Linguistics, vol. 1: The Formal Turn. P. Stalmaszczyk (ed.) Frankfurt: OntosVerlag, ISBN 978-3-86838-070-5, pp. 85-102.
11. Fintel, Kai von (2004). Would you believe it? The King of France is Back! (Presuppositions and Truth-Value Intuitions). In: Descriptions and Beyond, Reimer, M., Bezuidenhout, A. (eds.), Oxford: Clarendon Press, ISBN 0-19-927051-1, pp. 315 – 341.
12. Frege, G. (1884). Die Grundlagen der Arithmetik, Breslau: W. Koebner.
13. Frege, G. (1892). Über Sinn und Bedeutung. ZeitschriftfürPhilosophie

und philosophischeKritik, vol. 100, pp. 25-50.

14. Hajičová, E. (2008). What we are talking about and what we are saying about it. In: Computational Linguistics and Intelligent Text Processing, A. Gelbukh (Ed.), Berlin, Heidelberg: Springer-Verlag LNCS, vol. 4919, 241-262.
15. Jespersen, B. (2008). Predication and extensionalization. Journal of Philosophical Logic, vol. 37, pp. 479 – 499. Kripke, S., (1977). Speaker reference and semantic reference. In: Contemporary Perspectives in the Philosophy of Language, French, Uehling and Wettstein (eds.), Minneapolis: University of Minnestoa Press, p. 6-27.
16. Ludlow, P. (2007). Descriptions. Available from http://plato.stanford.edu/entries/descriptions/#2.
17. Neale, S., (1990). Descriptions. Cambridge: MIT Press Books.
18. Neale, S., (2004). This, that, and the other. In: Descriptions and Beyond, A. Bezuidenhout and M. Reimer (eds.), Oxford: Oxford University Press, pp. 68-182.
19. Russell, B. (1905). On denoting. Mind vol. 14, pp. 479-493.
20. Russell, B., (1957). Mr. Strawson on referring, Mind vol. 66, pp. 385-389.
21. Strawson, P. F. (1950). On referring, Mind vol. 59, pp. 320-334.
22. Strawson, P. F. (1952). Introduction to Logical Theory. London: Methuen.
23. Strawson, P.F., (1964). Identifying reference and truth-values, Theoria vol. 3, pp. 96-118.
24. Tichý, P. (1988). The Foundations of Frege's Logic, Berlin, New York: De Gruyter.

CHAPTER

6

Semantic Interoperability in E-Health for Improved Healthcare

Saman Iftikhar[1], Wajahat Ali Khan[1], Farooq Ahmad[1] and Kiran Fatima[2]

[1]School of Electrical Engineering and Computer Sciences National University of Sciences and Technology

[2]Department of Computer Sciences National University of Computer and Emerging Sciences, Pakistan

INTRODUCTION

One of the challenges faced nowadays by the healthcare industry is semantic interoperability. It is the ability of a healthcare system to share information

Citation: SamanIftikhar, Wajahat Ali Khan, Farooq Ahmad and Kiran Fatima (April 25th 2012). "Semantic Interoperability in E-Health for Improved Healthcare", Semantics in Action - Applications and Scenarios, Muhammad Tanvir Afzal, IntechOpen, DOI: 10.5772/36469.

and have that information properly interpreted by the receiving system in the same sense as intended by the transmitting system. Semantic Web (aka Web 3.0) provides the enabling technologies to achieve semantic interoperability. Web Services, as a catalyst in this process, provide seamless communication of information between healthcare systems thus providing better access to patient information and improved healthcare.

Semantic technologies are emerging and several applications ranging from business process management to information security have demonstrated encouraging prospects of its benefits. Role of semantics is also very vital for achieving interoperability in sharing of health records. The aim of this chapter is to establish research and development in the domain of Health Level 7 (HL7) as an application to provide e-health services for the diverse communities. Through this research process, we intend to develop HL7 interface software for healthcare information systems that will provide semantic interoperability between the communicating medical systems. The objective is to facilitate e-health services that are interoperable among a number of domains in this field such as laboratory, patient administration and pharmacy. After its development and testing in the end-user environment, this software solution will be made publicly available under an open-source license. Due to its cutting-edge nature, this software solution has the potential of establishing an international repute for Pakistan in the highly profitable and potent healthcare industry. Since healthcare is a sensitive and critical area as it involves life of human beings, this project will be conducted in a manner to ensure that the resulting software is secure, reliable and maintainable.

This mostly involves research and implementation challenges. Some initiatives are already underway such as Health Services Specification Project (HSSP). It is a joint-venture of HL7 and Object Management Group (OMG), providing standardized service interface specifications. Following the traces of HSSP, our proposal is aimed to design and implement concrete SOA model. The ultimate goal is to define the HL7 Web services as Semantic Web services. Web Services Modeling Framework will provide the platform for automatic web service discovery, composition, and invocation that makes the technology scalable. This purpose of this chapter is to bring improvement in electronic health records by integrating it with semantic web services and semantic registries that will eventually lead to healthcare interoperable systems. One important part is the integration of Service Oriented Architecture (SOA) with HL7. HL7 Pakistan NUST, more specifically, has designed a prototype for the laboratory domain and it has been successfully implemented at the CITI Lab (a local testing laboratory). This successful initial prototype has provided us the baseline to enhance it by embedding semantics in the system in order to enable semantic interoperability.

Background and Rationale

Healthcare systems are critical and demand high accuracy, prompt availability and interoperability. The right use of information and communication system can play vital role in achieving the said requirements; but unfortunately healthcare systems are used mostly as a replacement to manual patient logging. The critical need is to encourage healthcare systems to be more efficient and provide more workable solutions like other industries that have benefited from it e.g. banking, traffic systems and so on. When a patient moves from hospital to hospital, he needs to take all the records and reports with him which is difficult to manage especially in emergency situations. Manual healthcare data system is not only prone to error and loss but also it is not feasible to manage massive data and access any particular record from it. Using healthcare data electronically results in cost-effective, easily accessible, accurate and manageable data processing solutions. In Pakistan, very few healthcare organizations so far have become capable of storing healthcare data electronically but it comes without the ability to share the information. This is mostly due to lack of awareness and implementation of information exchange standards.

Standardization provides us an effective way of communication to achieve the goal of interoperability. HL7 is one of the healthcare standards that allow communication and integration of healthcare systems and allow sharing of data around the globe. The important requirement is to capture relevant information and then make it widely available for others. Therefore, the need is to have a standard that can provide best services in terms of efficiency and reliability. HL7, as it evolves, provides us with a technical business model to fulfill this vision of a diverse, integrated health information system.

The two most important issues that the healthcare industry is facing are integration and interoperability of systems. Countries are not willing to invest in healthcare industry until and unless the healthcare systems to be adopted by them provide interoperability. HL7 is a messaging standard that is used for the exchange of medical information between different communicating parties or devices. The most commonly used versions of

HL7 are HL7 V2.x and HL7 V3. HL7 V 2.x is mainly focused on the transfer of message from sender to the receiver rather on interoperability. HL7 V3 focused on the shortcomings of HL7 V2.x and overcome those by targeting semantic interoperability (Neotool). HL7 V3 is based on the standard model called Reference Information Model (RIM). Another potential capability is to make HL7 V3 based systems SOA complaint.

The innovation and the standardization of web services have set the concept of web services as the basic building blocks of information technology systems for Service Oriented Architectures (SOA) applications. SOA is a solution to handle complex business processes and to achieve interoperability.

Healthcare is a many-to-many business so to cater complexities and bring interoperability among heterogeneous systems; a business process model is required. SOA for our project requires certain standardized specifications to follow in order to claim the compliance with standards. These specifications are formulated mainly by coordination of HL7 and OMG group, under the name of Healthcare Services Specification Project (HSSP). HSSP gives Service Functional Models (SFM) which specifies interface specifications and not the implementation specifications. The document "Service Oriented Architecture and HL7 V3 Methodology" by Special Interest Group (SOA SIG), gives approach for implementing healthcare services in Healthcare domain. Another important document in this series is "The Practical Guide for SOA in Health Care" by HSSP gives concrete guidelines along with mega SOA architecture for Healthcare. These documents are providing main guidelines in our work for getting SOA workflows.

Although SOA framework can be used for designing interoperable systems yet it is not a proper solution for providing true interoperability, i.e. the semantic interoperability. Semantic interoperability is the way to intelligently interpret the transferred knowledge among communicating machines and provide accurate desired results. HL7 V3 provides specifications for different domains like patient administration, specimen, laboratory, observation etc. Every domain supports data and processes particular to that domain in addition to some common elements that are shared among multiple domains. The main focus of this thesis is to bring semantics in the interactions included in laboratory domain. This work refined the meaning of semantic interoperability by representing the interactions and other artifacts with ontologies rather only limited to the vocabulary representation supported by HL7 V3 (Beeler et al., 1999).

In HL7 the semantic interoperability can be seen from two perspectives; data and process. The potentials of semantic data interoperability remain incomplete without semantic process interoperability. Achieving interoperable data would be less effective if there is no semantics in the communication components which can only be achieved when the process is interoperable. Semantic data interoperability means understanding of the data communicated between sender and receiver in such a way that the receiver easily interprets the sender intension of sending the data and properly responds. On the other hand semantic process interoperability is the type of semantic interoperability, which helps in the decision process of the participating parties in communication of HL7 messages on the basis of data contents intended to be exchanged for automation. For bringing semantic interoperability in the HL7 processes, semantic web services are followed for the communication.

HL7 V3 claims to provide semantic interoperability but it only focuses on the semantic data interoperability and semantic process interoperability is still a grey area. HL7 V3 provides data interoperability in the form of terminologies by using vocabularies like SNOMED CT (SNOMED Clinical Terms, 2009), LOINC (LOINC) and HL7's own vocabulary. But semantic interoperability cannot be catered by only taking in to account specified terminologies. To achieve semantic interoperability there is a need of a framework that can support the required constructs for semantic interoperability. Web Service Modeling Framework (WSMF) provides Web Service Modeling Ontology (WSMO) which contains the entities like ontologies, mediators, web services and goals.

One technique for achieving semantic process interoperability is to use simple web services. Web services provide a standard means of interoperable communication between heterogeneous software applications. The complexity is increased for web services when semantic and syntactic heterogeneities are brought in to consideration for the transfer of messages between systems. Therefore, there is a need of using semantic web services for achieving semantic process interoperability. Semantic web services can be used for enhancing the web services capabilities in understanding semantics such that it can be more easily machine process able. This will result in better machine understanding of the web services and the communication would be more effective. Semantic web services should have proper precondition, post-condition, effects and assumptions. There are different approaches used for realizing semantic web services but WSMO is the most preferable as it is the most effective and complete approach amongst all.

There is a need to explore such sophisticated SOA technologies that make the discovery of services for requested users appropriate. In service oriented computing services are used to develop fast, economical, interoperable, evolvable, and extremely distributed applications. Services are self-governing, platform-independent entities that can be described, published, discovered, and loosely coupled. Semantic registries are required for the handling and accessing meaningful information over the semantic web. In present, the services are described, registered and accessed without semantics which is not efficient if the services are to be discovered precisely. In semantic registries the discovery of services is all about the finding of desirable services semantically which have knowledgeable significant properties and relationships. Therefore, the services have to be expressed semantically in semantic registries, so that the semantically described services can be machine comprehensible and precisely used by applications for interoperability of processes through semantic registries and results in semantic SOA.

The issue in using such standards like HL7 V3 is to provide tools and encourage its usage through making them integrated with the existing healthcare systems. Also these standards can be more utilized by following frameworks such as SOA and WSMF. These frameworks can help HL7 standard to achieve true interoperability. In this project our emphasis is to make such open source tools that will help the healthcare industry in achieving such targets.

Scope and Objectives

- To develop standardized services that should be reusable, cost effective and self-maintainable; setting the stage for interoperability in healthcare services.
- To create a hybrid platform by incorporating HL7 V3 standard and Service-Oriented Architecture.
- To model complex healthcare processes in well-defined business language and to capture real life business scenarios, rather than technology-specific terminologies and grammar.
- To contribute the developed platform to the open-source community so other healthcare organizations and hospitals, within and outside the, country can reuse and customize this solution to their specific requirements with minimum efforts.
- To train a reasonable number of professionals and researchers as HL7 based IT researchers, developers as well as users of the HL7 application in the medical related discipline.

Methodology

The HLH studio architecture as shown in Figure 1 will be used initially to create and parse HL7 V3 message using Java SIG API. The Java SIG API supports generation and parsing of any type of V 3 messages while making corresponding Hierarchical Message Description's (HMD) available. During creation of HL7 message, the HL7 builder tool consumes in-memory Refined Message Information Model (RMIM) objects and taking meta-data from HMDs to create valid serialized XML based message specified by HMD, while in message parsing, the parser tool consumes XML message, validates it against HMD and creates in memory RMIM object graph.

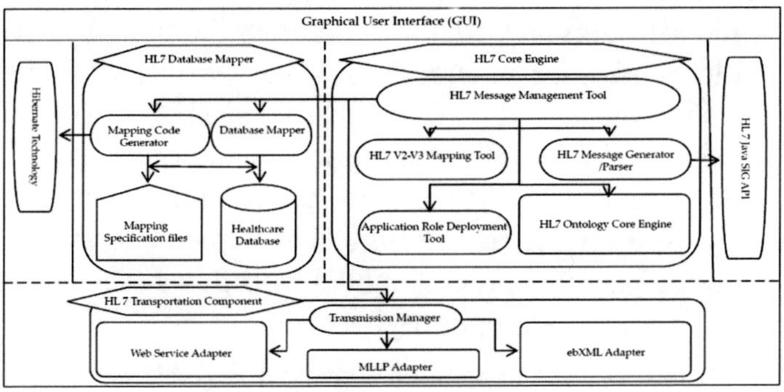

Figure 1. Architecture for HL7 Studio [14].

The message generation and parsing is only limited to the Laboratory and Patient Administration domains, their specifications are provided in the HL7 Normative, 2009. The message generation and parsing is the first step towards interoperability. This standard message can then be communicated between communicating parties.

HL7 is a standard used for information exchange among healthcare systems. SOA, on the other hand, is an architecture that enables business agility through the use of common services. HL7 stakeholders realized that by bringing these two realms at one place will generate revolutionary benefits for healthcare. SOA architecture mainly causes interoperable and easy accessible communication which HL7 V3 conventional Messaging Infrastructure (MI) cannot provide.

SOA framework, unlike MI, encompasses service creation, hosting and communication capabilities at one place. Our project needs the basic three elements of SOA; i.e. Producer, Consumer and registry to be realized for rejuvenating our healthcare environment. The producers will be the healthcare organizations, and the consumers are the patients, doctors and other healthcare community. As SOA provides communication according to business case, it supports the academic and business community to get enormous potentials for research and development in healthcare sector. The underlying infrastructure is based on web services, for which HSSP is providing specifications.

Based upon the lessons learned from HSSP specifications, for SOA framework there are some steps that are to be followed. As we are analyzing laboratory and patient administration domain for our case study to be implemented, the laboratory domain artifacts would be analyzed initially. We have to identify services in the laboratory domain by investigating application roles and their interactions. This will lead to decision on operations by studying storyboards, constraints, HL7 information model (DMIM) and trigger events. The description of interface specifications by studying HSSP services' specifications is carried out. The services are then implemented by Web service basic profile and implement orchestration and choreography using business process model workflows. The last step will be registering the services in a proper registry.

Once the HL7 services have been exposed as Web Services, it will be available for everyone to use over the web. The advancement in the Semantic Web has now shifted the simple Web services to the Semantic Web Services. The Semantic Web (SW) approach is to develop languages and mechanisms for expressing information in machine understandable form. The web services that are identified in the SOA framework are to be upgraded to semantic web services. In order to achieve this goal Semantic Web Service (SWS) Architecture review including WSMO, WSML and WSMX should be performed. The identification of process flows in HL7 is important for achieving the goal of semantic process interoperability. WSMO entities (ontologies, services, goals and mediators) modeling are the next step to be performed. For HL7 processes we would require to model Interaction ontology and Message Ontology. The interaction ontology would contain all the process artifacts (application roles, trigger events, message types and interactions) while the Message Ontology would contain information related to HL7 V3 message like transmission wrapper, control act wrapper and message payload. The WSMO entities should be modeled using WSMT tool for the semantics to completely take effect. The Adapter component implementation is also an important step as conversion from XML to WSML and WSML to XML is required for overcoming heterogeneity problem and bringing interoperability. To completely utilize the WSMO entities an execution environment WSMX should be implemented. Semantic web services will bring automatic service discovery which will make the timely information transfer of patient resulting in quick access to patient care.

The semantic services are required to be stored, published and retrieved in a repository. The semantic registry would be required for registration/ publication of patient and lab domain services semantically, so that the services can be accessed for medical research, decision support systems. Analysis of HL7 standardized referenced information models will be done for semantic information management. Identification of semantic discovery and semantic matchmaking algorithms based on inference and reasoning will be done for best retrieval of requested information services. Analysis of different data exchange mechanisms will be done to exchange medical information across the interlinked semantic registries. Analysis of semantic SOA techniques to make our semantic registries service orientated to ensure semantic interoperability, flexibility and extensibility across heterogeneous environments. Analysis of different electronic health records for its feasibility and integration with semantic SOA semantic registries using HL7 V3. The semantic services related to patient and lab domain will be stored, published and retrieved from the semantic registry that would be helpful for medical research, medical education and diagnosing and curing several diseases.

Figure 2 shows the generic architecture of how the SOA, semantic web services using WSMF and semantic registries would work together. The discovery would be of the services that are without semantics and semantics based discovery. The discovery without semantics would be through UDDI registry of the web services that are created in SOA framework. The semantic web service discovery would take place by Web Service Execution Environment (WSMX) and the bridge between semantic web services and simple web services is provided by a mechanism called grounding in WSMO.

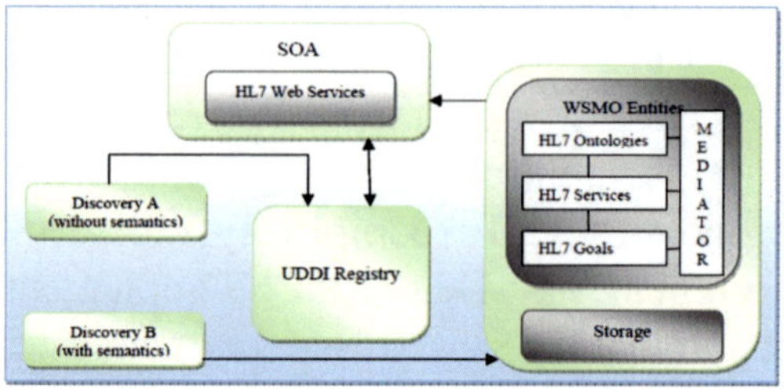

Figure 2. Generic Architecture of SOA and semantic web services.

SEMANTIC ELECTRONIC MEDICAL RECORD (SEMR) SYSTEM AS SAAS SERVICE MODEL

The advancement in Information and Communication Technology (ICT) is playing increasing role in healthcare and has managed to improve the efficiency of health services to common people. Health informatics plays a vital role in the integration of ICT in healthcare domain. The critical need is to encourage healthcare systems to be more efficient and provide more workable solutions that have benefited from ICT (HIMSS, 2011).

Current syntax based healthcare data systems are not only prone to error and loss but also it is not feasible to manage massive data and access any particular record from it. Therefore healthcare organizations are facing difficulties in managing the large amount of information as well as technological infrastructure. Information retrieval and analysis has turned into a very important challenge for healthcare domain. These challenges can effectively be handled with the help of semantics and cloud computing. Managing healthcare data with semantics results in cost-effective, easily accessible, accurate and manageable data processing solutions. At present EMR systems are designed for hospital operations within the premises, but now have to be modified to support primary care settings of patients, mostly outside of the walls of the hospital. The traditional primary care teams also have to redesign the workflow as they add new care coordination staff and EMR technology to achieve the desired goal of improving the clinical outcome at reduced costs (Ginsburg, 2006).

Interoperability is the ability of a healthcare system to share information and have that information properly interpreted by the receiving system in the same sense as intended by the transmitting system. Standardization provides us an effective way of communication to achieve the goal of semantic interoperability. HL7 is one of the healthcare standards that allow communication of healthcare systems and allow sharing of data around the globe. The important requirement is to capture relevant information and then make it widely available for others. Therefore, the need is to have a system that can provide best services in terms of meaningful data sharing and discovery. HL7, as it evolves, helps us with a technical business model to fulfill the vision of standard based information exchange in diverse, integrated health information systems (HL7, 2011; HLH, 2011; HL7, 2009).

In the era of Semantic Web and cloud computing, there is a need and demand of such an EMR system where timely, accurate and rapid availability of healthcare services can be possible that can manage patient's health data and helps physicians and patients. EMR is basically a part of local standalone Health Information System (HIS) that is an organization's legal proprietary, it includes hospitals as well as doctors, clinicians and physicians. The basic functionality of an EMR is to allow storage, retrieval and manipulation of records. In order to communicate the information of an EMR system between different branches of a healthcare organization, there is a need to follow a standard that provides interoperability. Since healthcare is a most demanding area as more people are concerned about their health, this system should be scalable, fault tolerant, reliable, secure, timely respondent, sustainable and maintainable.

It is a rarity to deploy an Electronic Medical Record (EMR) system on cloud. Also another challenging task is to incorporate semantic web technologies in EMR's and presenting the complex medical data in a meaningful and intelligent manner in healthcare. This will require the integration of Semantics Web and SaaS model (Software as a Service, 2011) with best featured existing EMR for developing an efficient healthcare semantic web services for the cloud. Some initiatives are underway worldwide such as Health Services Specification Project (HSSP), a joint-venture of HL7 and Object Management Group (OMG, 2011), providing standardized service interface specifications.

Therefore, there is a need to design and implement semantic based healthcare service on cloud for storage, retrieval and manipulation of patient data and medical records. Thus SEMR (Semantic Electronic Medical Record) system will provide the solution for highly intensive patient and medical data sharing, semantic interoperability and management with its availability for larger community access through cloud infrastructure.

Related work

Some of the current open source EMR systems are listed below with their functionalities and drawbacks.

OpenEMR is an open source clinical practice management system (OpenEMR, 2011). The system can track patient demographics, patient medical records, scheduling, billing, multilingual support and prescription. In short the system provides all basic functionalities that any hospital EMR system can provide but it is restricted to a hospital.

OpenEMR Virtual Appliance (OpenEMR Virtual Appliance, 2011) is a comprehensive open source Medical Practice Management Software Appliance, which provides office scheduling, electronic medical records, prescriptions, insurance billing, accounting and access controls. This appliance has many possible applications, such as a fully functional demo, a testing/developing platform, and as the starting point in real world clinic applications. It can be run on any operating system that supports the VMware Player.

OpenMRS (OpenMRS, 2011) is a full open source healthcare system and has the ability to configure the system to new requirements without programming and to interoperate with other systems whether open or closed. Both of these open source systems are refined under Health Insurance Portability and Accountability Act (HIPAA, 2011) and CCHIT (CCHIT, 2011; CCHIT EMR, 2011) certified.

SequelMed EMR (SequelMed EMR, 2011) is a secure, patient centric, medical record, integrated with Sequel Systems' medical billing software (SequelMed EPM). The system can automate clinical documentation and have Decision Support Tools and Alerts, Integrated Patient Education Protocols, wireless and internet access to medical records.

ClearHealth (Clear-health, 2011) is open source software and include five major areas of healthcare practice operations including scheduling, billing, EMR, HIPAA Security and accounts receivables."

XChart (XChart, 2011) is a paper based project by the Open Healthcare Group that promotes EMR, based in XML.

SmartCare (SmartCare,2011) is software that develops EMR programs and particularly used in Zambia.

Zimbra (Zimbra, 2011) gives e-mail solution for government offices, education institutes and other business environments. Medical professionals can also benefit from its fast backup and recovery of mailboxes, anti-spam and anti-virus protection, this software has also support for BlackBerry and other mobile devices, and their flexible applications. All of these systems are open source and primary care systems.

These systems provide basic clinical practice that is helpful for patients' medical record but do not support interoperability among different workflow components such as laboratory, medical reports, patient administration, pharmacy, insurance, billing, and prescription among medical repositories, hospitals, pharmacies and clinics.

Methodology

In order to avoid the burden of management of technological infrastructure, SaaS based solution should be used to develop the system on top of cloud infrastructure. To achieve full potential of machine process able SaaS service model based EMR, semantics need to be added. Semantics bring the benefits of unambiguous definition of service functionality and the external interfaces of services reduce human effort in integrating services to SOA, improve dynamism and stability to Web services. Our proposed system will ensure timely delivery of health care information and will ensure its confidentiality. The proposed healthcare system will be developed as semantic web services based on SaaS model and will be deployed on cloud infrastructure. This work will bring significant improvements in current EMR systems through interoperable, automated and seamless meaningful communication.

The ultimate goal is to exploit the EMR system's functionalities as semantic web services. Web Services Modeling Framework (WSMF) will provide the platform for automatic web service discovery, composition, and invocation that makes the product efficient. As EMR system, software will be developed as a service, semantic web technologies will be used to incorporate semantics in the services and the communication will take place through web services and would ensure timely delivery of medical information.

SEMR (Semantic Electronic Medical Record) system will be used to capture and manage patient's data and information by using these two approaches: Semantic Web and Software as a Service (SaaS) service model on cloud. These are emerging approaches that can bring novel way to properly manage patient's data and medical records. SOA and SaaS establish a SaaS service model by leveraging the benefits of SaaS solution and SOA infrastructure. SOA enhances reliability, reduces hardware acquisition costs, leverages existing development skills, and accelerates movement to standards based server and application consolidation. In this way SOA provides a data bridge between incompatible technologies.

Furthermore SaaS solution will provide data and system availability, secure and reliable performance, and maximum system throughput. Communication in the system will be handled by HL7 for semantic interoperability. This system is based on HL7 standard based data exchange format.

The important part of this project is the integration of Semantic Web and SaaS model with best featured existing EMR for developing an efficient healthcare semantic web services for the cloud. This mostly involves research and implementation challenges exist within best featured existing EMR for developing an efficient healthcare semantic web services for the cloud.

Proposed architecture

The proposed system will be semantic based SaaS service model developed on top of cloud for healthcare domain. SOA and SaaS establish a SaaS service model by leveraging the benefits of SaaS solution and SOA infrastructure. SOA enhances reliability, reduces hardware acquisition costs, leverages existing development skills, accelerates movement to standards-based server and application consolidation, provides a data bridge between incompatible technologies (SOA, 2010).

In the requirement gathering phase literature review and analysis of basic functionalities of EMR systems and SaaS service model would be carried out. Therefore SaaS service model based EMR system would be designed in the first phase. In order to avoid the burden of management of technological infrastructure, we will use SaaS based solution by developing our proposed system on top of cloud infrastructure. To make SaaS service model based EMR and machine process able and achieve its full potential, semantics needs to be added.

Semantics brings the benefits of unambiguous definition of service functionality and external interfaces reduce human effort in integrating services to SOA, improve dynamism and stability to Web services (Semantic SOA, 2011). Therefore the next phase is to upgrade SaaS service model based EMR to Semantic EMR system as SaaS service model for healthcare. In this phase the literature review, analysis and design of semantic web services identification and development for the purpose of fulfilling patient administration requirements would be carried out.

HL7 provides semantic interoperability; therefore the communication in our proposed system is based on HL7 standard based data exchange format. This step will embed HL7 standard in our proposed system for medical data communication.

In the final step an interface of this system can also be provided for smart-phones for physicians and patients to access our system also from outside the patient care premises.In the architecture four types of services are categorized for SEMR system SaaS service model. The EMR services are part of these categories that are semantic based.

Architectural layout of SaaS based SEMR system

The layered architecture is categorized as presentation layer, business logic layer, data management layer and database layer. The layered architecture is shown in Figure 3.

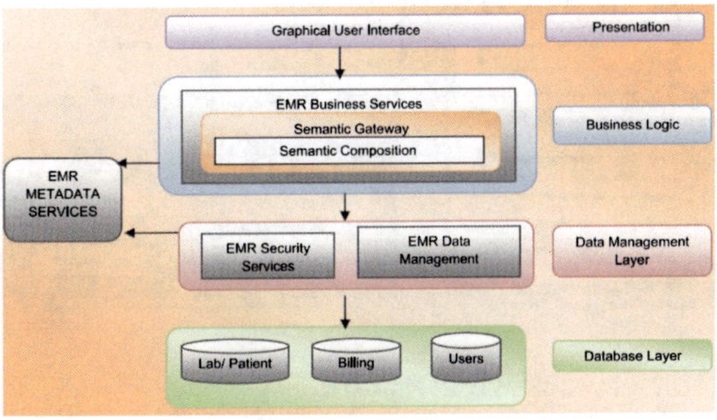

Figure 3. Architecture for SaaS based SEMR system.

- **Business process services:**These services perform the logic of business processes with the help of other services. Business logic is fulfilled by the management of processes and data through data management services. For example request for patient referrals would be fulfilled through underlying data management service provided through message generation service.
- **Data management services:**These services manage the data for business process services.
- **Metadata services:**These services provide metadata specifications and standards for message generation, database mapping, and data integration, interoperability, through data modeling, data transformation and data workflows. These services help data management services.

- **Security services:**These services are responsible for the authorization and authentication of data transmitted and stored for the working of data management services.

The elaborated services architecture is given in Figure 4. We demonstrated the sequence of functionality of Patient Administration service in the following paragraph. In order to use Patient Administration service from our SEMR SaaS service based system we presented patient registration scenario where a doctor registers a patient through our SEMR system Interface. The doctor will give patient demographic information in the form by using our system. As our system is semantic based, the Semantic Gateway service will perform semantic composition. The query of the doctor will be standardized with the help of Message Generation Data Management service that will generate an HL7 message.

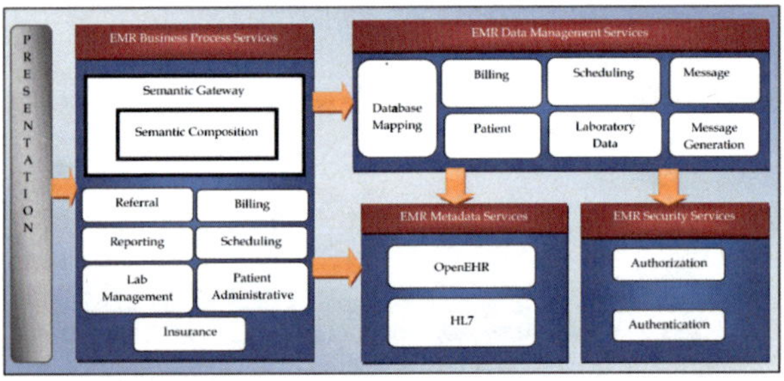

Figure 4. Elaborated Services Architecture.

The Semantic Gateway service will then discover, select and invoke Patient Administration Business Process service through HL7 message parsing. The Patient Administration service will call the Patient data service for data management. The Patient data service will call the Authorization service to authorize the patient for viewing his medical data. This service will assign user name and password to the patient. Then the Patient data service will store the registered patient in the patient database.

Semantic Gateway uses Semantic Gateway service as a part of business process services that is used for taking information from the user and resolving it by using the combination of other services. This provides the semantic annotations to services. Service ontology and Domain ontology are defined for semantic execution. Services and Ontology repositories will be the knowledge bases for the Semantic Gateway service. Reasoner is used in Semantic Gateway for inference about services semantics at runtime. Services of EMR system will be discovered semantically through Semantic

Composition business process service. The business logic of this service will perform parsing, choreography, ranking and selection with the help of Semantic Gateway. Semantic gateway is shown in Figure 5. Semantic Gateway is discussed in following sections.

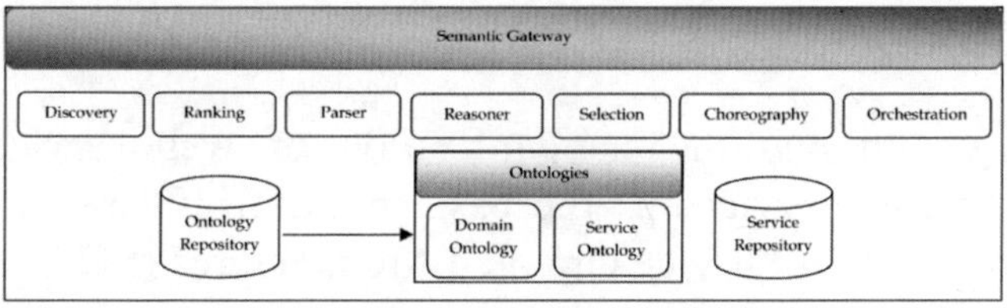

Figure 5. Semantic Gateway.

Semantic gateway

The advancement in Information Technology is playing increasing role in healthcare and has managed to improve the efficiency of health services to common people. Health informatics plays a vital role in the integration of Information Technology in healthcare domain. However healthcare organizations are facing problems related to communication of right information to appropriate. Due to data deluge, information retrieval and analysis has become an important problem in various fields including healthcare. Semantic web technologies provide extensible, flexible and efficient information.

The innovation and the standardization of web services provide basic building blocks for information exchange. To exploit web services to their full potential, semantics must be specified. Semantic web technologies play a pivotal role in bringing automation in the process flows. OWL-S provides ontologies for describing web services with the help of semantic constructs in an unambiguous and machine interpretable form. OWL-S follows layered structure of markup languages as HTML, XML, RDF and has built on OWL recommendation of W3C. Its ontologies describe domain concepts of services (e.g., travel, e-business, healthcare information) and business logic. The data flow and controls of the services are related to the domain ontologies through inputs, outputs, preconditions and effects. OWL-S ontologies divide service descriptions in four main parts: process model, service profile, service grounding and the service.

Currently WSMX framework provides automatic service discovery, composition and execution of web services. It provides information exchange between users and service providers and fulfill user specified goal by invoking end point web services. The main strength of WSMO over other semantic web technologies is its discovery mechanism. WSMO is based on the Web Service Modeling Framework (WSMF). WSML is used to describe services' description into Ontologies, Web services, Goals and Mediators (WSMO).

The innovation and the standardization of web services have set the concept of web services as the basic building blocks of information technology systems for Service Oriented Architectures (SOA) applications. The idea is to explore such sophisticated SOA technologies that make the discovery of services for requested users appropriate (Erl, 2005). SOA ensures interoperability, flexibility and extensibility across heterogeneous environments. In service oriented computing services are used to develop fast, economical, interoperable, evolvable, and extremely distributed applications. Services are self-governing, platform-independent entities that can be described, published, discovered, and loosely coupled (Papazoglou, 2007).

Traditional approaches to services publication and discovery have generally relied on the existence of pre-defined registry services like Universal Description, Discovery and Integration (UDDI) (Clement, 2004). Often the description of a service is limited in existing registry, with little or no support for problem specific descriptions. Semantic registries with the use of OWL-S attempt to overcome this limitation and provide a rich semantic description based on ontologies. Semantic matchmaking generally focuses on the problem of identifying services on the basis of the capabilities that they provide. We proposed an OWL-S based Semantic Registry for healthcare information provision. This chapter also presents healthcare service ontology (Iftikhar et al., 2010) developed through the specifications of HL7 Service Functional Model, which is used in our Semantic Registry for publishing and discovering HL7 compliant healthcare semantic web services. HL7 is a well-known healthcare standard that provides specification for standardization of information exchanged among healthcare applications.

In paper (Srinivasan, 2004), Authors have proposed OWL-S/UDDI Matchmaker as an extension of UDDI. Before registering OWL-S based Web Services on UDDI, OWL-S/UDDI Matchmaker converts service profile of these services to UDDI data structure and then stores them on UDDI. During web service discovery, OWL-S/UDDI Matchmaker translates the services back into OWL-S format. Matching takes place between the service request and the published services advertisements present in the registry. The proposed solution enhances the UDDI registry for semantic based searching and capability based matching. UDDI registry has some inherent limitations including lack of semantic representations of contents. The matching process proposed in this paper is restricted to Inputs and Outputs matching of the service profile.

The DAML-S Matchmaker (Paolucci, 2002) was developed by the Intelligent Software Agents Group at Carnegie- Mellon University. The matchmaking system is a database where service providers can register their Web services via DAML-S descriptions through a Web interface. The system then allows service requesters to upload their service requests. The matchmaking algorithm matches the types associated with each input or output parameter. For each parameter (either input or output) there are several degrees of matching, depending on the semantic relationship between the parameters of the advertisement and the request. Based on these results a global matching result is determined.

ebXML Registry (Dogac et al., 2008) give industry groups and enterprises the ability to share business semantic information and business process interfaces in form of XML. This registry has some extensions for medical data registration, annotation, discovery and retrieval in form or archetypes data definitions where registry semantic constructs are used. They provide archetype metadata ontology and describe the techniques to access archetype semantics through ebXML query facilities. They also provide mechanism, how archetype data can be retrieved from underlying clinical information systems by using ebXML Web services.

The FUSION Semantic Registry (Kourtesis and Paraskakis, 2006) is a semantically-enhanced Web service registry based on UDDI, SAWSDL and OWL. This registry augments and enhances the discovery facilities of typical UDDI registry and based on UDDI without changing its implementation. This registry performs matchmaking at data-level and developed by SEERC in the context of research project FUSION and released as open source software. Fusion registry has no matchmaking based on inputs, outputs, preconditions and effects capabilities of services.

Artemis project (Dogac et al., 2006), exploits ontologies based on the domain knowledge exposed by the healthcare information standards like HL7, CEN TC251, ISO TC215 and GEHR. Artemis Web service architecture has no any globally agreed ontologies; rather healthcare institutes resolve their semantic differences through a mediator component. The mediator component works in a P2P manner and uses ontologies in order to facilitate semantic negotiation among involved institutes.

CASCOM is an agent-based approach used for semantic service discovery and coordination in mobile eHealth environment (Fröhlich et al., 2007).

Cesar Caceres is another approach that focuses on Agent-Based Semantic Service Discovery for medical-emergency management (Cáceresc et al., 2006).

COCOON Glue is a prototype of WSMO Discovery engine for the healthcare field to find out the most appropriate advice services (Emanuele and Cerizza, 2005).

Registries are important in a large scale, distributed environment, such as the semantic web. They provide the necessary functionality that allows service providers to expose information of their services to potential users. Various types of approaches that are being followed for storing and accessing information over the web are registry-based discovery mechanisms (Willmott, 2005), indexing methods (UDDI) (Clement, 2004) and publish/subscribe approach (Nawaz et al., 2007). In healthcare domain there is no such mechanism of binding healthcare service providers and requesters in order to discover healthcare data for use in emergency situation. There is lack of registries that provide publish and retrieval of healthcare data through web services. There is no any healthcare services publish in a semantic way for the interoperability of health information exchanged in an efficient manner. Healthcare information is more complex and has diverse dimensions. UDDI (Paolucci, 2002; Srinivasan, 2004) and ebXML (Dogac et al., 2008) do not provide such semantic interoperability in healthcare domain.

Methodology

We proposed a framework based on OWL-S semantic layer which would provide automatic service discovery, composition, invocation and execution of web services for healthcare service providers and end users. Our proposed Semantic Registry would be the key foundation block upon which electronic information is exchanged in an interoperable manner among disparate communities through web services semantics. It would be an Ontology based semantic description model explicitly represents information semantics in abstract and concrete level and resolve heterogeneity.

The system will consist of entry points for the communication to take place. The OWL-S/WSDL grounding mechanism would be used for end point service invocation. In our framework, we proposed to perform goal-oriented discovery with semantic matchmaking of OWL-S ontologies. The proposed use of semantic web services specification language such as OWL-S for describing web services semantically would result in better information exchange. We will incorporate three views of services into user demand to satisfy the requirements of end users in healthcare domain. These views are: customization (who is demanding information), situation (when and where the demand is occurred) and quality (how important the demand is). Service provider, who is going to provide their services for use by appropriate users, will take advantage of the complementary strengths of OWL-S, and these three views of services.

OWL-S has classes of WSDLGrounding for realizing specific elements within WSDL for OWL-S/WSDL Grounding mechanism. This mechanism is more mature as compared to WSMX. WSMX required lowering and lifting mechanism and XSLT transformations for WSMO/WSDL groundings. WSMX also uses RDF and XML as a carrier between WSML and WSDL for grounding mechanism, where loss of semantics can be observed. WSMO provides goal oriented discovery and mediation between ontologies, web services and goals that are not provided by OWL-S. In OWL-S, there is no clear distinction between choreography and orchestration. OWL-S Process Model defines choreography and orchestration. There is no need of separate management for these two processes. In WSMO, the choreography and orchestration are specified clearly. WSMX has interfaces for choreography element (provides the necessary information for communicating with the service), and the orchestration class element, (describes how the service makes use of other services in order to achieve the goal). OWL-S has no Semantic Registry for web service discovery, selection and invocation mechanism, it depends on UDDI for web services discovery. Whereas WSMX framework has three steps of discovery, Goal Discovery, Semantic Web service Discovery and End point service Discovery using any one of the approach: keyword based, light weight and heavy weight discovery.

Our framework would work with both central and distributed computing infrastructures as shown in Figure 1. It will provide services for healthcare information provision and for collaboration of Personal Health Record (PHR) systems, Electronic Health Record (EHR) systems, Health Information Management (HIMS) systems, and other hospital and clinical systems.

Our OWLS Semantic Registry is used for HL7 compliant healthcare semantic web services and metadata publication, discovery, composition and invocation in healthcare domain. One of our major concerns is to describe the HL7 compliant healthcare services publication and discovery. Our vision is to have a Semantic Registry as the key foundation block upon which electronic health information would be exchanged among disparate communities. We already have a proactive approach for efficient discovery based on service category that utilizes semantic-based publish-subscribe model in conjunction with UDDI. In the Service discovery process we analyzed that there are less updates and frequent searches hence push model is the right approach to use. Through our web based Semantic Registry in Figure 6 users can publish and request service descriptions from Service Publish Interface and Service Discovery Interface. The service descriptions stored in OWL-S Profile Repository as OWL-S service profile. The matching algorithm semantically enhances ontology mappings for providing services descriptions to requesters. It assigns scores to individual concepts of the advertised service by concept matching with that of the requested one and then assigns overall ranking to advertisement on the basis of individual scores. The results have shown a significant increase in precision and recall of service discovery as compared to UDDI approach. The users of the UDDI registry can also switch between traditional syntax-based and proposed semantic-based searching. Normal users can access OWL-S profiles and WSDL advertisements through inquiry API provided by UDDI registry. Semantic Matchmaker used in this work (Capability Matching Module) performs Inputs, Outputs, Preconditions and Effects and Service Category Matching. Capabilities of OWL-S web services; Preconditions and Effects represent a "state" before and after the execution of a service respectively. In this paper we enhance the OWL-S semantic web services capability matching to Inputs, Outputs, Preconditions and Effects. In this way this work will cover data as well as functional semantics modeling aspects.

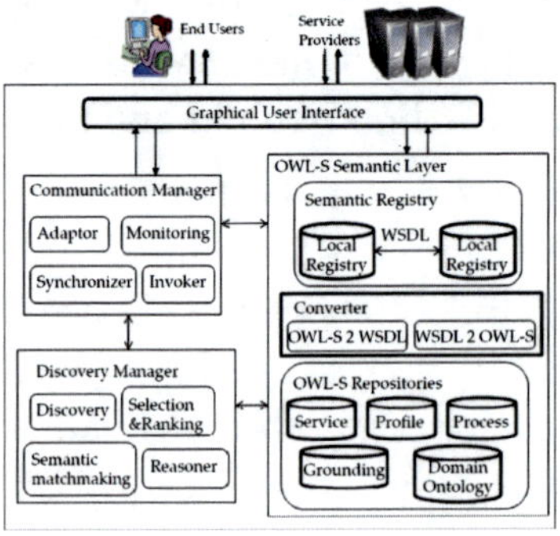

Figure 6. Semantic Framework.

Our proposed framework Figure 6 consists of following components:

- Communication Manager
  - **Adaptor:** End user request will be converted into OWL-S to make it adaptable to internal environment. OWL-S annotations of end user request will be provided to discovery component, which will perform the user oriented discovery with the help of SR, semantic matchmaking, selection & ranking components
  - **Monitoring:** This component will send the request to best selected end point web service candidate.
  - **Invoker:** The response from the end point web service will be given to the user through this component. This component will synchronize all responses from more than one end point web services.
- OWL-S semantic layer
  - **OWL-S ontologies:** Semantic descriptions of web services provided by service provider.
  - **Semantic Registry (SR):** SR manages semantic annotations of services provided by service providers in repository and handles discovery process. It also provides OWL-S to WSDL and WSDL to OWL-S translations with the help of OWL-S ontologies.
  - **Repository:** OWL-S ontologies' semantic annotations would be stored in repository to be accessed latter for discovery purpose.
  - o **Services domain ontology**
- Discovery Manager:
  - **Discovery:** This component will perform keyword based, light weight and heavy weight discovery.
  - **Semantic matchmaking:** During discovery process similar ontologies and web services will be mediated semantically.
  - **Selection & Ranking:** Best candidate end point web service will be selected from the ranked list of web service.
  - **Reasoner:** This component will help selection & ranking component for choosing best candidate.

We developed a healthcare domain services hierarchy through HL7 Service Functional Model (Healthcare Services Specification Project (HSSP)). That services classification is used as healthcare service ontology in our registry for discovery purpose Figure 7.

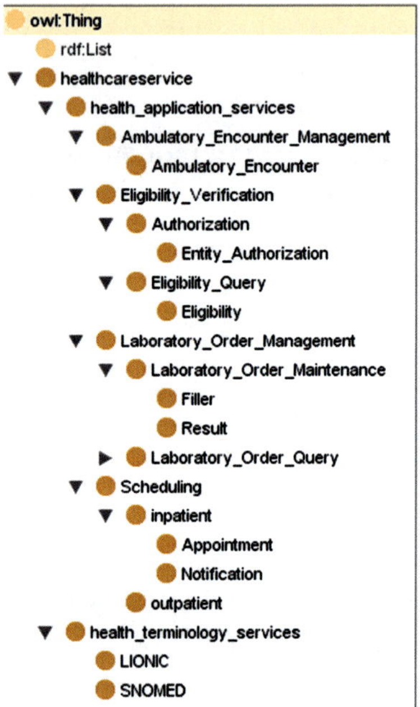

Figure 7. Healthcare Service Ontology.

In order to define HL7 service model specification as in Table 1 for healthcare services publication and discovery through Semantic Registry we consider these two types of services:

1. Business Services provide specific business functionality, such as "Patient Appointment", "Lab Order Management" and so on. These are often further subdivided into "Process Services" and "Core Business Services".
2. Infrastructure (Technical) Services are provided to support the business services and are not specific to healthcare, but are often subject to specific requirements derived from regulation of healthcare information, for example by professional bodies or national legislatures. Examples include: Authorization, Logging, and Transformation.

Table 1.HL7 Service Specifications.

Service specifica-tions	**HL7 v3 Artifacts Used [5]**
Service	Domain, Topic, Application Role, Trigger Events e.g Lab domain
Interface	Domain, Topic, Application Role, Trigger Events
Capabili-ties	DIM/D-MIM, Application Role, Storyboards, Activity Diagrams, Use Cases, Trigger Events, (Interaction, CIM/R-MIM, LIM/HMD, Message Type – if using message oriented level constructs) e.gApplicationLevelAck, ControlActProcess etc.
Message	RIM, DIM, CIM/R-MIM, CMETs, Vocabulary and Data Types (LIM, HMD, Message Type and Schema – if using actual message level constructs)

OWL-S Service profile generated through Jena and OWL-API is as follows:

<?xml version=”1.0”?>

<rdf:RDFxmlns:rdf=”http://www.w3.org/1999/02/22-rdf-syntax-ns#”xmlns:xsd=”http://www.w3.org/2001/XMLSchema#”xmlns:rdfs=”http://www.w3.org/2000/01/rdf-schema#”xmlns:owl=http://www.w3.org/2002/07/owl#

<owl:versionInfordf:datatype=”http://www.w3.org/2001/XMLSchema#string”>

-----OWL ontology for all parameters (input, output, are subclasses of parameters) ----

</owl:Ontology>

<rdfs:Classrdf:ID=”Parameter”/>

<owl:Classrdf:about=”#Parameter”>

</owl:Class><rdfs:Classrdf:ID=”Output”/>

<rdfs:subClassOfrdf:resource=”#Parameter”/>

<rdfs:Classrdf:ID=”Input”/><owl:Classrdf:ID=”ServiceCategory”>

<owl:Classrdf:ID=”Result”>

<rdfs:label>

Result

</rdfs:label>

-----Preconditions-----

```
<owl:ObjectPropertyrdf:ID="hasPrecondition">
<rdfs:domainrdf:resource="#Process"/>
<rdfs:rangerdf:resource="&expr;#Condition"/>
</owl:ObjectProperty>
-----Conditional Effects and Effects and Outputs bundled in Results-----
<owl:ObjectPropertyrdf:ID="inCondition">
<rdfs:label>
inCondition
</rdfs:label>
<rdfs:domainrdf:resource="#Result"/>
<rdfs:rangerdf:resource="&expr;#Condition"/>
</owl:ObjectProperty>
<owl:ObjectPropertyrdf:ID="hasEffect">
<rdfs:label>hasEffect</rdfs:label>
<rdfs:domainrdf:resource="#Result"/>
<rdfs:rangerdf:resource="&expr;#Expression"/>
</owl:ObjectProperty>
```

Profile is a subclass of OWLs Service Profile defined below. It is used to acknowledge that there may be different ways to profile services that are different from the way we expressed it so far (HSSP). OWL Profile ontology has no classes for modeling IOPE's. Profile instances will be able to define IOPE's using the schema offered by the Process.owl ontology defined by OWL.

Additional Classes, needed to specify details of the OWL-S service profile, are also specified for publication and discovery purpose. These are Service Category, Service Parameters and Quality Rating. We have also specified the definition of Profile that provides a definition of the Profile class. Non-Functional Properties are also defined those provide a definition of properties such as name of the service, contact information, quality of the service, and additional information that may help to evaluate the service. We have also specified Functional Properties like IOPE (Input/Output/Precondition/Effects) that help with the specification of what the service provides. The hasParameter property relates Profile instances to process:Parameter instances. In addition, the following properties relate Profile to expr:Condition and process:Result: hasPrecondition and hasResult as follows:

- hasResultVar (a Variable) - A variable scoped to the Result block, bound by the result condition.
- inCondition (a Condition)
- withOutput (an OutputBinding of an Output Parameter of the process to a value form)
- hasEffect (an Effect)

The working of the system consists of following phases:

- Information/Web services publication from service providers
- Demand oriented user discovery for healthcare information

OWL-S based semantic web service is consists of three modules: Service Profile, Process Model, and Service Grounding. Service profile is used for advertisement purpose and provides data semantics. In paper (Iftikhar et al., 2010) HL7 compliant health service capabilities were provided for publication to Semantic Registry. In order to provide functional semantics in the service description, process model is also defined for functional description of services. Figure 8 explains information publication.

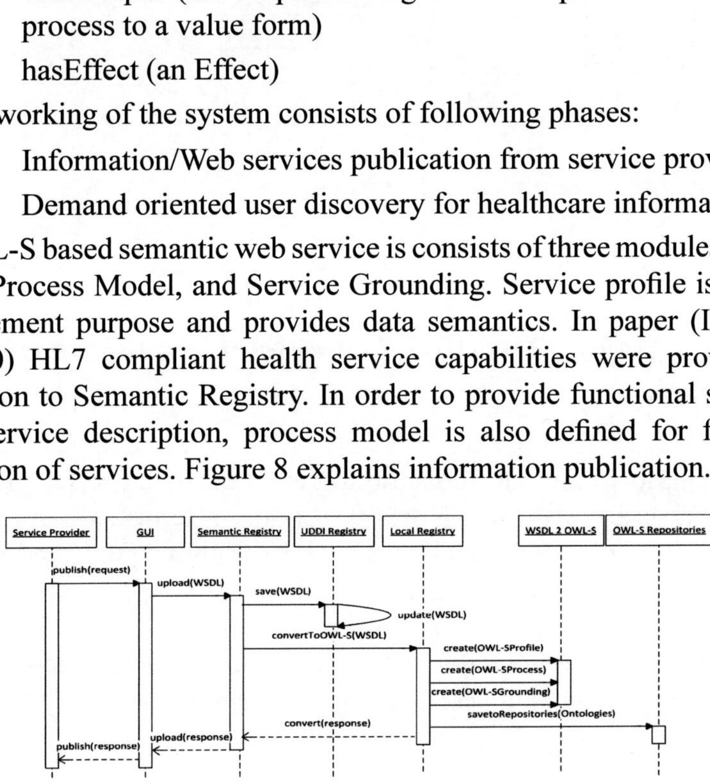

Figure 8. Healthcare information publication.

The Physician and patients can now query the Semantic Registry by providing service inputs, output, preconditions or effects. As service discovery will use OWL-S service profile and service process model, the service requester have to provide the required service criteria on the basis of service inputs, output, preconditions or effects. Figure 9 explains the working of the demand oriented information provision.

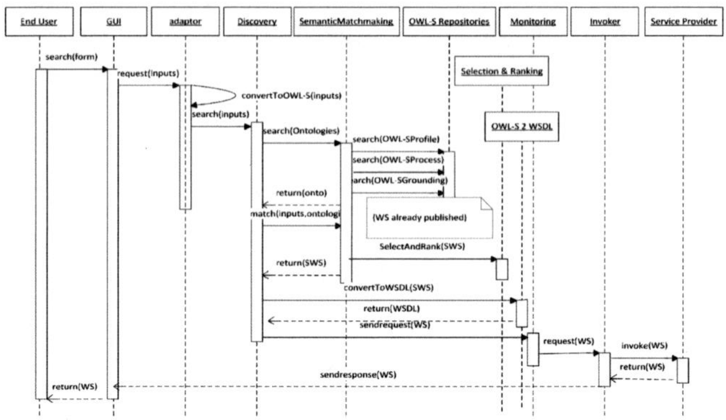

Figure 9. Healthcare information provision.

Results

A. FindLabReportResult HL7 compliant healthcare web service scenario

We described a "FindLabReportResult" HL7 compliant healthcare web service scenario where our Semantic Registry allows a service provider to give service descriptions of his health service in terms of service inputs, output, preconditions and effects. Service descriptions published with data as well as functional semantics in the Semantic Registry. Our Semantic Registry also allows a service requester to query the HL7 compliant semantic web health service on the bases of service inputs, output, preconditions or effects. We implemented this scenario in our Semantic Registry.

Service publishing

OWL-S based semantic web service is consists of three modules: Service Profile, Process Model, and Service Grounding. Service profile is used for advertisement purpose and provides data semantics. In this paper HL7 compliant health service capabilities are provided for publication to Semantic Registry. In order to provide functional semantics in the service description, process model is also defined for functional description of services. FindLabReportResult scenario is published in the Semantic Registry by defining service profile and service model.

Service profile of FindLabReportResult described below is the capabilities of web services in terms of its inputs, outputs, preconditions and effects. The service profile is described using OWL protégé APIs (protégé API). This service profile is used for publishing health service in the Semantic Registry.

- Service Category: Health_application_services
- ServiceName : FindLabReportResult
- Precondition: The service should be the member of ControlActProcess class of HL7 artifacts.
- Inputs: The service provider enters findResult and labReport as inputs.
- Outputs: The service provider enters resultStatus as output.
- Effects: The service provider mentions that the service should receive an acknowledgement of type ApplicationLevelAck.

Process Model of FindLabReportResult described below is the functional description of the service where the service functionality is termed as a process. One atomic process is defined for the service Inputs, output, preconditions and result, where result contains condition, output constraints and effects to come true for the result outcome.

```
process:AtomicProcessrdf:ID="findResult">
<process:hasInputrdf:resource="#labRepot"/>
<process:hasInputrdf:resource="#findResult"/>
<process:hasOutputrdf:resource="#resultStatus"/>
<process:hasPreconditionisMember(ControlActProcess)/>
<process:hasResult>
<process:Result>
<process:inCondition>
<expr:SWRL-Condition>
correctfindResultInfo(labReport,findResult)
</expr:SWRL-Condition>
</process:inCondition>
<process:withOutputrdf:resource="#resultStatus
<valueTyperdr:resource="#findResultMsg">
</process:withOutput>
<process:hasEffect>
```

<expr:SWRL-Condition>

ApplicationLevelAck(labReport,findResult)

</expr:SWRL-Condition>

</process:hasEffect>

</process:Result>

</process:hasResult>

</process:AtomicProcess>

The service provider publishes service profile and functional service descriptions of health service in OWL-S Profile Repository of Semantic Registry of Figure 2. Service metadata is stored in database for permanent storage purpose. Process model is used in this work to describe the atomic process of service profile. This model will be used further in our future work for service invocation process.

Service discovery

The service requester can now query the Semantic Registry by providing service inputs, output, preconditions or effects. As service discovery will use OWL-S service profile and service process model, the service requester have to provide the required service criteria on the basis of service inputs, output, preconditions or effects. After service publication in OWL-S Profile Repository as described in Figure 2, service requester can query the Semantic Registry. The Capability Matching Module searches the UDDI registry and OWL-S Profile Repository for the requested service parameters. The Capability Matching Module then executes the matchmaking algorithm with OWL-S Service Profile defined through Jena APIs as described below and with healthcare Service Ontology. Healthcare Service ontology is the upper ontology used by our Semantic Registry for implementing service profile publishing and discovery phases. The searched results and matching levels are provided based on scoring and ranking (degree of match: exact match, plugin match, subsume match, no match). The OWL-S Service Profile used for Service Discovery is as follows:

<profile:Profile>

<profile:serviceName>

FindLabReportResult

</profile:serviceName>

<profile:textDescription>

An HL7 compliant semantic web healthcare service

</profile:textDescription>………

How a Physician and a Patient bound on OWL-S Semantic Registry as shown in Figure 6 is better explained through a scenario. We implemented a scenario where a patient registered in a hospital through our semantic registry. The required steps for publishing and discovery phases included as follows:

- Publishing phase
  - 2 Web services (WSDL)
  - `WSDL 2 OWL-S conversion
  - OWL-S Annotations for these 2 WSDL
  - Service, Profile, Process Model, Grounding
  - Stored in Repositories
- Discovery phase
  - User request
  - Convert into OWL-S
  - Map user request, OWL-S Annotations
  - Semantic matchmaking, Selection, Ranking
  - OWL-S 2 WSDL conversion
  - WSDL information from UDDI Registry
  - Service invocation and execution
  - Information provided to End user

B. Publishing phase implemented scenario

The web services description in WSDL for Web service name addPatient is as follows:

```
<message name=”addPatient_Request”>
<part name=”Name” type=”xsd:string”>
<part name=”location” type=”xsd:string”>
</message>
<message name=”addPatient_Response”>
<part name=”patientId” type=”xs:string”>
</message><portType name=“addPatientPortType”>
```

```
<operation name="addPatient">
<input message="addPatient: addPatient_Request "/>
<output message="addPatient:addPatient_Response"/>
</operation>
</portType>
<binding name="addPatientSoapBinding" type="addPatient:addPatientPortType">
<soap:binding style="rpc" transport="http://schemas.xmlsoap.org/soap/http"/>
<operation name="addPatient">
</operation></binding>
```

The detailed OWL-S annotations for patient registration web service are as follows:

1. Service

```
<service:Servicerdf:
ID="regPatient_Service">
<service:presents rdf:resource="http://www.regPatient.com/regPatient.wsdl/regPatient_Profile#regPatient_Profile"/>
<service:describedBy rdf:resource="http://www.regPatient.com/regPatient.wsdl/regPatient_ProcessModel#regPatient_ProcessModel"/>
<service:supports rdf:resource="http://www.regPatient.com/regPatient.wsdl/regPatient_Grounding#regPatient_Grounding"/>
</service:Service>
```

2. Service Profile

```
<profile:serviceName>
patientReg
</profile:serviceName>
<profile:textDescription/>
<profile:hasInputrdf:resource=" #regPatientPortType _patientReg_Name_IN"/>
<profile:hasInputrdf:resource="#regPatientPortType _ patientReg_Location_IN"/>
<profile:hasInputrdf:resource=" #regPatientPortType _ patientReg_
```

isCritical_IN"/>

<profile:hasOutputrdf:resource="#regPatientPortType _ patientReg_patientId_OUT"/>

<profile:hasOutputrdf:resource="#regPatientPortType _ patientReg_hospitalName_OUT"/>

<profile:hasOutputrdf:resource="#regPatientPortType _ patientReg_contactNo_OUT"/>

</profile:Profile>

3. Process Model

<process:AtomicProcessrdf:ID="#regPatientPortType _ patientReg">

<process:hasInputrdf:resource=" #regPatientPortType _ patientReg _ Name_IN"/>

<process:hasInputrdf:resource="#regPatientPortType _ patientReg _ Location_IN"/>

<process:hasInputrdf:resource="#regPatientPortType _ patientReg_ isCritical_ IN"/>

<process:hasResult>

<process:Result>

<process:hasOutputrdf:resource="="#regPatientPortType _ patientReg_ patientId_OUT"/>

<process:hasOutputrdf:resource="="#regPatientPortType _ patientReg _hospitalName_OUT"/>

<process:hasOutputrdf:resource="="#regPatientPortType _ patientReg _contactNo_OUT"/>

</process:Result>

</process:hasResult>

</process:AtomicProcess>

4. Grounding

<grounding:WsdlGroundingrdf:ID="regPatient_Grounding">

…………rdf:ID="WSDLGrounding_regPatient_ patientReg ">

<grounding:owlsProcess rdf:resource="http://www.regPatient.com/regPatient.wsdl/regPatient_ProcessModel#regPatientPortType_patientReg"/>

<xsd:uriReferencerdf:value="http://www.regPatient.com/regPatient.

wsdl# patientReg"/>

<grounding:wsdlInputMessage>

// inputs

<xsd:uriReference rdf:value="http://www.regPatient.com/regPatient.wsdl#patientReg_Request"/>

……………………………<xsd:uriReferencerdf:value="http://www.regPatient.com/regPatient.wsdl#Name"/>

……………………………..<xsd:uriReferencerdf:value="http://www.regPatient.com/regPatient.wsdl#Location"/>

………………..<xsd:uriReference rdf:value="http://www.regPatient.com/regPatient.wsdl#isCritical"/> // Outputs

…………….<xsd:uriReference rdf:value="http://www.regPatient.com/regPatient.wsdl#hospitalName"/>

…………………..<xsd:uriReference rdf:value="http://www.regPatient.com/regPatient.wsdl#contactNo"/>

</grounding:wsdlOutputMessageParts>

C. Discovery phase implemented scenario

- User request (goal oriented request)
- Inputs: saman, seecs, true
- Output: patient id, hospital name, contact no
- Discovered OWL-S Profile

<profile:serviceName>

</profile:serviceName>

<profile:textDescription/>

<profile:hasInputrdf:resource=" saman"/>

<profile:hasInputrdf:resource=seecs"/>

<profile:hasInputrdf:resource=" true"/>

<profile:hasOutputrdf:resource="patient Id"/>

<profile:hasOutputrdf:resource="hospital name"/>

<profile:hasOutputrdf:resource="contact no"/>

</profile:Profile>

Discussion

We ranked the web services based on service level matching and it varies from 5 as the highest and 0 as the lowest. Ranking helps in displaying the best matching results on top of the list. The default lower bound has the value 3 which filters all the results and displays only those services which have Ranking of 3 or above. We also described concept level matching with these possible degrees of match. (1) Exact Match is applicable when concepts mach exactly. (2) Plug-in Match and Subsume Match are applicable when both request and advertisement have direct parent-child relationship. (3) Enclosure match is applicable when request and advertisement is not direct parent-child but still match in the ontology hierarchy. (4) Unknown matches or Fail when there is no concept in the ontology. Table 2 shows the ranking and degree of matches for the requested service with the advertised services. Similarly the same results achieved for other capabilities of services such as service outputs, preconditions and effects.

Table 2. Ranking of Found Services

Profile Name	Rank	Degree of Match
FindLabReportResult	5	Exact Match
Laboratory Service	4	Subsume Match (Parent Match)
Health-application-service	4	Subsume Match (Parent Match)
....	.....	....

The performance analysis of the system is represented in form of time taken for ontology to be loaded into the memory. Analysis also contains the results of the system in terms of number of relevant results produced by our system comparing with the results of the syntax based systems without ontologies.

The Figure 10 shows the performance of the parsing based approach with the protégé-OWL API. We used protégé-OWL API approach for creation of OWL-S profiles. Though it takes more time as compared to parsing based approach but it captures all required semantics for OWL-S Profiles.

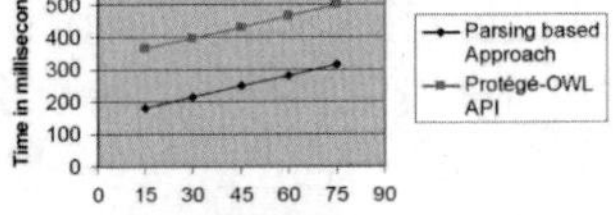

Figure 10. Performance Analysis of Publishing OWL-S Profile.

For service discovery analysis the system was tested on 100 service profiles. We tested our semantic based approach with the syntax based approach of UDDI. The figure shows the average result of different queries executed on both the systems under same conditions. The relevant result of the syntax based approach is much lower than that of the semantic based approach. With syntax based approach 95 service profiles retrieved out of which 50 were relevant. With our semantic based approach 70 profiles retrieved out of which 62 were relevant. The result is based on the exact matches of IOPE of service capabilities for both systems as shown in Figure 11.

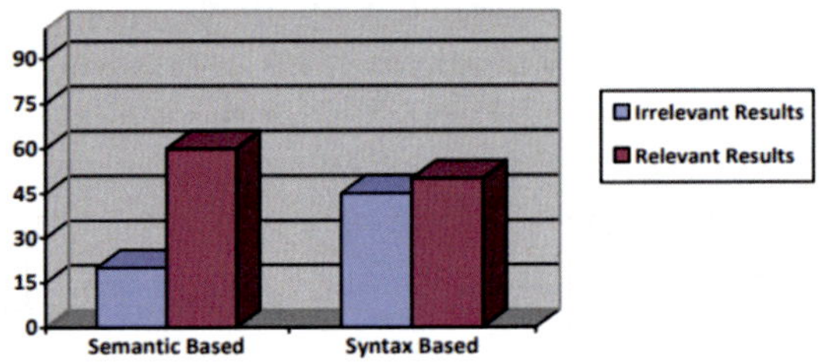

Figure 11. Performance Analysis of Service Discovery.

Our semantic based registry or OWL-S framework that provides services and metadata to manage healthcare information and processes in a consistent way that would be compliant with emerging international standards. Our Solution would provide collaboration and give hospitals and clinics the ability to share healthcare semantic information. Semantic web technologies can provide extensible, flexible and efficient information. Semantics can provide interoperable, automated and seamlessly meaningful communication in healthcare domain.

CONCLUSION

This chapter is based on discussion of two major problems of healthcare industry: interoperability and integration. We presented two designing architecture to handle the two common problems and manage large scale medical data, patient records and the technological infrastructure. Healthcare domain is facing challenges of information sharing, interoperability and efficient discovery. These challenges can be handled with the help of semantic web technologies, service oriented architecture and cloud computing by providing automated semantic web health services. This will lead to extensible and flexible data storage, retrieval and sharing among physicians and patients and efficient discovery of information related to diseases and clinical processes.

Cloud computing will change the rules of healthcare service provision globally with adding values to existing platforms as SaaS and will automate processes and knowledge networks through semantic interoperability. The SEMR system will develop a semantic based SaaS service model on top of cloud for healthcare domain to resolve the above mentioned problems. This will result in efficient healthcare provision to patients in a timely manner (Iftikhar et al., 2011).

A framework for semantic registry based on OWL-S - an ontology web language for web services is used for semantic composition. We implemented a scenario where we bound a physician and a patient for registering to a hospital. We also provide service advertisement publication and discovery of service profiles and process model of HL7 compliant healthcare web services. The service description capabilities of Semantic Registry incorporated functional semantics where we also defined preconditions and effects. The service discovery is also more efficient as matchmaking algorithm is also considering service preconditions and effects for fulfilling the user requests. The whole working of the service publication and discovery is described through FindLabReportResult HL7 compliant healthcare semantic web service scenario. The results are evaluated through implementing the UDDI Publish APIs and Inquire APIs as these are without semantics and do not provide discovery on the basis of preconditions and effects (Iftikhar et al., 2011).

ACKNOWLEDGMENTS

This work is part of Health Life Horizon project initiated at NUST SEECS (http://hl7.niit.edu.pk/index.htm) and is funded by National ICT R&D Funds, Pakistan, http://ictrdf.org.pk.

REFERENCES

1. Dogac A., Laleci G., Kirbas S., Kabak Y., Sinir S., Yildiz A., and Gurcan, Y.: "Artemis: deploying semantically enriched web services in the healthcare domain". Proceedings of Information systems journal (Elsevier), 2006, 31, (4–5), pp. 321– 339
2. Dogac, Asuman.,Gokce, B. Laleci., Kabak, Yildiray., Unal, Seda., Beale, Thomas., Heard, Sam., Elkin, Peter., Najmi, Farrukh., Mattocks, Carl., Webber, David. (2008). Exploiting ebXML Registry Semantic Constructs for Handling Archetype Metadata in Healthcare Informatics. Proceedings of International Journal of Metadata, Semantics and Ontologies (IJMSO-08).
3. apazoglou, M.P. and W-J. van den Heuvel, "Service-Oriented Architectures: Approaches, Technologies and Research Issues. Proceedings of VLDB J., vol. 16, no. 3, 2007, pp. 389-415.
4. Beeler, George W., Stan Huff, Wesley Rishel, Abdul-Malik Shakir, Mead Walker, Charlie Mead, Gunther Schadow. (1999) Message Development Framework. Version 3.3, December 1999, Copyright 1999 by Health Level Seven, Inc.
5. CASCOM: Nadine Fröhlich, HeikkiHelin, HeimoLaamanen, Thorsten Möller, Thomas Schabetsberger, HeikoSchuldt, and Christian Stark. (2007). Semantic Service CoOrdination for Emergency Assistance in Mobile e-Health Environments. Proceedings of Workshop on Semantic Web in Ubiquitous Healthcare, collocated with the 6th International Semantic Web Conference (ISWC2007), 2007.
6. Cesar Cáceresc, Alberto Fernández, SaschaOssowski, Carlos Matteo Vasirani. (2006). AgentBased Semantic Service Discovery for Healthcare: An Organizational Approach", IEEE Intelligent Systems, vol. 21, no. 6, 2006, pp. 11-20.
7. Clement, L. Hately, A. Riegen, C. and Rogers, T. "UDDI Version 3.0.2". OASIS, 2004. UDDI Spec Technical Committee Draft. Available at http://www.uddi.org.
8. Cocoon: Emanuele Della Valle, and Dario Cerizza. "The mediators centric approach to automatic Web Service discovery of Glue". CEUR Workshop Proceedings, vol. 168, 2005, pp. 35–50.
9. Ginsburg, Mark. Interface Considerations in a Pediatric EMR. Proceedings of 12th Americans Conference on Information Systems, Acapulco, Mexico, August 4-6, 2006.

10. Iftikhar, Saman., Khan, Wajahat Ali., Hussain, Maqbool., Afzal, Muhammad., Ahmad, Farooq. (2011). Design of Semantic Electronic Medical Record (SEMR) system as SaaS service model for Efficient Healthcare. Proceedings of International Health Interoperability Conference, March, 2011.
11. Iftikhar, Saman., Ahmad, Farooq., Fatima, Kiran. (2011). A framework based on OWL-S for health care information provision, Proceedings of 7th IEEE International Conference on Emerging Technologies, Islamabad, Pakistan, September, 2011.
12. Iftikhar, Saman., Nawaz, Falak., Ahmad, Farooq., Fatima, Kiran. (2011). Introducing Semantics in DHTs for Grid Services in a Semantic Registry. Proceedings of 6th IEEE International Conference on Emerging Technologies, pp 382 - 387, 18-19 Oct. 2010
13. Nawaz, F., Pasha, M., Ahmad, F., Suguri, H., (2007). Pushing Semantic Web Service Profiles to Subscribers for Efficient Service Discovery. Proceedings of the 3rd International Conference on Semantics, Knowledge and Grid (SKG '07) Xi'an, China, October 2007.
14. N. Srinivasan, M. Paolucci, K. Sycara. (2004). An Efficient Algorithm for OWL-S based Semantic Search in UDDI. Proceedings of first International Workshop on Semantic Web Services and Web Process Composition, SWSWPC 2004 96-110.
15. Paolucci, M., T. Kawamura, T. Payne, K. Sycara, "Semantic Matching of Web Services Capabilities. Proceedings of the First International Semantic Web Conference on The Semantic Web, p.333-347, June 09-12, 2002.
16. Willmott, S., Willmott, H. Ronsdorf, K. Krempels. (2005)Publish and search versus registries for semantic web service discovery. Proceedings of Web Intelligence, 2005.
17. World Wide Web Sites and Other Electronic Sources
18. Benefits of SOA, Website 2010, http://www.devshed.com/c/a/WebServices/Introduction-to-Service-Oriented-Architecture-SOA/2/ [(Last Visited march 2011)]
19. Benefits of Semantic SOA, http://members.sti2.at/~jacekk/education.sti2.org/slides/1- graham-soa.pdf [(Last Visited march 2011)]
20. Clear-health-improving practice management. http://www.clear-health.com/ [(Last Visited march 2011)]
21. CCHIT. http://en.wikipedia.org/wiki/Certification_Commission_for_

Healthcare_ Information_Technology/. [(Last Visited march 2011)]

22. CCHIT EMR. http://www.mtbc.com/cchit-emr.aspx/ [(Last Visited march 2011)]
23. Cocoon. 2011. Available from: http://www.cocoon-health.com
24. Health Level Seven, http://www.hl7.org/ [(Last Visited March 2011)]
25. Health Life Horizon (HLH), http://hl7.seecs.nust.edu.pk/ [(Last Visited march 2011)]
26. HL7 V3 Interoperability Standard, Normative Edition 2009
27. Health Services Specifications Project (HSSP) http://hssp.wikispaces.com/ [(Last Visited march 2011)]
28. HIPPA, http://en.wikipedia.org/wiki/Health_Insurance_Portabity_and_Accountability_ Act/ [(Last Visited march 2011)]
29. HL7 V3 Interoperability Standard, Normative Edition 2009.
30. HIMSS "Selecting the Right EMR Vendor," http://www.himss.org/content/files/selectingemr_flyer2.pdf [(Last Visited March 2011)]
31. Healthcare Services Specification Project (HSSP) HL7 Services Oriented Architecture SIG; 2011. Available from: http://hssp.wikispaces.com.
32. LOINC. 2011. Accessed from http://loinc.org/
33. Neotool "The HL7 Evolution, Comparing HL7 Version 2 to Version 3, Including a History of Version 2"
34. Object Management Group (OMG), http://www.omg.org/ [(Last Visited march 2011)]
35. OpenEMR, http://en.wikipedia.org/wiki/OpenEMR/ [(Last Visited march 2011)]
36. OpenEMR Virtual Appliance, http://en.wikipedia.org/wiki/OpenMRS/ [(Last Visited march 2011)]
37. OpenMRS, http://en.wikipedia.org/wiki/OpenMRS. [(Last Visited march 2011)]
38. Protégé API. Jena, 2011. Available from: http://jena.sourceforge.net/.
39. SequelMed EMR. http://www.sequelmed.com/Products/electronic_medical_records.aspx/. [(Last Visited march 2011)]
40. SaaS and Healthcare Internet Business Models http://microarray.wordpress.com/2009/01/24/saas-and-healthcare-internetbusiness-models/ [(Last Visited march 2011)]

41. Software as a Service (SaaS) http://msdn.microsoft.com/en-us/library/aa905332.aspx#enterprisertw_topic4/ [(Last Visited march 2011)]
42. SmartCare. http://en.wikipedia.org/wiki/SmartCare/ [(Last Visited march 2011)]
43. SNOMED Clinical Terms User Guide January 2007 Release
44. Understanding HIPPA: Health Insurance Portability And Accountability Act. http://www.googobits.com/articles/p0-2899-understanding-hippa-healthinsurance-portability-and-accountability-act.html. [(Last Visited march 2011)]
45. WSMO. http://www.wsmo.org/
46. Web Services Modeling Ontology. http://www.wsmo.org/
47. Xchart. http://www.openhealth.org/XChart/ [(Last Visited march 2011)]
48. ZIMBRA- open source email and collaboration. http://www.zimbra.com/ [(Last Visited march 2011)]
49. Erl, T., (2005). "Service-Oriented Architecture (SOA). Concepts, Technology, and Design". Prentice Hall PTR.
50. Kourtesis D. and Paraskakis I. (2008). Combining SAWSDL, OWL-DL and UDDI for Semantically Enhanced Web Service Discovery. In Bechhofer S. et al.(Eds.): ESWC 2008, Lecture Notes in Computer Science 5021, Springer-Verlag Berlin Heidelberg 2008, pp. 614-628.

CHAPTER

7

CCMF, Computational Context Modeling Framework – An Ontological Approach to Develop Context-Aware Web Applications

Luis Paulo Carvalho[1] and Paulo Caetano da Silva[2]

[1]UNIFACS-University of Salvador/IRT-InstitutoRecôncavo de Tecnologia

[2]UNIFACS-University of Salvador Brazil

INTRODUCTION

The purpose of software is to help people to perform their activities and fulfill their objectives. In this regard, the human-software relationship could be enhanced if software could adapt to changes automatically during its utilization (Brézillon, 1999). Context is defined by (Dey, 2001) as any type of information which characterizes an entity. An entity is any person,

Citation: Luis Paulo Carvalho and Paulo Caetano da Silva (April 25th 2012). "CCMF, Computational Context Modeling Framework - An Ontological Approach to Develop Context-Aware Web Applications", Semantics in Action - Applications and Scenarios, Muhammad Tanvir Afzal, IntechOpen, DOI: 10.5772/38281.

place or object that is relevant to the interaction between users and software. According to (Dey&Abowd, 1999) context-awareness is the capability of software to use context to offer services to users. For instance, a context-aware system may trigger an alarm in a device near to a user to remind him of the departure time of a planned trip (Yamato et al. 2011). In this example, context is used to provide a service to the user: the reminding of a personal activity. It is not, however, a trivial task to associate context with software in the same level of abstraction as humans do when they communicate with each other. (Dey&Abowd, 1999) considers that such ability is naturally inherited from the richness of the human languages and the common understanding of how the world works and from an implicit understanding of daily situations. Thus, with the intention of enhancing the offering of services from software to humans, it is important to transmit these capacities to computational environments.

As maintained by (Sheng &Benatallah, 2005), web services have become a promising technology for the development of internet-oriented software. Services are autonomous platform-independent software that executes tasks ranging from providing simple answers to users requests to the execution of complex processes. Web services are services that utilize the internet and its open technologies, e.g. WSDL, Web Service Description Language, SOAP, Simple Object Access Protocol, UDDI, Universal Description, Discovery and Integration, and XML, eXtensible Markup Language, to supply functionalities to other applications (Berbner et al. 2005). (Kapitsaki et al. 2009) assure that the handling of context is of vital importance to web services, since it promotes dynamic behavior, content adaptation and simplicity of use to end users. However, the association between web services and context is not easy to achieve because adequate mechanisms are not offered to developers in order to support the description and representation of context-related information and its later utilization by web services.

Considering the lack of appropriate technologies to extend software to integration of context and web services, this work proposes:

1. A framework, CCMF (Carvalho& Silva, 2011), Computational Context Modeling Framework, which relies on the reuse of artifacts and tools to automate analysis and development activities related to the making of context-aware web applications;
2. The instantiation of CCMF considering 2 different case studies: (a) Integration of CCMF and CCMD (Carvalho& Silva, 2011),

Computational Context Modeling Diagram (to be presented in Section 3.1); (b) The embedding of ontologies in CCMF. Both cases intending to enable the development of context-aware web applications;

3. The analysis of the coupling between the framework and the 2 targeted technologies (CCMD and Ontologies) in order to evaluate the advantages and disadvantages of each approach.

This work is organized as follows: Section 2 presents related works. The framework is described in Section 3. In Section 4, CCMF is coupled with CCMD and ontologies to develop a context-aware web application (both approaches are compared). Section 5 enfolds conclusions and future works.

RELATED WORKS

(Carvalho& Silva, 2011) gathered requirements from related literature - e.g. (Topcu 2011), (Hoyos et al. 2010), (Dey et al. 2001), (Vieira, 2008), (Bulcão, 2006), (Schmidt, 2006) - with the intention of enumerating important characteristics for the modeling of the information which influences the utilization of software and to provide guidelines to base the creation of the framework. Table 1 lists the requirements.

Table 1. Requirements for developing context-aware software (Carvalho& Silva, 2011)

<table>
<tr><th></th><th>Requirement</th><th>Purpose</th></tr>
<tr><td>I</td><td>It must support the development of context-aware software as a two-phase task: specification of context information (structure) and adaptation</td><td>The separation into two phases promotes the decoupling of aims, allowing designers to focus on specific activities related to each development phase</td></tr>
<tr><td>II</td><td>It must categorize the information into context dimensions</td><td rowspan="2">By modeling the context focus and dimensions, designers are able to orderly identify and structure context information, promoting the readability of the model</td></tr>
<tr><td>III</td><td>It has to identify the context focus of a task</td></tr>
<tr><td>IV</td><td>It must support the transfer of context information and artifacts between development phases</td><td>The effort required to perform next development steps (e.g. modeling of adaptation) is lessened by the input of artifacts from previous phases (e.g. modeling of structures)</td></tr>
<tr><td>V</td><td>It must promote the diversity of context information in a domain-independent manner</td><td>So that designers can model context-aware systems to automate tasks of a variety of scenarios</td></tr>
<tr><td>VI</td><td>It has to support the reuse of distributed computing systems such as services</td><td>To base context adaptation on web services API, e.g. Google Agenda API (GAgenda, 2011)</td></tr>
</table>

The following works were evaluated against the requirements (listed in Table 1):

1. CMS-ANS (Bonino et al. 2007), Context Management Service/ Awareness and Notification Service, a framework that allows context sources to publish information and client software to be notified when specific contexts are acquired;

2. CONON (Wang et al. 2004), CONtext Ontology, a two-layered ontology intended to promote the sharing of context structures among agents and services;
3. CMP (Simons, 2007), Context Modeling Profile, uses stereotypes to extend the class diagram of UML to model context. In the same way, ContextUML (Sheng &Benatallah, 2005) adds stereotypes to the UML (in specific, to the class diagram) to model contextaware web services;
4. CEMantTIKA Case (Patrício, 2010), composed of a set of customized diagrams - based on the Eclipse platform and JBoss Drools (JBDrools, 2009) - that model context structures and adaptations of context-aware software;
5. (Bastida et al. 2008) proposes WSBPEL (WSBPEL, 2007), Web Service Business Process Execution Language, to model adaptation based on context information extracted from software requirements;
6. (George & Ward, 2008) modify the WSBPEL engine to support the addition of context variables and sources (i.e. the sources are used to fill information in the variables);
7. CAMEL (Grassi&Sindico 2009), Context-Awareness ModEling Language, composed of UML-oriented diagrams made specifically to model context structures and adaptation;
8. (Yamato et al. 2010) proposes dynamic adaptations of composite web services utilizing semantic context metadata to select equivalent functionalities from clusters of web services.

Table 2.shows the result of the evaluation of the works against the proposed requirements (filled cells indicate that the requirement was fulfilled).

Since the aforementioned related works do not fulfill all of the requirements (described in Table 1), CCMF is proposed as set of activities intended to automate the analysis and development of context-aware web applications. In Section 3, the framework is described and it is discussed its association with reusable development languages, tools and artifacts. A case study in which CCMF is applied is presented in Section 4.

Table 2. Evaluation of related works against the requirements (Carvalho& Silva, 2011).

	I	II	III	IV	V	VI
CMS-ANS		■				■
CONON		■			■	
CMP	■				■	
ContextUML	■			■	■	■
CEManTIKA Case	■		■	■	■	
(Bastida et al. 2008)	■			■	■	■
(George and Ward 2008)	■			■	■	■
CAMEL	■			■	■	
(Yamato et al. 2010)				■	■	■

CCMF, Computational Context Modeling Framework

CCMF is composed of a set of analysis and development activities which are intended to lessen the effort demanded by the development of context-aware web applications. This is achieved from: (a) the reuse of artifacts and third-part tools, modeling languages and technologies and (b) the automation of the execution of targeted activities, which are described in next paragraphs.

As shown in Figure 1, the framework is composed of two layers containing specific activities to be carried by developers. Its upper layer comprises the activities related to the definition of structures of context information and its externalization to the adaptation modeling mechanism, a WSBPEL diagram. Such externalization is made possible by the transformation of the context structures into a context medium. Provided that XML-based languages enable the interoperation of computational agents, e.g web services (Alboaie et al. 2003), XSD (XSD, 2001), XML Schema Definition, documents are used by the framework to enable the utilization of context by web services integrated to the WSBPEL diagram. Respectively, the definition of context structures and the transformation of these structures into context mediums are performed by the activities identified by numbers 1 and 2.

Once the context medium is created, it can be transformed into language-specific context classes. Considering, for instance, JAVA as the development language, XMLBeans API (XMLBeans, 2009) can be used to transform the XSD schema into JAVA serializable classes. The resulting classes can be instantiated as objects that are capable of encapsulating their attributes into XML documents. Later on, web services can rely on such documents to exchange complex context data between each other, i.e. the serialization via

XML documents is necessary to interoperate web services in a manner that the information about context is used to parameterized the adaptation. The generation of the serializable classes is performed by the activity number 3.

After having modeled the context structures, the developer must define how the context information must be used to automate adaptations. This activity (identified by number 4), the first one of the framework´s lower layer, depends on WSBPEL to base the context adaptation on web services. In this case, web services must be gathered and integrated to a WSBPEL diagram in order to utilize context information to parameterize responses to situations of use. Along with the deployment of the composite context-aware web service (by activity number 5), a WSDL document is created. This document describes the web service with the purpose of allowing the remote calling of its functionalities by other computational agents (e.g. handheld-embedded applications, other web services). To ease the effort required by the creation of these agents, the WSDL document can be transformed into language-specific source code (by executing the activity identified by the number 6). The source code is intended to provide ways to client software to access the composite web service in order to be served by adaptation functionalities.

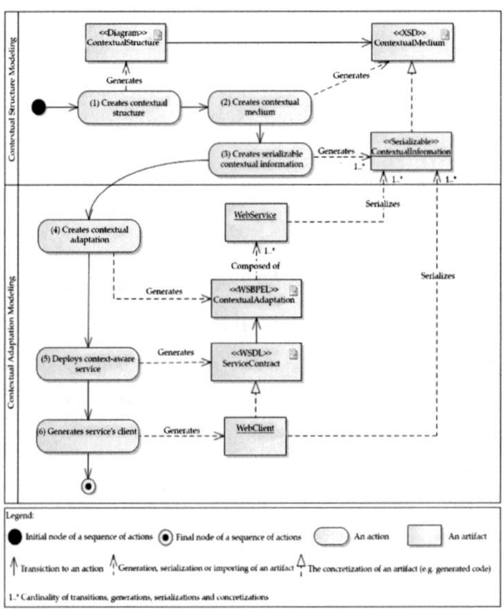

Figure 1. CCMF – Computational Context Modeling Framework (Carvalho& Silva, 2011).

Provided the activities depicted in Figure 1, CCMF is capable of:

1. Modeling structures of context information (upper layer of the framework) and the adaptation (lower layer of the framework);
2. Enabling the reuse of development artifacts, e.g. by transforming a context medium (a XSD document) into XML-based classes in order to serialize complex context data between web services;
3. Supporting the reuse of distributed computing systems such as web services. In this case, the adaptation mechanism is placed "in the cloud" and it can be reused by other computational agents over the internet.

In Section 3.1, it is described a diagram, CCMD, Computational Context Modeling Diagram, which automates the execution of activity number 1 of CCMF, the modeling of context structures, i.e. CCMD can be coupled with the upper layer of CCMF to define the sets ofinformation which may interfere in situations of use of software. In Section 3.2 ontologies are introduced as a replacement for CCMD, being analyzed what are the necessary adaptations to be applied to the framework in order to enable the use of ontologies to model context-aware web applications.

CCMD – Computational Context Modeling Diagram

CCMD is composed of a set of stereotypes which allows the creation of diagrams to model concepts related to computational context, e.g. the context focus and dimensions. According to (Brézillon&Pomerol, 1999) the context focus corresponds to a step in the solution of a problem or in a decision making process. (Vieira, 2008) states that the focus can represent a relationship between an agent and a task, in which the agent is responsible for performing the task. For instance, referring to the modeling of software that bases the scheduling of meetings on computational context, the focus might indicate that a secretary (the agent) must perform the task "prepare meeting". The focus is important to context modeling because it enables developers to identify specific sets of context information in relation to the task executed by an agent. Once the focus is identified, the related information can be grouped as context dimensions. As indicated by (Brézillon&Bazire, 2005) the context dimensions enables the categorization of context information and have the main purpose of helping software designers to specify, model and fill information into adequate structures (Bulcão, 2006). CCMD models the following context dimensions identified by (Abowd&Mynatt, 2000):

1. "Location" represents spatial characteristics of the context information;
2. "Temporal" ("Time") comprises any date/time-related information of the context;
3. "Participant" represents entities (other than the agent) which participates in the execution of the task;
4. "Motivation" ("Preferences") is related to the objectives of the agent and participants;
5. "Activity" corresponds to activities performed during the execution of the task.

The task, the context focus and dimensions are illustrated in Figure 2. Number 1 points to the task. The context focus is represented by the stereotype linked to number 2. Number 3 is associated with the stereotypes that represent the context dimensions.

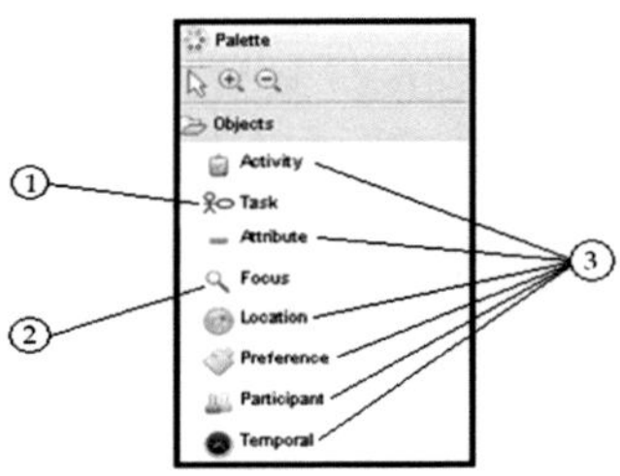

Figure 2. Stereotypes of CCMD (Carvalho& Silva, 2011).

A concrete implementation of the stereotypes of CCMD can be generated via EuGENia (EuGENia, 2011) plugin to embed the modeling of context in the Eclipse IDE. EuGENia defines a declarative language which abstracts away the details of the coding of diagrams. The declarative metadata of CCMD is transformed by EuGENia into artifacts which input graphic-related data into Eclipse's GMF (GMF, 2010), Graphical Modeling Framework, and EMF (EMF, 2009), Eclipse Modeling Framework. As a result, it is generated a diagram (CCMD) to be used via Eclipse IDE to model context information structures. The graphical elements of CCMD are shown in Figure 3. Next to number 1, it is represented the "Task" from which the context focus is extracted. The "Focus" is placed next to number 2. The "Preference" is modeled by the element next to the number 3. Each "Participant" is symbolized by the element pointed by number 4. The "Location" is positioned near to number 5. The "Activity" is represented by the element next to number 6.

The "Temporal" ("Time") dimension is situated nearby the number 7.

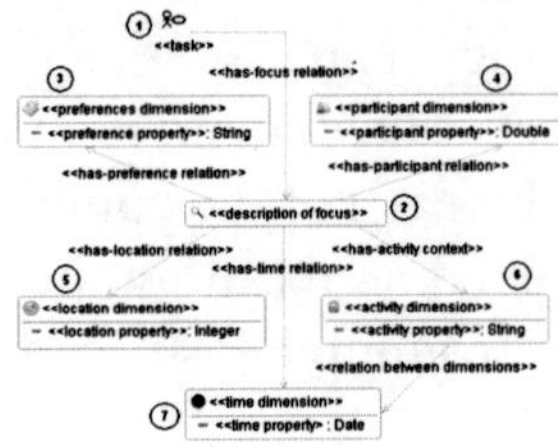

Figure 3. Concrete implementation of CCMD stereotypes (Carvalho& Silva, 2011).

The instantiation of CCMF and its coupling with CCMD is described in Section 4.1. The framework is used to implement a context-aware web application. The modeling activities enumerated in Figure 1 are exemplified as well as the reuse of tools and artifacts.

Ontologies

As stated by (Noy, 2004; Chen et al. 2004), ontologies are believed to be a key feature in the making of context-aware distributed systems due to the following reasons:

1. Ontologies enable the sharing of knowledge by open dynamic agents (e.g. web services);
2. Ontologies supply semantics for intelligent agents to reason about context information;
3. Ontologies promote the interoperability among devices and computational agents.

Considering that the abovementioned advantages ensure that ontologies side with the purpose of CCMF, which is to promote the reuse and interoperability of distributed computational agents (e.g. web services) with the intention of automating the creation of context-aware web applications, it is proposed the coupling of CCMF with an ontological approach. In this case, it must be surveyed how ontologies are capable of supporting the representation of context structures and the generation of context-aware adaptations mechanisms.

(Bontas et al. 2005) defines ontology reuse as the process in which available (ontological) knowledge is used to generate new ontologies. By reusing existent ontologies the cost of implementation is reduced, since it avoids the manual codification of a new one. Moreover, two different ontologies can be bound together as one to represent concepts of broader domains, i.e. a given ontology can be associated with others with the intention of modeling concepts of a domain in order to represent the sum of the information represented by each of the combined ontologies. Therefore, the framework must be evolved as to allow the collecting and binding of ontologies with the intention of supplying structures of information to model computational context.

Another aspect of ontologies that motivates modifications on the development activities of CCMF is related to their capability of having a dual purpose (Reinisch et al. 2008): ontologies are able to represent knowledge and also to store and generate instances of such knowledge to interoperate agents. In comparison with the set of activities of the former framework (Figure 1), the handling of CCMD and the XSD/XML-based artifacts can be replaced by ontologies, because they can be accessed directly by the web services of the context-aware composition in order to enable the saving and retrieval of the context information. As a consequence, the effort required to model a context-aware composite web service is lessened, because it is not necessary to deal with the instantiation and manipulation of serializable objects and XML documents, i.e. the utilization of ontologies causes the removal and substitution of activities from the original framework (the one illustrated in Figure 1 of Section 3).

The modified framework is shown in Figure 4. The activity identified by number 1 represents the collecting and binding of existent ontologies in the making of a new one, which must be suitable to model information of the context-aware application's domain. The second activity is that of customizing the ontology to better represent context information. This activity can be exemplified by the definition of associations between natively dissociated classes and/or the addition of new classes and attributes to candidate ontologies. The third activity creates the context adaptation and bases it on the utilization of composite web services. The web services of the composition are able to add and select instantiated individuals from the ontology in substitution to serializations via XML documents. The deployment of the composite web service is performed by activity number 4. The generated WSDL contract is reused in the making of client software by activity number 5.

Thus, the adapted framework, hereafter O-CCMF, Ontology-driven Computational Context Modeling Framework, is able to (re)use ontologies through a smaller set of activities dedicated to the development of context-aware web-applications.

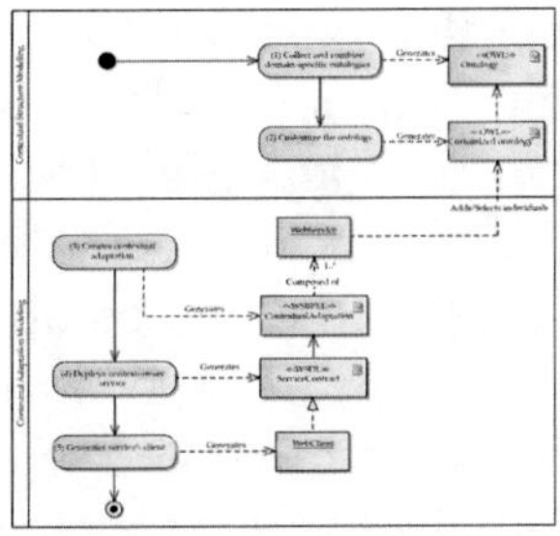

Figure 4. O-CCMF – Ontology-Driven Computational Context Modeling Framework.

The two versions of CCMF, the one coupled with CCMD and O-CCMF are exemplified as study cases in Section 4. They are used to develop the same context-aware web application. Later on, both approaches are evaluated against the requirements identified in Section 2 (Table 1).

CASE STUDIES

As a proof of concept of the application of CCMF and O-CCMF, it is proposed the creation of a context-aware meeting alert application. The frameworks are used to model and develop an application that must send alerts to participants of meetings according to the requirements defined by (Antoniou et al. 2007):

1. If the participant is located near to the place where the meeting is going to happen, he must receive an alerting message 5 minutes before the meeting;
2. If the participant is located in a place far from where the meeting is going to happen, the message must be sent within 40 minutes;
3. If the meeting is going to happen in the rush hour, 10 minutes are added to the interval;
4. If it is raining, another 10 minutes are added;
5. If the meeting's subject is about giving a class, 30 minutes are added in order to allow the participant to prepare himself for the class.

Developing the meeting alert application with CCMF

The first activity of the framework is that of modeling the context information structures. Figure 5 shows a graphical instantiation of CCMD which is used to represent the context data that parameterizes the context adaptation of the meeting alert application. The element next to number 1 represents the task under which a context focus is identified (next to number 2). The focus aids designers in determining the specific set of context information that is necessary to enable the adaptation, i.e. the combination of tasks and focus helps designers to restrain the scope of analysis of context structures. Once the focus is identified, the datasets of context information can be added to CCMD. The meeting is symbolized by the element next to number 3. The location of the meeting is represented by the element next to number 5. The temporal dimension is represented by the element identified by number 6 and contains information about the starting and ending datetime of the meeting. The list of participants is represented by the element next to number 4. Each participant has its own geographic location (latitude/longitude coordinates) which is represented by the element next to number 7. The locations of the participants are used to calculate their distances from the location of the meeting. The preferable weather condition is represented by the element next to number 8.

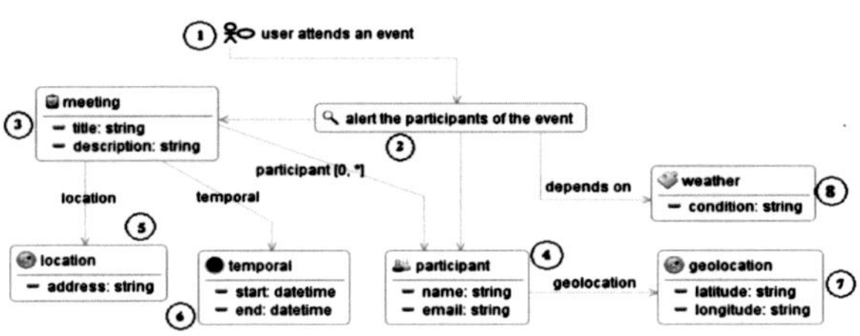

Figure 5. Meeting alert context information modeled by CCMD (Carvalho& Silva, 2011).

```
<complexType name="meeting">
 <sequence>
  <element name="location" type="gagenda:location" minOccurs="1" maxOccurs="1"/>
  <element name="temporal" type="gagenda:temporal" minOccurs="1" maxOccurs="1"/>
  <element name="participant" type="gagenda:participant" minOccurs="0"
maxOccurs="unbounded"/>
 </sequence>
 <attribute name="title" type="string"></attribute>
 <attribute name="description" type="string"></attribute>
</complexType>
```

Figure 6. Context medium exported by CCMD as a XSD document (Carvalho& Silva, 2011).

After using CCMD to define context structures, a context medium must be generated (activity 2 of the framework). The purpose of the context medium is to integrate the framework with different sources of context information (e.g. CCMD). Figure 6 shows an excerpt from a XSD document generated by the CCMD that represents the meeting and its location, its participants and the date/time-related information.

The context medium (XSD document) enables the framework to transform the context structure into other formats of reusable artifacts. For instance, in order to interoperate the web services, with the purpose of implementing the context adaptation of the meeting alert software, the XSD document can be converted into serializable JAVA classes (by the XMLBeans API). This transformation corresponds to the third activity of the framework and it generates a library that makes possible the exchanging of context data between web services, e.g. a certain web service fills context information into a serializable object, which automates the creation of a XML document that is serialized toward other web services. By receiving the XML document as an input, the targeted web service deserializes the context information back into a high level JAVA object. Figure 7 illustrates an example of a XML document which serializes context information related to a meeting.

```
<data:meetings title="Meeting professor Paulo Caetano"
 description="Meeting professor Paulo Caetano to talk about the dissertation"
xmlns:data="http://www.data.agenda.adapters.google.unifacs.edu.br">
 <data:location address="Rua Ponciano de Oliveira, 126, Rio Vermelho, CEP 41950-275, Salvador,
Ba, Brasil">
 </data:location>
 <data:temporal start="2011-08-23T17:30:00.000-03:00" end="2011-08-23T18:30:00.000-03:00">
 </data:temporal>
 <data:participant name="luis paulo" email="luispsc@yahoo.com.br"></data:participant>
 <data:participant name="paulo caetano" email="paulocaetano.dasilva@gmail.com">
</data:participant>
</data:meetings>
```

Figure 7. XML-based serializable information (Carvalho& Silva, 2011).

Once the modeling of the context structures is made available, it must be defined how the software is adapted to situations of use. Prior to designing the adaptation, using the BPEL Visual Designer for Eclipse IDE (BPELEclipse, 2010), web services has to be found so to make possible the collecting and processing of the context data. Table 3 lists services API's used to automate the adaptation of the meeting alert application.

Table 3. Services API's used to automate the adaptation of the meeting alert application

API/Service	Usage
Google Agenda	It supplies information about meetings
Yahoo Weather Forecast	It offers information about weather conditions
Google Geocoding (GGCoding, 2011)	It converts address-based locations of meetings to geographic coordinates
Google Geodirections API (GDirections, 2011)	It calculates the distance from each participant to to meeting's location

The XML document in Figure 7 contains data retrieved from a web service based on the Google Agenda API. Figure 8 shows an example of an event added to the user's agenda. Next to number 1, it is shown the title of the event. Its description is placed near to number 2. Next to 3, the event's starting and ending date and time are shown. Event's location is identified by the number 4. The list of participants is placed near to number 5.

Figure 8. Google Agenda as a source of context information (Carvalho& Silva, 2011).

The WSBPEL diagram illustrated in Figure 9 models a workflow in which the web services of Table 3 are used to automate the context adaptation. The action identified by the number 1 request events from Google Agenda.

The location of the event is processed to determine the weather condition in the area where the meeting is going to happen. This is performed by the action identified by number 2. Since the location of the event is not expressed as a latitude-longitude pair, Google Geocoding is executed to translate the address of the event into geographic coordinates (next to number 3).

The distance from each participant to the event's location is calculated by Google Directions (near to the number 4). Once all of the context information is retrieved and processed by the web services, the WSBPEL diagram evaluates the amount of time within which the alert messages must be sent to participants.

If the participant is located near to event's location1, the message is sent within 5 minutes. If not, the message is sent within 40 minutes (conditional test next to number 5).

If it is goingto rain (test placed near to number 6), another 10 minutes are added. If the event happens during the rush hour, the interval is increased in 10 minutes (condition evaluated next to number 7).

If the event is about giving a class2, another 30 minutes are added to the interval so that the participant will be able to ready himself in order to give the class.

Figure 9. Context adaptation based on WSBPEL (Carvalho& Silva, 2011).

After the modeling of the context adaptation, the BPEL designer is able to generate a WSDL document that externalizes the new generated composite web service to client applications. Figure 10 shows an example of the result of the adaptation supplied by the meeting alert web service.

> To participant identified by 'luispsc@yahoo.com.br' the alert message must be sent within 50 minutes!
> To participant identified by 'paulocaetano.dasilva@gmail.com' the alert message must be sent within 15 minutes!

Figure 10. Adaptation supplied by the meeting alert web service (Carvalho& Silva, 2011).

Coupling CCMF and Ontologies

The O-CCMF can, as well, be used to develop the meeting alert application. In this section, its activities are performed to re-implement the software. The first activity of O-CCMF is that of finding the appropriate ontologies to enable the modeling of context information. For instance, in relation to the meeting alert application, SOUPA, Standard Ontology for Ubiquitous and Pervasive Applications, (Chen et al. 2004) can be used for this purpose. SOUPA comprises two sub-ontologies, SOUPA Core and SOUPA Extension, which contain, among others, classes suitable for the representation of meetings. In Figure 11, such classes are highlighted (in yellow).

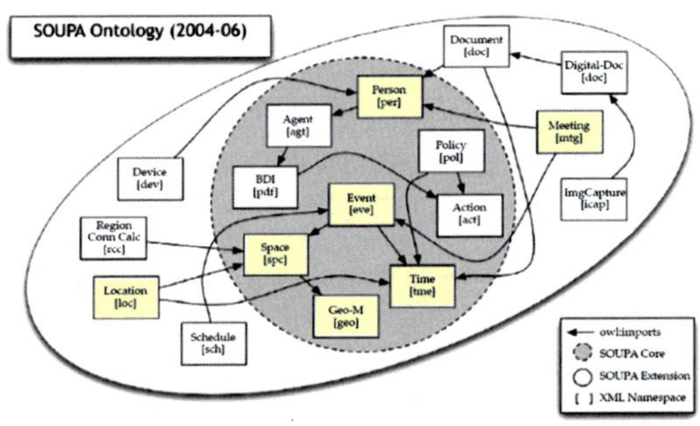

Figure 11. Classes of SOUPA (Chen et al. 2004).

Considering the set of context information contained in Figure 5, SOUPA must be coupled with other ontology in order to represent weather conditions, since the adaptation requires the evaluation of such information prior to furnishing context adaptation. With that purpose, the $O_{WEATHER}$, Weather Ontology, (Gajderowicz, 2008) is bound to SOUPA to provide classes which enable the modeling of weather-related information. Figure 12 showsthe three layers of abstraction of the $O_{WEATHER}$ ontology. The upper layer, Class Level 1, contains a top generic Weather class under which grouping classes (e.g. Wind, Precipitation at Class Level 2) are defined. Class Level 3 contains classes that represent specific natural phenomena (e.g Gusting, Rain).

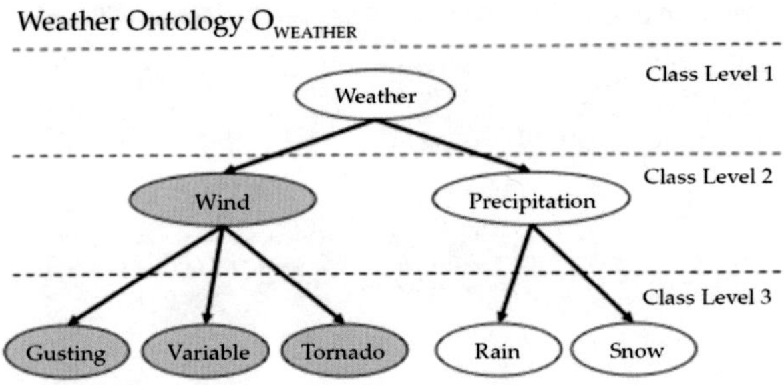

Figure 12. Classes of OWEATHER (Gajderowicz, 2008).

The union of SOUPA and $O_{WEATHER}$ produces a new ontology, MAO (Meeting Alert Ontology), which enables the modeling of the context structures for the meeting alert application. Table 4 relates the classes contained in MAO to the context information defined using CCMD (in Figure 5).

Table 4. Ontology classes to represent context information.

Source ontology	Ontology classes	CCMD classes
SOUPA	Meeting + Event (MeetingEvent)	Meeting
	Location	Location
	Time	Temporal
	Geo-M	Geolocation
	Person	Participant
OWEATHER	Weather	Weather

The resulting ontology can be populated by information related to meetings. In Figure 13, number 1 points to a "MeetingEvent" individual (instance of the "MeetingEvent" class of MAO) being exhibited by Protégé (Protégé, 2011). Protégé is a free, open-source platform that provides a suite of tools to construct domain models and knowledge-based applications with ontologies. Number 2 identified the class-to-class properties of the event, i.e. its relation with other complex classes of the ontology. The "hasParticipant" element represents an association between an event and its participants, i.e. the individuals "LuisPaulo" and "PauloCaetano" that are instances of the class "Person". The "hasStart" and "hasEnd" elements are related, respectively, to the starting and ending date and time of the event (they are instances of the "Time" class). The "locatedAt" element is intended to represent the spatial location of the event, i.e. the place where the meeting is intended to happen. The ontology also supplies information about the meeting's title and description (elements pointed by number 3).

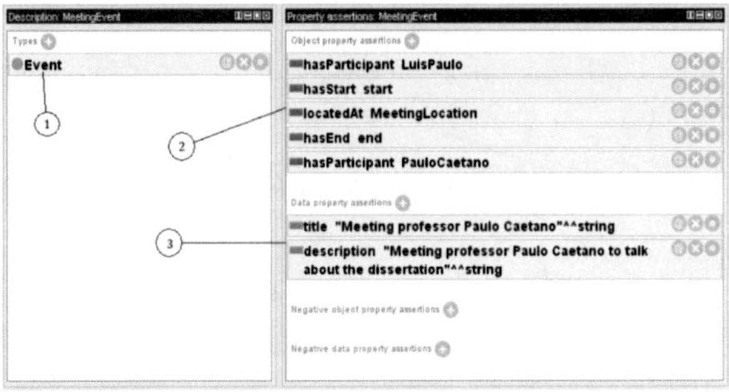

Figure 13. The "Event" individual of the meeting alert ontology.

Although, it is possible to combine different ontologies in the production of a new one, e.g. the combination of SOUPA and $O_{WEATHER}$ produces MAO, it is necessary to adapt the ontology to better express the context information. For instance, Event and Meeting were two dissociated concepts of SOUPA, but, considering the meeting alert application, they had to be combined in a single class, MeetingEvent, so that it would supply a unique way to represent meeting-related events. This adaptation exemplifies the execution of activity 2 of the O-CCMF (as illustrated in Figure 4).

The meeting event information of Figure 13 was retrieved from a web service based on the Google Agenda API and stored in MAO using the OWL API (OWLAPI, 2011). The composite web service (the one illustrated in Figure 9 of Section 4.1) was altered with the intention of using the OWL API and ontologies (SOUPA and $O_{WEATHER}$ grouped in MAO) as a replacement for the XML serializable classes (i.e. the JAVA XML Beans classes originated from XSD documents). In this case, the ontologies promote the sharing of a common vocabulary that replaces the serialization of context information via XML documents. As a concrete example of this form of interoperability, Figure 14 illustrates how individuals retrieved from Google Agenda are added to MAO with the intention to parameterize the execution of other web services, e.g. the one originated from the Google Geocoding API. This is done by the "getEventEntries" method that selects event entries found in user's agenda and inserts them in the meeting alert ontology. Once the Geocoding converts the address of the meeting to geographic coordinates, they are compared to the current location of the participants to determine how far/near they are from meeting's location. The location is also used by Yahoo Weather Forecast to evaluate the rain likelihood, i.e. the service analyzes the weather-related information to determine if it is going to rain in the area where the meeting is intended to happen.

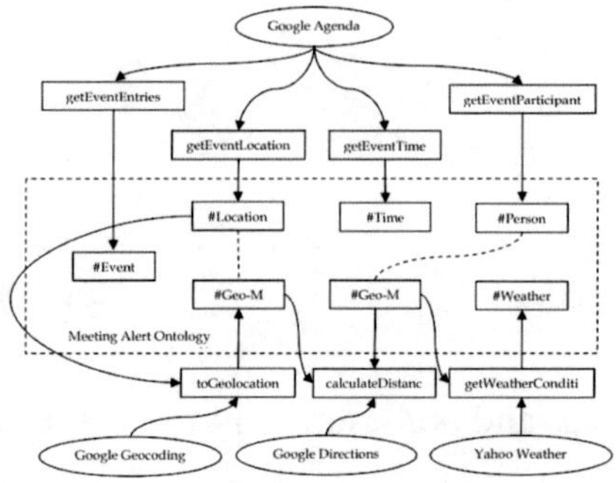

Figure 14. Using the MAO ontology to interoperate web services.

Considering the scenario depicted in Figure 14, the context adaptation is less influenced by the overhead of modeling serializations via XML. In the making of the meeting alert web application, for instance, it was possible to produce web services which took no parameters as input and, likewise, returned no output, because the context information was selected and saved directly to the ontology (no serialization of context information needed). As a consequence, the modeling of the context adaptation can rather rely on choreographed web services in substitution to orchestrations. Figure 15 illustrates the difference between orchestration and choreography (Gábor et al. 2004). The orchestration (left side of Figure 15) requires that the execution of web services is controlled by one agent which describes how services interact with each other. The WSBPEL, for instance, is an orchestrator of web services. In a choreography (right side of Figure 15), each web service involved in the process describes the part they play in the interaction which is performed in a collaborative manner.

The choreography can be exemplified by the interaction between the Geocoding and Directions web services. The Directions web service is able to extract the geographic coordinates inserted into the ontology by the Geocoding web service. This is performed in a i.e. choreographed manner, since the direct manipulation of the meeting alert ontology bythe web services promotes an internalized sharing of context information, without the intervention of controlling agents, such as an orchestration mechanism. As an opposite example, the WSBPEL diagram (e.g. the one illustrated in Figure 9, Section 4.1) is responsible for transferring the context information from one service to other, i.e. using WSBPEL, software designers must model an appropriate sequence of actions so that the context information is interchanged among services. In this case, the WSBPEL workflow acts like a controlling agent.

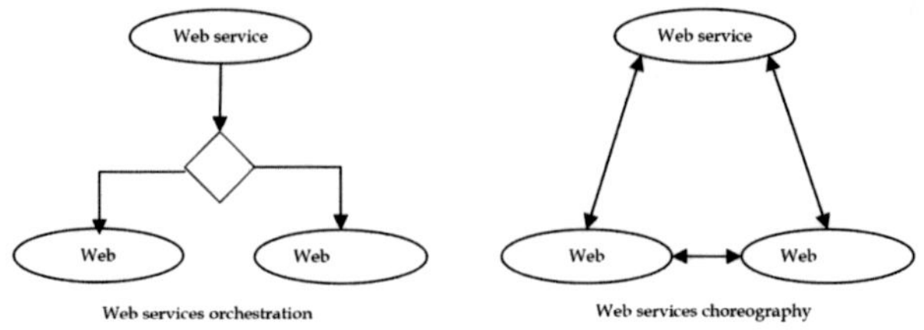

Figure 15. Choreography and orchestration of web services (Peltz, 2003).

Comparing CCMF and O-CCMF

Provided the two scenarios of development of context-aware web applications, the ontological approach, O-CCMF, leads on a reduced framework in comparison with the former version, CCMF, because ontologies have the characteristic of being artifacts suited for both the storage and sharing of information among computational agents. The meeting alert ontology, for instance, represents structures of context information and, too, it encloses the instances of its own ontological classes (individuals). On the contrary, considering that CCMF utilizes CCMD to only model the context information with no regard as to afford the mechanisms to allow the direct storage and instantiation of its classes as concrete objects, it is required from CCMF the transformation of CCMD into XSD/XML documents to support the sharing of context information. Consequently, as computational agents are able to add and select individuals directly from ontologies, the context adaptation can be automated by a workflow that groups and interoperates web services in a collaborative manner, i.e. the adaptation is served to client software by choreographed web services as a replacement to orchestrated ones, in a way that the orchestration eases the modeling of the adaptation by not requiring the provision of serializations.

Table relates the requirements identified in Section 2 (Table 1) to CCMF and O-CCMF, indicating how they were fulfilled by each framework.

CCMF and O-CCMF are capable of assisting developers in the creation of context-aware web applications. Adopting one or the other as development framework is a matter of deciding what it is the intended context information source: diagrams such as CCMD or ontologies. Another criterion would be the intended method of creating composite web services to serve context adaptation to client software: orchestrated (CCMF) or choreographed (O-CCMF) web services.

Table 5. Evaluating the frameworks against the requirements.

Requirement	CCMF	O-CCMF
It must support the development of context-aware software as a two-phase task: specification of context information (structure) and adaptation	CCMD is coupled to the framework to represent context structures. WSBPEL diagram models the adaptation	CCMD is replaced by combined ontologies to represent context information. WSBPEL is maintained to create the adaptation
It must categorize the information into context dimensions	CCMD contains stereotypes that represent the context focus and dimensions	No specific data structures represent the focus and dimensions. It could be, though, added to ontologies (e.g. MAO) during the execution of the customization activity (activity 2 of the framework)
It has to identify the context focus of a task		
It must support the transfer of context information and artifacts between development phases	The transference is performed by XML documents and XML serialization API's	The usage of ontology is twofold: it represents the context and it enables the interoperability of web services by instantiated individuals
It must promote the diversity of context information in a domain-independent manner	CCMD does not constrain the domain	Although ontologies are known for representing specific knowledge domains, they can be combined to support broader concepts
It has to support the reuse of distributed computing systems such as services	Achieved by the usage of orchestrated web services	Achieved by the usage of choreographed web services

CONCLUSION AND FUTURE WORK

Related works, as those described in Section 2, are likely to subject the modeling and development of context-aware applications to the utilization of ontologies or diagramsoriented solutions (e.g. stereotyped UML class diagram). By introducing CCMF, a modeldriven framework, and its ontology-oriented variation, O-CCMF, this work points to a heterogeneous scenario where context information is collected from different sources and adaptations are served by varied web services. Such diversification demands adaptive approaches from development solutions, as, for instance, the ability to deal with different modeling technologies (e.g. ontologies, diagrams) in a decoupled manner. Instead of favoring one specific form of development of context-aware web applications, CCMF and OCCMF promote the reuse of a mixed set of artifacts, tools, API's, information and functionalities sources.

In regard to CCMF, its coupling with CCMD intends to grant to developers an immersive environment in which concepts of computational context (context focus and dimensions)orients the design of context information and adaptation.

An advantage that is not provided by O-CCMF. However, contrary to ontologies, CCMD (and CCMF, consequently) does not rely on a single artifact to represent classes and instances of context information. Thus, CCMF has to be coupled with extra mechanisms (e.gserializable JAVA classes) to workaround such limitation which is naturally overcame by O-CCMF.

Both frameworks rely on web services to automate context adaptation and to serve it to remote clients across the internet. One advantage that arises from this approach is that of making possible the addition of further context information and adaptation steps to enhance context-awareness mechanisms.

For instance, improvements in the Google Agenda API can be automatically propagated to client software without needing to distribute modification patches. Conversely, faulty web services might lessen the quality of served adaptations. For example, in case a specific functionality of the Google Agenda API either becomes deprecated or fails to retrieve some important context information, client software may not succeed in supplying context-awareness to end users.

Currently, the following tasks must be carried out in order to supplement this work:

1. The ontology-driven framework must be evaluated against further study cases to analyze weather the WSBPEL diagram can be decoupled from the framework in order to favor other composition mechanisms, e.g. the WSCI, Web Service Composition Interface (Gábor et al. 2004), which is representative of the choreography approach;
2. Reasoning mechanisms based on the semantics supplied by ontologies must be surveyed in order to enhance the adaptation. For instance, the conditional test that evaluate if the participant is the same location of the event could be inferred from the ontology by the web service that schedules the alerts;
3. The ontological approach promotes the binding of existent ontologies in the definition of domain-specific context information. Therefore, the searching for fitting available ontologies must be adequately supported by the framework. It must be surveyed how this activity can be better assisted by the coupling O-CCMF with available third-part tools and processes.

REFERENCES

1. Abowd, G. D. &Mynatt. E. D. (2000). Charting past, present, and future research in ubiquitous computing. ACM Trans. Comput.-Hum. Interact. 7, pp. 29-58
2. Alboaie, L.; Buraga, S. C. &Alboaie, S. (2003). tuBiG: a layered infrastructure to provide support for Grid functionalities, Proceedings of the second international conference on Parallel and distributed computing, Washington, DC, USA, pp. 9-14
3. Antoniou, G.; Bikakis, A.; Karamolegou, A. &Papachristodoulou, N. (2007). A contextaware meeting alert using semantic web and rule technology. International Journal of Metadata, Semantics and Ontologies 2007, Vol. 2, No.3, pp. 147 – 156
4. Bastida, L.; Nieto, F. J. &Tola, R. (2008). Context-aware service composition: a methodology and a case study, Proceedings of the 2nd international workshop on Systems development in SOA environments, New York, USA, pp. 19-24
5. Bonino, L. O.; Wijnen, R. P. &Vink, P. (2007). A service-oriented middleware for contextaware applications. In Proceedings of the fifth international workshop on middleware for pervasive and ad-hoc computing. New York, NY, USA
6. Bontas, E. P.; Mochol, M. &Tolksdorf, R. (2005). Cases on Ontology reuse. Proceedings of the 5th International Conference on Knowledge Management BPELEclipse (2010).
7. BPEL Eclipse Designer. Available from http://www.eclipse.org/bpel
8. Brézillon, P. (1999). Context in problem solving: a survey. Knowl. Eng. Rev. 14, 1, pp. 47-80.
9. Brézillon, P. &Bazire, M. (2005). Understanding Context Before Using It. 5th International and Interdisciplinary Conference, CONTEXT-05, v. LNAI 3554, Springer Verlag, Paris, France, pp. 29-40
10. Brickley, D. & Miller, L (2003). FOAF vocabulary specification. RDFWeb Namespace Document, RDFWeb, xmlns.com.
11. Bulcão, R. (2006). Um processo de software e um modeloontológico para apoioaodesenvolvimento de aplicaçõessensíveis a contexto. Serviço de pós-graduação do ICMC-USP, São Carlos, São Paulo, Brasil
12. Carvalho, L. P. & Silva, P. C. (2011). CCMD – Computational Context

Modeling Diagram – And WSBPEL Integration. IADIS Applied Computing International Conference. Rio de Janeiro, Brasil, November

13. Chen, H.; Perich, F.; Finin, T. & Joshi, A. (2004). SOUPA: Standard Ontology for Ubiquitous and Pervasive Applications. 1st Annual Int'l Conf. on Mobile and Ubiquitous Systems: Networking and Services, August
14. Dey, A. K. (2001). Understanding and Using Context. Personal and Ubiquitous Computing, Special issue on Situated Interaction and Ubiquitous Computing 5, 1, pp. 4-7
15. Dey, A. K. &Abowd, G. D. (1999). Towards a better understanding of context and contextawareness, Proceedings of the first international symposium on handheld and ubiquitous computing, H. Gellersen, Ed. Lecture Notes in computer science. Springer-Verlag, London, England, pp. 304-307
16. Dey, A. K.; Abowd, G. D. &Salber, D. (2001). A conceptual framework and a toolkit for supporting the rapid prototyping of context-aware applications, Human-computer interaction, vol. 16
17. EMF (2009). Available from http://www.eclipse.org/modeling/emf
18. EuGENia (2011). Available from http://www.eclipse.org/gmt/epsilon/doc/eugenia/
19. Gábor, V.; Andersson, B. &Wohed, P. (2004). An Ontology based Analysis of BPEL4WS and WSCI. Proceedings of the 3rd Nordic Conference on Web Services (NCWS 2004), ISBN 91-7636-431-3. Växjö, Sweden
20. GAgenda (2011). Google Agenda API. Available from http://code.google.com/intl/ptBR/apis/calendar/
21. Gajderowicz, B. (2011). Using decision trees for inductively driven semantic integration and ontology matching. Thesis, Ryerson University, Program of Computer Science. Available from http://www.scs.ryerson.ca/~bgajdero/msc_thesis/document/bgajderowicz-msc-thesis.pdf GDirections (2011). Google Directions API. Available from http://code.google.com/intl/ptBR/apis/maps/documentation/directions/
22. GGCoding (2011). Google GeoCoding API. Available from http://code.google.com/intl/ptBR/apis/maps/documentation/geocoding/
23. GMF (2010). Graphical Modeling Framework (Graphical Modeling Project - GMP). Available from http://www.eclipse.org/modeling/gmp

24. George, A. A. & Ward, P. A. (2008). An architecture for providing context in WS-BPEL processes, Proceedings of the 2008 conference of the center for advanced studies on collaborative research: meeting of minds, New York, NY, USA, Article 22
25. Grassi, V. &Sindico, A. (2009). Model driven development of context aware software systems, Proceedings of International Workshop on Context-Oriented Programming, New York, USA, pp. 1-5
26. Hoyos, J. R.; Molina, J. G. &Botia, J. A. (2010). MLContext: A Context-Modeling Language for Context-Aware Systems, Proceedings of Electronic Communications of the European Association of Software Science and Technology JBDrools (2009).
27. JBoss Drools. Available from http://www.jboss.org/drools/drools-flow
28. Noy, N. F. (2004). Semantic integration: A survey of ontology-based approaches. SIGMOD Record, 33(4), Dec. 2004
29. OWLAPI (2011). The OWL API. Available from http://owlapi.sourceforge.net/index.html
30. Patrício, R. F. (2010). CEManTIKA CASE: umaferramenta de apoioaodesenvolvimento de SistemasSensíveisaoContexto, UFPE, Recife, Pernambuco, Brasil
31. Peltz, C. (2003). Web Service Orchestration and Choreography. Available from http://wpage.unina.it/rcanonic/didattica/at/documenti/wsOrchestration.pdf
32. Protégé (2011). Protégé Ontology Editor. Available from http://protege.stanford.edu/
33. Reinisch, C.; Granzer, W.; Fraus, F. &Kastner, W. (2008). Integration of Heterogeneous Building Automation Systems using Ontologies. Proc. of the 34th Annual Conference of the IEEE Industrial Electronics Society (IECON '08), Nov. 2008, pp. 2736–2741
34. Schmidt, D. C. (2006). Guest Editor's Introduction: Model-Driven Engineering. IEE Computer 39(2), pp. 25-31
35. Sheng, Q. Z. &Benatallah, B. (2005). ContextUML: A UML-based modeling language for model-driven development of context-aware web services, Proceedings of the International Conference on Mobile Business, Washington, DC, USA, pp. 206-212
36. Simons, C. 2007. CMP: A UML context modeling profile for mobile distributed systems, Proceedings of the 40th Annual Hawaii International Conference on System Sciences, Hawaii, USA

37. Topcu, F. (2011). Context modeling and reasoning. Available from http://www.snet.tuberlin.de/fileadmin/fg220/courses/SS11/snet-project/context-modeling-andreasoning_topcu.pdf
38. Vieira, V. 2008. CEManTIKA: A domain-independent framework for designing contextsensitive systems, Centro de Informática - UFPE, Recife, Pernambuco, BrasilXMLBeans (2009). Apache
39. XML Beans 2.5. Available from http://xmlbeans.apache.org/
40. XSD (2001). W3C XML Schema 1.1. Available from http://www.w3.org/XML/Schema
41. Yamato, Y.; Nakano, Y. & Sunaga, H. (2010). Context-aware service composition and change-over using BPEL engine and semantic web. Intech Open Access Publisher. Rijeka, Croatia
42. YWForecast (2011). Yahoo Weather. Available from http://developer.yahoo.com/weather/
43. Wang, X. H.; Gu, T.; Zhang, D. Q. &Pung, H. K. (2004). Ontology based context modeling and reasoning using OWL, Proceedings of the 2004 communication networks and distributed systems modeling and simulation conference, San Diego, CA, USA
44. WSBPEL (2007). OASIS Web Service Business Process Execution Language (WSBPEL) 2.0. Available from http://www.oasis-open.org/committees/wsbpel/

CHAPTER

8

Three Types of Episodic Associations for the Semantic/Syntactic/Episodic Model of Language Prospective in Applications to the Statistical Translation

Zi-JianCai

CaiFortune Consulting, Suzhou, China

ABSTRACT

Recently, it was proposed by Cai a new semantic/syntactic/episodic model of language encompassing the sentential meanings, while deriving three corresponding principles from it for machine translation, respectively as first to establish the dictionary of words/phrases, second to translate the

Citation: Cai, Z. (2017), "Three Types of Episodic Associations for the Semantic/Syntactic/Episodic Model of Language Prospective in Applications to the Statistical Translation". Open Access Library Journal, 4, 1-12. doi: 10.4236/oalib.1103830.

grammar, and third to determine the meanings of some words/phrases of multiple meanings by statistical translation. In this article, it is discovered three types of episodic associations for this linguistic model, prospective in applications to statistical translation, as: 1) It is classified the living/natural words and phrases of multiple meanings by behavior, adopting both the zoological/organizational/physical/categorical and affective/behavioral/logic/characteristic/changing characters to classify the nouns and verbs, the affective/behavioral/logic/characteristic/changing/spatial/temporal characters to the adjectives and adverbs, helpful to discern the meanings of them using these episodic associations with others within the sentence. 2) Likewise, it is classified the sentence/paragraph into the category of natural/social subjects like physics, biology, art, economy, etc., which was improved by the Chinese people in television from my original sentential/thematic category. 3) It is suggested to collect the frequent word- pairs during statistical translation, such as "bank money", "war declaration", etc., helpful to determine the episodic associations of some prepositions or terminal "which" clauses. It is suggested to use word episodic symbolization to apply them to computer. It is therefore improved the third principle of machine translation as third to determine the meanings of some words/ phrases of multiple meanings by episodic associations with others using the behavioral classification of words, the categorization of sentence/paragraph and the collection of frequent word-pairs.

Subject Areas: Artificial Intelligence, Information and Communication Theory and Algorithms, Linguistics, Neuroscience

Keywords: Semantic/Syntactic/Episodic Linguistic Model, Behavioral Classification of Words, Sentential/Paragraphic Categorization, Frequent Word-Pairs, Word Episodic Symbolization, Statistical Translation

INTRODUCTION

The natural language of humans is organized from word to sentence to story, making the language able to contain and deliver almost all kinds of information and intention at ease [1] .

Recently, the author proposed a new semantic/syntactic/episodic model of three kinds of linguistic processes in brain, so as to encompass the sentential meanings to the linguistic processes [1] [2] .

From this semantic/syntactic/episodic linguistic model, the author has also derived three principles for guidance of software design of translation machines [2] , as followings: 1) Principle 1 is the necessity to establish the dictionary for translation of words and phrases in machine translation. 2) Principle 2 is the necessity to install the linguistic grammar for reading and forming the sentence from words and phrases in machine translation, arranging such parts of speech as noun, verb and adjective into order. 3) Principle 3 is the necessity to check with statistics for the words and phrases of multiple meanings and figure out one correct meaning of them in machine translation.

The Principles 1 - 2 of machine translation are regular and fixed in contents or rules, while the Principle 3 nowadays popularly present as the statistical translation requires to store and rectify the statistical concurrence of word pairs with the accumulation of translation. It is relatively most flexible in application, and accordingly it would be helpful if provided with some common methods to help coordinate the technological applications. In this article, it is newly demonstrated three types of episodic associations for the semantic/syntactic/episodic linguistic model to prospectively help and improve the statistical translation nowadays, while other improvements to statistical translation from visual, auditory inputs and so on are not considered in this paper.

THE BRIEF SEMANTIC/SYNTACTIC/EPISODIC MODEL OF LANGUAGE

Recently, Cai extended the present declarative/procedural model of Ullman and Pinker [1] [3] [4] [5] underlying two kinds of linguistic processes to a new semantic/syntactic/episodic model of three kinds of linguistic processes in brain [1] [2] , able to encompass the sentential meanings to the linguistic processes that the declarative/procedural model of Ullman and Pinker has neglected [1] [2] [3] [4] [5] .

Pinker, Ullman and so on integrated a declarative/procedural model for linguistic processing in brain. They suggested that the linguistic lexicon of word- specific knowledge should subserve the storage of meanings of words and phrases, and depend on the temporal-lobe substrates of declarative memory for the storage and usage of facts and events [1] [3] [4] [5] , while the linguistic grammar should subserve the sequential combination of lexical items by procedural rules into complex sentences, and depend on a network of specific frontal, parietal, basal-ganglia and cerebellar structures of procedural memory in the brain [1] [3] [4] [5] . There are many evidences in support of this declarative/ procedural model of language [1] [3] [4] [5] .

To extend this declarative/procedural model to a new semantic/syntactic/ episodic model of three linguistic processes in brain, Cai added that, besides the declarative/procedural processes of language, the episodic coordination of cortical modality by reticular formations was also required for language performance and organization in addition [1] [2] .

Many neurobiological evidences supported this suggestion [1] [2] , as in the followings: 1) The reticular dopaminergic system may be involved in the linguistic modality organization, as the dopaminergic antagonists [1] [2] [6] [7] alleviate while the dopaminergic genes [1] [2] [8] phenotype the stuttering. 2) From the drugs in many assisting therapies of aphasia, it is implicated that the ascending reticular cholinergic projections, noradrenergic projections and nonspecific activating projections from intralaminar thalamic nuclei may participate in episodic coordination of cortical modalities in linguistic processes [1] [2] [9] [10] . 3)

It is evidenced by numerous reports that the gamma bands of high frequency, subject to modulation by the reticular cholinergic system [11] [12] , associate with the word congruency at sentential level [1] [2] [13] [14] [15] , and the episodic coordination of cortical modalities.

Now that it is well evidenced for the episodic coordination of cortical modalities at the sentential level, it is reasonable to in further consider it for story narration. Complex stories certainly require more episodic coordination of cortical modalities. Language disorders occur in narrative discourse skills in patients with various pathologies [16] [17] [18] , demonstrating diversity in cortical modalities. Besides, stuttering is also a disorder of discourse sometimes, as narrative therapy is auxiliary to treatment of stuttering [19] [20] . These facts implicate that episodic modality coordination of cortices is also required at high level during story narration.

In summary, herein it is briefly demonstrated that there are three semantic/ syntactic/episodic linguistic processes present in the human brain.

THREE PRINCIPLES FOR MACHINE TRANSLATION DERIVED FROM THE SEMANTIC/SYNTACTIC/EPISODIC NEUROLINGUISTICS

At present, there are two types of machine translation, adopting two different strategies of design respectively. One is early in method following which to translate the individual words and grammar of sentence [21] . The difficulty of this type of machine translation lies in that many words have multiple meanings, so that the translation often makes mistakes due to this reason. Another is the recent method called as statistical machine translation [22] [23] , in which the machine translation is made according to the statistical concurrence of words and contents. The difficulty of this type of machine translation lies in that the statistical concurrence of words and contents is various and limitless from collection, so that it is necessary to further find out some rules to make it more effective, which is difficult.

Because of the lack of scientific guidance from linguistics, the present machine translation has mostly chosen one of the two types of methods, and therefore only adopted two linguistic processes rather than the recently revealed three brain linguistic processes. In this regard, the results of machine translation are quite unsatisfactory at present, and the translational mistakes occur everywhere [21] [22] [23] .

With the recent semantic/syntactic/episodic model of three linguistic processes [1] , it is possible to derive three corresponding principles from them for guidance of software design of translation machines [2] .

From word comprehension as remote declarative memory associations in brain, it can be formulated the first principle for design of translation machines as followings (Table 1):

Principle 1: Corresponding to the word comprehension as memory associations, it is necessary to establish the dictionary for translation of words and phrases in translation machine.

From grammatical rule as procedural memory in brain, it can be formulated the second principle for design of translation machines as followings:

Principle 2: Corresponding to the grammatical rule as procedural memory, it is necessary to install the linguistic grammar for reading and forming sentence from words and phrases in translation machine, arranging such parts of speech as noun, verb and adjective into order.

From episodic coordination of language in brain, it can be formulated the third principle for design of translation machines as followings:

Principle 3: Corresponding to the episodic coordination of language, it is necessary to check with statistics of concurrence for the words and phrases of multiple meanings, and figure out one correct meaning of them in translation machine.

Table 1. Three principles of machine translation from semantic/syntactic/episodic neurolinguistics.

	Neurolinguistic processes in brain	Principles of machine translation
Principle 1	Semantics as memory associations	Make dictionary of words/phrases
Principle 2	Syntax as procedural memory	Install linguistic grammar
Principle 3	Episodic coordination of language	Statistically check word meanings

BEHAVIORAL CLASSIFICATION OF LIVING/NATURAL WORDS

In this article, it is mainly considered the episodic association of words for the semantic/syntactic/episodic linguistic processes to prospectively improve the statistical translation.

To determine the meaning of a word or phrase of multiple meanings in the sentence or clause, the episodic association of the word with other words in the sentence or clause can provide some important clues. For example, for the word "charge" as noun, it can be interpreted as 1) the duty, 2) the necessity of payment, 3) the amount of money necessary to pay, or 4) the electrical character and quantity, quite different in meanings. Its meaning varies in episodic association with other words in the sentence or clause. Statistical translation with episodic association is helpful to determine one correct meaning.

It is useful to find some common clues for identification of the word or phrase of multiple meanings in the sentence or clause. The word "he" and "she" can think or behavior as a living life, whereas the word "it" cannot in most situations except it means an animal. This is the further classification of pronouns in the present English. Besides, the present verbs have also been further classified into Vt, Vi and link Verb.

The author suggests that many words can similarly be further classified according to the characteristics of them to possibly behave as a living entity or a natural matter, just as the present pronouns "he", "she" and "it". With such further classification of words by behavior, it is helpful to determine the meaning of some words or phrases of multiple meanings in the sentence or clause.

With the above noun "charge" as example, its meanings as duty and the necessity of payment contain the zoological or organizational mind and behavior, while its meanings as the amount of payment and the electrical character or quantity do not contain the living meaning, but the natural character. Herein, it is demonstrated that this clue is useful to identify the meaning of noun "charge", even though not completely.

It is especially important to point out that all contents expressed in language can fall into a special category of sciences. At the individual level, all sentential contents can fall into either physical sciences or life sciences, while at the organizational level; all sentential contents can fall into either natural sciences or social sciences. In this regard, the physical and zoological category can contain all nouns at the individual level, while the categorical and organizational category can contain all nouns at the organizational level. For example, the noun "worker" is zoological, and the noun "team" is organizational, while the noun "hydrogen" is physical, and the noun "element" is categorical.

The nouns in the physical and zoological category adopt different verbs to manifest their behaviors respectively. The physical verbs can correspondingly be classified as characteristic, changing and consequential characters, while the zoological verbs can be classified as affective, behavioral and logic. Due to the logic nature of consequential character, herein it is classified the consequential character into logic too. For example, the noun "sun" is physical, the relevant verb "shine" is characteristic, the relevant verb "rotate" is changing, and the relevant verb "bring about" is logic. The noun "patient" is zoological, the relevant verb "fear" is affective, the relevant verb "cry" is behavioral, and the relevant verb "result from" is logic.

Because some nouns, such as "application", are derived from verbs, it is also appropriate to further classify the nouns using the verb classification above as affective/behavioral/logic/characteristic/changing. Therefore, all nouns can be classified into both zoological/organizational/physical/categorical and affective/ behavioral/logic/characteristic/changing characters. Likewise, the verbs can also resemble the nouns to be categorized into the zoological/organizational/physi- cal/categorical characters, with the affective/behavioral/logic verbs belonging to zoological/organizational, and the characteristic/changing/logic verbs belonging to physical/categorical.

Now that it is adopted the behavioral classification of the living/natural nouns and verbs into both the zoological/organizational/physical/categorical and affective/behavioral/logic/characteristic/changing characteristics, it is also possible to classify the adjectives and adverbs on their behaviors. With the adverb "along" as example, it can be interpreted as 1) altogether, 2) following others, 3) forward, 4) future, which can be classified into the 1) characteristic, 2) behavioral, 3) spatial, 4) temporal characteristics respectively.

Besides, such words as "horrible", "exciting" represent the affective psychology, such words as "aggressive", "diligent" represent the behavioral psychology, and such words as "consequent", "thus" represent the logic of the sentential meaning, which should be discerned apart. In these regards, the adjectives and adverbs can also be classified into the affective/behavioral/logic/characteristic/changing/spatial/temporal characters. Correspondingly, the characteristic/changing/logic/spatial/temporal characters are physical or natural, while the affective/behavioral/logic characters are zoological or social.

It is noted that the name of a person or pet is zoological in psychology, but is physical in body. Thus, the name of a person or pet can be either zoological or physical, while its meaning should be determined in association with the verb, adjective and adverb in the sentence as zoological or physical.

Herein, as shown in Table 2, it is classified the living/natural nouns and verbs into both the zoological/organizational/physical/categorical and affective/behavioral/logic/ characteristic/changing characteristics, the adjectives and adverbs into the affective/behavioral/logic/characteristic/changing/spatial/tem- poral characteristics. The advantages of the classifications are: (1) They result from the universal nature of words falling into either natural sciences or social sciences. (2) The behavioral classifications of words are applicable to all nouns, verbs, adjectives and adverbs, with the characteristic/changing/logic words associating with physical/ categorical, and the affective/behavioral/logic words associating with zoological/ organizational.

Table 2. Behavioral classification of the living/natural words.

	Physical/categorical words	Zoological/organizational words

Noun	Characteristic/changing/logic	Affective/behavioral/logic
Verb	Characteristic/changing/logic	Affective/behavioral/logic
Adjective	Spatial/temporal/characteristic/ changing/logic	Affective/behavioral/logic
Adverb	Spatial/temporal/characteristic/ changing/logic	Affective/behavioral/logic

SENTENTIAL/PARAGRAPHIC CATEGORIZATION

The words within one sentence mostly adapt to the meanings fitting the category of subject of the sentence, such as the physics, biology, art, economy, and so on, in the natural sciences or social sciences. Categorization of the sentential subject can certainly be adopted to help statistical translation. After the natural/social subject of the sentence is categorized as the physics, biology, art, economy, and so on, some words of multiple meanings can be determined to one correct meaning fitting the category of this subject falling in either the natural science or social science, therefore helpful to the statistical translation.

Still with the above noun "charge" as example, if the subject of sentence is categorized by other words as physics, chemistry, computer, and so on, then the meaning of "charge" is most likely to be the electrical character or quantity. Herein again, with this linguistic example it is demonstrated that the sentential categorization is useful to determine the meaning of "charge".

As mentioned above, complex story narration certainly belongs to the episodic linguistic process and requires more complex episodic coordination. Originally, I adopted the thematic subject of the whole essay or article to help determine the word meanings fitting the subject. However, the Chinese people in television, especially the old people's representatives in Beijing in television on January 11, 2017, strongly argued that they often deviated the main topic while making speech, so that the thematic subject should be improved to the paragraphic subject for the same purpose.

The paragraphic subjects are usually more complex than the sentential subject. Besides the natural/social subjects such as the physics, biology, art, economy, and so on, it is possible to extend the subject to the story of life, personal experience, environmental depiction, and so on successional situations.

COLLECTION OF FREQUENT WORD-PAIRS

In some situations, the episodic association of words or clauses in the sentence is very intricate. For instance, the prepositions like by, with, through and via can associate in meaning with either noun or verb in the sentence. It is necessary to refer to the frequent word-pairs to determine the episodic associations.

For example it is herein to compare two sentences as: 1) They agreed the war by declaration. 2) They agreed the war with consensus. Using the word-pair "war declaration", it is determined "by declaration" in sentence 1) to modify the noun "war", while using the word pair "consensus agree", it is determined "with consensus" in sentence 2) to modify the verb "agreed". Obviously, this example demonstrates that the collection of frequent word-pairs is necessary to the statistical translation of the episodic association of some prepositions.

For another instance, the terminal "which" clause may modify the last noun, and may also manifest the consequence of the former sentence. It is also necessary to use the frequent word-pairs to determine the episodic associations.

For example it is herein also to compare two sentences as: 1) Tomorrow I am going to the park, which is beautiful. 2) Tomorrow I am going to the park, which is expected. Using the word-pair "beautiful park", it is determined the "which" clause in sentence 1) to modify the noun "park", while using the word pair "I expected", it is determined the "which" clause in sentence 2) to modify the former sentence "Tomorrow I am going to the park". Obviously, this example demonstrates that the collection of frequent word-pairs is also necessary to the statistical translation of episodic associations of terminal "which" clauses.

WORD EPISODIC SYMBOLIZATION FOR COMPUTER APPLICATIONS

Each meaning of a word or phrase belongs the semantic meanings of the word. For the words and phrases of multiple meanings, there are several semantic meanings of the words/phrases, with each of them belonging to their own behavioral classification and subject category as well as possessing their own word- pairs with others, manifesting three different types of episodic associations.

It is necessary to consider how to implement the application of them to computer. These episodic associations may be easily processed in computer as various databanks for SQL or Oracle. For the behavioral classification and subject category of words, the databank of semantic translation can be designed to contain and promote various relevant episodic associations, as illustrated in the following paragraph. For the collection of frequent word-pairs, they can be collected and stored directly in the specific databank of frequent word-pairs, separate from the data bank for behavioral classification and subject category.

The databank for storing and processing the behavioral classification and subject category of words deserves special demonstration. For a word or phrase of multiple meanings, herein it is recommended to use the symbol ⊥ to separate the multiple meanings. For example, the noun "charge" has several meanings as "duty ⊥ money-payment ⊥ payment-amount ⊥ electrical-quantity". With this symbol, a word of multiple meanings can be processed as if one data including all meanings in the databank.

Herein it is recommended to use another symbol <> to characterize the behavioral classification and subject category of each meaning of the word or phrase of multiple meanings. For example, the noun "charge" can be better stored as one complex data in databank as "duty ⊥ money-payment ⊥ payment-amount ⊥ electrical- quantity ". This is herein called as the word episodic symbolization.

With word episodic symbolization, all words and phrases of multiple meanings in a sentence or clause can be stored in analogy to the form of the noun "charge". In translation, all words and phrases of multiple meanings in the sentence or clause are directly transformed into the complex stored form from the databank. Then, according to the contents in the <>, the computer makes additional processing of the sentence or clause. If the sentence is about physics, then the electrical-quantity matches the meaning of "charge". If the sentence is about the job, then the duty matches the meaning of "charge". In this way, it is prospective for the word episodic symbolization to help discern one correct meaning for the word and phrase of multiple meanings in sentence.

Word episodic symbolization can store the various episodic associations of a word with the characteristic episodic symbols affiliated with the word, make the computer easy to process the various episodic meanings in the sentence, which would bring about significant progression to the automatic comprehension and translation of language.

DISCUSSIONS

Based on the semantic/syntactic/episodic linguistic model, it has been derived the three corresponding principles for machine translation, respectively as first to establish the dictionary of words/phrases, second to translate the grammar, and third to determine the meaning of some words/phrases of multiple meanings by statistical associations with others [2] . In this article, it is further demonstrated three types of episodic associations for this neural model of language, prospectively to improve the statistical machine translation, concretely as the behavioral classification of the living/natural words, the categorization of sentence/paragraph and the collection of frequent word-pairs.

It is noted that the word episodic symbolization herein can store the various episodic associations of a word with the characteristic episodic symbols affiliated with the word, which would be a breakthrough for the computer to process the various episodic meanings in the sentence.

In this regard, due to the prospective improvement of statistical translation by these methods, the third principle of machine translation should correspondingly be improved by using these three methods, as the followings: third to determine the meaning of some words/phrases of multiple meanings by episodic associations with others using the behavioral classification of the living/natural words, the categorization of sentence/paragraph and the collection of frequent word-pairs.

It is necessary to point out that there are still some other methods able to improve the statistical translation, such as using the visual, auditory inputs and associations, and so on. This article only deals with the improvement of statistical translation prospectively brought about from the three new type of episodic associations demonstrated here, while does not consider those from others.

CONCLUSION

In this article, it is newly demonstrated three types of episodic associations for the semantic/syntactic/episodic neural model of language, prospectively to help and improve the statistical translation. It is adopted the behavioral characteristics both as zoological/organizational/physical/categorical and affective/beha- vioral/logic/characteristic/changing to further classify the living/natural nouns and verbs, the affective/behavioral/logic/characteristic/changing/spatial/tem- poral characteristics to the living/natural adjectives and adverbs, so as to help discern the meaning of words/phrases of multiple meanings with these episodic associations within the sentence or clause. For the same purpose, it is also classified the sentence and paragraph into the category of natural/social subjects such as physics, biology, art, economy, and so on, so as to help discern the meaning of words/phrases of multiple meanings with episodic associations. It is further required to collect the frequent word-pairs during statistical translation, so as to help determine the episodic associations of some prepositions or some terminal "which" clauses. Finally, it is suggested to use word episodic symbolization to apply them to computer. In these respects, it is herein improved the third principle of machine translation as third to determine the meaning of some words/phrases of multiple meanings by episodic associations with others using the behavioral classification of the living/natural words, the categorization of sentence/paragraph and the collection of frequent word-pairs.

HIGHLIGHTS

- Behavioral classifying the living/natural words helps the statistical translation.
- Sentential/paragraphic categorization is useful to statistical translation.
- Collection of frequent word-pairs is necessary to statistical translation.
- Word episodic symbolization is useful to make databank in computer.
- These methods can help the statistical translation significantly.

CONFLICT OF INTEREST

The author declares no conflict of interest or financial support for this work.

ACKNOWLEDGMENTS

It is herein acknowledged that MingxunCai paid the Open Access publication fee of this paper.

REFERENCES

1. Cai, Z.J. (2015) Semantic Memory Association, Procedural Grammar Syntax and Episodic Modality Coordination as Three Interactive Neural Processes Organizing Language: A Model. Open Access Library Journal, 2, Article ID: e1718. http://dx.doi.org/10.4236/oalib.1101718
2. Cai, Z.J. (2016) Principles Derived from Neurolinguistics of Brain for Design of Translation Machines. Open Access Library Journal, 3, e2704. http://dx.doi.org/10.4236/oalib.1102704
3. Pinker, S. (1991) Rules of Language. Science, 253, 530-535. https://doi.org/10.1126/science.1857983
4. Ullman, M.T., Corkin, S., Coppola, M., Hickok, G., Growdon, J.H., Koroshetz, W.J. and Pinker, S. (1997) A Neural Dissociation within Language: Evidence that the Mental Dictionary Is Part of Declarative Memory, and that Grammatical Rules Are Processed by the Procedural System. Journal of Cognitive Neuroscience, 9, 266-276. https://doi.org/10.1162/jocn.1997.9.2.266
5. Ullman, M.T. (2004) Contributions of Memory Circuits to Language: The Declara- tive/Procedural Model. Cognition, 92, 231-270. https://doi.org/10.1016/j.cognition.2003.10.008
6. Maguire, G.A., Yu, B.P., Franklin, D.L. and Riley, G.D. (2004) Alleviating Stuttering with Pharmacological Interventions. Expert Opinion on Pharmacotherapy, 5, 1565- 1571. https://doi.org/10.1517/14656566.5.7.1565
7. Stager, S.V., Calis, K., Grothe, D., Bloch, M., Berensen, N.M., Smith, P.J. and Braun, A. (2005) Treatment with Medications Affecting Dopaminergic and Serotonergic Mechanisms: Effects on Fluency and Anxiety in Persons Who Stutter. Journal of Fluency Disorders, 30, 319-335. https://doi.org/10.1016/j.jfludis.2005.09.004
8. Lan, J., Song, M., Pan, C., Zhuang, G., Wang, Y., Ma, W., Chu, Q., Lai, Q., Xu, F., Li, Y., Liu, L. and Wang, W. (2009) Association between Dopaminergic Genes (SLC6A 3 and DRD2) and Stuttering among Han Chinese. Journal of Human Genetics, 54, 457-460. https://doi.org/10.1038/jhg.2009.60
9. Small, S.L. and Llano, D.A. (2009) Biological Approaches to Aphasia Treatment. Current Neurology and Neuroscience Reports, 9, 443-450. https://doi.org/10.1007/s11910-009-0066-x
10. Berthier, M.L., Pulvermüller, F., Dávila, G., Casares, N.G. and

Gutiérrez, A. (2011) Drug Therapy of Post-Stroke Aphasia: A Review of Current Evidence. Neuropsy- chology Review, 21, 302-317. https://doi.org/10.1007/s11065-011-9177-7

11. Cape, E.G., Manns, I.D., Alonso, A., Beaudet, A. and Jones, B.E. (2000) Neuroten- sin-Induced Bursting of Cholinergic Basal Forebrain Neurons Promotes Gamma and Theta Cortical Activity Together with Waking and Paradoxical Sleep. The Jour- nal of Neuroscience, 20, 8452-8461.
12. Mena-Segovia, J., Sims, H.M., Magill, P.J. and Bolam, J.P. (2008) Cholinergic Brain- stem Neurons Modulate Cortical Gamma Activity during Slow Oscillations. The Journal of Physiology, 586, 2947-2960. https://doi.org/10.1113/jphysiol.2008.153874
13. Wang, L., Zhu, Z. and Bastiaansen, M. (2012) Integration or Predictability? A Fur- ther Specification of the Functional Role of Gamma Oscillations in Language Com- prehension. Frontiers in Psychology, 3, 187. https://doi.org/10.3389/fpsyg.2012.00187
14. Vidal, J.R., Freyermuth, S., Jerbi, K., Hamamé, C.M., Ossandon, T., Bertrand, O., Minotti, L., Kahane, P., Berthoz, A. and Lachaux, J.P. (2012) Long-Distance Ampli- tude Correlations in the High γ Band Reveal Segregation and Integration within the Reading Network. The Journal of Neuroscience, 32, 6421-6434. https://doi.org/10.1523/JNEUROSCI.4363-11.2012
15. Weiss, S. and Müller, H.M. (2013) The Non-Stop Road from Concrete to Abstract: High Concreteness Causes the Activation of Long-Range Networks. Frontier in Hu- man Neuroscience, 7, 526. https://doi.org/10.3389/fnhum.2013.00526
16. Miniscalco, C., Hagberg, B., Kadesjö, B., Westerlund, M. and Gillberg, C. (2007) Narrative Skills, Cognitive Profiles and Neuropsychiatric Disorders in 7-8-Year-Old Children with Late Developing Language. International Journal of Language and Communication Disorders, 42, 665-681. https://doi.org/10.1080/13682820601084428
17. Ash, S., Menaged, A., Olm, C., McMillan, C.T., Boller, A., Irwin, D.J., McCluskey, L., Elman, L. and Grossman, M. (2014) Narrative Discourse Deficits in Amyotroph- ic Lateral Sclerosis. Neurology, 83, 520-528. https://doi.org/10.1212/WNL.0000000000000670
18. Youse, K.M. and Coelho, C.A. (2009) Treating Underlying Attention Deficits as a Means for Improving Conversational Discourse in Individuals with Closed Head Injury: A Preliminary Study.

Neurorehabilitation, 24, 355-364.

19. DiLollo, A., Neimeyer, R.A. and Manning, W.H. (2002) A Personal Construct Psy- chology View of Relapse: Indications for a Narrative Therapy Component to Stut- tering Treatment. Journal of Fluency Disorders, 27, 19-40. https://doi.org/10.1016/S0094-730X(01)00109-7
20. Leahy, M.M., O'Dwyer, M. and Ryan, F. (2012) Witnessing Stories: Definitional Ce- remonies in Narrative Therapy with Adults Who Stutter. Journal of Fluency Dis- orders, 37, 234-241. https://doi.org/10.1016/j.jfludis.2012.03.001
21. Zhang, M., Duan, X.Y. and Chen, W.L. (2014) Bayesian Constituent Context Model for Grammar Induction. IEEE/ACM Transactions on Audio, Speech, and Language Processing, 22, 531-541. https://doi.org/10.1109/TASLP.2013.2294584
22. Xiong, D.Y., Zhang, M. and Li, H.Z. (2011) A Maximum-Entropy Segmentation Model for Statistical Machine Translation. IEEE Transactions on Audio, Speech, and Language Processing, 19, 2494-2505. https://doi.org/10.1109/TASL.2011.2144971
23. Xiong, D.Y., Zhang, M. and Wang, X. (2015) Topic-Based Coherence Modeling for Statistical Machine Translation. IEEE/ACM Transactions on Audio, Speech, and Language Processing, 23, 483-493. https://doi.org/10.1109/TASLP.2015.2395254

SECTION 3 MATHEMATICAL ALGORITHMS AND NATURAL LANGUAGE

CHAPTER

9

Language and Mathematics: Bridging between Natural Language and Mathematical Language in Solving Problems in Mathematics

Bat-Sheva Ilany[1], Bruria Margolin[2]

[1]Beit-Berl College, Israel;

[2]Levinsky College of Education, Israel

ABSTRACT

In the solution of mathematical word problems, problems that are accompanied by text, there is a need to bridge between mathematical language that requires an awareness of the mathematical components, and natural language that requires a literacy approach to the whole text. In this paper we present examples of

Citation: Ilany, B. & Margolin, B. (2010). "Language and Mathematics: Bridging between Natural Language and Mathematical Language in Solving Problems in Mathematics". Creative Education, 1, 138-148. doi: 10.4236/ce.2010.13022.

mathematical word problems whose solutions depend on a transition between a linguistic situation on one side and abstract mathematical structure on the other. These examples demonstrate the need of treating word problems in a literacy approach. For this purpose, a model for teaching and learning is suggested. The model, which was tested successfully, presents an interactive multi-level process that enables deciphering of the mathematical text by means of decoding symbols and graphs. This leads to understanding of the revealed content and the linguistic situation, transfer to a mathematical model, and correspondence between the linguistic situation and the appropriate mathematical model. This model was tested as a case study. The participants were 3 students: a student in the sixth grade, a student in the ninth grade and a college student. All the students demonstrated an impressive improvement in their mathematical comprehension using this model.

Keywords: Mathematical Language, Word Problems

NATURAL LANGUAGE AND MATHEMATICAL LANGUAGE

In the solution of word problems, that is to say in the solution of mathematical problems that are accompanied by text, the student is faced with two languages mixed together (Kane, 1970): natural language and mathematical language. One of the limitations of natural language is the fact that it works in a diachronic manner; the meanings it represents are interpreted according to a time frame. The perception of the world, and in fact the meaning of the world, depends on field synchronicity, the reciprocal relations with the environment. Furthermore, the field as a whole gives meaning to its parts, and each part of the field contributes meaning to the whole. In other words, to read a word problem in mathematics and to give it meaning, it is necessary to perceive the problem as a textual unit and not as a collection of data. A textual unit is a linguistic unit larger than a sentence. It's semantic structure "consists of those elements and relations that are directly derived from the text itself [...] without adding anything that is not explicitly specified in the text" (Kintsch, 1998, p. 103). The linguistic unit is coherent from a content and linguistic point of view (Brown & Yule, 1983; Halliday & Hassan, 1976; Van Dijk, 1980; Widdowson, 1979), and is used for communication (Sarel, 1991, Margolin, 2002). Identification of the constituent parts of a text depends on meta-awareness of the function of the form, the function of the word, and the function of the sentence in a text, especially awareness of symbols and syntactic awareness (Herriman, 1991 in MacGregor, & Price, 1999).

Indeed, exercises like addition and subtraction or multiplication and division are important for the understanding of the mathematical language, but the perception of the textual structure is a process by which you can identify textual components and carry out different logical operations. Mathematical language is a language of symbols, concepts, definitions, and theorems. Mathematical language needs to be learned and does not develop naturally like a child's natural language. In mathematical language the child learns to recognize, for example, numbers as objects, one to one of their similar and different properties. The child perceives the numbers as signs by means of which it is possible to calculate calculations and to do various manipulations. Syntax, generally, deals with configuration rules according to which sentences and words are constructed. The syntax of mathematical language includes lists of symbols, configuration rules for constructing language patterns, axioms, a deductive system, and theorems.

Mathematical terms and symbols must be defined unambiguously. Likewise, every assertion in mathematical language is also unambiguous—every mathematical pattern has one deep structure that is determined by operational rules. We will not expand on definitions and theorems in mathematics, but each definition of a mathematical concept is the result of a complex process. Each definition contains additional concepts that also need to be defined. All mathematical theorems in all branches of mathematics are characterized by the fact that they are derived logically, deductively, and consistently from a system of elementary theorems – axioms. Our central argument is that there is a bridge between mathematical language that necessitates seeing the mathematiccal components, and natural language that demands textual literacy for the text as a whole. In other words, there is a bridge between the mathematical components and the literal components. When knowledge gaps in the mathematical language are large, natural language must supply what is missing, and be clear and explicit. However, when knowledge gaps in the mathematical language are small, natural language does not need to supply what is missing.

DIFFERENCES BETWEEN NATURAL LANGUAGE AND MATHEMATICAL LANGUAGE

The fundamental differences between natural language and mathematical language derive first and foremost from the fact that mathematical language is more precise and less flexible than the structure of natural language. In natural language there are differences between surface structure and deep structure of the utterance, there are ambiguous statements that derive from ambiguous words, and there is a wealth of language. This wealth of language derives from the diversity of nouns, and from the diversity of words expressing relation - all the verbs and adjectives. On the other hand, in mathematical language for each surface structure there is one deep structure, all statements are unambiguous, and there is a paucity of language that expresses itself in the fact that there is only one type of noun – numbers, functions, etc., and that there are two relational signs – equality and inequality (Bloedy-Vinner, 1998). Different concepts are interpreted in the different languages – natural language and mathematical language – in different ways. The structure of mathematical language is more precise and less flexible than the structure of natural language, thus great tension is created in the use of natural language in mathematical problems. Let us take for example the concept diagonal. Diagonal in mathematical language is a straight-line segment that joins two non-adjacent vertices in a polygon. The diagonal can also pass through points outside the polygon, and can be at different angles. On the other hand, in natural language no mathematical rules apply to the diagonal and as evidence we can give as an example the following advert. According to the advert, it is forbidden to cross the road on a diagonal that is at an angle different from 90 degrees between the crossing and the sidewalk. The diagonal in the advert is not a mathematical diagonal, since it does not join two vertices of a polygon. Like the diagonal, the straight line is also different in mathematical language than in natural language. Whereas in natural language a straight line is a segment with a beginning and an end, in mathematical language it is a fundamental undefined concept, with no beginning and no end.

TRANSLATING FROM NATURAL LANGUAGE TO MATHEMATICAL LANGUAGE IN MATHEMATICAL WORD PROBLEMS

A mathematical problem is a situation in which an individual or a group of people are asked to perform a task for which there is no immediately available algorithm that completely defines a solution method. Solving mathematical problems requires the implementation of a sequence of operations by means of which some final target is attained (Lester, 1978). A word problem in mathematics is an independent unit of text that comprises a question sentence and a speech event (Nesher, 1988; Nesher & Katriel, 1977). Sometimes the unit of text describes an event from daily life. The aim of the description is to give expression to the logical structure that dictates a particular arithmetic operation. The difficulty with the solution of mathematical word problems is the need to translate the event described in natural language to arithmetic operations expressed in mathematical language. The transition from natural language includes syntactic, semantic, and pragmatic understanding of the discourse.

Word problems in mathematics are divided into two types according to the topics they relate to. One type is mathematical word problems that deal with mathematical relationships between objective sizes, like: What is the number that is twice as big as the sum of 25 and 17? The other type is mathematical word problems that deal with real life situations, like: It takes 3 workers 5 hours to plough a field. How many hours would it take 2 workers to plough the same field?

In this paper we will relate to every mathematical problem accompanied by text as a word problem in mathematics. There is a tendency in the professional literature to relate to a word problem as a textual unit that describes an everyday event, and the majority of papers and researches relate to problems not accompanied by an authentic background story as mathematical problems and not as word problems. Thus, this problem: "Find the equation of the straight line that is parallel to the straight line $3x - 7y = 4$ and passes through the point (0, 10)" is not considered to be a word problem, rather a mathematical problem, since it is not accompanied by an authentic background story. An example for this could be Polya's treatment in his book How to Solve It (1945) of mathematical problems accompanied by text as problems, although at the same time he suggested that for the problem to be understood it is first of all necessary for the verbal version to be understood. In our opinion, those problems must be defined as word problems since such problems include text that the solver needs to understand.

We attempted to implement the teaching and learning model proposed in this paper with two kinds of mathematical problems: one, accompanied by an authentic background story that is considered to be a word problem in the professional literature; and another, not accompanied by an authentic background story, that is not considered to be a word problem in the professional literature. We argue that a mathematical problem with the following properties is a word problem even when it is not accompanied by an authentic background story: it constitutes a coherent textual unit in terms of content and language; it has clear boundaries; it is used for communication; it contains two different languages mixed together: natural language and mathematical language (see the case of Shiri later). Following are examples of mathematical word problems, in which the solution of the problem depends on converting a linguistic situation into a mathematical model. These examples differ from each other in many varied aspects.

The Soldiers and the Bus Problem

Translation from natural language to mathematical language in mathematical word problems is problematic also because of the difference between solving an authentic realistic problem and solving a word problem in mathematics. An example of this is "The soldiers and the bus problem": An army bus can transport 36 soldiers. 1128 soldiers need to be bused to training camp. How many buses are needed?

The appropriate calculation is: 1128:36 = 31(12). The answer to the problem is 32 buses. 12 soldiers will go in the 32nd bus (or less than 36 soldiers will travel in some of the buses bus). In a research that was conducted among 13-year-old students only 23% answered this correctly, 19% answered 31 buses, and 29% gave as the answer 31 buses remainder 12 (Silver, Shapiro, & Deutsch, 1993). Contrary to the previous problem, where there was an attempt to connect the answer to the real situation, in this problem there is no such attempt. Apparently this is because of the fact that the arithmetical solution is easily arrived at, and thus there is no need to connect the problem to the real situation.1

The Sheep and the Dogs Problem

Students make the transition from natural language to mathematical language automatically even in problems that do not have a mathematical solution, because the norm in school is that if a problem is given, then it must have a solution. For example: Five dogs guard 125 sheep. How old is the shepherd? (Baruk, 1989) Students try to find a calculation, and they try to solve the problem through trial and error. They try to check different possible solutions by using the given numbers and ignoring the situation. They try solutions according to arithmetic operations, from the easy to the difficult, as follows:

1. By adding: 5 + 125 = 130
2. When the number seems to them to be too big to be a person's age, the students try to solve the problem by subtracting: 125 – 5 = 120

3. When this number is also seems to be too big, they try to solve the problem by dividing: 125: 5 = 25. This solution seems to them to be reasonable.

The Students and the Professor Problem

An example of a mathematical problem and of the difficulty of translating from natural language is The Students and the Professor Problem (Kaput & Clement, 1979). This problem, which exposed the reversal in translation mistake, has been investigated in various researches (e.g., Clement, 1982; Rosnick, 1981), and has been explained in different ways (BloedyVinner, 1998). Write an algebraic expression using the variables S and P that will represent the following assertion: "In this university the number of students is 6 times greater than the number of professors". Use S for the number of students, and P for the number of professors. When this problem was given to 150 first year engineering students and 47 social science students, 37% of the engineering students and 57% of the social science students got it wrong. Two thirds of the wrong answers contained reversed equations of the type 6S = P instead of 6P = S. The mistake derived from the fact that in natural language the order of the words determines the meaning. The quantifier 6 appears beside the noun (students) and equality in the mathematical equation is not con sidered. According to natural language, the students were represented by S, the arithmetic operation was represented by multiplication, and finally the professors were represented by P, and thus 6S = P.

The problem of the students and the professor was given to eight fourth-year students specializing in mathematics for elementary school at a teachers' training college in Israel. Apart from one student who solved it correctly, all the other students erred, writing 6S = P instead of 6P = S. Here also, as in the above-mentioned cases, the mistake arose from the fact that in natural language the order of the words determines the meaning. The quantifier 6 appears beside the noun (students) and equality in the mathematical equation is not considered.

The Reduced Number Problem

Another example of a mathematical problem for which there is a need for transition from natural language to mathematical language is "The number that was reduced": Write an equation, using the variable X, which represents the following assertion: "In this college a quarter of the number of students, which was reduced by 5, are mathematics students". When this problem was given to students of mathematics education in a teachers' training college, the following expressions were given:

$$1.\ \frac{X-5}{4}$$

$$2.\ \frac{X}{4}-5$$

The two above expressions are correct. The difference between them derives from the fact that the surface structure expressed in the assertion represents two deep structures. For each deep structure there is a different mathematical expression. In the first expression, the quarter was of the number of students in the college reduced by 5. Whereas in the second expression, the quarter was of all the students in the college, and only then was the number reduced by 5. Both answers are correct.

The Combinations Problem

Another example of a word problem for which misunderstanding the literal meaning caused a misunderstanding of the mathematical problem is Combinations (Woolf, 2005). The problem was presented during a fourth grade mathematics lesson: In a parking lot there are 66 wheels, some of them belonging to cars, and some of them belonging to tricycles. What combinations of cars and tricycles can you find that have 66 wheels altogether? How could you know whether you have found all possible combinations?

The combinations problem documented in Woolf's paper describes students' inability to cope with the problem due to the fact that they did not understand the word combinations. Solution of the mathematical problem described above focused on understanding the word combinations and understanding the logical structure of the whole text.

To understand the problem, students are required more than command of the language. They need to learn to construct a meaningful body of knowledge from the information in the question, including data and a solution scheme.

In other words: they need to make a connection between natural language and mathematical language.

TOWARDS BRIDGING BETWEEN NATURAL LANGUAGE AND MATHEMATICAL LANGUAGE

As we saw above, the knowledge gaps between mathematical language and natural language emerge especially in the solution of word problems. Problem solving is an all-encompassing concept that includes many cognitive processes like, among others, literal and syntactic processing, changes of representation, and algorithmic processing. Representation is an important area for problem solving and little is known about the relationship between inner comprehension and its external representation. To bridge between natural language and mathematical language it is necessary to educate towards mathematical-linguistic literacy2 , at the level of the addressor (speaker or writer) and at the level of the addressee (listener or reader). From the point of view of the addressor, he/she must ensure that the references in the text are related to suitable referents, that the expressions are not ambiguous, and that all the problematic terms are made clear. In other words, the addressor must display consideration for the recipient by supplying easily accessible and acceptable information. The addressor must take into account that the meaning of the text is a product of the interactions between the addressor's schema and deductions, and the addressee's schema and conclusions. Thus the addressor must first determine precise assumptions about the addressee's knowledge and deductive ability, to produce text as explicit as possible by means of linguistic implementation of his/her ideas.

The addressor must predict detractors and obstacles that are liable to disturb understanding, and take steps to prevent them (Folman, 2000). As for the addressee, to extract the full meaning from the text he must fill in the missing information that is not found in the text. In other words, he/she must identify the information in the text in three circles of connection. The adjacent and literary connection (co-text) is the connection formed inside adjacent linguistic units. The circumstantial pragmatic connection (context) includes different components like the identity of the addressor and the addressee, the time and place of the discourse, the addressor's intentions, and the communication medium (Nir, 1989). The connection with the universe of discourse that is in fact the connection formed between the text and the world (Sarel, 1991), is based on our previous knowledge of the particular subject area. The knowledge gaps in problem solving are between the textual unit and the hidden mathematical structure. The linguistic units in the text not only function as signs that have their signified object or idea in the world external to linguistics but also are connected to other fundamentals in the text, so that their meanings arise from the way the linguistic components are organized in the text. Moreover, not all the information is given explicitly in the text. There is information that can be derived by mathematical means on the basis of the explicit information. To bridge the gaps between natural language and mathematical language it is necessary to develop an awareness of these gaps by means of meaningful interactions between the student and his/her environment in the context of authentic activities. These authentic activities are activities that represent situations that describe a reality that is connected to the world of students and teachers in school and in the community (BenChaim, Keret, & Ilany, 2006).

A language develops by means of meaningful interactions between the individual and his/her environment in the context of authentic activities (Gee, 1996). The context of authentic activities enables education towards linguistic-mathematical literacy, because the interprettation of the discourse is based to a great extent on analogy to our past experience, meaning that it is based on our socio-cultural knowledge (Brown & Yule, 1983). According to Greer (1997), the concepts addition, subtraction, multiplication, and division forcefully create models for situations, and students have to differentiate between the model and the situation and to assess whether the model is appropriate to the situation. The process of creating meaning for the context is multi-layered and is carried out at every layer of the text: at the syntactical, the semantic, and the pragmatic layers, at different levels of focusing. The interaction between the reader's schemas and the schemas of the text necessitates communicative-cognitive effort. The communicative effort is expressed by the identification of the situation described, and the cognitive effort is expressed by the composition of the problem from new while combining within it the mathematical model. Bridging between natural language and mathematical language necessitates connecting the two faces of the word problem: the linguistic situation on one side and the abstract structures on the other (Greer, 1997).

According to the professional literature, the bridging can be carried out in two different ways: by translation of the linguistic situation into abstract structures (Polya cited in Reusser & Stebler, 1997), and by organization of the unit of mathematical content (Freudental, 1991). In this paper we suggest making an interaction between the two methods in a processive approach by a model for the Instruction and Learning of the Solution of Mathematical Word Problems. Many researches that deal with varied subjects in the learning of mathematics like, for example, real mathematics

(De Lange, 1987), dilemmas in mathematics instruction based on different representations of concepts (Ball, 1993), solution of verbal questions (Nathan, Kintch, & Young, 1992), and learning concepts like the concept of function (Kaput, 1993), maintain that development of modeling skills is one of the important aims of a mathematics curriculum, and serves as a central pedagogical tool.

INSTRUCTION MODEL FOR THE SOLUTION OF MATHEMATICAL WORD PROBLEMS

To bridge the gaps between natural language and mathematical language in solving word problems in Mathematics the researchers of this study developed an instruction model for the solution of mathematical word problems. The two researchers are teachers in two colleges in Israel.

One of them is a teacher of Mathematics and the other is a teacher in Linguistics. The teacher of Mathematics has encountered many difficulties of students in solving word problems. She realized that the difficulties emerged from understanding the text literally and mathematically. She decided to build a tool with a teacher in Linguistics to bridge the gaps between Mathematics and Linguistics. The two researchers began interviewing children asking what where the difficulties in solving word problems. A nine - stages instruction model was built after the interviews. In several cases, a third party, a colleague who teaches Mathematics was involved, and took part in the deliberation process until agreement was reached. After the model was built it was validated by six experts in Mathematics and Mathematics education. The nine–stage model was validated by 34 student-teachers specializing in mathematics teaching at a teachers' seminary in a college in Israel. Only then it was used on three students: a student from elementary school, a student from Junior high school and a college student. The data were taken from word problems in Mathematics, in which these students were asked to answer in two stages: first they were asked to answer them without any instruction and then they were asked to answer them with this instructional model. Following is our nine-stage instruction model for the solution of mathematical word problems (schemas appear in the diagram that follows):

Reading the Problem

The first stage involves reading the problem from the bottom up, as a way of collecting the details. The action of reading at this stage is an exposure to the meaning, where the location of the meaning is in the text. The process of reading is an accumulative process from the smallest units (the words) to the largest units (the whole text).

Understanding the Linguistic Situation

The next stage involves reading the problem for a second time. The action of reading at this stage will be called in this paper the warming up stage: a multi- directional search as a way of brainstorming. At this stage the reader will ask himself the following questions:

1. Are all the words clear?
2. Are all the sentences clear?
3. What are the keywords?
4. Do I understand the keywords?
5. What is the question?
6. Do I understand the question?
7. How can I describe the problem in my own words?

Understanding the Mathematical Situation

We define the mathematical situation as the mathematical context of the problem, which relates to two types of information: the data and the question. The data relate to all the expressions that we assume to exist in the problem. They can appear in explicit form or in implicit form. The explicit data are those that are mentioned in the text, and the implicit data are axioms, theorems, and implicit facts that can be used in the solution of the problem. The question points in the direction of the expression we want to find. To understand the mathematical situation there is a need to examine the data and the question and to have a good grasp of the subject at hand. It is possible to be assisted, when necessary, by taking apart, demonstration, exercise, and illustration. In the first stage it is possible to break up the given problem into explicit data, implicit data, and a question, and in the second stage it is possible to demonstrate the problem with specific instances and to interpret the problem by means of a picture, a table, a diagram, or a graph, that can help to simplify the problem. A problem solver needs to identify the known facts and the logical-mathematical conditions of the problem—the connections and relationships between the mathematical data and the logical analysis of the problem. In other words, the connections between the classical elements—nouns connected to numerical quantifiers in different sentences of the text and time-space relationships between objects or events that appear in the text—and the semantic relationship between the classical elements that are the verbs that appear in different sentences of the text (Nesher & Katriel, 1977; Hershkovitz & Nesher, 1996).

At this stage the reader will ask himself the following questions:

1. What is my relationship with the mathematical subject of the problem?
2. Is there a difficulty in the problem?
3. Are all the data clear?
4. Are there implicit data in the problem? (For example: in a problem that describes a working week, is the intention 7, 6, or 5 working days, as is usual nowadays?)
5. Are there superfluous data? (For example: in a problem accompanied there superfluous by a background story, are there superfluous data about the heroes?)
6. Do I understand the connection between the data in the question?
7. Is it possible to demonstrate the problem in particular instances?

Matching the Mathematical Situation to the Linguistic Situation

This stage involves reading the problem once more, from the top down. The action In the course of acquiring schemas the learner meets new cases and acts on them according to his/her previous schemas connected to the same matter. The learner expects a particular outcome. If the result marches his/her expectations, then an expansion of his/her existing schema takes place. If not, then there occurs a violation that could cause changes in the schema and the acquisition of a new schema. At this stage the solver needs to process the literal information for the of reading at this stage is the application of schemas on the text, where the location of the meaning is in the reader's knowledge schemas. The process of reading at this stage is an accumulative process from the combining of mathematical knowledge schemas with the schemas in the text. A schema is a mental representation characterized by a fixed internal network of relationships that is created at a high level of abstraction or generalization and serves as a template that is used to clarify specific events (Brown & Yule, 1983; Hiebart & Carpenter, 1992). The schema is an activity pattern (Piaget, 1980) that enables its owner to act under the same conditions in a consistent manner by habit, and in addition it has a dynamic characteristic that allows it to expand in new conditions. Different definitions of schemas by different researchers appear in Hershkovitz and Nesher (2003). purpose of changing it into a mathematical exercise or an algebraic equation while focusing on the syntactic structure and the semantic structure of the problem. The problem with processing the information necessary for solving the word problem is one of the main difficulties in the solution of mathematical word problems. Processing the literal information for the purpose of changing it into a mathematical exercise or an algebraic equation is done by understanding the literal clues, that is the words that support (helpful clues) or the words that deceive (misleading clues) as clues for choosing the arithmetic operations needed to solve the problem. For example: the use of the words more or less (Nesher, Greeno & Reilly, 1982). At this stage the reader will ask himself the following questions:

1. Do the nouns in the question appear again in a more general unit? (For example: given apples and later fruits. It is important that the problem solver understands that apple is a fruit.)
2. Do the connectives that appear in the question relate to different mathematical sizes? (For example: if some number is 7 and the product is x what is the multiplying number?)
3. Are there literal clues in the problem that is certain words that help as a clue for choosing the arithmetic operation required for solving the problem?
4. Is it possible to demonstrate the problem by means of a picture, a table, a diagram, or a graph?

Bringing up Ideas for a Solution The meaning of solving a problem is to find an arrangement of steps starting from the given situation (in the problem) until the desired goal is reached, such that each step is derived from its predecessor by logical operations (acceptable in the context of the given problem).

The process leading to a solution of the problem is connected to a suitable choice that is a search for a method, idea, or steps. It may be necessary to analyze the problem in different ways, to identify the problem before attempting its solution (Schoenfeld, 1980). To change the search to systematic, it is necessary to know problem-solving strategies. There exist general strategies, and strategies specific to different types of problems. Usually, students are given problems similar to those they solved in the past. Therefore, according to Polya (1945), there raises the question: Do you know a problem close to this one? In most cases there is no difficulty, according to Polya in bringing up problems that are already solved and are close in some way to the present problem. As far as using Polya's theory, indeed we have not explained it in as much detail as Polya did, and the significance of his theory is much greater than presented here, yet from our experience and from case studies presented in this paper it is possible to see that for practical purposes the questions appearing in this section are likely to help the problem solver.

At this stage the learner will ask the following ques- tions: 1. Is the problem unique 2. Have I encountered similar problems? 3. Is it possible to construct a schema for solving the problem on the basis of past experience?

Screening the Ideas After raising different ideas for a solution of the problem, it is necessary to check each one of them, whether it truly helps to solve the problem. It is necessary to screen them, and to retain only relevant ideas. At this stage the learner will ask the following questions: 1. Does the idea help to solve the question? 2. How does the idea help to solve the question?

Building a Mathematical Model

Researchers who are concerned with the process of building a mathematical model for a phenomenon agree that the meaning of the process is mathematization of a phenomenon (Yerushalmi, 1997) or, according to Ormell's (1991) version, a mathematical description of the whole phenomenon instead of checking isolated parameters in the phenomenon. Consequently, we define mathematical model building as constructing representations in mathematical language like an exercise or an equation. At this stage the learner will ask the following questions:

1. What will I do as a first stage to solving the problem?
2. Do I know how to solve the problem and to build an appropriate mathematical model?
3. What mathematical model should I use to solve the problem?

The learner will construct a schema that represents the network of connections between his/her previous knowledge and the schemas in the mathematical text by means of an interaction with the following operations: defining the problem and comprehending the situation it describes; building a mathematical model of the mathematical principles relevant to the problem; understanding the relationships and the conditions pertaining to the problem; and using of the mathematical model.

Finding the Solution

After finding the mathematical model, it is necessary to solve it to reach the expected solution. It is important to check if this is a unique solution or if there is another possible solution; all possible solutions must be found. At this stage the learner will ask the following questions: 1. Is the solution unique? 2. What are all the possible solutions to the problem?

Control

It is necessary to check that the solution to the problem is suitable to the problem itself. That is to say, it is necessary to return to the original problem, to read it again, and to check:

1. Does the solution make sense?
2. Is the solution appropriate to the linguistic situation?
3. Is the solution appropriate to the mathematical situation?
4. Does the mathematical model that I used fit the problem?

This stage is the most important, because many times it seems as if we have found the solution, but the solution does not make sense (for example, we got 2.2 people), and so we need to redo the process from the beginning. It is worthwhile testing the solution, and checking all the steps that lead from the data to the solution.

It is important to note that in every word problem it is necessary to pass through all the stages.

However different learners need to focus on different stages (since some of the stages are already automatic).

During instruction it is necessary to go over a different stage each time, and to locate the stages with specific difficulties for different learners and to focus on them (examples will follow).

Mathematicians focus also on a further stage—the efficiency stage. They check whether the solution is efficient, whether it is possible to solve in a different manner, and whether there exists a shorter method of solution. A sketch of the teaching and learning model appears in the following diagram (Figure 1):

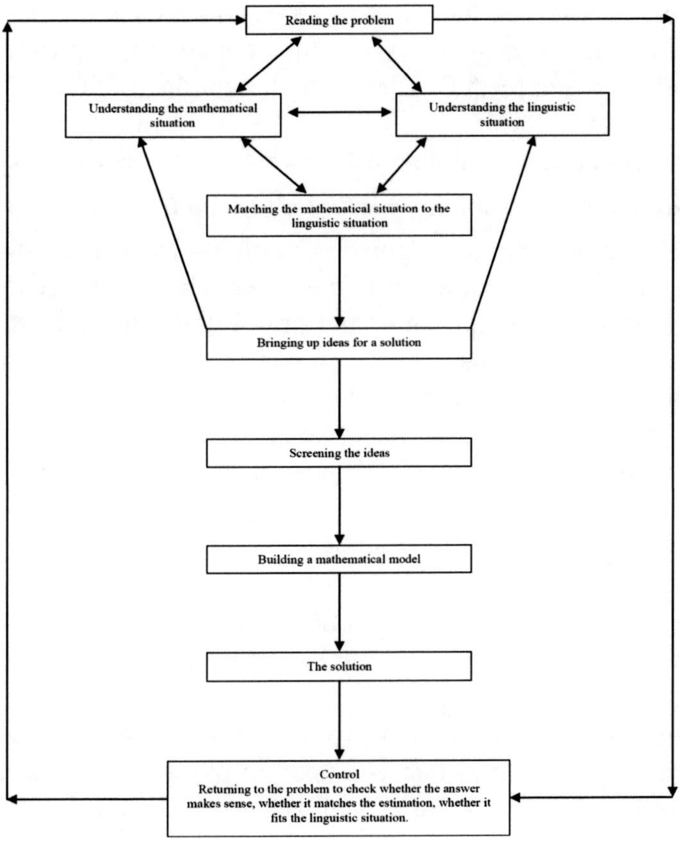

Figure 1. Diagram of the teaching and learning model for the solution of mathematical word problems.

APPLICATION OF THE TEACHING AND LEARNING MODEL

To illustrate the model we bring 3 case studies: a student in the fifth grade, a student in the ninth grade and a college student. We attempted to apply the model both to mathematical word problems accompanied by an authentic background story, and to mathematical word problems not accompanied by a background story.

The Case of Yael

Yael is a college student specializing in mathematics teaching at a teachers' college in the center of the country. She was given the Students and Professors Problem described above, and she made the typical mistake, as found in the literature: 6S = P. After being taught the model, she solved the problem and got the correct solution: 6P = S. The student wrote down her working-process according to the instructional model as follows:

1. Reading the problem –First of all I read the problem.
2. Understanding the linguistic situation – Next, I read the problem again. I asked myself if it is all clear (words and sentences), if I understand the question, and how I could describe the problem in my own words. Once it was clear to me that I understood all the words in the problem, I marked the key words: "times greater than", "the students", and "the professors". I asked myself, what do they want me to do? What is the P and what is the S? And here is my description of the problem: The number of students is 6 times greater than the number of professors.
3. Understanding the mathematical situation – I checked whether I needed to describe the problem with an equation with letters. I think that it is not a problem that I need to find an actual result for, but that I have to give an equation. Then I realized that I have trouble with this sort of problem. The given information seems to be clear, but in fact you need to pay attention the concept "6 times". It is important to analyze and understand which given is 6 times the other one. Understanding the relationship between the two givens is important for the solution.
4. Matching the mathematical situation to the linguistic situation – I looked for verbal clues that might help me solve the problem. In our case, the concept "times greater than" tells us to multiply by some amount and so that is the arithmetic operation we need to perform. Here, I started to draw a diagram to bring the given information into focus: Students Professors S P Their number is 6 times greater
5. Bringing up ideas for a solution – To solve the problem at this stage I have to build a schema. I've met problems like this in the past, and that will help me build the schema. I met problems with the concept "greater than"; to see links between a particular number and another. My ideas for the solution are: 6P = S; 6S = P; 6S > P; 6P > S
6. Screening the ideas – To solve the problem I check whether the

ideas I came up with are relevant to the problem, and whether they help me to solve it. I think that the inequality 6P > S does not make sense because the number of students is 6 times bigger than the number of professors. The inequality 6S > P makes sense, but does not solve the problem, because I multiplied the number of students by 6, and then made it even bigger. From the information given in the problem I know that S > P. That is, I did not add anything that helps me to solve the problem. For that reason I also discard the solution 6S = P.

7. Building a mathematical model – As I said in the previous stage while screening the ideas, I need to understand the situation - the correct representation of the problem - and to see whether I understood correctly the connections between the given pieces of information. In the previous stage I ruled out all the possibilities: 6S = P; 6S > P; 6P > S. Therefore the only solution that remained is
8. Finding the solution – In this case there is no numerical result, so the solution is 6P = S or in another form it could be written S: 6 = P.
9. Control – I chose to read the problem again, and again I noticed the fact that the number of students is 6 times bigger than the number of professors. It seems to me that my solution makes sense. In addition, I substituted numbers and checked myself, since I know that I have trouble with this type of problem and sometimes I do the opposite.

The Case of Shiri

Shiri is a good student in the ninth grade. She, however, had some difficulties in understanding and solving the following word problem that did not describe every day event and was not accompanied by an authentic background story. Shiri, was given the following problem in a school test: Find the equation of the straight line, parallel to the line 3x – 7y = 4, passing through the point (0, 10). In the school test Shiri answer incorrect to this problem. We interviewed Shiri and in the interview she claimed that she did not know how to solve this problem: "I do not understand what is written in the problem, so …either I do something or I do not do anything. Therefore, in the test I wrote y = 3x + 10 and that was not the correct answer". Shiri explained that she took the 3x from the original equation and added 10 because the line passes through the point (0, 10)). To enable Shiri to solve the problem we used all the steps of the above model.

1. Reading the problem – At the first stage Shiri was asked to read the problem aloud.
2. Understanding the linguistic situation – At this stage, once it was clear that Shiri understood all the words in the problem, we asked her to mark the keywords. Shiri marked them as follows: "equation of the straight line", "parallel", and "passing through the point".
3. Understanding the mathematical situation – Despite the fact that Shiri understood all the words linguistically and marked the keywords, she did not yet understand the mathematical context. Shiri was asked to express what she thought the problem was about. She said, "To find a new line". Shiri was asked whether the given information was clear and whether she understood the connections between the pieces of information and the problem. Shiri did not understand the connection between the given information and the problem, despite the fact that the general conceptual frame of the problem was clear to her – she knew what a straight line and a parallel line are.
4. Matching the mathematical situation to the linguistic situation – At this stage Shiri needed to process the verbal information to turn it into a mathematical exercise (equation). Shiri was asked a general question about straight lines, "What is the equation of a straight line?" Shiri answered and wrote down $y = mx + n$, but she claimed that in the question there was no equation of a straight line. Shiri was asked what she though "parallel" meant, and she answered, "A line that has the same (slope) m". At this stage integration took place between Shiri's schemas concerning the equation of a straight line and her schemas concerning the text. Shiri was asked to look at the equation written in the problem and to think how it might be possible to convert it into the equation of a straight line like the one she just wrote. Then Shiri said, " I need to convert the equation into the equation of a straight line. Oy! In the test I made a mistake. In the test I took the coefficient of x, the 3, and I related to it as if it were the slope and that is wrong. It is forbidden to relate to the coefficient of x as if it were the slope, like I did in the test".

5. Bringing up ideas for a solution – Shiri suggested moving the 3x to the right-hand side and wrote $-7y = 4 - 3x$. Shiri did not know what to do, and said, “This is still not the familiar equation of a straight line. I do not know what to do with the minus”. Then Shiri was asked, “On the basis of your past experience, can you convert this equation to the equation of a straight line?” Shiri said, “In fact I can move the $-7y$ to the other side’ and then I would not have the problem of the minus”.
6. Screening the ideas – Shiri was asked, “Which idea would you chose to solve the problem?” Shiri showed the equation $7y = 3x - 4$ and claimed that it reminds her of the equation $y = mx + n$ because there is no minus before the y.
7. Building a mathematical model – Shiri was asked, “What can you do now to bring the equation to the same form as the equation $y = mx + n$?” Shiri looked again at the equation and said that in her opinion she needs to “get rid of” the 7.
8. Finding the solution – After Shiri’s insight concerning the equation of a straight line and the meaning of a line parallel to the given line, Shiri solved the problem correctly. Shiri was asked whether this was the only solution. She answered, “Since this is a line parallel to a given line and passing through a certain point there is only one solution.”
9. Control – Shiri was asked whether the solution made sense and met the conditions of the problem. She answered, “I think so.” When asked how she could check it, she substituted the point (0, 10) into the equation of the line and said, “I got a true statement, and the line is parallel to the given line, so my solution is correct.”

The Case of Sivan

Sivan is a 6th grade student, who had some difficulties in understanding and solving word problems. She said: “I cannot understand word problems. They have too many words in them and I do not understand what I have to do”. Sivan was given the following problem and was asked to solve it: Tom has a bottle containing three quarters liter of milk. He drank one third of the milk.

How much did he drink? Sivan did not understand the problem and she said: “I do not know what to do”. To enable Sivan to solve the problem we used all the steps of the above model.

1. Reading the problem – First of all Sivan read the problem.
2. Understanding the linguistic situation – Next, she read the problem again, and she found the key words: "drank" "containing" "three quarters liter of milk" "one third of the milk".
3. Understanding the mathematical situation – Sivan pointed out that she needed to pay attention to the two givens: "three quarters of" and "one third of". Sivan said that she doesn't like fractions.
4. Matching the mathematical situation to the linguistic situation – Sivan was asked if there are clues that might help her to solve the problem. She said: "I think that one third of the milk tells me to multiply or maybe to subtract but I don't know what to do".
5. Bringing up ideas for a solution – To solve the problem at this stage Sivan was asked if she met similar problems. She said that she had met problems like this in the past but only with integer numbers. We asked her to create a problem with integer numbers. She created a problem, as follows: "Tom has a bottle containing six liters of milk. He drank one third of the milk. How much did he drink?" Sivan's ideas for the solution of this problem were: 6 X1/3 or 6-1/3.
6. Screening the ideas – To solve the problem Sivan checked whether the ideas she came up to the problem that she created were relevant to the problem, and whether they helped her to solve it. She decided to implement her ideas for her problem to our problem and she said: "my ideas for the problem are: 3/4 X1/3 or 3/4 -1/3".
7. Building a mathematical model –Sivan did not know which idea is right and therefore she decided to draw a picture of the problem. Sivan decided that the subtraction did not make sense because of the picture that she drew. She said: "I can see in the picture what it means 1/3 of 3 /4". Sivan built the mathematical model: $3/4 \times 1/3$ (Figure 2).
8. Finding the solution – Sivan found the solution: Tom drank ¼ liter of milk. She said that she is certain that this is the only solution because of her drawing.
9. Control – Sivan read the problem again and said: "The solution is logical, because of the drawing. In the drawing it is very clear that if you divide 3/4 to 3 you get 1/4".

CONCLUSION

In this paper we have tried to show how it is possible to bridge gaps between natural language and mathematical language in solving mathematical problems by means of an instructional model, whereby the addressee processes the text cognitively. The process of dealing with the verbal text of the mathematical problem is multi-staged, and necessitates the implementation of a number of cognitive actions: interpreting symbols and graphs, understanding the substance, understanding the linguistic situation, finding a mathematical model, and matching between the linguistic situation and the appropriate mathematical model. This nine-stage instruction and learning model transforms into a complex thought process when fully understood and internalized. It is a meta-cognitive process that contributes to students' conceptualization (Natstasi & Clements, 1990). Knowledge of meta-cognitive processes assists in problem solving and improves the ability to achieve goals. We recommend teachers to "hitch" mathematical language to natural language: to avoid problems that have no connection with reality, to avoid ambiguous problems, to explain to the students the differences between natural and mathematical languages and the possibility of combining them. We recommend teachers to make intelligent use of the instruction and learning model suggested above, that is, to adapt the model and its various stages both to different populations of students and to the nature of the problems and their complexity. The instruction and learning model suggested here is suitable for students in the upper grades of elementary school, in middle and high schools, and in teacher training colleges. In elementary school, the majority of problems available to students have a numerical solution with real –life meaning, and so it is important to understand the situation described in them. In their continued studies in middle and high school students will have to cope with problems that do not necessarily have a numerical solution, and will have to use algebra to solve them. Graduated work on solution methods of word problems using schemas built in previous work on simply word –problem solving will enable students to cope with more complex problems. Moreover, adapting the model for different students will enable teachers to help every student according to his/her needs and to pinpoint the focus of difficulty for each student. Intelligent use of the suggested model of instruction and learning will also help student teachers, both in their training and in their teaching practice. Understanding the model will allow the starting teacher to understand that meta-linguistic awareness, syntactic and semantic awareness, and awareness of mathematical schemas are necessary for solving problems in mathematics. Furthermore, the way the problem is worded and its correspondence to reality can significantly affect students' ability to solve the problem.

REFERENCES

1. Ball, D. H. (1993). With an eye on the mathematical horizon: Dilemmas of teaching elementary school mathematics. The Elementary School Journal, 93, 373-397. doi:10.1086/461730
2. Ben-Chaim, D., Keret, Y., & Ilany, B. (2006). Yahas veproporzia – Mehkar vehoraha behachsharat morim lematematica (Ratio and proportion- research and teaching in mathematics teacher training). Tel-Aviv: Mofet Inst. Press.
3. Bloedy-Vinner, H. (1998). The understanding of algebraic language in university preacademic students. Ph. D. dissertation, Jerusalem: Hebrew University.
4. Brown, G., & Yule, G. (1983). Discourse analysis. Cambridge: Cambridge University Press.
5. Clement, J. (1982). Algebra word problem solution: Thought processes under- lying a common misconception. Journal for Research in Mathemat ics Education, 13, 16-30. doi:10.2307/748434
6. De Lange, J. 1987 (1987). Mathematics insight and meaning. Utrect, Holland: Rijksuniversiteit.
7. Fischbein, E. (1987). Intuition in science and mathematics: An educational approach. Dordrecht, Holland: Reidel Pub.
8. Folman, S. (2000). Hafakat Mashmaut mitext: Hebetim Hakaratiim-tiksortiim shel Heker Hasiah (Decoding meaning from a text: Cognitive and communicational aspects of discourse analysis). Tel-Aviv: Tel-Aviv University.
9. Freudenthal, H. (1991). Revising mathematics education. Dordrecht, South Holland: Kluwer.
10. Gee, J. P. (1996). Social Linguistics and Literacy, Ideology in Discourse. Bristol, PA: Taylor & Francis.
11. Gravermeijer, K. (1997). Commentary on solving word problems: A case study of modeling?. Learning and Instruction, 7, 389-397. doi:10.1016/S0959-4752(97)00011-X
12. Greer, B. (1997). Modeling reality in the mathematics classroom: The case of word problems. Learning and Instruction, 7, 293-307. doi:10.1016/S0959-4752(97)00006-6
13. Halliday, M. A. K., & Hassan, R. (1976). Cohesion in English. London: Longman.

14. Hershkovitz, S., & Nesher, P. (1996). The role of schemes in designing computerized environments. Educational Studies in Mathematics, 30, 339-366. doi:10.1007/BF00570829
15. Hershkovitz, S., & Nesher, P. (2003). The role of schemes in solving word problems. The Mathematics Educator, 7, 1-24.
16. Hiebert, J., & Carpenter, T.P. (1992). Learning and teaching with under- standing. In: D. A. Grouns (Ed.), Handbook of research on mathematics teaching and learning (pp. 65-92). New York: Macmillan.
17. Kane, R. B. (1970). The readability of mathematics textbooks revisited. The Mathematics Teacher, 63, 579-581.
18. Kaput, J. J. (1993). The urgent need for proleptic research in representation of quantitative relationships. In: T. A., Romberg, E. Fennema and T. R. Carpenter (Eds.), Integrating research on graphical representation of functions (pp. 273- 311). London: Lawrence Earlbaum Associates.
19. Kaput, J. J., & Clement, J. (1979). Letter to the editor of JCMB. Journal of Children's Mathematical Behavior, 2, pp. 208.
20. Kintsch, W. (1998). Comprehension: A Paradigm for Cognition. Cambridge, England: Cambridge University Press.
21. Lester, F. K. (1978). Mathematical problem solving in the elementary school: Some educational and psychological considerations. In: L. L Hatfield and D. A. Bradbard (Eds.), Mathematical problem solving: Papers from a research workshop (ERIC/SMET). Columbus, Ohio: Columbus.
22. MacGregor, M., & Price, E. (1999). An exploration of aspects of language proficiency and algebra learning. Journal for Research in Mathematics Education, 30, 449-467. doi:10.2307/749709
23. Margolin, B. (2002). Al defusey lechidut bein tarbutiim [On intercultural coherence patterns]. Script – Journal of the Israel Association for Literacy, 5-6, 81-89.
24. Nastasi, B. K., & Clements, D. H. (1990). Metacomponential functioning in young children. Intelligence, 14, 109-125.
25. Nathan, M. J., Kintsch, W., & Young, E. (1992). A theory of algebra-word- problem comprehension and its implications for the design of learning environments. Cognition and Instruction, 9, 329-389. doi:10.1207/s1532690xci0904_2
26. Nesher, P. (1988). Multiplicative school word problems: Theoretical

approaches and empirical findings. In: J. Hiebert and M. Behr (Eds.), Number concepts and operations in the middle grades (pp. 19-41). Mahwah, NJ: L. Erlbaum Associates.

27. Nesher, P., Greene, J. G., & Riley, M. S. (1982). The development of semantic categories for addition and subtraction. Educational Studies in Mathematics, 13, 373-394. doi:10.1007/BF00366618
28. Nesher, P., & Katriel, T. (1977). A semantic analysis of addition and subtraction word problem in arithmetic. Educational Studies in Mathematics, 8, 251-269. doi:10.1007/BF00385925
29. Nir, R. (1989). Semantika hivrit mashmaut vetikshoret (Hebrew semantics meaning and communication. Tel-Aviv: Open University.
30. Ormell, C. (1991). How ordinary meaning underpins the meaning of mathe- matics. Learning of Mathematics, 11, 25-30.
31. Piaget, J. (1980). Experiments in contradiction. Chicago and London: University of Chicago Press.
32. Polya, G. (1945). How to Solve it?. Princeton, NJ: Princeton University Press.
33. Reusser, K., & Stebler, R. (1997). Every word problem has a solution - the social rationality of mathematical modeling in school. Learning and Instruction, 7, 309-327. doi:10.1016/S0959-4752(97)00014-5
34. Rosnick, P. (1981). Some misconceptions concerning the concept of variable. Are you careful about defining your variables?. Mathematics Teacher, 74, 418-420, 450.
35. Sarel, Z. (1991). Mavo Lenituah Hsiah (Introduction to discourse analysis). Tel-Aviv: Or-Am.
36. Schoennfeld, A. H. (1980). Teaching problem-solving skills. American mathematical monthly, 87, 794-805. doi:10.2307/2320787
37. Silver, E. A., Shapiro, L. J., & Deutsch, A. (1993). Sense making and the solution of division problems involving remainders: An examination of middle school student's solution processes and their interpretation of solution. Journal for Research in Mathematics Education, 24, 117-135. doi:10.2307/749216
38. Van Dijk, T. A. (1980). Macrostructures: An interdisciplinary study of global structures in discourse. Mahwah, N.J.: L. Erlbaum Associates.
39. Widdowson, H. G. (1979). Explorations in Applied Linguistics. Oxford, England: Oxford University.

40. Woolf, N. (2005). Lilmod lelamed Mathematica leshem Havana beezrat mentorim (Teaching how to teach Mathematics for understanding with mentors). In: R. Lidor, et al (Eds.), Zematim Bamehkar Hahinuhi (Cross-Roads in Educational Research) (pp.223-248), Tel-Aviv: Mofet Inst. Press.

41. Yerushalmi, M. (1997). Mathematizing qualitative verbal descriptions of situations: A language to support modeling. Cognition and Instruction, 15, 207-264. doi:10.1207/s1532690xci1502_3

CHAPTER 10

Spanish Language Grammatical Context—Acknowledging Specific Language Characteristics

Joel Laffita Rivera

Faculty of Applied Communication (FAC), Multimedia University, Selangor, Malaysia

ABSTRACT

The current research article exposes a linguistic-outline-analysis about the use of Nouns-Object/Thing/Place, Definite and Indefinite Articles and Descriptive Adjectives in the writing and speaking context of Spanish language communication. The teaching and learning of these Spanish grammar themes continue to be subject of interest among scholars due to

Citation: Rivera, J. (2019), "Spanish Language Grammatical Context—Acknowledging Specific Language Characteristics". *Open Journal of Modern Linguistics*, **9**, 215-228. doi: 10.4236/ojml.2019.93020.

the level of complexities that these syntaxes present in terms of Second Language Acquisition (SLA) (Bialystok, 1981) . The article collected appropriate literature-materials from different sources and added new-contextual-insights into its frame to adhesive an analytical-database with emphasis on Spanish Language Grammatical Contexts that tap into the subject-matter-discussed. Being consecutive to this, the study aimed to provide valuable material as a reference to teach and study these Spanish grammar subjects in Spanish foreign language classes.

Keywords: Learning-Language-Retention, Translation, Grammar-Patterns, Communication-Insights, Methodology-Schemes

INTRODUCTION

The grammar of the Spanish language is by logical definition "the Spanish grammar", redundant definition but denotes the "authenticity" of this discipline referring to the Spanish language in particular. The following statement quotes that grammar is part of Linguistics which studies the elements of a language as well as the way in which these are organized and combined (Diccionario de la lengua española, 2015) . The Spanish language possesses unique grammar shapes and grammatical structures that make this language exclusive and different from other languages. For instance, in Spanish the nouns form a two-gender system and are marked for number. This is a fact that reflexes on nouns-object/thing/place. The definite articles, excluding the neuter "lo", and indefinite articles are also marked for gender and number. All grouped "nine in total" and with unique grammar-shapes. Although the adjectives and descriptive adjectives do not have gender in Spanish; they are subjected to follow the same patterns (gender and number) when they adhered to these grammar themes (article/noun) (Batchelor, José, & Ángel, 2010) . The way with which these syntaxes components are treated referring to the use of gender (masculine/feminine) and the number (singular/plural) and the arrangement (words order) of nouns, articles and descriptive adjectives into the writing and speaking context of Spanish language communication makes more challenging the teaching and learning of these grammar themes in Spanish FL classes, essentially when working with 2L learners whose native-language does not apply the "gender/number/words-order" as Spanish does. As a result, the acquisition and development of the linguistic and communicative competences that involve the use of these Spanish grammar themes cannot produce successful language-outputs without acknowledging these distinct-syntaxes-patterns-usages. Based on this overall respect, the research article is addressing its headings and sub-headings.

LEARNING LANGUAGE RETENTION

Memory plays a vital role in the acquisition of the L2. Learning is to save some memory, and to recall it when it is necessary. Memory and learning, therefore, are closely related. The memory is defined as the test of the learning. This definition of memory as a test of the learning gets relevance when it comes to adequately apply the gender and number in all the linguistic aspects of Spanish language that requires it. It has been cited by many scholars that Spanish 2L learners at all levels mistake in this regard (Rutherford & Sharwood Smith, 1988) . My professional opinion agrees with that of those scholars. According to the finding of this research-article I would say that many of the errors made by 2L learners whose native-language does not apply the "gender/number" as Spanish does are directly or indirectly related to the way that that subject-knowledge was acquired, predominantly when it comes to Learning-Language-Retention. The mind of 2L learners for instance will choose the easy way of acquiring knowledge versus the hard mode. This means that knowing the "meaning" of a particular phrase that they want to say/write in the L2 rather than studying the linguistic elements that make it up will be sufficient to comprehend it at all. So, in order to achieve the L2-target in a faster way, they will translate from the L1 to L2, but, without taking into account that each language has its own linguistic-characteristics and own linguistic-speaking and writing standards applications context. Even though the use of translation can facilitates the acquisition and development of the speaking-skill; it does not work in the case of applying correctly the gender and number and words-order in nouns-object/thing/place, definite/indefinite articles and descriptive adjectives in Spanish if the learners do not acknowledge these distinct-syntaxes-patterns and their usage. Thus, understanding that the mind of the 2L learners does not conceived the acquisition of grammar and grammatical structures of the L2 without using the knowledge that it has already been conceived by the L1, it will lead us to emphasis on the significant of acknowledging the L2 own-grammar-patterns in translation by considering the fact that in Spanish nouns-object/thing/place and definite/indefinite articles are marked for gender and number; that the descriptive adjective are subjected to the gender-number-nature of nouns/articles; that it is necessary to know the words-order of nouns/articles/adjectives into the speaking and writing context of Spanish; that there are communication-linguistic-structures that require to be knowledgeable about the use of these Spanish-syntaxes for applying them correctly in this specific field. Furthermore, that there are rules and exceptions related to the use of L2-grammar. In practice, failing in doing this could have adverse effects to the mind of 2L learners leading to distortion and inadequate Language-Learning-Retention.

GRAMMAR PATTERNS-NOUNS OBJECT/THING/PLACE

One of the most questionable Spanish language topics in Spanish FL classes is the use of the gender, mostly referring to its application in nouns-object/thing/place. For 2L learners whose native-language does not apply the gender in nouns-object/thing/pace in the way Spanish does. This often becomes a difficult Spanish language-issue to comprehend and digest. The main reason points to the inference of the L1-mind-subconscious which does not apprehend such irrational-view, I would say. However, from the point of view of language-learning-retention is clear that the keyword required is "acknowledging". It might seem not logical classifying the nature of an object, thing or place in the same way that we do in the case of people or animals when we refer to their gender (male/female). Nonetheless, this is well-seen linguistic-phenomenon in the case of Spanish language own-linguistic-characteristics as well as in others European Languages such as French, Germany, Portuguese and Italian (see Table 1).

Table 1. Nouns object/thing/place gender.

Nombres/Nouns	Masculine	Feminine
auto/car	-	
casa/house		-
aula/classroom	-	
agua/water	-	
sofá/sofa	-	
cine/cinema	-	
machete/machete	-	
banquete/banquet	-	
calle/street		-

llave/key		-
art/arte	-	
air/aire	-	
librería/bookshop		-
universidad/university		-
educación/education		-
profesión/profession		-
hospital/hospital	-	
libertad/liberty		-
universo/universe	-	-

As can be observed from the above Table 1; it could be difficult to recognize a masculine or feminine noun in the case of objects/things/places. If we think for instance how variable and distinct they are, it could be also a real challenge to master this topic. I essentially say this because in Spanish all nouns referring to objects/things/places have their own-orthography/spelling which cannot be changed in terms of gender-application. In this respect it is necessary to acknowledge these specific-linguistic-traits. For this reason the study has outlined the statements below to provide a clear understanding regarding to the use of gender/number and singular/plural in Objects/Things/Places according to the writing system of Spanish language:

- Usually, the nouns that end in a vowel "o" are masculine (anillo/palacio/auto/libro) etc. Generally, nouns ending in a vowel "a" are feminine; excluding exceptions of nouns that end in a vowel "a" but are masculine (agua/mapa/alba/sofá) ext.
- Nouns that end in a vowel "e" can be masculine or feminine. However, by considering that the predominant way in terms of the use of gender in Spanish is "masculine one" and that the number of masculine nouns ending in "e" is much greater than that of the feminine one, identifying the female between these kinds of nouns is a thing of going for the masculine one. Of course, learners need to count on the help of the Spanish teacher to do so: (cine/restaurante/machete/banquete/pacquete/panque/aceite/arete/calle/llave/clase) ext.
- Usually nouns ending in the vowel "i" are masculine (rubí/maní) ext.
- The nouns beginning in a vowel "a" are usually masculine

(amanecer/atardecer/ambiente/arte) ext.

- Note: Nouns ending in "consonants" can be male or female. However, among these kinds of nouns are those that the following references (syllable) telling us the gender to which they belong.
- Nouns ending in "al"/"ón"/"or" are male (hospital/portal/cristal)/ camión/proyector/tractor) ext.
- Nouns ending in "ad"/"zión"/"ción"/"xión" are female (universidad/popularidad/amistad/profesión/educación/ crucifixión) ext.

GRAMMAR PATTERNS-SINGULAR/PLURAL-NOUNS

The singular and plural is generally applied to all nouns. It is easy to recognize the singular nouns since the vast majority of them do not have "s" at the end of the word that referred to them as such. So, the "s" at the end of these words will determine also the plural in all these cases: casa/casas/ libro/libros/pueblo/pueblos ext. If the nouns end in a "vowel with tilde" the "es" is added, excluding some exceptions: rubí-rubíes/sofá-sofás/café-cafés ext. The "es" is added to nouns ending in consonants as well: proyectores/ universidades. Nouns' ending in "z" this letter is changed by the "c" and "es" is added: cruz/cruces/lápiz/lápices ext.

GRAMMAR PATTERNS-DEFINITE AND INDEFINITE ARTICLES

The acquisition and application of definite/indefinite articles in Spanish FL language classes is another complex issue to comprehend and digest for 2L learners whose native-language does not apply these syntaxes in the way Spanish does. Nevertheless, knowing theses linguistic-application-views it will lead to certain analyzes and understanding: in Spanish the definite articles are used to determine and to give a connotation to the nouns they refer to. For example, saying "The white horse". It is not the same as to say "A white horse". In the first case we refer to a specific horse among many. In the second case we refer to any horse among many. The definite articles are also the grammatical components which determine the gender of nouns ending in "e"/"ista"El estudiante./La estudiante./El dentista./La dentista. In the case of "neutrality and cognation" the article "lo" is used, but it followed by a masculine adjective Lo Bueno./Lo malo. Lo intersante.

On the other hand, the indefinite articles do not give the same connotation to the nouns they refer to as the definite articles do. However, when it comes to "determiners" they do as quantifiers (un/una instead of uno which means one). The definite articles are the English equivalent of "the", while the indefinite articles are the English equivalent of "a, an, some/few" (see Table 2). Despite the differences between these two grammar themes; both, definite and indefinite articles show agreement in gender and number (see Table 3).

Table 2. English/Spanish definite and indefinite articles.

English Definite Article	Spanish Definite Articles		
The	el	los	lo
	la	las	
English Indefinite Articles	Spanish Indefinite Articles		
A, an	un		unos
	una		unas

Table 3. Definite and indefinite articles gender and number.

Articles	Singular/Masculine	Singular/Feminine	Plural/Masculine	Plural/Feminine
Definite	el	la	los	las
Indefinite	un	una	unos	unas

GRAMMAR PATTERNS-ADJECTIVES

When it comes to noun-description for instance, color, size, quality, etc., it is impossible to do without using adjectives. In this regard the function of these grammar themes in the writing and speaking context of Spanish language communication is similar to other languages. However, the application of adjectives and descriptive adjectives in Spanish is subjected to the characteristics (male/female/singular/plural) of the nouns they described. The same-patterns apply when the adjectives are preceded by definite/indefinite articles. So, once again the keyword to better understand the use of adjectives and descriptive adjectives is "acknowledging". Generally, there are basic rules to apply adjectives in Spanish: the adjectives ending in "o" are masculine, to get the feminine therefore it matches the feminine-nature of the noun "o" is replaced by "a" (Hombre alto./Mujer alta.). Adjectives ending in "consonant" are masculine, to get the female therefore it matches the feminine-nature of the noun an "a" is added after the consonant (habador/ habladora). This rule applies to living creatures only. Adjectives ending in "e" and "ista" are neuter; they do not have gender. These kinds of adjectives agree with the nouns they describe in singular and plural only:

Auto grande. Casa grande./Autos grandes. Casas grandes.

Hombre optimista. Hombres optimistas./Mujer optimista./Mujeres optimistas.

ADJECTIVES-OUTSTANDING-NOTE

When it comes to noun-color/origin-description; it would be very useful to acknowledge that colors are adjectives and to define the origin of people, objects, things, and places we have to use adjectives of nationality. So, there are also basic rules to apply them into the writing and speaking context of Spanish language communication: colors ending in "o" are masculine, to get the feminine therefore it matches the feminine-nature of the noun "o" is replaced by "a". Colors ending in "e" "a" "consonant" are neuter, they agree with the nouns they describe in singular and plural only. Adjective of nationality ending in "o" and "consonant" are masculine. To get the feminine therefore it matches the feminine-nature of the noun "o" is replaced by "a" and an "a" is added after those ending in consonant. The adjectives of nationality ending in "e" "i" "a" are neuter, they agree with the nouns they describe in singular and plural only. The adjective of nationality are not written with capital letters in Spanish:

Auto blanco. Casa blanca./Cinto verde. Camisa verde./Zapato azul. Pantufla azul.

Chico japonés. Chica japonesa./Chicos japoneses./Chicas japonesas.

Barco español./Música española.

GRAMMAR PATTERNS-AGREEMENT AND WORDS-ORDER

In Spanish language there is something that we call "concordancia", this is nothing else than linking many linguistic components into a mutual agreement, I would say. A true example of "concordancia" is the linguistic and lexical agreement between definite/indefinite articles, nouns and adjectives in the speaking and writing context of Spanish language communication (El auto rojo./Un auto rojo.). I would personally name such extraordinary arrangement "The three Musketeers of the Spanish language" due to the undoubted value in terms of gender and number usage. Apart from this insight, one thing to ponder is the position the adjectives in phrases/sentences. In Spanish adjectives are written after the nouns, although there are some exceptions in relation to this, it is a general rule. Even though some scholars recommend using the similarity that exists between Spanish and other languages to acquire and enhance the Spanish-lexical (Erichsen, 2015) . Spanish second-language-learners have to acknowledge in their minds that each language uses the lexicon according to its own linguistic standards. One example of writing-context to cite is the composition of adjective-phrases in English which translated to Spanish they become noun-phrases:

An easy language./Una lengua fácil.

The White House./La Casa Blanca.

A wonderful day./Un día bonito.

A big university./Una universidad grande.

An interesting book./Un libro interesante.

Anold friend./Un viejo amigo.

Along distance./Una distancia larga.

The red dress./El vestido rojo.

The blue sky./El cielo azul.

The black cat./El gato negro.

A small chair. Una silla pequeña.

An ancient text. Un texto antiguo.

The short girl. La chica baja.

The handsome boy. El chico guapo.

An excellent idea./Una idea excelente.

A green apple./Una manzana verde.

COMMUNICATION-INSIGHTS

According to Rivera (Rivera, 2019) communication is instigated to express human experiences and traits. It is the channel through which an individual can communicate his thoughts. The most common approach used by an individual for communicating is through speaking or writing. These skills require a good understanding of language to be used, particularly its grammar. In this regard having a good command of Spanish grammar concerning the use of nouns-object/thing/place; definite/indefinite articles and descriptive adjectives will give an individual the advantage to organize the language in the writing and speaking context of Spanish language communication. To support this insight the study provides various examples of Spanish language communication setting and subsequent-explanations:

Q & A

Transmitter: ¿Cómo está el café?

Receiver: bueno, malo, caliente, frío.

Transmitter: ¿Cómo está la pasta?

Receiver: buena, mala, deliciosa.

Referring to the title.

El señor./La señora. El doctor./La doctora./Quiero hablar con el/la señor-a.

Responding to the reference pointed.

¿Qué es esto/eso/aquello?

Un libro/una pizarra/un lápiz/una goma

Describing physical characteristics.

Yo tengo el pelo negro, corto y liso./Yo tengo los ojos negros./Yo tengo la piel morena.

Asking and responding the mode.

¿Cómo está el café?/¿Cómo está la leche?/¿Cómo están los pasteles/¿Cómo están las galletas?

Bueno, malo, amargo, dulce ext./Buenas, malas, saladas ext.

Expressingpreferences and wishes.

Me gusta el café./Me gusta la leche./Me gustan los dulces./Me gustan las frutas./Quiero comerpollo frito./Quiero beber jugo de mango./Quiero tomar helado de chocolate./Quiero tomar sopa de pescado.

Asking and responding the opinion.

¿Qué tal el libro que te presté? ¿Qué tal la película de ayer?

Interesante/bueno/interesante/buena

Expressing the existence.

Hay un auto en el garaje./Hay una casa en esa esquina.

Expressing possessions.

Tengo un auto nuevo./Tengo una bicicleta nueva. Tengo unos libros muy interesantes. Tengo unas revistas de moda muy interesante. El mío./La mía./ Los míos./Las mías.

Making comparisons.

El pescado es mejor que el huevo./La carne es mejor que las verduras./Los dulces son mejores que las frutas./Las frutas son mejores que las golosinas.

Expressing the superlative.

El mayor/la mayor/los mayores/las mayores/el más joven/la más joven/ los más jóvenes/las más jóvenes.

The examples illustrated show how relevance is the use of nouns, definite and indefinite articles and descriptive adjectives in these cases of communication. In the first example I referred to two ways of communication in which the articles and nouns agree in gender and number. So, the adjectives used in the answers respond to the gender and number of the nouns used in the questions. In the second example I referred to the title, in Spanish we use the definite articles in dependence to the male/female/singular/plural to refer to the title that a person holds. In the third example I referred to how to answer the reference pointed, in such case we use indefinite articles before the nouns. In the fourth example I referred to how to ask and answer mode, something that is impossible to do without using nouns, definite articles and descriptive adjectives in such situation. In the fifth example I referred to express preferences, in such situations the definite articles always precede the nouns in the grammar construction of I like.../I don't like... mainly referring to things. In case of expressing wishes; usually the definite articles don't precede the Spanish nouns "I want to eat..."/"I want to drink..." In the sixth example I referred to ask and answer the opinion, such situation requires the use of definite articles and adjectives. In the seventh example I referred to expressing the existence, something that requires the use of the indefinite articles "un/una" if it is wanted to quantify the existence of "a person, an object, a place". In the eighth example I referred to express possession, in this situation is common to use indefinite articles to emphasize in Spanish. In the ninth example I referred to make comparisons, the use of definite articles is required in these situations in Spanish. In the tenth and last example I referred to express the superlative, this grammar subject requires the use of definite articles in Spanish. As could be seen; using nouns-object/ thing/place, definite/indefinite articles, and descriptive adjectives in Spanish language is a relevance subject-matter. The main reason regarding "language-difficulties" is due to the use of gender and number and the words-order with which they are treated in Spanish grammar (Gómez Torrego, 2006) . This is nothing else than "own linguistic typologies", a Spanish-linguistic-fact that must be conscious to achieve it.

METHODOLOGY-SCHEMES

At present, the acquisition of Spanish grammar through the use of inductive learning is most recommended by academics as per Linguistics. The inductive approach allows learners to develop through analytical ways and cognitive skills. Learners observe and analyze a feature of the target language first and then they study the rule that explains that feature. On the other hand, the deductive approach focuses on the learning of grammar from the perspective of "grammar rules" first (Prince & Felder, 2006) . In the inductive approach, if the grammatical content only presents a limited number of variables and the function rule is evident, using it may be the most appropriate. However, when the linguistic content that one wants to teach presents many irregularities or the rule is not obvious, then the inductive teaching may be too time consuming, and effort wasting compared to the deductive. Therefore, the most effective strategy may be the combination of inductive and deductive teaching (Castañeda, 1997) . In this respect (combination of inductive and deductive teaching) setting appropriate methods for teaching and learning the three Spanish grammar themes presented in this research article should be a matter of concern among Spanish Language Teachers. According to the outline of the common European framework for languages(Consejo de Europa, 2001) as well as the American Council on the Teaching of Foreign Languages (2012) ; the teaching and learning of nouns, definite/indefinite articles and descriptive adjectives corresponds to the levels A1 and A2. This means that these linguistic themes are to be taught from the beginning of the teaching and learning process of Spanish language. Thus, let us remember as Spanish language teachers that the own-linguistic-characteristics of Spanish language will allow the introduction of these Spanish grammar themes from the very beginning too, particularly when it comes to nouns and adjectives. For instance, which Spanish teachers have not been questioned by students when they are taught something as simple as: Buenos días./Buenas tardes./ Buenas noches. The usual question from the students: why buenos and buenas and buenas? What is the difference? This seems to be a simple thing, but if we analyze the grammatical and lexical components used in these phrases we would realize that they are "adjectives and nouns" in which the use of gender and number is presented. So, considering this reality, the first thing we should do is to give students the response based on what is said, which does not take long. Then, and not to lose the first chance in helping students to begin acknowledging this necessary Spanish language-topic, giving to them as "a task" studying the didactic material that explains explicitly the use of gender and number in nouns-object/thing/place, definite/indefinite articles, and descriptive adjectives. It is necessary explain to students about this use as it will be required in the class on the alphabet. The class of the alphabet is often taught after the introduction of greetings and farewells. Well, here we have another chance to deepen further in teaching and learning these syntaxes. Ask students to make up an alphabet of nouns-object/thing/place, present it in class and then identify the gender of these words, this can be done through a game if desired, for which the new technologies (computer tools applications) can be used, for example, "Kahoot". During the class-topic-discussion set an exercise which consists in writing nous-phrases. For example, if the letter A is said and written the word "auto", with the use of definite/indefinite articles and descriptive-adjectives one can say/write a phrase: "El auto blanco"./Un auto blanco. These examples of phrases show the concordance between the articles + noun + adjectives and they are addressed to empower the acquisition of the linguistic competence with regard to the use of (gender, number, and word-order) in the writing and speaking context of Spanish language communication.

Example

Abecedario/Artículos D/I + Nombre + Adjetivo

A. auto _______ auto ___________

COMMUNICATIVE COMPETENCE APPROACH

The Communicative competence is the ability of a person to behave effectively and appropriately in a given speech; and this demands from speakers to have a good command of the language (grammar, vocabulary, phonetics, semantics) ext. Hence, it is impossible to ignore the role of "linguistic competence" in "communicative competence" if the speech requires the use of nouns-object/thing/place, definite/indefinite articles and descriptive adjectives. So, with emphasis on both, the linguistic/communicative-competences; we can provide to students a set of exercises based on Q/A that requires the obligatory use of these Spanish grammars themes:

Example

¿Qué es esto/eso/aquello?

Un libro/una pizarra/un lápiz/una goma

¿Cómo es el/la libro/goma?

Blanco-a./pequeño-a.

OBJECTIVE OF THE RESEARCH

The core intention of this study has been to provide a valuable script as reference for teaching and learning Spanish grammar on the topics of Nouns Object/Thing/Place, Definite and Indefinite Articles and Descriptive Adjectives. In line with the main objective of the manuscript the research article has displaced throughout its headings and sub-headings significant among of collected and added data which can validate the research article-literature and prove its authenticity. In order to corroborate confidentiality in the finding of this research-article; the results; discussion and conclusion as follow.

RESULTS AND DISCUSSION

This study was conducted based on close observations in teaching and learning Nouns Object/Thing/Place; Definite and Indefinite Articles; Descriptive Adjectives in Spanish language classes at Multimedia University (MMU), Malaysia. These observations were based on analyzing the acknowledgement of Spanish language own linguistic characteristics. The reference topics were the role of memory in SLA; the application of grammar; the act of communication. The results showed that Spanish 2L language learners whose native-language does not apply the grammar themes questioned in this research-article the way Spanish does are prone to commit mistakes in correctly applying them in Spanish. The reasons can be traced to factors such as learning-language-retention which cause is based on no acknowledging own language grammar characteristics; Direct and inappropriate translations; Insufficient knowledge about the usage of nouns-object/thing/place, definite/indefinite articles and descriptive adjectives; The influence of negative external sources in terms of learning choices and the design of specific teaching and learning Spanish grammar lessons to overcome the challenges that the current grammar teaching methodology (grammar must be acquired by students in an inductive way) suggested. Regarding methodology the study discussed the use of inductive and deductive approaches in teaching Spanish grammar and the significant of the methodology provided in this research article as appropriate vehicle in teaching and learning the Spanish grammar-themes highlighted. This reference-method has already been used in Spanish language classes conducted at Multimedia University (Malaysia). To validate its efficacy a statistical analysis was carried out among a group of students from level A1 once they had finished the course. This analysis was carried out through a set of questions. The questions were directed to investigate the level of understanding; acquisition; application of the linguistic aspects of Spanish grammar discussing in this manuscript. According to the responds the results showed a significant improvement in the acquisition and develop of cognitive skills and language competences. Thus, this study discussed the significant of acknowledging specific language characteristics in order to acquire and develop the linguistic-competence that involves the use of nouns-object/thing/place, definite/indefinite articles and descriptive adjectives in the speaking and writing context of Spanish language communication. Generally, this is focused “Spanish-grammar-topic”, and although the degree of difficulty that Spanish grammar presents has led many to drop out from Spanish school-classes and also stacking many students with regard to the study of the grammar, this discipline continues to be the arbiter that regulates the writing and speaking context of this language, irrespective of pragmatic and socio-cultural factors that also determine its use. Even though it is not an easy task for Spanish 2L language learners retain in their minds the use of gender and number and the words-order with which these Spanish grammar themes presented are treated in the writing and speaking context of Spanish language communication; the literature-content of this research-article-paper will allow these learners and Spanish language teachers managing the subject-matter discussed accordingly.

CONCLUSION

On examining the data provided throughout the headings and sub-headings in this research article, one could conclude that the manuscript contains significant literature sources corresponding to the main objective of the research article. The data presented in the manuscript contextualize clearly the subject-matter (Acknowledging Specific Language Characteristics). In this respect, the study has presented a suitable literature material and methods with emphasis on Spanish Language communication setting such as Nouns-Object/Thing/Place; Definite and Indefinite Articles and Descriptive Adjectives. Among many significant finding-results, the study has drawn the attention of a phenomenon (learning-language-retention) and its cause, which is an open door to be studied by the field of Neurolinguistics. By considering the professional view from other researchers about the interest shown among scholars related to the high level of complexities that these Spanish syntaxes present in terms of Second Language Acquisition (SLA), I would respectfully say that this study-research is a response to that concern and an upright-modest contribution letting at the disposition of readers and the specialized critics for its evaluation.

ACKNOWLEDGEMENTS

The author is very thankful to all the associated personnel in any reference that contributed in/for the purpose of this research.

FUNDING

The research is not funded through any source.

CONFLICTS OF INTEREST

The research holds no conflict of interest.

REFERENCES

1. (2015). Diccionario de la lengua española (23rd ed.). Madrid: Espasa.
2. American Council on the Teaching of Foreign Languages (2012). https://www.actfl.org/publications/guidelines-and-manuals/actfl-proficiency-guidelines-2012
3. Batchelor, R. E., José, S., & Ángel, M. (2010). A Reference Grammar of Spanish. Cambridge: Cambridge University Press.
4. Bialystok, E. (1981). The Role of Linguistic Knowledge in Second Language Use. Studies in Second Language Acquisition, 4, 31-45. https://doi.org/10.1017/S0272263100004265
5. Castañeda, A. (1997). Aspectos cognitivos en el aprendizaje de una lengua extranjera. Granada: Lingüística y Método.
6. Consejo de Europa (2001). Marco Común Europeo de Referencia para las Lenguas: Aprendizaje, enseñanza, evaluación. http://cvc.cervantes.es/obref/marco
7. Erichsen, G. (2015). Grammatical Differences between Spanish and English.
8. Gómez Torrego, L. (2006). Hablar y escribir correctamente: GramÁtica normativa del español actual.
9. Prince, M. J., & Felder, R. M. (2006). Inductive Teaching and Learning Methods: Definitions, Comparisons, and Research Bases. Journal of Engineering Education, 95, 123-138. https://doi.org/10.1002/j.2168-9830.2006.tb00884.x
10. Rivera, J. (2019). Applied Linguistic-Tú and Usted Spanish Personal Subject Pronouns. Open Journal of Modern Linguistics, 9, 12-24. https://doi.org/10.4236/ojml.2019.91002
11. Rutherford, W., & Sharwood Smith, M. (1988). Grammar and Second Language Teaching. A Book of Readings. Rowley, MA: Newbury House.

ADDITIONAL BIOGRAPHY

12. August, D., Calderón, M., & Carlo, M. (2002). The Transfer of Skills from Spanish to English: A Study of Young Learners. Washington DC: Center for Applied Linguistics.
13. Austin, J. L. (1962). Cómo hacer cosas con palabras. Barcelona: Paidós.
14. Azahares, F., & Miladys, T. (2011). Características del inglés cuyo

conocimiento puedes ser útil al que se dispone a estudiarlo.

15. Bachman, L. (1990). Habilidad lingüística comunicativa (pp. 105-129).
16. Berlok, K. D. (2008). El proceso de la comunicación (introducción a la teoría y la práctica). El Ateneo.
17. Bertuccelli, M. (1993). Qué es la pragmática. Barcelona: Paidós.
18. Calderón, M., August, D., Durán, D., Madden, N., Slavin, R., & Gil, M. (2003). Spanish to English Transitional Reading: Teacher's Manual. Baltimore, MD: The Success for All Foundation.
19. Canale, M., & Swain, M. (1980). Fundamentos teóricos de los enfoques comunicativos. Signos, 17, 56-61.
20. De Bruyne, J. (1996). A Comprehensive Spanish Grammar. Hoboken, NJ: Wiley-Blackwell.
21. Giovannini, A., Martín Peris, E., Rodríguez, M., & Simón, T. (1996). Profesor en acción 2. Madrid: Edelsa.
22. Gómez Torrego, L. (2006). Hablar y escribir correctamente: Gramática normativa del español actual.
23. Hymes, D. H. (1972). Acerca de la competencia comunicativa (pp. 27-47).
24. Jiménez, M., Antonio, J., Muñoz Marquina, F., Mora, S., & Ángel, M. (2011). Lenguaje y comunicación. Lengua Castellana y Literatura.
25. Ortega Olivares, J. (1990). Gramática, pragmática y enseñanza de lenguas. Granada: Actasdel I Congresode ASELE.
26. Pérez, Á., Sala, R., & Santamarina, M. (1994). Cassell's Contemporary Spanish. London: MacMillan.
27. Vermunt, J. D., & Verloop, N. (1999). Congruence and Friction between Learning and Teaching. Learning and Instruction, 9, 257-280. https://doi.org/10.1016/S0959-4752(98)00028-0

CHAPTER

11

A Shallow Parsing Approach to Natural Language Queries of a Database

Richard Skeggs, Stasha Lauria

College of Engineering, Design and Physical Sciences, Brunel University, London, UK

ABSTRACT

The performance and reliability of converting natural language into structured query language can be problematic in handling nuances that are prevalent in natural language. Relational databases are not designed to understand language nuance, therefore the question why we must handle nuance has to be asked. This paper is looking at an alternative solution for the conversion of a Natural Language Query into a Structured Query

Citation: Skeggs, R. and Lauria, S. (2019), "A Shallow Parsing Approach to Natural Language Queries of a Database". Journal of Software Engineering and Applications, 12, 365-382. doi: 10.4236/jsea.2019.129022.

Language (SQL) capable of being used to search a relational database. The process uses the natural language concept, Part of Speech to identify words that can be used to identify database tables and table columns. The use of Open NLP based grammar files, as well as additional configuration files, assist in the translation from natural language to query language. Having identified which tables and which columns contain the pertinent data the next step is to create the SQL statement.

Keywords: NLIDB, Natural Language Processing, Database Query, Data Mining

INTRODUCTION

With the quantity of real-time data and the speed of data increases the need to search and extract data from multiple sources is becoming more important. Natural Language Processing can be useful for converting natural language text into a formal structure that can be processed by a computer program.

The growth in size and importance of data within society has led to the development of a new range of tools to query, examine and analyse data. Even the increasing use of tools like Siri, Bixby, Alexa and Google Assistant to perform searches is changing the way users look for information. With large quantities of data stored within databases or databased backed repositories providing an interface between a non-technical user and data is becoming increasingly important.

The use of natural language interface to a database enables non-technical users to search a database using natural language statements, whether that is the spoken or written word. The Natural Language Interface to Database (NLIDB) provides the interface between a natural query and a structured data query language like SQL. This allows for data retrieval without the need for technical knowledge or a detailed understanding of the Structured Query Language (SQL) or even knowledge of the underlying database.

A number of systems such as LADDER, CHAT-80, NaLIX and WASP [1] have all been developed to become the interface between natural language and the database but none of them have come into mainstream use. The issues these tools have struggled with revolve around natural language complexity. The most common one of these complexities has been understanding language nuance [2] [3] [4] . Other issues have revolved around the performance of the interface in converting the natural language query not only in a timely fashion but also with the accuracy of the returned results [5] .

This paper is proposing a solution to solve both the language nuance [3] [6] and performance issues with the use of shallow parsing [7] , which does not require an understanding of language nuances. The shallow parsing approach being proposed by this paper is the use of keywords [8] to identify characteristics that are important for the search. This paper will introduce the use of an index file containing keywords that can be used to enhance the performance. Jwalapuram & Mamidi [5] are among a number of authors who have carried out research into using keywords to enable NLIDB based systems to perform searches.

The keyword searching proposed in this paper unlike Jwalapuram & Mamidi [5] uses Part of Speech (POS) [5] processing and an index file which allows for individual words to be extracted from the natural language query. The individually extracted words can then be used to create the query for the NLIDB solution.

FOOTBALL EVENTS DATA

To test the performance of the NLIDB application an open data set was selected for benchmarking. The website Kaggle.com has several openly available large datasets that can be used freely. The Football Events dataset was chosen and is available via the following link (https://www.kaggle.com/secareanualin/football-events). The data contains two tables which ensure that the feature to join two tables together can also be tested. The concept of being able to join two or more tables together is important as this feature is often useful when searching data repositories as data can be held across multiple tables.

The dataset comes in the form of two comma separated value (CSV) files which are labelled EVENTS and GINF. The events recorded in the tables cover 9074 football games from across Europe. The two tables are in CSV format which makes it easier to load into a database whether that is a no-SQL or RDBMS version. The EVENTS table as shown in Table 1 contains details about each game. The data has been scrapped from bbc.com, espn.com and onefootball.com and has 941009 recorded items. The GINF table, details are shown in Table 2 contains metadata and market betting odds for each game and contains 10,112 entries. The odds for the dataset were supplied by oddsportal.com.

The two tables can be joined using the common key ID_ODSP, which is the unique identifier for the game.

Table 1. The EVENTS table describes the structure of the events database. The details of the event types can be found in Appendix B.

Column Name	Data Type	Description
ID_ODSP	String	Unique id of the game
ID_EVENT	String	Unique identifier of event (ID_ODSP + SORT_ORDER)
SORT_ORDER	Number	Chronological sequence of events in a game
Time	Number	Minutes into the match
Text	String	Description of event
EVENT_TYPE	String	Primary event. 11 unique events (1-attempt (shot), 2-corner, 3-foul, 4-yellow card, 5-second yellow card, 6-(straight) red card, 7-substitution, 8-free kick won, 9-offside, 10-hand ball, 11-penalty conceded)
EVENT_TYPE 2	String	Secondary event. 4 unique events (12-key Pass, 13-failed through ball, 14-sending off, 15-own goal)
Side	String	Home or away team (1-home, 2-away)
EVENT_TEAM	String	Team that produced the event (In case of Own goals, event team is the team that beneficiated from the own goal)
Opponent	String	Opposing team
Player	String	Player involved
Player 2	String	Player involved
PLAYER_IN	String	Player that came in (only applies to substitutions)
PLAYER_OUT	String	Player substituted (only applies to substitutions)
SHOT_PLACE	String	Placement of the shot (13 possible placement locations, available in the dictionary, only applies to shots)
SHOT_OUTCOME	String	4 possible outcomes (1-on target, 2-off target, 3-blocked, 4-hit the post)
IS_GOAL	Boolean	binary variable if the shot resulted in a goal (own goals included)
Location	String	Location on the pitch where the event happened (19 possible locations, available in the dictionary)

Body Part	String	Body part ball touches (1-right foot, 2-left foot, 3-head)
ASSIST_ METHOD	String	In case of an assisted shot, 5 possible assist methods (details in the dictionary)
Situation	String	In case of an assisted shot, 5 possible assist methods (details in the dictionary)
FAST_ BREAK	Boolean	Did a fast break occur

Table 2. The GINF table describes the features of the GINF table.

Column Name	Data Type	Description
ID_ODSP	String	Unique ID of the game
LINK_ODSP	String	Link to odd sportal page
ADV_STATS	Boolean	Availability of advanced statistics
Date	Date	Date of event
League	String	The league the match was played in
Season	Number	The year the season finished
Country	Number	The country the match was played in
Ht	String	Home team
At	String	Way team
Fthg	Number	Full time home goals
Ftag	Number	Full time away goals
ODD_H	Number	Highest home win market odds
ODD_D	Number	Highest draw market odds
ODD_A	Number	Highest away market odds
ODD_OVER	String	Highest over 2.5 market odds
ODD_UNDER	String	Highest under 2.5 market odds
ODD_BTS	String	Highest both teams to score market odds
ODD_BTS_N	String	Highest both teams NOT to score market odds

PROPOSED CONFIGURATION

This paper is proposing to use three index files to aid the conversion from natural language query to SQL. The files being proposed are the Grammar file, Join file and Index file. The use of these files ultimately describes the structure of the underlying database which will become the target for searching, while providing an index like data structure that can be used to identify the database table(s) and table columns relevant for the database search.

The files describe in this section can be created either manually or through scripting. The grammar file should be created through the collection of queries that been used to query the underlying database. With a historic record of prior questions, the grammar file can be enhanced.

Figure 1 shows an overview of the proposed architecture for the NLIDB solution being discussed in this paper. The details of which will be expanded in this section, but the first step is to parse the incoming natural language query using the grammar file to identify parts of the query and to be able to tag individual words appropriately. The second step is to translate the natural language into an SQL statement. The join file and the index file contain the information about the database; details of this process are discussed below. The final step is the query itself. Having created the SQL query the next step is to execute the query against the database.

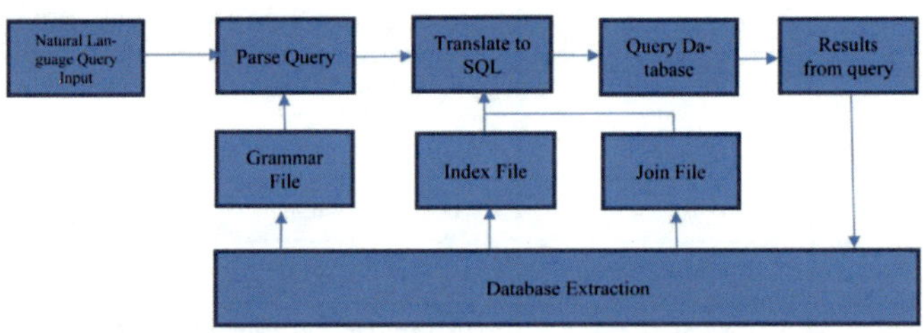

Figure 1. Shows an overview of the proposed system.

Grammar File

The database extraction process which provides data for the three configuration files manually extracts data from the target database. Thought the process is manual there is nothing about the structure of the configuration files nor the data used by the files which stop their creation from being automatic.

The first of these is the Apache Open NLP [9] grammar file which is used to identify words in the natural language query. The content from the database is used to create the grammar file, column names from the database tables and the database tables are used with the grammar file. Separate tags are assigned to each word which identifies words of importance that can be labelled as either a table name or column name. The convention for tags is that VB identifies a verb, N for noun and ADJ for adjective, a full list of tags can be found in Appendix A. The list of tags is used by convention rather than being statically defined, therefore custom tags can be created to fulfil a specific task. This paper uses a custom tag IRR to identify words that are irrelevant in the conversion from natural language to query language. In the example used for this paper, the grammar file is constructed from entries from both the GINF and EVENTS tables. Questions posed to the application are also used as part of the grammar file. Table 3 lists the column names from both source files that are used within the grammar file.

The index data extracted from the GINF table contain 10,643 entries which are made up of the original entries with some additional data. Entries from the Events table create an index file with 1201 unique entries in the data. The structure of the table is made up of potential questions that could be posed to the NLIDB application. Each word is assigned a tag representing how that word should be treated. The tags follow the appropriate word and are separated from it by an underscore.

The grammar file (an extract of which is Figure 2) for this paper uses a couple of tags, IRR which stands for irrelevant and ensures that the word will be ignored in the conversion from natural language to structure query language. The IRR tag is defined as being words or values not found within the underlying database as either table names, columns or values.

NP, which signifies that the word is important in the conversion process and states that is a value of significance and will be used within the search as this is the search criteria. Words tagged with AP signify the table that must be searched.

Table 3. Lists the entries extracted from the database for inclusion into the index file.

Events	GNIF
ID_ODSP	ID_ODSP
Side	Date
EVENT_TEAM	League
Opponent	Season

Player	County
Player 2	Ht
SHOT_PLACE	At
SHOT_OUTCOME	Fthg
	Ftag
	ODD_H
	ODD_D

```
Which_IRRevent_APhas_IRRabdoulaye#diaby_NPplayed_IRRin_IRR.

which_IRROpponent_APhas_IRRustaritz_NPfaced_IRR
what_IRRare_IRRthe_IRRodd_h_Non_IRRa_IRRgame_IRRwith_IRRan_IRRevent_APinvolving_IRRc
aro_NP
what_IRRare_IRRthe_IRRodds_Non_IRRan_IRRevent_APthat_IRRcaro_NPis_IRRinvolved_IRRwit
h_IRR
what_IRRare_IRRthe_IRRodd_h_Non_IRRan_IRRevent_APthat_IRRcaro_NPis_IRRinvolved_IRRwi
th_IRR
odd-h  N
event  AP
caro   NP
```

Figure 2. The table is an extract from the grammar file showing the data structure.

Finally, the tag N defines which column the search criteria could potentially be found in.

Index File

In addition, the grammar file is the index file. This file is currently created manually but there is nothing within the file that prevents its creation through automated scripts. The file contains elements from the database being searched; an extract from the index file is shown in Figure 3. The data is made up of three columns; the first column shows the relationship between the table, the table column and the database value. The index file uses the same tags as the grammar file to identify elements that are within the database such as the tables, columns and values. Figure 3shows that the AP tag is assigned to the value event, this represents the table. The second value is player which is assigned the tag N, which represents the column in the table. The third column shows a value in this case the name of a player (Abdoulaye Diaby) which has been assigned the tag NP.

From this, information the query is beginning to be built and simplistically the query is "select * from event". The second column describes which variable from the table to use as part of the condition. In the example below, the column is "player". This now means that the query is "select * from event where player =". The only element missing is the value to search on or in this case the player's name. This information comes from the third column labelled NP. From the extract in Figure 2, there is an extract of abdoulaye#diaby_NP, so the final query is now "select * from event where player = 'abdoulayediaby'".

```
event_APplayer_Nabdoulaye#diaby_NP

event_APplayer_Nabdoulaye#faye_NP
event_APplayer_Naboubakar#kamara_NP
event_APplayer_Nadam#federici_NP
event_APplayer_Naitor#cantalapiedra_NP
event_APplayer_Nalberto#garcia_NP
event_APplayer_Naleksandr#iakovenko_NP
event_APplayer_Nalende_NP
event_APplayer_Nalessandro#bastrini_NP
```

Figure 3. Extract from the index file.

Join File

The above example shows the first step into parsing a natural language query into simple SQL statement. Not all queries are that simplistic as some will require that tables are joined to extract the required data. A key aspect is how the joins between tables can be identified not just from the natural language query but also from the table structure. One possible solution is from the configuration within the index files.

This paper suggests using a join file which lists the table and the primary key for the table. This table (see Figure 4) allows two tables to be joined. The table contains two entries which are the table name and the primary key of the table. In the example below, both the Event table and the GINF table can be joined and both share the same primary key (ID_ODSP).

The process for creating the join file is manual but as discussed above in the section titled Proposed Configuration there is the possibility of automating this process. The caveat when creating an automatic script is to identify which tables have an identifiable relationship as well as what contrives to make that relationship. In the simple case discussed within this paper, the relationship is easy to identify and easy to create as only two tables exist. In larger more complicated database environments identifying these relationships may be harder to identify. Using deep learning techniques to identify which tables are related and how that relationship exists may be required.

CONVERSION STEPS

The solution proposed by this paper allows for the natural language query "What are the odds on a game involving caro?" to be converted into an SQL statement using the following steps:

1) Tag the natural language statement. The Open NLP tagger process takes the original statement and labels each word r component with a natural language tag. An example output from the tagging process will look like what_IRRare_IRRthe_IRRodds_NPon_IRRa_IRRgame_IRRevent_APinvolving_IRRcaro_NP.
2) Looking at Figure 1 the grammar file identifies that the word event has the tag "AP". The conversion process identifies AP as a table. Using this information, the first part of the query is "select * from event".
3) The next step taken by the proposed is to identify that the query should join the events and the GINF table together as the query is asking for odds from the GINF table and player (caro) from the events table. The join table specifies that the tables' event and ginf are joined by the column ID_ODSP. This creates the where clause "where event.id_odsp = ginf.id_odsp".
4) The final step is to identify that the player being searched for is "caro" (see above). This gives the final part of the query where player = "caro".
5) The query can now be joined into select * from events where event.id_odsp= ginf.id_odsp where player = "caro".
6) Currently, the select statement just uses "select * from". The next step is to retrieve just the requested data or columns from the database. Through the use and application of machine learning techniques it is anticipated that select everything could be reduced to selecting only relevant columns from the query.

```
event=id_odsp

ginf=id_odsp
```

Figure 4. The join properties file lists the table name with the primary key which allows multiple tables to be joined.

TRAINING THE MODEL

The Open NLP toolkit model uses machine learning algorithms at its core. Having created the configuration to be used as a model, the next step is training the Apache Open NLP model. Training the model is an important aspect of the Apache Open NLP process. The mathematical models used by the Open NLP application require that the model is trained. The training allows the model to perform the word tagging using the grammar file more accurately than would have been otherwise achieved. The machine learning models used by Open NLP for training include maximum entropy and perceptron-based machine learning.

The use of a maximum entropy model as described by Ratnaparkhi [8] , ensures that the model best represents the current state of knowledge. The current state of knowledge in the case of the model proposed by this paper is the training set of questions being asked by users to query the underlying data repository.

The solution allows for more questions to be added as the process evolves. The additional questions can be added as part of an automated process or manually. Each question added would need to be tagged and the process retrained. This allows for the continued evolution of the system.

The tagging model used for this solution is the Part of Speech (POS) tagger which converts every word into a token. Each token has an associated tag. Open NLP will use a probability model to predict the correct tag for each word in the sentence. The fewer the tags used the quicker the performance, this can be seen from testing and appears to be supported by Taghipour [10] but more thorough performance testing is required. The tests that were carried out were performed on whole sentences, which included tags that can be identified as having a database related value. An example of this would be where the name of a database table or table column appears in the natural language query. In the case of the natural language query "Which event has Abdoulaye Diaby played in.", "event" is an identifiable database table. The sentence can then be processed, and relevant tags will be applied to the parts of the query (see Table 1), irrelevant tags will be ignored.

The Open NLP model training task process output: The output from training the model against the grammar file, which contains the list of potential asked questions that is shown in Figure 5.

As can be seen from the training output, the test was run against a training file with approximately 36,000 entries that were processed and indexed. From the 36,432 source entries, 11,666 were identified as either significant or unique. The number of outcomes in Figure 5 refers to the number of possible outcomes from the model. For the shallow parsing approach proposed by this paper, the number is not significant. Though not significant for this paper the number of predicates could indicate the number of sentences in the data frame. The predicate identifies what is happening with the subject of a sentence. Though this might be helpful when trying to understand the content or meaning of the sentence for the shallow parse approach being taken by this paper the number of predicates is inconsequential.

EVALUATION

During the evaluation phase of the proposed system, the idea was to measure the performance of the natural language conversion to SQL. The Java Virtual Machine (JVM) usage was monitored and the code profiled. The details of the proposed system performance are discussed in this section.

```
Indexing events using cutoff of 5


    Computing event counts...  done. 36432 events
    Indexing...  done.
Sorting and merging events... done. Reduced 36432 events to 11666.
Done indexing.
Incorporating indexed data for training...
done.
    Number of Event Tokens: 11666
        Number of Outcomes: 3
      Number of Predicates: 2241
...done.
Computing model parameters ...
```

Figure 5. The output from the training model.

Computer System

The computer used for the development and testing of the application is of a standard desktop configuration. The very utilitarian nature of the computer used for developing and testing this solution supports the concept that the conversion process does not require a large, expensive dedicated server. The specifications of the test machine for the natural language to SQL conversion are shown in Table 4.

Java Virtual Machine

The Java Machine used for the development and testing of the application is again a standard build. The application does run on a single JVM instance, the settings for which are shown in Figure 6.

Performance Results

The profiling of software allows for some tangible method to measure software excellence [11] [12] . The tests performed on the software show the resources used for converting a natural language query into a SQL based query. A number of tools have been employed to monitor the performance of the application which includes Java Visual VM from Oracle, YourKit Java Profiler, and the Coverage tool from JetBrains IntelliJ Java IDE. These tools highlight the computer resources used by the code in terms of virtual memory allocation and call time per function.

```
JVM: OpenJDK 64-Bit Server VM (25.152-b8, mixed mode)

Java: version 1.8.0_152-release, vendor JetBrains s.r.o
Java Home: C:\Program Files\JetBrains\IntelliJ IDEA Community Edition 2017.3.1\jre64
JVM Flags: <none>
-Xms24m
-Xmx256m
-Dsun.jvmstat.perdata.syncWaitMs=10000
-Dsun.java2d.noddraw=true
-Dsun.java2d.d3d=false
-Dnetbeans.keyring.no.master=true
-Djdk.home=C:\Program Files\Java\jdk1.8.0_25
-Dnetbeans.home=C:\Program Files\Java\jdk1.8.0_25\lib\visualvm\platform
-Dnetbeans.user=C:\Users\rskeggs\AppData\Roaming\VisualVM\8u20
-Dnetbeans.default_userdir_root=C:\Users\rskeggs\AppData\Roaming\VisualVM
-XX:+HeapDumpOnOutOfMemoryError
-XX:HeapDumpPath=C:\Users\rskeggs\AppData\Roaming\VisualVM\8u20\var\log\heapdump.hprof
-Dsun.awt.keepWorkingSetOnMinimize=true
-Dnetbeans.dirs=C:\Program Files\Java\jdk1.8.0_25\lib\visualvm\visualvm;C:\Program
Files\Java\jdk1.8.0_25\lib\visualvm\profiler
```

Figure 6. The shows the setting for the Java Virtual Machine on the test server. The output was taken from the Java Visual VM application version 1.8.0_25 (build 140407).

Table 4. Server specifications.

Variable	Value
Operating System	Windows 7 Enterprise
Service Pack	SP1
Processor	Intel® Core™ i5-4570 CPU @3.2GHz
Installed Memory	8.00 GB
System Type	64-bit Operating System

The concept of benchmarking software performance provides a tangible metric to evidence the performance of a software solution as supported by Sims et al. [12] . The benchmarking work carried out by Siewiorek et al. [13] highlights the fact that monitoring memory is key to understanding the performance of a software solution. These techniques update the work by Gama et al. [14] and Whaley [15] .

The YourKit Java profiler was used to measure the CPU of a conversion from a natural query to SQL. The profile modelled the application through the required classes as part of the execution cycle. Figure 6 shows the performance in milliseconds that each class takes to complete a task. Figure 7 shows just how much of the code gets executed when converting a simple natural language query to an SQL statement. For the simple example used as part of the test the execution time to convert the natural language query to SQL took a total of 665 milliseconds.

The Java Visual VM tool provides detailed information about Java applications while being executed on a Java Virtual Machine. The performance figures highlight the fact that no specialist hardware is required to run the process, which could be hosted on commodity hardware. To substantiate this Figure 7 shows the screenshot from of the Visual Machine usage, that the largest resource allocation during testing was 42 Mb which accounted for 51% of all memory allocations by the virtual machine. Running tests against larger data will use more resources but the need to move to specialist hardware may not be a requirement, though further testing will need to be conducted to determine more accurately resource requirements. Tuning for performance in high throughput environments can also be managed by distributing resources across a platform when bottlenecks are identified. More in depth testing will need to be carried out to understand where and when these limits are reached (Figure 8).

Having completed a conversion and extraction of data from the dataset the next step was to compare performance the system discussed in this paper with other comparable systems. For this, the paper by Joshi, Akerkar [7] which proposed a similar approach using a Part of Speech based algorithm for converting natural language into an extraction-based query. The researchers compared the performance for two systems and the results are summarised in Table 5.

Table 5. Shows the performance figures from Joshi, Akerkar [7]

Type of Data No. of Words	Time Required by QTAG (Used in Enlight)	Time Required by Minipar (Used in Sapere)
News Extract Times of India (202 Words)	1.71 secs	2.88 secs
Reply START QA System (251 Words)	1.89 secs	3.11 secs

University Information NMU Broacher (226 Words)	1.55 secs	2.86 secs
Brazil Information Source: Wikipedia (226 Words)	1.67 secs	3.13 secs
Average	1.705 secs	2.995 secs

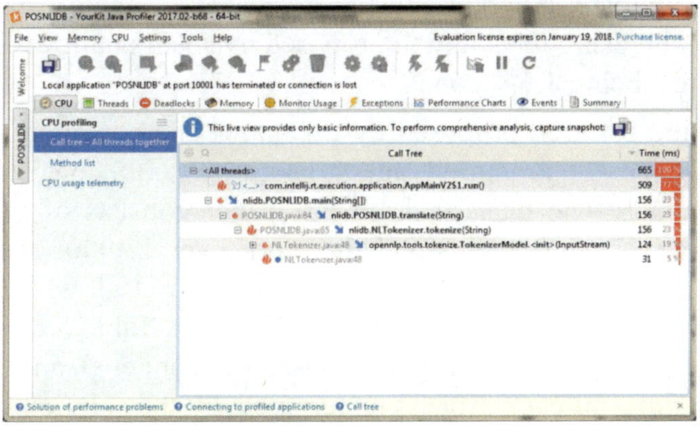

Figure 7. Shows the execution time the conversion process took courtesy of the YourKit Java Profiler.

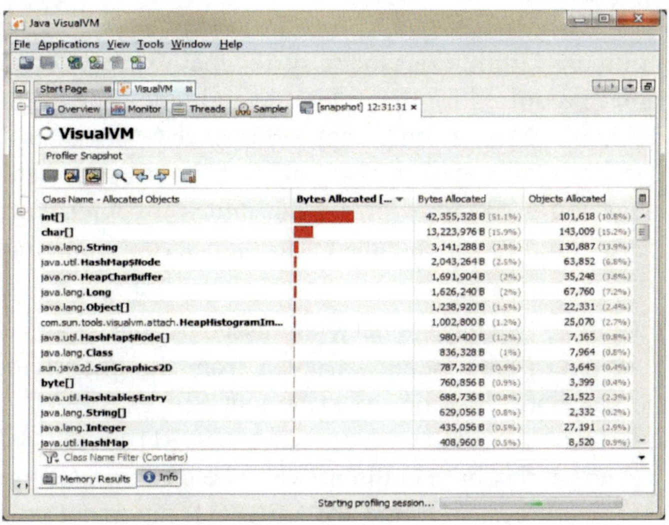

Figure 8. This shows the memory allocation of the NLIDB process. Courtesy of Oracle's Java VisualVM.

The paper [7] did not specify the specification of the computer used to carry out the benchmark. The questions used by the paper [7] were taken from the TREC-2005 Question Database but there was some ambiguity in identifying the actual datasets used for the benchmarking. In comparison, this paper has taken a much larger dataset and has added the additional complexity of creating a join between two tables. The natural language questions used by this paper were of a similar complexity to the questions used in testing carried out by Joshi, Akerkar [7] and are listed in Table 6. The average conversion time using the solution proposed by Joshi et al. was 1.7 seconds with the fastest being 1.5 seconds.

Testing the solution proposed by this paper the conversion time from natural language to structured query language took consistently under 700 milliseconds. The datasets from this paper consists of two files one containing over 36,000 events and the other over 11,000 (see Figure 5). Where also larger than the datasets used by Joshi et al. as these datasets contained approximately 220 records (see Table 5). Table 5 also shows the completion of time for the solution proposed by Joshi et al. and Table 7 also contains the times of each process to complete by the solution discussed in this paper. In summary, the tables highlight the improvements in performance the approach being taken by the paper as over existing solutions.

CONCLUSIONS

There are a number of limitations to the system being proposed in this paper. The storage space required for the index file and index file might make this solution unworkable. More testing against larger datasets is also required to understand the limitations and performance of the proposed solution. This paper has suggested a solution for joining tables together. Further testing would also be required to validate the performance of joining more than two tables.

The biggest issue that has not been addressed by this paper is that around the selection of data points being retrieved from the underlying database. Currently, the solution relies on the statement SELECT * which retrieves all data points from the tables being searched. Retrieving data from all columns in the target database could prove to be costly in terms of memory and processing resources. Refining the SELECT statement could possibly be achieved through the use of deep learning techniques. It may be possible to identify columns in tables that have a higher probability of being selected.

Table 6. Sample questions used for performance comparison by Joshi, AkerKer [7] .

Who killed militants?
Who did Forman defeat for his first heavyweight championship?
What do frogs eat?
Who visited Bill Clinton?
Who did France beat for the World Cup?
What Shiite leaders were killed in Pakistan?
What is the largest volcano in the Solar System?
What is the longest river in the world?

Table 7. Performance from the proposed system which includes the conversion from natural language to SQL.

College	SQL Conversion	Data Extraction
ginf.csv (19531 Words) events.csv (13697026 Words)	0.665 secs	0.9 secs

Regardless of the identifiable short comings from the proposed system, the paper has reinforced the benefits of using part of speech within a framework that translates natural language into a query language for searching a database. Performance of NLIDB solutions has been an issue that researchers are continually trying to improve upon [1] [3] [5] [7] [16] . As can be seen from this paper the performance of the proposed system is an improvement on the performance recorded by Enlight and Sapere (Table 7).

The shallow nature of the parsing through the use of the natural language part of speech also reduces the need to understand the complexity underpinning language nuance. Further work will be carried out to improve the performance of the proposed system as well as reduce the number of identifiable shortcomings. The proposed work will look at the use of deep learning to refine the select statement.

Conflicts of Interest

The authors declare no conflicts of interest regarding the publication of this paper.

APPENDIX A

The standard list of tags and definitions used by Apache Open NLP (These tags are not a definitive list and are used by convention).

CC Coordinating conjunction

CD Cardinal number

DT Determiner

EX Existential there

FW Foreign word

IN Preposition or subordinating conjunction

JJ Adjective

JJR Adjective, comparative

JJS Adjective, superlative

LS List item marker

MD Modal

NN Noun, singular or mass

NNS Noun, plural

NNP Proper noun, singular

NNPS Propernoun, plural

PDT Predeterminer

POS Possessive ending

PRP Personal pronoun

PRP$ Possessive pronoun

RB Adverb

RBR Adverb, comparative

RBS Adverb, superlative

RP Particle

SYM Symbol

TO to

UH Interjection

VB Verb, base form

VBD Verb, past tense

VBG Verb, gerund or present participle

VBN Verb, past participle

VBP Verb, non 3rd person singular present

VBZ Verb, 3rd person singular present

WDT Whdeterminer

WP Whpronoun

WP$ Possessive whpronoun

WRB Whadverb

APPENDIX B

The data is from the dictionary text file. The data contains a dictionary with the textual description of each categorical variable coded with integers event_type.

1) Announcement
2) Attempt
3) Corner
4) Foul
5) Yellow card
6) Second yellow card
7) Red card
8) Substitution
9) Free kick won
10) Offside
11) Hand ball
12) Penalty conceded

EVENT_TYPE 2

13) Key Pass
14) Failed through ball
15) Sending off
16) Own goal

SIDE
1) Home
2) Away
SHOT_PLACE
1) Bit too high
2) Blocked
3) Bottom left corner
4) Bottom right corner
5) Centre of the goal
6) High and wide
7) Hits the bar
8) Misses to the left
9) Misses to the right
10) Too high
11) Top centre of the goal
12) Top left corner
13) Top right corner
SHOT_OUTCOME
1) On target
2) Off target
3) Blocked
4) Hit the bar
LOCATION
1) Attacking half
2) Defensive half
3) Centre of the box
4) Left wing
5) Right wing
6) Difficult angle and long range
7) Difficult angle on the left
8) Difficult angle on the right

9) Left side of the box
10) Left side of the six yard box
11) Right side of the box
12) Right side of the six yard box
13) Very close range
14) Penalty spot
15) Outside the box
16) Long range
17) More than 35 yards
18) More than 40 yards
19) Not recorded

BODYPART

1) right foot
2) left foot
3) head

ASSIST_METHOD

1) None
2) Pass
3) Cross
4) Headed pass
5) Through ball

SITUATION

1) Open play
2) Set piece
3) Corner
4) Free kick

REFERENCES

1. Soumya, M.D. and Patil, B.A. (2017) An Interactive Interface for Natural Language Query Processing to Database Using Semantic Grammar. International Journal of Advance Research, Ideas and Innovations in Technology, 3, 193-198. [Citation Time(s):2]
2. Kim, M. and Kim, H. (2018) Dialogue Act Classification Model Based on Deep Neural Networks for a Natural Language Interface to Databases in Korean. IEEE International Conference on Big Data and Smart Computing, Shanghai, 15-17 January 2018, 537-540. https://doi.org/10.1109/BigComp.2018.00090 [Citation Time(s):1]
3. Bais, H., Machkour, M. and Koutti, L. (2018) An Arabic Natural Language Interface for Querying Relational Databases Based on Natural Language Processing and Graph Theory Methods. International Journal of Reasoning-Based Intelligent Systems, 10, 155-165. https://doi.org/10.1504/IJRIS.2018.092221 [Citation Time(s):3]
4. Li, Y.Y. and Rafiei, D. (2017) Natural Language Data Management and Interfaces: Recent Development and Open Challenges. Proceedings of the 2017 ACM International Conference on Management of Data, Chicago, 14-19 May 2017, 1765-1770.https://doi.org/10.1145/3035918.3054783 [Citation Time(s):1]
5. Jwalapuram, P. and Mamidi, R. (2017) Domain Independent Keyword Identification for Question Answering. International Conference on Asian Language Processing, Singapore, 5-7 December 2017, 95-98. https://doi.org/10.1109/IALP.2017.8300554 [Citation Time(s):5]
6. Voorhees, E.M. (2001) The TREC Question Answering Track. Natural Language Engineering, 7, 361-378. https://doi.org/10.1017/S1351324901002789 [Citation Time(s):1]
7. Joshi, M.R. and Akerkar, R.A. (2008) Algorithms to Improve Performance of Natural Language Interface. International Journal of Computer Science and Applications, 5, 52-68. [Citation Time(s):8]
8. Ratnaparkhi, A. (1996) A Maximum Entropy Model for Part-of-Speech Tagging. In: Conference on Empirical Methods in Natural Language Processing, Association for Computational Linguistics, Stroudsburg, 133-142.http://aclweb.org/anthology/W/W96/W96-0213 [Citation Time(s):2]
9. Baldridge, J. (2005) The OpenNLP Project. http://opennlp.apache.org/ [Citation Time(s):1]

10. Taghipour, K. and HweeTou, N. (2015) One Million Sense-Tagged Instances for Word Sense Disambiguation and Induction. In: Proceedings of the Nineteenth Conference on Computational Natural Language Learning, Association for Computational Linguistics, Beijing, 338-344. https://doi.org/10.18653/v1/K15-1037http://www.aclweb.org/anthology/K15-1037 [Citation Time(s):1]
11. Deuter, A. and Hans-Jürgen, K. (2015) Applying Manufacturing Performance Figures to Measure Software Development Excellence. In: Software Measurement, Lecture Notes in Business Information Processing, Springer, Cham, 62-77. https://doi.org/10.1007/978-3-319-24285-9_5 [Citation Time(s):1]
12. Sim, S.E., Easterbrook, S. and Holt, R.C. (2003) Using Benchmarking to Advance Research: A Challenge to Software Engineering. 25th International Conference on Software Engineering, Portland, 3-10 May 2003, 74-83.https://doi.org/10.1109/ICSE.2003.1201189 [Citation Time(s):2]
13. Siewiorek, D.P., Hudak, J.J., Suh, B.H. and Segal, Z. (1993) Development of a Benchmark to Measure System Robustness. The 23rd International Symposium on Fault-Tolerant Computing, Toulouse, 22-24 June 1993, 88-97.https://doi.org/10.1109/FTCS.1993.627311 [Citation Time(s):1]
14. Gama, K., Pedraza, G., Lévêque, T. and Donsez, D. (2011) Application Management Plug-Ins through Dynamically Pluggable Probes. Proceedings of the 1st Workshop on Developing Tools as Plug-Ins, Waikiki, 28 May 2011, 32-35.https://doi.org/10.1145/1984708.1984718 [Citation Time(s):1]
15. Whaley, J. (2000) A Portable Sampling-Based Profiler for Java Virtual Machines. Proceedings of the ACM Conference on Java Grande, San Francisco, 3-4 June 2000, 78-87.https://doi.org/10.1145/337449.337483 [Citation Time(s):1]
16. Brad, F., Iacob, R., Hosu, I. and Rebedea, T. (2017) Dataset for a Neural Natural Language Interface for Databases (NNLIDB). Proceedings of the 8th International Joint Conference on Natural Language Processing, Vol. 1, 13 p.http://arxiv.org/abs/1707.03172 [Citation Time(s):1]

CHAPTER 12

A Comparative Study to Understanding about Poetics Based on Natural Language Processing

Lingyi Zhang[1] and Junhui Gao[2]

[1]Wuxi No. 1 High School, Wuxi, China

[2]American and European International Study Center, Wuxi, China

ABSTRACT

This paper tries to find out five poets' (Thomas Hardy, Wilde, Browning, Yeats, and Tagore) differences and similarities through analyzing their works on nineteenth Century by using natural language understanding technology and word vector model. Firstly, we collect enough poems from these five poets, build five corpus respectively, and calculate their high-frequency words, by using Natural Language Processing method. Then, based on the

Citation: Zhang, L. and Gao, J. (2017), "A Comparative Study to Understanding about Poetics Based on Natural Language Processing". *Open Journal of Modern Linguistics*, **7**, 229-237. doi: 10.4236/ojml.2017.75017..

word vector model, we calculate the word vectors of the five poets' high-frequency words, and combine the word vectors of each poet into one vector. Finally, we analyze the similarity between the combined word vectors by using the hierarchical clustering method. The result shows that the poems of Hardy, Browning, and Wilde are similar; the poems of Tagore and Yeats are relatively close—but the gap between the two is relatively large. In addition, we evaluate the stability of our approach by altering the word vector dimension, and try to analyze the results of clustering in a literary (poetic) perspective. Yeats and Tagore possessed a kind of mysticism poetics thought, while Hardy, Browning, and Wilde have the elements of realism combined with tragedy and comedy. The results are similar comparing to those we get from the word vector model.

Keywords: Poets, Natural Language Processing, Word Vector Model, Similarity, Cluster Analysis

INTRODUCTION

Deep Learning is a new field in machine learning, a learning method based on the representation of data. The concept is derived from the study of artificial neural networks. By combining low-level features to form a more abstract high- level representation of attributes, categories, or features, the aim is to discover the distribution of data.

The earliest neural network in deep learning originated from the MCP artificial neuron model in 1943 (Bryant, 2016), which was used to simulate human neuronal responses by computers at that time. In 1958, Rosenblatt invented the perceptron algorithm that used MCP for machine learning (Rhys, 2017).

The deep learning in natural language began in 2006 when Hinton proposed the concept of Deep Belief Network (DBN) (Imagination Tech, 2017). Previously, the neural network was a complex one that was difficult to train, and only studied as a mathematical theory. In addition, Word vector model is the most common model used in natural language deep learning process. The core idea of this model is to symbolize the language into 1 and 0, a mode that is suitable for machine learning.

Andrew L et al. used a probabilistic model of documents, which learns semantically focused word vectors, to learn the word representations to encode word meaning—semantics (Maas, Andrew, & Ng, 2011).

Mikolov et al. proposed two new model structures for computing continuous vector representations of words from very large data sets to measure the similarity between syntactic and semantic words, and the results are compared to the previously techniques based on different types of neural networks (Mikolov, Chen, Corrado, & Dean, 2013).

Attabi et al. studied the effectiveness of anchor models to solve multiple emotion recognition problems from speech, based on the FAU AIBO Emotion Corpus—a database of spontaneous children's speech. Compared with generative model such as the Gaussian Mixture Models, the anchor models improve significantly the performance of GMMs by 6.2 percent relative in such problems (Attabi & Dumouchel, 2013).

Sreeja et al. discussed the automatic recognition of emotions in English poems, which included Love, Sad, Anger, Hate, Fear, Surprise, Courage, Joy and Peace, by using the Vector Space model with a total of 348 poems of 163 poets mined from the web (Sreeja & Mahalakshmi, 2016).

Zhou Yingying et al. conducted experiments on the Chinese Quora—Zhihu— by using the topic2vec vector model in Chinese corpora. They found out that the convolutional neural network (CNN) with topic2vec gained an accuracy of 98.06% for long content texts, 93.27% for short time texts and an improvement comparing with other word embedding models (Zhou & Fan, 2016).

According to a series of previous study in deep learning of natural language, we can find that some have studied the syntax and semantics of text on the basis of word vector models. Some, based on the study of their predecessors, compared the efficiency of different models applied to the similar task. Others did detailed research such as using plenty of poems as corpora to carry out emotion recognition. Based on the study above, we will use the traditional word vector model for comparative poetics study.

MATERIALS AND METHOD

We will describe them from data, word vector calculations, and comparative approaches among poets in the following content.

Materials

Four of the five selected poets are from England, including Thomas Hardy, Wilde, Browning, and Yeats. The one left is Tagore, a poet from India. We selected a total of 257 poems from Thomas Hardy (Poemhunter, 2017), 96 poems from Oscar Wilde (Poemhunter, 2017), 63 poems from Browning

(Blackcatpoems, 2017), nearly 400 poems from (Yeats, 1951 ; Blake, 2002), and 86 poems from Tagore (Tagore, 2011).

The main reason for selecting the five poems is to avoid the errors caused by all sorts of differences. Firstly, the origin version of poems of their works are all in English. In this way, we do not need to translate their works in which we get the second-hand poems containing the translation errors in order to get accuracy results from analysis. Secondly, the gaps between their living years are very small since nearly all of their works are produced in early nineteenth Century to mid twentieth Century, which was the golden years of the development of European poetry. Thus, the problems which may be caused by the differences between archaic words and modern words can be effectively avoid. For example, in old English, poets used "thou" in lieu of "you" to express you's nominative form and "thee" in lieu of "you" to express you's accusative form. The five poets who all gathered during nineteenth Century and twentieth Century almost eliminate the use of old English, although some old words may also appear in their poems rarely. In other words, we will not choose to compare Beowulf with Mark Twain's The Million Pound Note because they do not belong to different language systems at various times.

Word Vector Calculation

Although the research of natural language has already existed, traditional natural language study is a basic bottom-up study, from words, sentences, and paragraphs, and finally to the structures of text, but still can not let the computers understand the natural language well. One of the obstacles is the poor understanding of semantics. Before word2vec occurred, the research of semantic in NLP was mainly based on the understanding of latent semantic (LSA, Latent Semantic Analysis), and then its subsequent model (topic model) was introduced (Niketim, 2016).

Word2vec and topic models are completely different things. In the topic model, the basic granularity is still the word, and the topic is a probabilistic combination of words.

The semantics mined from the topic model of the article is at high level. In word2vec, however, the word "fundamental granularity" has a new expression, which is called the word vector (word embedding).

Before the occurrence of word vector, we often used the method called 1-of-N (or one-hot). In this representation, the great majority of elements is

0, and only one dimension is 1. This dimension represents the current word. Suppose that we have five words in our table: King, Queen, Man, Woman, Child. If we want to represent 'Queen', we can express it in 1-of N, as shown in Table 1.

This simple method has two drawbacks. One is the curse of dimensionality. Another is a phenomenon called "lexical gap", namely the isolation between any two words, and is unable to judge a synonym like "microphone" and "Mike".

The new method of word representation is called Distributed Representation. This method in representing word uses the position of a real vector to represent a word such as [0.792, −0.177, −0.107, 0.109, −0.542, …], as shown in Table 2.

For each poet, we combine all the poems we collected, and construct the corpus by NLTK. Then, the corresponding word vectors are generated by Word2vec.

Natural Language Toolkit, referred to as NLTK, is a Natural Language Processing kit and a often used Python library in NLP, which was developed by Steven Bird and Edward Loper in the information science department at University of Pennsylvania (Baike, 2017).

Comparative Approaches among Poets

For each poet, we find the common high-frequency words of him and other poets, and assume that each high-frequency word is a 100 dimensional vector, and finally combine all the vectors into one corresponding to the high-frequency words.

Then, we calculate the distance between the five vectors by cosine method. The cosine similarity is derived by the cosine value of the angle between the two vectors in the vector space to measure the difference between the two individuals.

Table 1. Expression in 1-of-N.

0	1	0	0	0
King	Queen	Man	Woman	Child

Table 2. Distributed Representation.

	King	Queen	Woman	Princess	...
Royaling	0.99	0.99	0.02	0.98	...
Mascalining	0.99	0.05	0.01	0.02	...
Feminin	0.05	0.93	0.999	0.94	...
Age	0.7	0.6	0.5	0.1	...
...	...	...	...	...	...

The closer the cosine is to one, the more the angle is closer to zero degrees, namely the close resemblance between the two vectors. This is called "cosine similarity" (Yuhushangwei, 2016).

After we get the distance between the five poets, the value is subtracted by 1, and we consider this value as the similarity between the five poets. Afterwards, we employ cluster analysis to analyze the relationship between the five poets. The difference between clustering and classification is that the classes divided by clustering are unknown. Clustering is a process that classifies data into different classes or clusters, so the objects in the same closer have great similarity, while objects between different clusters have great diversity. From the point of view of statistics, clustering analysis is a way to simplify date through data modeling.

There are many kinds of clustering methods, and here we use hierarchical clustering. This method decomposes the given date set as a hierarchical level until reaching a certain condition. Concretely, it can be divided into two programs: condensed and split. Hierarchical agglomerative cluster is a bottom-up strategy. Firstly, take each object as a cluster, and then combine these clusters into bigger clusters until all the objects are in one cluster, or a certain condition is reached. The great majority of the hierarchical clustering method belongs to this class, and only the definitions of the similarity between clusters are different. Split level clustering is opposite to hierarchical agglomerative cluster, by using strategy of top-down. It will first put all the objects into one cluster, and then gradually subdivided them into smaller clusters until each object form a cluster, or a certain condition is reached.

RESULTS

We will show our results from three aspects: statistics of high-frequency word, similarity calculation, and cluster analysis.

Statistics of High-Frequency Word

The statistics of the high-frequency words of the five poets are shown in Table 3. This table is arranged from left to right, and from top to bottom. The word in the upper left corner has the highest number of occurrence, which is 1225; The word in the lower right corner has the minimum number of occurrence, which is 392.

Similarity Calculation

We set the word vector dimension to 100, then calculate the word vector, and finally compare the similarity between the five poets, as shown in Table 4.

Cluster Analysis

Based on Table 4, we use hierarchical clustering, and the results are shown in Figure 1.

Table 3. Public High-Frequency Words (first 20).

word	times	word	times	word	times	word	times
one	1225	come	715	know	530	shall	432
would	999	day	661	time	504	upon	420
like	941	life	623	king	480	never	416
said	821	man	584	old	442	night	399
heart	786	love	531	could	441	let	392

Table 4. Similarity between the Five Poets.

	brown-ing	hardy	tagore	wilde	yeats
brown-ing	1.00	0.79	0.22	0.81	0.26
hardy	0.79	1.00	0.54	0.78	0.54
tagore	0.22	0.54	1.00	0.34	0.61
wilde	0.81	0.78	0.34	1.00	0.40
yeats	0.26	0.54	0.61	0.40	1.00

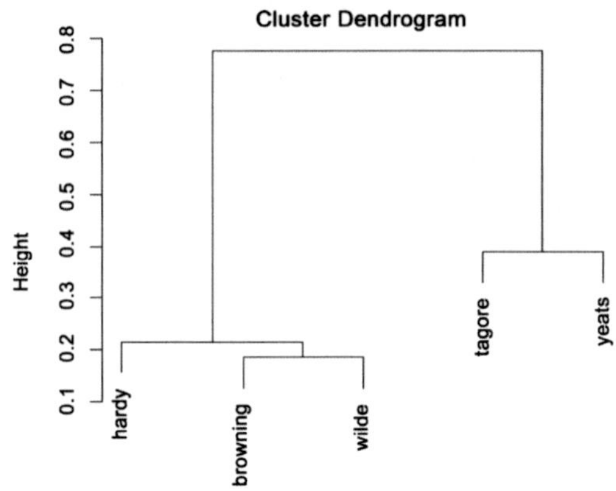

Figure 1. A Hierarchical Clustering Map of Five Poets by a 100 Dimensional Vector Model.

In Figure 1, the abscissa is five poets. The ordinate is the distance between those poets. The shorter the distance between the poets, the higher the similarity. From Table 1, Hardy, Browning, and Wilde are similar, with the difference of about 0.2, especially the latter two. Tagore and Yeats are close to each other, with the difference of about 0.4, not as close as the first three poets. However, the difference between the group of Hardy, Browning and Wilde and the group of Tagore and Yeats is large, with the value between 0.7 and 0.8 (the largest difference is 1).

DISCUSSION

As mentioned earlier, we talked about the definition of 100 dimensional computational vector of word, and obtained the results in Tables 1-4. In order to test the stability of the results, we also use 80 dimension and 120 dimension to calculate the word vector, and the result we get from the calculation is very close to that of 100 dimension. Take 120 dimension as an example. The clustering result we obtain is shown in Figure 2. The results of Figure 1 and Figure 2 are very close to each other, indicating that our method is stable and reliable.

From a literary perspective, Tagore is a patriotic poet, and his works reveal his patriotism and the spirit of Democracy. Yeats showed the reverence to Aestheticism and Romanticism in his early years. After he experienced the nationalist political movement in Ireland in his forties, the style of his poetry gradually went close to realism.

Tagore and Yeats developed their friendship because of poetry. They shared many points of view in literature. First of all, Tagore and Yeats had direct contacts in life. In 1912, they met each other due to "Gitanjali". Yeats admired Tagore's talent very much, and helped Tagore publish this collection and made the preface of it. Second, both of them possessed a kind of mysticism poetics thought. Tagore's belief is a mixture of religious philosophy while Yeat's belief is derived from his natural disposition, which is personal philosophy. Third, although they are modern poets, they do not belong to Modernism since both of them criticize the modernist literature in their poems. Therefore, the results we obtained from literary appreciation are similar to those gained from the cluster analysis above (Wang, 2012).

Wilde is one of the representative poets of aestheticism, with fairy tales as the main characteristic. His poems are full of the elements of duality, which shows the simultaneism of aesthetics and tragedy. Wilde is good at describing the contradiction between characters and the cruel social background. His tragic beauty and death consciousness contain his understanding about life (Sun, 2012).

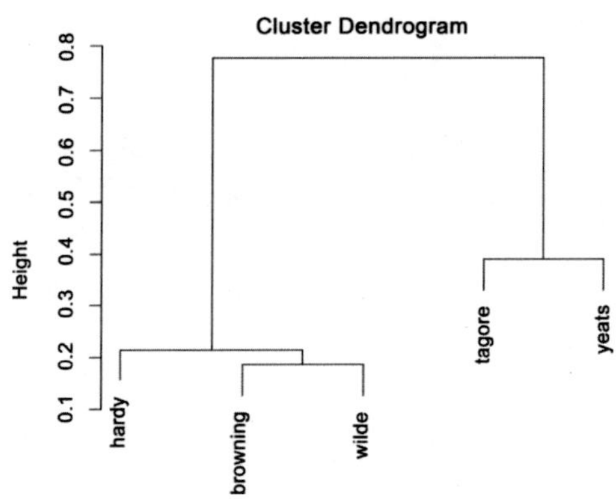

Figure 2. A Hierarchical Clustering Map of Five Poets by a 100 Dimensional Vector Model.

Likewise, the poems of Thomas Hardy also have tragic color, which is mostly the natural revelation of personal experience and emotion. Hardy believes that society is the root of pain; the personality of human beings leads to the suffering in the world; and the destiny is controlled by the universe. The analysis of these unique perspectives illustrates the ubiquitous tragedy and distress in his poems (Ma, 2009). Robert Browning is a British poet and a playwright. He creates a unique from of poetry, referred to as "dramatic monologue", using a cinematic narrative technique-Montageto restructure and integrate time and space. Browning loves to show the changes in characters' psychological and story scenes through personal confession. Owning the color of the mixture of tragedy and comedy, His poems express the complexities of the characters and their attitudes of life. To sum up, although the styles of the three poets belong to different genres, all of them do well in depicting tragedies, and showing the irreconcilable contradictions between man and society (Zhang, 2007). Thus, the results we obtained from literature perspective are similar to those gained from the cluster analysis above.

The main contribution of our work is that this research is the first work to study different poets' works by using the word vector model, which is pioneering and original. The drawback is that the number of the poets we used is limited. Also, the poet's geographical distribution was not uniform enough since of the five poets, four of them came from England, and one left came from India. Finally, the dimensions we used are limited that we only employed 80, 100, and 120 the three dimensions to calculate their difference, but larger ones have not been used.

CONCLUSION

This paper uses vector model and hierarchical clustering in deep learning to investigate the similarities between the works of the five poets—Thomas Hardy, Oscar Wilde, Robert Browning, William Yeats, and Rabindranath Tagore—in the nineteenth Century. Our research contributes to the field which combines mathematical analysis and literary analysis together. High frequency words picked from the five poets are analyzed by the word vector model in 100 dimensions. The results show that the poems of Hardy, Browning, and Wilde are similar; the poems of Tagore and Yeats are relatively close. We also have employed other dimensions such as 80 and 120 to test the stability of our results, which have been proved reliable then. In addition, we have obtained the similar results by analyzing the works of the poets from a literary perspective which indicate their similarity in the interpretation of the tragedy, and the conflicts between men and the society.

REFERENCES

1. Attabi, Y., & Dumouchel, P. (2013). Anchor Models for Emotion Recognition from Speech. IEEE Transactions on Affective Computing, 4, 1-11. https://doi.org/10.1109/T-AFFC.2013.17
2. Baike (2017). Natural Language Toolkit. https://baike.baidu.com/item/NLTK/20403245?fr=aladdin
3. Blackcatpoems (2017). Robert Browning. http://www.blackcatpoems.com/b/robert_browning.html
4. Bryant, L. J. (2016). The History of Deep Learning. CSDN Blog. http://blog.csdn.net/u012177034/article/details/52252851
5. Imagination Tech (2017). The History and Problems of Deep Learning in Natural Language. http://www.sohu.com/a/161325083_468740
6. Ma, L. (2009). On the Topics of Tradedy, Love & Marriage, and Christianity in Thomas Hardy's Novels and Poetry. M. Thesis in Aesthetics, Tianjing Normal University, 8-11.
7. Maas, A. L., & Ng, A. Y. (2011). A Probabilistic Model for Semantic Word Vectors. 1-8.
8. Mikolov, T., Chen, K., Corrado, G., & Dean, J. (2013). Efficient Estimation of Word Representations in Vector Space. Computer Science, 1-12.
9. Niketim (2016). The Introduction of Word Vector. CSDN Blog. http://blog.csdn.net/u013362975/article/details/53319002
10. Poemhunter (2017). Oscar Wilde Poems. https://www.poemhunter.com/oscar-wilde
11. Poemhunter (2017). Thomas Hardy Poems. https://www.poemhunter.com/thomas-hardy
12. Rhys (2017). Rosenblatt's Perceptron Algorithm. http://blog.sina.com.cn/s/blog_166b82f8b0102xcu3.html
13. Sreeja, P. S., & Mahalakshmi, G. S. (2016). Comparison of Probabilistic Corpus Based Method and Vector Space Model for Emotion Recognition from Poems. Asian Journal of Information Technology, 15, 908-915.
14. Sun, C. W. (2012). Literature Review of Research on Wilde's Works in the Past Thirty Years (pp. 1-4). Shenyang: Liaoning University.
15. Tagore, R. (2011). Gitanjali. Annals of Neuroscience, 18, 66.
16. Wang, X. S. (2012). The Comparison of Tagore and Yeats' Poetic Thoughts (pp. 1-3). M.Sc. Thesis, Chongqing: Chongqing Southwest

University.

17. Yeats, W. B. (1951). The Collected Poems of W.B. Yeats. Wordsworth Poetry Library, 1, 118-134.
18. Yuhushangwei (2016). The Calculation Method and Application of Cosine Similarity. http://blog.csdn.net/yuhushangwei/article/details/48541891
19. Zhang, W. (2007). On the Cinematic Narrative Feature of Robert Browning's Poetry (pp. 5-7). M.Sc. Thesis, Hangzhou: Zhejiang University.
20. Zhou Y. Y., & Fan, L. (2016). Deep Learning on Improved Word Embedding Model for Topic Classification. Computer Science and Application, 6, 629-637. https://doi.org/10.12677/CSA.2016.611077

CHAPTER

13

Computers and Language Learning

Junia Rocha[1], Alexsandro Soares[2], Mauro Honorato[3], Luciano Lima[4], Nayara Costa[4], Elvio Moreira[5], Eduardo Costa[4]

[1]Department of Informatics, Federal Institute of Triangulo Mineiro, Patos de Minas, Brazil

[2]Department of Computer Science, Federal University of Uberlandia, Uberlandia, Brazil

[3]Department of Informatics, Federal Institute of Sao Paulo, Barretos, Brazil

[4]Department of Electrical Engineering, Federal University of Uberlandia, Uberlandia, Brazil

[5]Department of Education, Federal University of Uberlandia, Uberlandia, Brazil

Citation: Rocha, J. , Soares, A. , Honorato, M. , Lima, L. , Costa, N. , Moreira, E. and Costa, E. (2015), "Computers and Language Learning". Creative Education, 6, 1456-1465. doi: 10.4236/ce.2015.613146..

ABSTRACT

This paper investigates how computers together with Internet technologies help people in the learning of languages. To achieve this goal, it analyses open source libraries that a teacher can use to build educational applications. The text contains a short discussion on how to build such tools, using methods of programming proposed by Richard Stallman and Paul Graham. It also shows that computers help to improve language skills in those children with low reading abilities. Finally, it provides an overview of linguistic and computational tools that a teacher can use to check a student's grammar. Of course, in order to build a practical grammar checker, the reader must have a working knowledge of Lisp and Prolog. In few words, the reader will not only see the magic of programs that understand English grammar, but learn how one can reproduce it.

Keywords: Rasch Model, Natural Language Processing, Automatic Grammar Checker

INTRODUCTION

When one hears about computer aided language learning, she thinks immediately in Artificial Intelligence, and machines that can talk, translate all English Wikipedia entries to Esperanto, perform automatic caption, and accept speech-to-text input. Everybody knows that such intelligent applications exist, and help millions of people in their dealings with a multi-language world. Therefore a large portion of the present paper concerns Artificial Intelligence and programming. However, the greatest help that computers bring to language learning is the possibility of publishing books.

While doing graduate studies in Cornell in the seventies, one of the authors of this work dedicated himself to space science and linguistics. His main concern at the time was learning Ancient Greek. As a space scientist, he had access to good computers to perform numerical calculations. However, electronic publishing did not exist at the time, and the powerful Cray computer available to engineers was of little use for reproducing Greek documents.

In 1984, Donald Knuth made TeX available (Knuth, 1984) . TeX allowed for the typeseting of Greek books. Therefore, students could learn to read Greek by typesetting their own edition of Plato's Republic.

With the invention of eInk, publishing a book became even easier. Now students can carry around whole libraries in a device weighting less than

200 g. While reading a book, the student can touch a word whose meaning is unknown, and get its definition in 20 languages.

Another way that computers help language learning is to connect learners to native speakers through the Internet. For instance, the authors observe that children that are learning Chinese in the United States spontaneously contact people living in China.

Computer aided language learning has two kinds of tool. Typesetting, dictionary construction and connectivity do not require Artificial Intelligence. On the other hand, automatic caption, translation and speech-to-text input require a good deal of artificial intelligence.

Let us end this section with a short discussion on programming. Students of computer science learn their trade by trying to write programs from scratch. In summary, the students open a blank buffer in a text editor like emacs and start filling it with code. Stallman (2015) thinks that such an approach is wrong. In his opinion, the student should start with an open software application, and adapt it to her needs, fix bugs and extend its functionality. To make a long story short, if the computer scientist does not start with the accumulated work of linguists and teachers, she is doomed to failure.

There are many open source tools that a language teacher can use to build parsers. The easiest of these to install and use is the open source version of RASP (Briscoe, 2015) . In order to make this conversation easier, let us introduce Nia, a fictitious female character that performs natural language processing for a living. Nia downloads and expands the archive in her work space, and runs the Makefile script in the application home directory.

```
~/wrk/rasp3os$ make
```

Since Nia has a limited knowledge of shell commands, she asks for help from Bob and Alice, who work in the Cryptography Department, as anyone familiar with the world of Computer Science fictitious characters already knows. After a few minutes, there appears the Clozure Common Lisp together with the RASP system in Nia's machine. Nia checks what comes ready to go.

```
~/rasp3os/scripts$ echo "cats chase rats" | ./rasp.sh -p'-os'
(|cat+s:1_NN2| |chase:2_VV0| |rat+s:3_NN2|) 1 ; (-8.936)
sparkle: 1
("S" ("NP" "cat+s:1") ("VP" "chase:2" ("NP" "rat+s:3")))
```

It seems that, after learning Lisp, Nia will be able to build a simple grammar checker on top of RASP.When dealing with languages, one needs a parser. Following Stallman philosophy, the parser should be open source and written in a language that facilitates contributions from the linguist. The computer languages that satisfy this last requisite are Lisp and Prolog.The focal point of this introductory section is that one should not start a programming project on an empty buffer. The most effective approach to programming is to build code on top of existing tools, as recommended by Richard Stallman.

LISP

A small team that wants to write an educational natural language application should rely on one of the libraries available on line. However, it is a good idea to build a small prototype, in order to learn programming, and understand how libraries work.

Lisp has two features that one cannot find in other languages, and makes it specially suitable for Artificial Intelligence. For one thing, Lisp has a strong mathematical foundation. Mathematics does not become obsolete. People use books written by Gauss 200 years ago, or by Archimedes, 2000 years ago, and they are considered state of the art. Although Lisp is the oldest computer language that is widely used, the very best works in Artificial Intelligence are coded in Lisp even today. After all, Lisp has remained unchanged for decades, while generations of mathematicians and physicists add code to complex applications.The syntax of Lisp is extremely simple: Programs and data are represented by a list of elements between parentheses. When that list represents a program snippet, the first element is an operation, i.e., a command or a function call. When a list is data, it is prefixed by a quotation mark. Let us define a small vocabulary, and a few syntax rules.

```
;; Store this program in file cyk.lisp

(defparameterwrds
          '((cat n)
            (rat n)
            (thedet)
            (to prep) (chasestverb)))

(defparameter rules
          '( (pp prep np)
             (npdet n)
             (svtverbnp)
             (phrasenpsv)))
```

The parameter words represents a list of words, where each word is associated with its grammatical class. For example, cat is a noun, therefore its dictionary entry is the sublist (cat n). The grammar is written in the so called Chomsky Normal Form. The rule (npdet n) means that a noun phrase is made of a determiner followed by a noun.

Representing the dictionary and the grammar as lists means that the computer would need to loop through all entries. Loops are both inefficient and hard to code. They should be used only when necessary. Dictionary lookup must be performed with a hash table.

```
;; Continuation of the cyk.lisp file

(defparameter gr (make-hash-table :test 'equal))

(defparametervy (make-hash-table :test 'equal))

(loop for (hd nt1 nt2) in rules do(setf (gethash (list nt1 nt2) gr) hd))

(loop for (w cat) in wrds do (setf (gethash w vy) cat))
```

The above snippet creates two hashtables, that use the lisp predicate #'equal for comparison. This predicate is able to check whether two lists are equal.

To test the program, the linguist needs a text editor and a lisp. The text editor must be emacs. One can find emacs and the sbcl Lisp on the Internet.

Since Nia has already installed the RASP library, she decided to use it. A Read Eval Print Loop prompt appears on the window. Below one can see how Nia tested the program.

```
~/wrk/rasp3os$ bin/x86_64_darwin/ccl
Welcome to Clozure Common Lisp Version 1.8-r15286M
? (load "cyk.lisp")
#P"/Users/ufu/wrk/rasp3os/cyk.lisp"
? (gethash 'cat vy)
N
T
? (gethash '(det n) gr)
NP
```

It seems that everything is working fine. Now Nia will write a snippet that retrieves grammar rules, and use them to rewrite an input list. Of course, with such a small vocabulary in the hash table, the input sentence must be something like the cat chases the rat.

```
(defunrp(s) (gethash (list (first s) (second s)) gr ))

(defunky(input)
        (loop for s = input then (if (rp s) (cddr s) (cdr s))
          for hd = (if (rp s) (rp s) (car s)) while s collect hd))

(defunnxt(fn s &optional (z (funcallfn (car s))))
          (if (equal (car s) z) s (nxtfn (cons z s))) )

(defunnr (n) (lambda(guess)
        (- guess (/ (- (expt guess 2) n)(* guess 2.0))) ))

(defun tree(words)
        (nxt #'ky (list(loop for w in words collect (gethash w vy) ) words)))
```

Lisp has an extremely simple syntax: The first element of a list is the operation and the other elements are arguments. For instance, (rp s) picks the left hand side of a rule, (first s) produces the first element of s, and so on.

The nxt program repeatedly applies a function to the first element of a series until the series converges to a fixed value. Before proceeding to syntactical analysis, let us test the nxt program with a subject that is easier than natural language, something like mathematics.

The nr is the famous Newton algorithm that calculates the square root of a number. Before trying to understand it, Nia checks whether it works.

```
* (load "cyk.lisp")
T
* (nxt (nr 16) #'equal '(3))
(4.0 4.0000014 4.003333 4.1666665 3)
* (car '(a x b e))
a
* (cdr '(a x b e))
(x b e)
* (cons 'top '(a x b e))
(top a x b e)
```

It seems that it works. The series converges to the square root of 16. Function nxt finds the limit of a series by repeatedly applying a function that adds the next element of a series to the head of list s. Of course, Nia will not learn Lisp in a short paper. However, she can understand an amazing fact. One can represent almost everything with lists. Nia has seen that she can use lists to represent grammar, sentences, arithmetic series and syntactical trees. Besides this, one needs only four functions to process lists.

The car and the cdr, in the theory of algebraic data types, are called selectors. These two functions take a list apart: (car s) calculates the head of s, while (cdr s) calculates the tail, which is the remaining part of the list when its first element is removed. The (cons a s) is called constructor, and builds a list whose car is a and the cdr is s. The predicate (null s) checks whether a list is empty.

Function nxt keeps adding elements to the head of the list until an element converges to the same value as the previous one. Function fn calculates the next element of the series. Nia noticed that fn is passed as a parameter to nxt. This is necessary because this fn changes from one application to another.

Expression (nr n) builds a function that calculates the next approximation of the square root of n. Yes, Lisp functions can build other functions as easily as Python builds intergers.

Lisp has two mechanisms that allow programs to build programs: closures and macros. There are two books that one can use to learn more about closures and macros. The first one was written by Paul Graham(Graham, 1993) . Nia prefers Paul Graham's book, but the most popular one is Practical Common Lisp, by Peter Seibel (Seibel, 2005) .

Let us go back to English grammar. One can use nxt to build a series of syntactic trees that converge to the representation of a phrase.

```
~/wrk/rasp3os$ rlwrap bin/x86_64_darwin/ccl
Welcome to Clozure Common Lisp Version 1.8-r15286M
? (load "infix.cl")
#P"/Users/ufu/wrk/rasp3os/infix.cl"
? (load "cyk.lisp")
#P"/Users/ufu/wrk/rasp3os/cyk.lisp"
? (tree '(the cat chases the rat))
((PHRASE) (NP SV) (NP TVERB NP)
(DET N TVERB DET N)
(THE CAT CHASES THE RAT))
```

The function ky picks each pair of symbols and checks whether there is a grammar rule able to rewrite the pair. After reading the first and second chapter of Practical Common Lisp, the interested reader will have no problem in understanding this short program.

RECOVERING FROM BLIND ALLEYS

The problem with the parser described in program cyk. lisp is that the choice of a grammar rule may lead the algorithm down a blind alley, where there is no way to backtrack from the mistake. What is worse, the deterministic cyk algorithm has no mechanism to choose a rule with high probability of success. In fact, it does not even deal with probability.

Most people implements the cyk algorithm with arrays. This paper shows a list based implementation, because one can easily add backtrack to stateless data structures such as lists. The interested reader can use the screamer library to build a backtracking version of the cyk. lisp parser.

The work that gave rise to this paper uses both probabilities and backtrack. The rule with greatest probability of success is chosen first. This point deserves a comment. Consider the following rule:

$$S \rightarrow NP\ VP$$

The probability of S is the product of the probability of the rule by the probabilities of the subtrees NP and SP. To overcome the problem of estimating the probabilities of NP and VP before the full expansion of the tree, one solution is to accept backtracking in case of failure. With backtracking, a rough estimation of the subtree probabilities is acceptable.

ASSESSMENT

The previous section states that the probability of a construction occurring is used to resolve ambiguities in the grammar formalism. The main contribution of the present paper is a method for calculating the probability of a student committing a given mistake. To unify the framework, one describes mistakes as grammar rules. For instance, there are grammar rules for the lack of agreement between the verb and its subject. Therefore, a set of rules accept a sentence like The cat chase mouses, and tags it as a mistake.

In order to estimate probabilities, the teacher needs to model the student, and assess his/her evolution. The method explained here is amply used to evaluate learning.

In any kind of measurement, there is a variable that one wants to evaluate. Variables like weight, temperature or height can be measured directly with scales, thermometers, measuring tapes, calipters, etc. Unobservable variables like skill and difficulty are not so easy to measure. One can describe such latent variables, but cannot compare them to a standard meter, since they lack physical dimensions. However, one needs to assess them to appraise student evolution.

In order to estimate the value of a latent variable, Rasch, Lord and Lazarsfeld developed independently a branch of statistics known as Measurement Theory. There is strong evidence found in Measurement Theory that leads educators to consider its superiority over classical test theory. Therefore, making it the preferred method for scoring high stake tests, like SAT.

Scales

Let us consider two students C and V. Suppose a teacher wants to discover the most common types of errors her students commit. In order to do this, one needs to compare the ability of the student in relation to a given grammatical rule.

The teacher's best option would be to write a grammar for mistakes. Let us examine exactly what a grammar for mistakes is. A very commoner or among students of English as a Second Language is lack of agreement between subject and verb. For instance, the subject may be in the third person singular and the verb in the plural: She walk in beauty. One can write a grammar that accepts this kind of sentence, and use it to compare how often it appears in texts that two students C and V have written. Let us ignore those results where both C and V commit the same mistake or both of them avoid it.

At first glance, it may seem strange that the counter ignores when an instance of the error occurs with both students. To understand that such a procedure does not alter the distance between the two students, let us consider Table 1.

C committed this particular kind of mistake 5 times. V made the mistake 8 times. The difference is 3. If one ignores the cases where both C and V hit the mistake together, then the final count for C drops to 2, and for V is reduced to 5. The difference between them is still 3.

The probability of C committing a mistake r is given by P_{cr} and the probability of avoiding it can be calcu- lated by $(1-P_{cr})$. On the other hand, the probabilities of V committing and avoiding the mistake are given by P_{vr} and $(1-P_{vr})$ respectively. Let N_{10} be the notation of how many times C stumbles upon a mistake and V avoids it. On the same token, let N_{01} denote the number of times that C makes a mistake and V stays away from it. The ratio between N_{10} and N_{01} is given below

$$\frac{N_{10}}{N_{01}} = \frac{P_{cr} \times (1 - P_{vr})}{(1 - P_{cr}) \times P_{vr}}$$

Specific Objectivity

One can say that C is more prone to mistakes than V if the rate N_{10}/N_{01} does not change with the kind of mistake. This property is called specific objectivity and when it holds, one has the equality below.

$$\frac{P_{cr} \times (1 - P_{vr})}{(1 - P_{cr}) \times P_{vr}} = \frac{P_{cs} \times (1 - P_{vs})}{(1 - P_{cs}) \times P_{vs}}$$

Odds is the ratio of the probability of an event occurring to the probability of it not occurring. One can rewrite this equality in order to obtain the odds of C committing the mistake r

$$\frac{P_{cr}}{(1 - P_{cr})} = \frac{P_{cs}}{(1 - P_{cs})} \times \frac{(1 - P_{vs})}{P_{vs}} \times \frac{P_{vr}}{(1 - P_{vr})}$$

Origin

The next step is to choose the origin for the measurement scales that one intends to introduce. Let us consider a student o whose tendency to make mistakes matches the easiness of anitem o. In this case, the student will stumble upon the mistake in half of the trials, and the error will fail to defeat the student for the other half. This student is said to be at the origin of the inability scale, and the item is at the origin of the easiness scale. Since the student commits the mistake half of the times, the probability of failure is $P_{oo} = 0.5$. Let us compare C with the student of the origin.

$$\frac{P_{cr}}{(1 - P_{cr})} = \frac{P_{co}}{(1 - P_{co})} \times \frac{(1 - P_{oo})}{P_{oo}} \times \frac{P_{or}}{(1 - P_{or})}$$

Since P_{00} is 0.5 one has that $(1 - P_{oo})/P_{oo} = 1$. Therefore

$$\frac{P_{cr}}{(1 - P_{cr})} = \frac{P_{co}}{(1 - P_{co})} \times \frac{P_{or}}{(1 - P_{or})}$$

Let's take the logarithm from both sides of this equation

$$\ln\left(\frac{P_{cr}}{(1-P_{cr})}\right)=\ln\left(\frac{P_{co}}{(1-P_{co})}\times\frac{P_{or}}{(1-P_{or})}\right)$$

$$\ln\left(\frac{P_{cr}}{(1-P_{cr})}\right)=\ln\left(\frac{P_{co}}{(1-P_{co})}\right)+\ln\left(\frac{P_{or}}{(1-P_{or})}\right)$$

$$\ln\left(\frac{P_{cr}}{(1-P_{cr})}\right)=\ln\left(\frac{P_{co}}{(1-P_{co})}\right)-\ln\left(\frac{(1-P_{or})}{P_{or}}\right)$$

If one defines

$$F_c=\ln\left(\frac{P_{co}}{(1-P_{co})}\right)$$

$$E_r=\ln\left(\frac{(1-P_{or})}{P_{or}}\right)$$

The equation becomes:

$$\ln\left(\frac{P_{cr}}{(1-P_{cr})}\right)=F_c-E_r$$

Notice that F_c does not depend on the grammar rule r and E_r does not depend on the student c. This finding is the greatest contribution made by Georg Rasch to the Measurement Theory (Wright & Mok, 2004) .

The definition of the logarithm yields the following expression for the odds of committing a given mistake:

$$\frac{P_{cr}}{(1-P_{cr})}=e^{F_c-E_r}$$

$$P_{cr}=e^{F_c-E_r}-P_{cr}\times e^{F_c-E_r}$$

$$P_{cr}\times\left(1+e^{F_c-E_r}\right)=e^{F_c-E_r}$$

$$P_{cr}=\frac{e^{F_c-E_r}}{\left(1+e^{F_c-E_r}\right)}\ \text{Logistic equation}$$

One often refers to parameters F_c and E_r as an individual's inability and an item easiness respectively.

Table 1. VS agreement, where 1 represents a mistake.

C	1	0	0	1	0	0	1	1	1	0
V	1	1	1	0	1	1	0	1	1	1

Calibration

In the previous section, the reader saw that probability depends on parameters like easiness and inability. Calibration is thus the process of determining these parameters. To meet this goal, an iterative algorithm must force raw data onto the logistic curve.

The first step of the iteration calculates row and column averages to estimate initial easiness and inability vectors for the data matrix Xn.

```
(defparameterXn
        #2A (1.0 1.0 0.0 1.0 0.0)
       (0.0 0.0 1.0 1.0 0.0)
       (0.0 1.0 1.0 1.0 1.0)
       (0.0 0.0 1.0 0.0 0.0)
       (0.0 0.0 0.0 1.0 0.0)
       (0.0 0.0 1.0 1.0 1.0) ))

(defparameter d0 (array-dimension Xn 0))

(defparameter d1 (array-dimension Xn 1))

(defun hits(m)
         (make-array (list d0) :initial-contents
           (loop for i from 0 below d0 collect
            (loop for j from 0 below d1
       when #i(m[i,j]==1) sum 1.0 into s1
              finally (return #i(s1 /d1))) )))

(defunina_logit
          (vet&optional (v_logit (make-array d0)))
          (loop for i from 0 below d0 do
       #i(v_logit[i]=log(vet[i]/(1-vet[i])))) v_logit)

(defun misses(m)
         (make-array (list d1) :initial-contents
           (loop for j from 0 below d1 collect
            (loop for i from 0 below d0
       when #i(m[i,j]==1) sum 1.0 into s1
              finally (return #i(s1 / d0))) )))

(defuneas_logit(vet &optional(v_logit(make-arrayd1)))
         (loop for i from 0 below d1 do
        #i(v_logit[i]=log((1-vet[i])/vet[i]))) v_logit)
```

The next step is to adjust the easiness vector by subtracting the average from each element. The function probability calculates the odds, and stores its value in a two dimensional array.

```
(defunavg-vector (vet)
    (loop for x across vet
    sum x into s count x into c
      finally (return (/ s c))))

(defunadj_dif_logit (vet avg)
    (map 'vector (lambda(x) (- x avg)) vet))

(defun probability (A Dadj&optional (m (make-array (list d0 d1))))
    (loop for i from 0 below d0 do
      (loop for j from 0 below d1 do
    #i(m[i,j] := (exp (A[i] - Dadj[j])) /
              (1.0 + (exp (A[i] - Dadj[j])))) )) m)
```

In order to update the inability and easiness vectors,one must calculate the residual between the current andthe previous probability matrix.

```
(defun residual(mi me &optional (rs (make-array (list d0 d1))))
    (loop for i from 0 below d0 do
      (loop for j from 0 below d1 do
    #i(rs[i,j] := mi[i,j] - me[i,j]) )) rs)

(defunresidual_sum(m &optional (sum (make-array d0)))
    (loop for i from 0 below d0 do
      (loop for j from 0 below d1 do
    #i(sum[i]:=sum[i]+m[i,j]))) sum)
```

Now, one needs to calculate the variance of the probability matrix.

```
(defun variance (m &optional (mv (make-array (list d0 d1))))
    (loop for i from 0 below d0 do
      (loop for j from 0 below d1 do
    #i(mv[i,j]:=m[i,j]*(1-m[i,j])))) mv)

(defunsum_row_mat(m)
    (make-array (list d0) :initial-contents
      (loop for i from 0 below d0 collect
        (loop for j from 0 below d1 sum
          #i(-m[i,j])))) )

(defunsum_col_mat(m)
    (make-array (list d1) :initial- contents
      (loop for j from 0 below d1 collect
        (loop for i from 0 below d0 sum
    #i(-m[i,j])))) )
```

After summing up the residual and variance for each of the two dimensional arrays along each row, one is ready to update the easiness and inability vectors. These steps must be repeated until the sum of the squares of the residuals becomes sufficiently small.

```
(defunnewF(A rsvrc
        &optional (nAbil (make-array d0)))
         (loop for i from 0 below d0 do
        #i(nF[i]:=A[i]-rs[i]/vrc[i])) nF)

(defunnewE (D rsvrc&optional (nDif (make-array d1)))
         (loop for i from 0 below d1 do
        #i(nE[i] := D[i]-rs[i]/vrc[i]) ) nE)
```

The calibration algorithm produces Table 2 containing the probabilities of each student committing a given mistake.

CONCLUSION

The authors are convinced that natural language processing has reached a stage that makes building of automatic grammar checking possible. Another interesting application of these new technologies is the construction of models that facilitate the planning of grammar drilling. The abstract of the present paper was written by a person with limited knowledge of English, and corrected by natural language processing tools. The reader will find the original text below.

Table 2. Probabilities.

	You + is	She + go	It + stay	He + have	She + give	Inability
Porgy	0.2329	0.4890	0.8640	0.9525	0.4890	0.6810
Std 2	0.0784	0.2113	0.6401	0.8489	0.2113	−0.5463
Std 3	0.5267	0.7781	0.9588	0.9866	0.7781	1.9686
Std 4	0.0185	0.0561	0.2831	0.5550	0.0561	−2.0104
Std 5	0.0185	0.0561	0.2831	0.5550	0.0561	−2.0104
Std 6	0.2329	0.4890	0.8640	0.9525	0.4890	0.6810
Easiness	2.0564	0.8420	−1.2528	−2.4914	0.842	

This paper investigates how computers and communication can help people in learning languages. The authors will present both tools developed by themselves and by third parties. The text contains a short discussion on how to build such tools, using methods of programming proposed by Richard Stallman and Paul Graham. A longitudinal survey that the authors performed along three decades shows how computers improved the language learning environment. This article will provides enough information about linguistic and libraries for the reader building a program able to check of English prose composition. Of course, in order to build a practical grammar checker, the reader must have a working knowledge of Lisp and Prolog. In fewer words, this article intends not only to show the magic of programs that understand English grammar, but reveal how one can reproduce the effects.

REFERENCES

1. Briscoe, T., Buttery, P., Carroll, J., Medlock, B., Watson, R. Andersen, O., & Parish, T. (2015). RASP, a Robust Parsing System for English. Cambridge: iLexIR. http://users.sussex.ac.uk/~johnca/rasp/
2. Graham, P. (1993). On LISP: Advanced Techniques for Common LISP. Upper Saddle River, NJ: Prentice Hall.
3. Knuth, D. E. (1984). The TEXbook. New York: Addison-Wesley Professional.
4. Seibel, P. (2005). Practical Common Lisp. New York: Apress. http://dx.doi.org/10.1007/978-1-4302-0017-8
5. Stallman, R. (2015). The Best Way to Learn Programming. https://www.youtube.com/watch?v=dvwkaHBrDyI
6. Wright, B. D., & Mok, M. M. C. (2004). An Overview of the Family of Rasch Measurement Models in Introduction to Rasch Measurement (pp. 1-24). Maple Grove: JAM Press.

SECTION 4
NATURAL LANGUAGE PROCESSING IN MOBILE COMPUTING

CHAPTER
14

Automatic Approach of Sentiment Lexicon Generation for Mobile Shopping Reviews

Jun Feng[1], Cheng Gong[1], Xiaodong Li[1] and Raymond Y. K. Lau[2]

[1]College of Computer and Information, Hohai University, Nanjing 211100, China

[2]Department of Information Systems, City University of Hong Kong, Hong Kong

ABSTRACT

The dramatic increase in the use of smartphones has allowed people to comment on various products at any time. The analysis of the sentiment of users' product reviews largely depends on the quality of sentiment lexicons. Thus, the generation of high-quality sentiment lexicons is a critical

Citation: Jun Feng, Cheng Gong, Xiaodong Li, and Raymond Y. K. Lau, "Automatic Approach of Sentiment Lexicon Generation for Mobile Shopping Reviews", Journal on Wireless Communications and Mobile Computing, Volume 2018, Article ID 9839432, 13 pages, https://doi.org/10.1155/2018/9839432.

topic. In this paper, we propose an automatic approach for constructing a domain-specific sentiment lexicon by considering the relationship between sentiment words and product features in mobile shopping reviews. The approach first selects sentiment words and product features from original reviews and mines the relationship between them using an improved point wise mutual information algorithm. Second, sentiment words that are related to mobile shopping are clustered into categories to form sentiment dimensions. At each sentiment dimension, each sentiment word can take the value of 0 or 1, where 1 indicates that the word belongs to a particular category whereas 0 indicates that it does not belong to that category. The generated lexicon is evaluated by constructing a sentiment classification task using several product reviews written in both Chinese and English. Two popular non-domain-specific sentiment lexicons as well as state-of-the-art machine-learning and deep-learning models are chosen as benchmarks, and the experimental results show that our sentiment lexicons outperform the benchmarks with statistically significant differences, thus proving the effectiveness of the proposed approach.

INTRODUCTION

With the rapid development of smartphones, mobile shopping, which is already popular, is expected to grow faster. After shopping, people provide a large number of reviews about different kinds of products on the Internet. Different products could be preferred by different consumer groups. Hence, it is becoming increasingly important to learn about a customer's emotional inclinations and favorite products through online reviews. Sentiment classification can be performed using machine-learning, lexicon-based, and hybrid approaches. Sentiment lexicons are important resources for these approaches. The analysis of sentiment orientation is widely known as a domain-specific task. However, almost all the existing sentiment lexicons are general lexicons, which are not suitable for the analysis of product reviews on the Internet. Thus, automatic construction methods for sentiment lexicons have attracted increasing attention recently, especially methods for constructing sentiment lexicons aimed at mobile shopping.

Sentiment analysis, which is also called opinion mining, review mining (appraisal extraction), or attitude analysis, is the task of detecting, extracting, and classifying opinions, sentiments, and attitudes concerning different topics [1]. In a machine-learning approach, sentiment analysis can be considered as a supervised classification task. Pang et al. [2] solved the sentiment classification problem by training the classifier. However, most machine-learning approaches rely on features that are engineered by machine-learning methods. In a lexicon-based approach, a dictionary is created to judge whether the polarity of words in the text is positive or negative. For example, Turney [3] scanned a review for phrases that matched certain patterns (adjectives and adverbs) and then added up all sentiment orientations to compute the orientation of a document. A hybrid approach combines both the above approaches and has a relative advantage in sentiment analysis. Ortigosa et al. [4] developed a lexicon from a corpus and then chose sentiment words along with the labeled class as the input features for a machine-learning classification method. Sentiment lexicons play a key role in a majority of the above methods.

A sentiment lexicon (or an opinion lexicon) is a list of words and phrases that are commonly used to express positive or negative sentiments [5]. Researchers have proposed many approaches to compile these sentiment words. Technically, the existing automatic lexicon construction methods for both English and Chinese languages are mainly divided into corpus-based and knowledge-based methods. Turney [3] developed a corpus-based method in which the sentiment orientation of a word was judged by using point wise mutual information (PMI) to describe the closeness of the word and seed words. Knowledge-based methods require a relatively complete knowledge base. Hu and Liu [6] constructed a sentiment lexicon by searching for the synonyms and antonyms of a word in WordNet. For a specific domain, the sentiment lexicon constructed from the corresponding domain corpus is more practical. When building a sentiment lexicon for online product reviews, the product features modified by sentiment words are also very important factors [7]. However, the existing general sentiment lexicons usually include only limited common words, and these words are divided into binary or other fixed categories according to the sentiment orientation.

In this paper, we present a novel method to construct a domain-specific sentiment lexicon by mining the relationship between sentiment words and product features in a specific corpus. In our approach, first, a sentiment matrix is constructed based on the relationship between sentiment words and product features. Every row of the sentiment matrix is regarded as a vector representation of the sentiment word. The sentiment words in the matrix space are clustered based on the distance between the vectors. Second, sentiment words that are related to mobile shopping are clustered into categories to form sentiment dimensions. In the process of building the sentiment matrix, the idea of term frequency–inverse document frequency (TFIDF) is utilized to screen the product features. Furthermore, the traditional PMI algorithm is improved to obtain a new algorithm called EPMI, which is more suited to mobile shopping reviews. Extensive experiments are performed on seven different domain product reviews, which include reviews in both Chinese and English. Compared to two popular general lexicons as well as state-of-the-art machine-learning and deep-learning models, our lexicon can obtain satisfactory classification performance. The experimental results also show that the filtering of product features and the application of the EPMI algorithm can greatly improve the performance of our lexicon for mobile shopping reviews.

The rest of the paper is structured as follows. Discussions on sentiment classification and lexicon generation and a review of the most recent research are presented in Section 2. Our methods for constructing the sentiment lexicon for mobile shopping reviews and a walk-through example of our methods are presented in Section 3. The experimental setup and results are described in Section 4. The conclusions of the paper are summarized in Section 5.

RELATED WORK

This section is structured as follows. In the first part of this section, we review previous works on sentiment classification approaches. In the second part, we summarize works on approaches for sentiment lexicon creation. In addition, we briefly introduce the sentiment dimensions considered in the lexicon and product feature identification for product reviews.

Sentiment Classification

Sentiment classification aims to automatically classify the text of reviews written by customers into positive or negative opinions. Sentiment classification techniques can be roughly divided into machine-learning, lexicon-based, and hybrid approaches [8].

Machine-Learning Approaches. In such approaches, the analysis of customers' emotional inclinations is considered to be a problem of polarity classification. Pang et al. [2] applied three machine-learning methods (naive Bayes (NB), maximum entropy, and a support vector machine (SVM)) to sentiment classification as a form of traditional topic-based categorization. Zhang et al. [9] used machine learning (NB and SVM) to classify the sentiments expressed in restaurant reviews written in Cantonese. Li et al. [10] adopted extreme learning machine and deep-learning architecture to improve feature representations for text classification. Enríquez et al. [11] showed how a vector-based word representation obtained via Word2Vec can help in improving the results of a document classifier based on the bag-of-words model. However, these supervised machine-learning techniques require a large corpus of training data, and their performance is acceptable only if the match between the training and test data is good.

Lexicon-Based Approaches. These approaches adopt a lexicon to perform sentiment analysis by counting and weighting sentiment words that have been evaluated and tagged [12]. Nasukawa and Yi [13] developed a method to determine subject favorability by creating a sentiment lexicon containing 3513 sentiment terms. Qiu et al. [14] used a lexicon-based approach to identify sentiment sentences in contextual advertising. The most common lexicon resources are SentiWordNet, WordNet, and ConceptNet, and among these resources, SentiWordNet is the most widely used [15].

Hybrid Approaches. Nowadays, researchers are also using combined approaches, in which two or more approaches are combined to achieve better accuracy. Sindhwani and Melville [16] presented a unified framework in which lexical background information, unlabeled data, and labeled training examples can be effectively combined. Li et al. [17] set up a system to analyze the market impact by combining the stock price and news sentiment. Ortigosa et al. [4] performed sentiment classification and sentiment change detection on Facebook comments using a hybrid approach. They combined lexicon-based and machine-learning methods by considering a lexicon as the source of features and using a classification model to evaluate the lexicon; this approach is similar to the one used in our experiments in this study.

Lexicon Creation

A sentiment lexicon is an important tool for identifying the sentiment polarity of reviews provided by mobile users [18]. Two methods are commonly used to generate sentiment lexicons: knowledge-based and corpus-based methods.

Knowledge-Based Methods. These methods exploit available lexicographical resources such as WordNet or HowNet. Hu and Liu [6] developed a lexicon by searching for the synonyms and antonyms of a word in WordNet. Kamps [19] inferred that the greater the closeness of two words, the smaller the number of iterations required to determine the synonymous relationship between the words. Both these studies used the relationship between words in a knowledge base. The main strategy in these methods is to first manually collect an initial seed set of sentiment words and their orientations and then search for their synonyms and antonyms in a knowledge base to expand this set [12]. However, very few complete and robust knowledge bases are available for the Chinese language.

Corpus-Based Methods. These methods depend on syntactic patterns or patterns that occur together along with a seed list of opinion words to find other opinion words in a large corpus [20]. Hatzivassiloglou and McKeown [21] found that, with a change in the emotional polarity in the text, the turning point appears but concatenation does not. Based on the idea that the emotional polarity of a word tends to be consistent with the emotional polarity of its neighboring words, Turney and Littman [22] constructed a dictionary from a large corpus. Both these works [21, 22] are based on a corpus rather than a knowledge base. The corpus-based approach has a major advantage in that it can find domain-specific words and their orientations if a domain-specific corpus is used in the discovery process. Therefore, our work also focuses on a corpus-based approach. In addition, PMI is commonly used in this approach to exploit the syntactic patterns of cooccurrence patterns. Turney and Littman [22] used PMI and latent semantic analysis to measure the correlation between two words, and this method, which uses PMI to calculate the correlation between a word and seed word, is called semantic-orientation PMI (SO-PMI). Yang et al. [23] introduced a method based on SO-PMI to construct a sentiment lexicon and improved the SO-PMI model based on user behavior. In the process of our lexicon construction, we improve the traditional PMI to make it more suitable for mobile shopping reviews.

In the process of lexicon construction, we focus on two issues: the sentiment dimensions of the lexicon, and feature or topic identification in product review domains.

Sentiment Dimensions. Ekman [24] found that humans have six basic emotional categories: happiness, sadness, fear, surprise, anger, and jealousy. Ekman's theory, which is accepted by numerous psychologists and linguists, is widely used in the field of sentiment analysis. Rubin et al. [25] presented an empirically verified model on the basis of the idea [26] that an emotion can be divided into eight categories with two major bipolar dimensions: positive and negative effects. Although early approaches simply focused on this binary classification [27], we not only consider the two polarities but also anticipate that sentiment words can be reasonably clustered into finer-gained categorizations.

Feature Identification. Considering that many words in different fields may have different sentiment polarities, it is necessary to explicitly extract the sentiment words and topics or product features, especially in the mobile review domain. Fast et al. [28] found out that using experts or crowdsourcing to construct domain-specific sentiment lexicons is very difficult. Zhang et al. [29] proposed a hybrid method that combined Apriori and PMI to extract product features. Mishne [30] chose the part of speech (POS) and word counts as features in a text classification task. In our research, the primitive product feature extraction also uses the POS as a selection criterion.

METHODS

In this section, we present our proposed framework to generate domain-specific sentiment lexicons for mobile shopping. Figure 1 shows the framework of our method. The domain-specific lexicon is based on the relationship between sentiment words and product features modified by the sentiment words. A sentiment matrix is adopted to represent the relationship between the sentiment words and product features. First, we use PMI to express the relationship between sentiment words and product features. Second, we use TFIDF to filter product features so as to reduce the matrix dimension. Finally, we improve the traditional PMI to develop a new algorithm called EPMI, which is used to build a new sentiment matrix. Each row in the sentiment matrix is a vector representation of the sentiment word. After obtaining the sentiment matrix, we cluster the sentiment words into several categories based on the distance between their vector representations. The mathematical symbols used in the process of construction are listed in Table 1.

Table 1. Mathematical symbols and their meanings.

Symbol	Meaning
A, B, F	Sentiment matrix
C	Matrix of relationship between features
$E = \{e_1, e_2, \ldots, e_n\}$	Set of sentiment words
$M = \{m_1, m_2, \ldots, m_p\}$	Set of primitive product features
$M' = \{m'_1, m'_2, \ldots, m'_t\}$	Set of product features after filtering
$D = \{d_1, d_2, \ldots, d_n\}$	Set of reviews

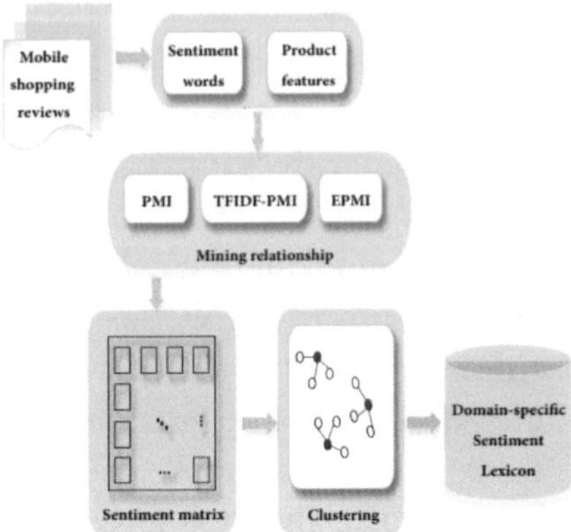

Figure 1. Framework of method used for constructing domain-specific lexicon for mobile shopping.

Building of Primitive Sentiment Matrix

To perform the key step of mining the relationship between sentiment words and product features, we need to determine the sentiment words and product features in the corpus. To choose the terms from the corpus as candidate words, we use the POS.

Sentiment words are commonly used to express positive or negative sentiments. Sentiment lexicons usually contain such words, which can indicate the sentiment polarity (e.g., "good" and "wonderful" indicate positive opinions, whereas "rubbish," "cheap," and "terrible" indicate negative opinions). In mobile shopping reviews, a number of verbs can also indicate the sentiment polarity (e.g., "like" and "love" indicate positive opinions, whereas "dislike" and "refund" indicate negative opinions). In some previous studies [31, 32], the words whose POS is an adjective or adverb are considered as sentiment words. The sentiment lexicons developed or used in some other studies [6, 33] are also mainly concerned with adjectives and adverbs. In addition, product features in the product review domain are usually nouns or noun phrases found in review sentences [6]. Therefore, we choose adjectives, adverbs, and verbs as sentiment words and choose nouns as primitive product features. For instance, in the hotel review "The food in the dining room is really good, the breakfast tastes good," the product features are "dinning," "breakfast," and "food," and the sentiment words are "good" and "tastes."

If a sentiment word A modifies a product feature B, we consider that there is a relationship between them. In mobile shopping reviews, this relationship can be shown as a phenomenon of cooccurrence. We use PMI to quantify this type of cooccurrence relationship. PMI is defined as

$$\mathrm{PMI}\left(word_1, word_2\right) = \log_2\left(\frac{\mathrm{p}\left(word_1, word_2\right)}{\mathrm{p}\left(word_1\right)\mathrm{p}\left(word_2\right)}\right) \quad (1)$$

Here, $p(word_1, word_2)$ is the cooccurrence probability of $word_1$ and $word_2$ in the local window and is expressed as

$$\mathrm{p}\left(\mathrm{word}_1, \mathrm{word}_2\right) = \frac{\mathrm{count}\left(word_1, word_2\right)}{N} \quad (2)$$

where N is the total number of words contained in the corpus. $count(word_1, word_2)$represents the number of occurrences of the two words in the local window. Similarly, the frequency of each word can be obtained as

$$\mathrm{p}\left(\mathrm{word}\right) = \frac{\mathrm{count}\left(word\right)}{N}$$

In (1), $p(word_1)p(word_2)$ gives the probability of cooccurrence if these two words are statistically independent. Te ratio of $p(word_1,word_2)$ to $p(word_1)p(word_2)$ is thus a measure of the degree of statistical dependence between the words.

The PMI value between the sentiment words and product features can reflect the relationship between them. By calculating the PMI value between all the sentiment words and product features, we can obtain a sentiment matrix that contains the relationship between the sentiment words and product features. Let us denote $E = \{e_1, e_2 \ldots e_n\}$ as the set of sentiment words and $M = \{m_1, m_2, \ldots m_p\}$ as the set of product features. Matrix A, as shown below, consists of n rows and p columns.

Definition 1. Sentiment matrix A: the rows represent the sentiment words, whereas the columns represent the product features. The value of each cell w_{ij} is given by $\mathrm{PMI}(e_i, m_j)$.

$$A = \begin{bmatrix} w_{11} & w_{12} & \cdots & w_{1p} \\ w_{21} & w_{22} & \cdots & w_{2p} \\ \vdots & \vdots & \ddots & \vdots \\ w_{n1} & w_{n2} & \cdots & w_{np} \end{bmatrix} \quad (4)$$

In the above matrix, each sentiment word e_i can be represented as a vector $\vec{e_i} = [w_{i1}, w_{i2}, \ldots, w_{ip}]$. Sentiment matrix A is the primitive sentiment matrix, and this matrix is optimized, as described in the next subsection.

Filtering of Product Features

So far, we have obtained the primitive sentiment matrix A, and each sentiment word e in the matrix can be represented as a vector. According to our approach, these vectors should be clustered into several categories. However, we found that the number of product features is very large because we consider all nouns as product features. Consequently, the word vector will face the dimension disaster problem. The clustering of high dimensional data is still a challenging problem because of the curse of dimensionality [34]. In addition, the use of high dimensions will result in low computational efficiency, especially in mobile computing. In Hu and Liu's study [6], only those product features regarding which many people have expressed their opinions are reserved. Similarly, we also select key product features from the primitive nouns. Next, we will describe our feature selection method in detail. The high-dimension problem stems from the large number of nouns in the corpus. The number is large because we choose all nouns as product features. For instance, consider the product review "Tis hotel is great, I can recommend my mom to live next time." The word "mom" and "time" will be treated as product features, but these words do not represent any features of the hotel. In addition, this type of nouns can be found everywhere in mobile shopping reviews. Therefore, it is necessary to filter out the key product features rather than choose all nouns as the product features. Product features should be nouns that frequently appear in a particular category of product reviews and rarely appear in other categories. Therefore, we use the idea of TFIDF to select real product features. TFIDF is defined as

$$\text{TFIDF}(\textit{word}) = \text{TF}(\textit{word}) \times \text{IDF}(\textit{word}) \tag{5}$$

Here, TF(word) means the term frequency of the word in the document. IDF(word) means the inverse document frequency, that is, whether the word is common or rare across all documents. It is important to note that the TFIDF value of the same word may be different in different documents. However, TFIDF is usually used for documents rather than pieces of reviews. There may be thousands of comments about a single product. We just need to merge the same kind of comments together to form the corresponding document.

From (5), we can obtain the TFIDF value of words in different documents. Unlike the analysis described in the previous subsection, here, we choose the nouns whose TFIDF values are relatively high in the document as product features of the product. Unexpectedly, we find that the nouns whose TFIDF values are relatively high happen to be words that are closely related to the reviewed product. For example, if there are numerous reviews about a hotel, we can retrieve words such as "bathroom" and "air-conditioning" from the corresponding document. When we are commenting on a hotel, we often refer to the "bathroom" or "air-conditioning" in the hotel. However, these two words rarely appear in the reviews of products from other domains such as the electronics domain. We can certainly defne a threshold α that the TFIDF value of real product features must reach. Let us denote $M' = \{m'_1, m'_2, \ldots, m'_t\}$ where $M' \subseteq M$ as the set of the remaining product features after filtering by TFIDF. Accordingly, we can obtain another sentiment matrix that is similar to sentiment matrix A. Tis matrix (sentiment matrix B) consists of n rows and t columns.

Definition 2. Sentiment matrix B: this matrix can be considered to be part of sentiment matrix A. The rows represent the sentiment words, whereas the columns represent the product features after filtering by TFIDF. The value of each cell w_{ij}, which is the same as that in sentiment matrix A, is given by $PMI(e_i, m'_j)$.

In matrix *B*, each sentiment word e_i can be represented as a vector $\vec{e_i} = [w_{i1}, w_{i2}, \ldots, w_{it}]$. Here, t can be considerably less than when the threshold α is set appropriately. Compared to sentiment matrix *A*, sentiment matrix *B* can effectively solve the high-dimension problem in word embedding. However, there are still some defects in the sentiment matrix, which will be elaborated in the next subsection.

Optimization of Sentiment Matrix by EPMI

Here, we introduce an example from hotel reviews to further explain the defect in sentiment matrices A and B. We focus on two sentiment words (e_1 = "rich" and e_2 = "hearty") and two product features (m_1 = "food" and m_2 = "breakfast"). Both these sentiment words can be used to express opinions about a wide variety of foods. The meanings of these two sentiment words are very similar, and these words are commonly used in the hotel review domain. If we just consider the two features m_1 and m_2, e_1 and e_2 can be represented as $\vec{e_1} = [w_{11}, w_{12}]$ and $\vec{e_2} = [w_{21}, w_{22}]$ in the sentiment matrix. w_{ij} is given by $PMI(e_i, m_j)$. As is well known, the distance or angle between word vectors can be considered to be the similarities between words. The greater the similarity between two words, the shorter the distance between them. However, in a hotel review, the two sentiment words (e_1, e_2) and two product features (m_1, m_2) can be matched with each other flexibly. Although some customers may usually modifym$_1$ with e_1 and m_2 with e_2, they may rarely modify m_1 with e_2 and m_2 with e_1. Tis means that the PMI value of (e_1, m_1) and (e_2, m_2) is relatively high, but the PMI value of (e_1, m_2) and (m_2, e_1) is very low. Therefore, an illusion is created that e_1 and e_2 are irrelevant in the two dimensions of m_1 and m_2.Tis irrational result stems from the flexibility of product reviews and the diversity of vocabulary in mobile shopping reviews. Although e_1 rarely modifies m2, it cannot be simply considered to be irrelevant.

```
Input:
        M = {m_1, m_2, ..., m_p}, M' = {m'_1, m'_2 ..., m'_t}, D = {d_1, d_2, ..., d_n}
Output: Matrix C[t][p]
        i = 1, C[t][p] = zero matrix
        while i ≤ t do
          j = 1
          while j ≤ p do
            for each d ∈ D do
              if (m'_i, m_j) in d && m'_i ≠ m_j then
                C[i][j] = C[i][j] + 1
            j = j + 1
          i = i + 1
        For each row row ∈ C[t][p] do
          row = normal(row)
        Return C
```

Algorithm 1. Mining relationship between product features.

When we consider the relationship between a sentiment word and product feature, it is not sufficient to just calculate the PMI value of these two words directly. We still need to consider the relationship between the sentiment word and other product features that are related to the initial product feature. In the mobile shopping reviews about a hotel, there are many features related to m_2 (breakfast), such as "food" and "dinning." Therefore, when we calculate the PMI value of e_1 and m_2, we consider the cooccurrence of not only e_1 and m_2 but also e_1 and m_1 or other product features related to m_2. We use u_{ij} □ [0, 1] to reflect the degree of correlation between the two product features m_i and m_j. The larger the value of u_{ij}, the more relevant m_j to m_i. $u_{ij} = 0$ indicates that the two features m_i and m_j are irrelevant. In particular, if the features m_i and m_j represent the same feature, the value of u_{ij} between them is zero. Considering all the p product features contained in the corpus, we define EPMI as

$$\mathrm{EPMI}\left(e_i, m_j\right) = \mathrm{PMI}\left(e_i, m_j\right) + \sum_{k=1}^{p} u_{jk} * \mathrm{PMI}\left(e_i, m_k\right) \quad (6)$$

Once we know the value of u_{ij} between any two features m_i and m_j, we can obtain the EPMI value on the basis of the PMI value. Considering that we can screen the features according to the method described in the previous subsection, we focus on the correlation between the remaining product features after filtering and all the primitive features. We assume that the more frequently two features appear in the same review, the higher the correlation between them is. The pseudocode for mining the relationship between them is presented in Algorithm 1.

Following the earlier definitions, M is still the set of all product features for a given kind of production, and M′ is the set of product features obtained by carrying out filtering using the approach described in the previous subsection. D is the set of reviews related to the product (m'_i, m_j) in d means that features m'_i and m_j appear together in review d. The function normal () is a simple normalization function that is used to ensure that every element in the vector belongs to [0, 1].Tis algorithm is an effective algorithm in the sense that it can find the features that are the most relevant to a specific feature. We can obtain matrix C using the above algorithm. After obtaining matrix C, we can use EPMI to build a new sentiment matrix.

Definition 3. Sentiment matrix F can be determined by (7). The only difference between sentiment matrices F and B is that matrix F is obtained using our approach (EPMI) rather than the traditional PMI. In other words, each cell of sentiment matrix F represents the EPMI value between the sentiment words and product features rather than the PMI value between them.

$$F[n][t] = B[n][t] + A[n][p] * C^T[t][p] \qquad (7)$$

So far, we have obtained three sentiment matrices *A*, *B*, and *F*. The sentiment words can be represented by the vectors in each of the sentiment matrices.

In mobile shopping reviews, customers often use different sentiment words to modify different product features. In addition, customers may have a good feeling about some features of a product, but they may be dissatisfied with some other features at the same time. Therefore, different product features also reflect different feelings. We assume that sentiment words can be divided into different categories according to the relationship between them and the product features.

Therefore, we cluster the sentiment words into several categories rather than into binary or other fixed categories. In other words, the sentiment dimension of a word in our domain-specific lexicon is flexible rather than having only limited emotional polarity. For each sentiment dimension, each sentiment word can take the value of 0 or 1, where 1 indicates that it belongs to a particular category whereas 0 indicates that it does not belong to that category. If we cluster the sentiment words into five categories, the representation $\vec{e} = [0,0,1,0,0]$ means that the word e belongs to the third category. The flexibility of sentiment dimensions is a main characteristic of the domain-specific lexicon built using our approach.

Walk-Through Example

Here, we will elaborate on the differences between EPMI and PMI using an example. Suppose that we want to determine the semantic correlations between the sentiment words e_1 = "丰富" (rich) and e_2= "丰盛" (hearty), and the five sentences listed in Table 2 are our corpus. This small corpus is a part of Chinese mobile shopping reviews about hotels.

Table 2. Sample product reviews.

1	早餐 很 丰盛, 餐厅 非常 大。 (Breakfast is very hearty, the dining room is very large)
2	食物 种类 丰富, 那里 有 免费 的 早餐。 (The food is plentiful and there is a free breakfast)
3	餐厅 免费 供应 丰盛 的 早餐。 (The dinning serves a hearty breakfast for free)
4	餐厅 里 的 食物 挺 丰富 (The food in the dinning is rich)
5	餐厅 食物 真不错, 早餐 尝起来 很 好吃 (The food in the dinning is really good, the breakfast tastes good)

Here, N is 33 because these five comments contain 33 Chinese words. In this example, there are four nouns (or primitive product features), i.e., $M = \{m_1 \sim m_4 \mid$ "食物" (food), "早餐" (breakfast), "餐厅" (dining room), "种类" (variety). To keep our example simple and understandable, we focus on only two features, m_1= "食物" (food) and m_2= "早餐" (breakfast). Therefore, M′ can be $\{m'_1, m'_2\}$. count (e_1) is 2 because the word e_1 appears only twice in this small corpus. Similarly, count (e_2) is 2, count (m_1) is 3, and count (m_2) is 4. The size of the local window of cooccurrence is set as 3. count (e_1, m_1) is 2 because e_1 and m_1 cooccur twice in the second and fourth comments within the window. Similarly, (e_2, m_2) is 2, (e_1, m_2) is 0, and (e_2, m_1) is 0. Using (1), we can obtain $\mathrm{PMI}(e_1, m_1) =$

$\log_2(p(e_1,m_1)/p(e_1)p(m_1)) = (2/33)/((2/33)(3/33)) = 3.46$ and $\mathrm{PMI}(e_1,m_2) = 0$. Similarly, $\mathrm{PMI}(e_2,m_1) = 0$ and $\mathrm{PMI}(e_2,m_2) = (2/33)/((2/33)(4/33)) = 3.04$. Therefore, the two sentiment words e_1 and e_2 can be represented as $\vec{e_1} = [3.46, 0]$ and $\vec{e_2} = [0, 3.04]$, respectively, in sentiment matrices *A* and *B*.

Table 3. Number of instances of cooccurrence of features.

	m_1	m_2	m_3	m_4
m_1'	0	2	2	1
m_2'	2	0	3	1

We calculate u_{ij} using Algorithm 1. First, by iterating through these five comments, we obtain the number of instances of cooccurrence of m_i' and m_j (Table 3). In this table, each cell shows the number of times that two features appear together in the same comment. The values in this table are similar to those in matrix C obtained in Algorithm 1.

Next, we normalize this table or matrix. We choose the min–max normalization function as the normal() function in the algorithm. Finally, we obtain $u_{12} = 1$, $u_{13} = 1$, $u_{14} = 1/2$, $u_{21} = 2/3$, $u_{23} = 1$, and $u_{24} = 1/3$. Note that u_{11} and u_{22} are 0.

Using (6), we obtain $\mathrm{EPMI}(e_1,m_2) = \mathrm{PMI}(e_1,m_2) + u_{21}\mathrm{PMI}(e_1,m_1) + u_{22}\mathrm{PMI}(e_1,m_2) + u_{23}\mathrm{PMI}(e_1,m_3) + u_{24}\mathrm{PMI}(e_1,m_4) = 3.65$ and $\mathrm{EPMI}(e_1,m_1) = 5.48$. Similarly, $\mathrm{EPMI}(e_2,m_1) = 6.08$ and $\mathrm{EPMI}(e_2,m_2) = 6.08$. The two sentiment words e_1 and e_2 can be represented as $\vec{e_1}' = [5.48, 3.65]$ and $\vec{e_2}' = [6.08, 6.08]$ in sentiment matrix *F*.

It is obvious that the distance between $\vec{e_1'}$ and $\vec{e_2'}$ is considerably closer than that between $\vec{e_1}$ and $\vec{e_2}$, irrespective of the Euclidean or cosine distance. This result reflects the difference between our EPMI algorithm and PMI. These two sentiment words are very similar and are commonly used in hotel reviews. The greater the similarity between the two words, the shorter the distance between them. In the clustering model, the vectors that are located at shorter distances are easier to be clustered into the same category.

EXPERIMENTS

To evaluate the domain-specific lexicon developed using our approach, we design an experimental setup using which we compare the proposed domain-specific lexicon with two popular general lexicons and with state-of-the-art machine-learning and deep-learning approaches that do not use a lexicon. We mainly evaluate different lexicons and approaches using document-level classification tasks in the domain of online product reviews. For hybrid sentiment classification methods, we consider the features of the document vector representation as the lexicon. We use the F1-measure as our main evaluation index and choose NB and SVM as the classifiers. In the following subsections, the details of the experiments and their results are described.

Dataset

The dataset includes both Chinese and English shopping reviews. These reviews are for seven types of products. The detailed statistics of this dataset are listed in Table 4.

Table 4. Statistics of dataset.

Polarity	Chinese			English			
	Hotel	Cloth	Fruit	Books	Kitchen	DVD	Electronics
Positive	5321	5000	5000	1000	1000	1000	1000
Negative	2444	5000	5000	1000	1000	1000	1000

The Chinese product reviews include three domains: hotel, cloth, and fruit. The hotel reviews are provided by Dr. Tan (http://download.csdn.net/download/lssc4205/9903298), and the cloth and fruit reviews are crawled from a mobile shopping application JD (https://www.jd.com/). The English reviews are obtained from the famous Amazon product review dataset collected by Blizter et al. [35]. It is widely used as a benchmark dataset for cross-domain sentiment classification. Four domains—book, DVD, electronics, and kitchen—are included in this dataset. For each domain, 1000 positive and 1000 negative reviews are included.

Experimental Design

We use the open-source software jieba (https://pypi.python.org/pypi/jieba/) to carry out preprocessing tasks on the Chinese product reviews, including Chinese word segmentation and POS tagging. For the sentiment classification approaches that do not use a lexicon, we compare our method with the classical bag-of-words and deep-learning model Word2Vec [36]. Furthermore, we compare the domain-specific sentiment lexicon with two popular general sentiment lexicons. We use the scikit-learn [37] python library implementation of the classifier. The detailed differences between the three test groups are described below.

(a) No Lexicon

(BOW) The classical method to express the document involves the use of the bag-of-words model [2]. Each document d is represented by a feature-presence vector $\vec{d} = [0, 1, \ldots, 0]$.

(W2V) In addition to the bag-of-words classical representation, we use the encoding of words provided by Word2Vec, which is a deep-learning tool released by Google in 2013. This tool adopts two main model architectures—the continuous bag-of-words model and continuous skip-gram model—to learn the vector representations of words [38]. To use Word2Vec for document-level tasks, a method is required that can unify all word vectors and generate a single vector representing the entire document [11]. Thus, the final representation is obtained according to the number of words contained in the document as follows:

$$\overrightarrow{v_d} = \frac{\sum_{i=0}^{n} \overrightarrow{v_i}}{n} \quad (8)$$

We use the genism (https://radimrehurek.com/gensim/models/word2vec.html) python library implementation of Word2Vec. We use the default values for almost all the parameters and use vectors with 200 dimensions.

(b) General Lexicon

For this test group, we use the hybrid sentiment classification approaches. That is, we consider the words in the lexicon, the sentiment dimensions of the lexicon, and a combination of the words and dimensions as the features for the machine-learning classifier. First, we choose a general sentiment lexicon DUTIR [39] for Chinese reviews. The DUTIR lexicon contains 27446 common Chinese words. The sentiment polarity of these words is labeled as positive, negative, or neutral.

(DUTIR) We consider only the words contained in the DUTIR lexicon as features, as in the case of the bag-of-words model. Therefore, the review d can be represented as $\vec{d}_0 = [0,1,\ldots,1]$.

(Only 3) We consider the three polarities of the sentiment words in the DUTIR lexicon. We represent the product review d by a three-dimensional vector $\vec{d_1} = [k_0, k_1, k_2]$, where k_0, k_1, and k_2 are the number of words with the three types of polarities in the review.

(DUTIR+3) Here, we combine the above two representations. The product review d can be represented as $\vec{d} = \vec{d}_0 + \vec{d}_1 [0,1,...,1,k_0,k_1,k_2]$.

For the English reviews, we choose a general sentiment lexicon SentiWordNet (http://sentiwordnet.isti.cnr.it/). SentiWordNet assigns three sentiment scores to each synset of WordNet: positivity, negativity, and objectivity. In other words, both the sentiment dimensions of the words for these two general sentiment lexicons in Chinese and English are 3.

(SentiWordNet) As in the case of the DUTIR lexicon, we focus on the words contained in the SentiWordNet lexicon. The review d can be represented as $\vec{d}_0 = [0,1,...,1]$.

(Only 3) We represent the product review d by a three-dimensional vector $\vec{d_1} = [k_0, k_1, k_2]$. Here, k_0 is the sum of the positivity scores of the words in the review d. Similarly, k_1 and k_2 represent the sum of the negativity and objectivity scores, respectively.

(SentiWordNet+3) As in the case of the DUTIR lexicon, the product review d can be represented as $\vec{d} = \vec{d_0} + \vec{d_1} = [0, 1, \ldots, 1, k_0, k_1, k_2]$.

(c) Domain-Specific Lexicon

We use hybrid approaches to evaluate the domain-specific lexicon developed using our method. We set the window size as 3 and α as 0.01 (as mentioned in Section 3.2). We use *k*-means (http://scikit-learn.org/stable/modules/clustering.html#k-means) to cluster the sentiment words into k categories based on the distance in the matrix space. Unlike the general lexicons, the sentiment dimension of words in our domain-specific lexicon is k. Note that we select k through a fivefold cross-validation on the training set. The details of the selection of k are explained in the next subsection. In our experiment, the number of clusters is not more than 30. In the following discussion, the domain-specific lexicon built using our method is denoted as DS.

(DS) We consider the sentiment words contained in the domain-specific lexicon as features, as in the case of the bag-of-words model. Accordingly, the review d can be represented as $\vec{d}_0 = [0,1,...,1]$.

(Only *k*) We cluster the sentiment words into k categories using *k*-means. We represent the product review k by a k(k≥2) –dimensional vector . Obviously, $\vec{d_1} = [m_0, m_1, .., m_{k-1}]$ represents the number of sentiment words that belong to the (t+1) category in the review.

(DS+k) Here, we combine the above two representations. The product review d can be represented as $\vec{d} = \vec{d_0} + \vec{d_1} = [0, 1, \ldots, 1, m_0, m_1, .., m_{k-1}]$.

Three different sentiment matrices are considered in our lexicon construction process. The sentiment word representations in different matrices are very different. Therefore, the clustering result would also be different. We use (PMI), (TFIDF-PMI), and (EPMI) to represent the clustering results of sentiment matrices *A*, *B*, and *F*, respectively. We discuss the different results of the three matrices in the next subsection.

In addition, we evaluate the lexicon in terms of the coverage and usage. We assume that the test set contains N unique words and that these N words include T sentiment words, which are contained in the sentiment lexicon. We also assume that the size of the lexicon that is used to train the classification model is S. Therefore, the coverage of the lexicon is T/N, and the usage of lexicon is T/S. If the coverage of the lexicon is low, the classification performance will be unsatisfactory. If the usage of the lexicon is low, computing resources will be wasted, which should be avoided especially for mobile devices. Considering these two evaluation indexes, we propose an average evaluation index such as the F1-measure. Let V,U , and T represent the coverage, usage, and average of the lexicon, respectively. Then, T is defined as

$$T = \frac{2 * V * U}{V + U} * 100\% \qquad (9)$$

Results and Discussion

Overall Results. Table 5 lists the overall classification results. All the tasks are balanced two-class problems. The best result for each domain review is marked in bold font, and the second-best result is underlined.

Table 5. F1-measure classification results for shopping domain reviews (NB).

Method	Chinese			English			
	Hotel	Cloth	Fruit	Books	Kitchen	DVD	Electronics
No lexicon							
BOW	<u>81.9</u>	<u>86.4</u>	<u>88.8</u>	74.0	79.3	77.6	77.0
W2V	61.2	68.2	69.8	61.5	67.1	63.8	61.7
General lexicon							
DUTIR	71.5	75.0	73.8	-	-	-	-
SentiWordNet	-	-	-	72.3	79.0	76.8	76.5
Only 3	68.8	70.7	70.2	65.1	62.3	68.4	61.9
DUTIR+3	72.6	74.8	74.2	-	-	-	-
SentiWordNet+3	-	-	-	74.9	79.8	78.5	77.9
Domain-specific lexicon							
DS	80.3	84.9	86.8	<u>77.7</u>	<u>81.1</u>	<u>79.5</u>	<u>79.0</u>
Only *k*	70.3	71.2	71.5	61.6	64.9	62.7	63.2
DS+*k*	**83.6**	**87.6**	**89.5**	**78.9**	**82.5**	**80.6**	**80.5**

First, for the domain-specific and general lexicons, DS+k achieves the best results for all the seven domain reviews whereas DS achieves the second-best results for four of the reviews. DS outperforms the general lexicons DUTIR and SentiWordNet. These results indicate that the domain-specific lexicon, which is constructed from the corresponding corpus, shows better performance for sentiment classification tasks on shopping reviews.

Second, for no lexicon approaches, the classical bag-of-words model obviously performs better than the deep-learning model Word2Vec in terms of sentiment classification tasks. BOW achieves the second-best results for three of the reviews, whereas W2V shows nearly the worst performance for both Chinese and English reviews. The poor performance is unexpected, and a large corpus of training data is perhaps required for training Word2Vec [40].

Third, for sentiment dimensions, the performances of Only 3 and Only k are relatively worse for both Chinese and English reviews. That is, it is not sufficient to just consider the sentiment dimensions when we use the lexicon as the source of the features to express the reviews. However, the performance of DS+k is better than those of DS and Only k for both Chinese and English reviews. This result indicates the effectiveness of combining the words and sentiment dimensions of the lexicon.

Note that, in Table 5, k represents (EPMI). Considering that (DS+k) provides the best performance, we analyze the differences among the results of DS+k(PMI), DS+k(TFIDF-PMI), and DS+k(EPMI) in detail.

EPMI versus PMI and TFIDF-PMI. Table 6 lists the classification results of (DS+k) with the three different methods mentioned in Section 3. First, we find that the classification performance of DS+k(EPMI) is better than those of DS+(PMI) and DS+(TFIDF-PMI). In particular, the performance of DS+k(PMI) is relatively poor. According to a t-test, the differences among the results of the three methods are significant ($p<0.05$). This result reflects the advantages of EPMI over traditional PMI in sentiment classification.

Table 6. Classification results of DS+ with three different methods.

DS + *k*	Chinese			English			
	Hotel	Cloth	Fruit	Books	Kitchen	DVD	Electronics
k(PMI)	81.0	85.2	87.3	77.3	81.5	79.0	79.2
k(TFIDF-PMI)	82.8	87.1	89.0	78.4	82.1	80.1	79.9
k(EPMI)	**83.6**	**87.6**	**89.5**	**78.9**	**82.5**	**80.6**	**80.5**

Second, we discuss the differences among the three methods in terms of time efficiency. Figure 2 shows the average clustering times required by the three different sentiment matrices. The time consumed by sentiment matrices B and F is considerably less than that consumed by sentiment matrix A. This is because in matrices B and F, the dimension of the vector in the matrix space is reduced by using the method described in Section 3.2. The dimension reduction leads to a substantial increase in the efficiency and accuracy of classification. Therefore, sentiment matrix *F* constructed using EPMI shows the best performance.

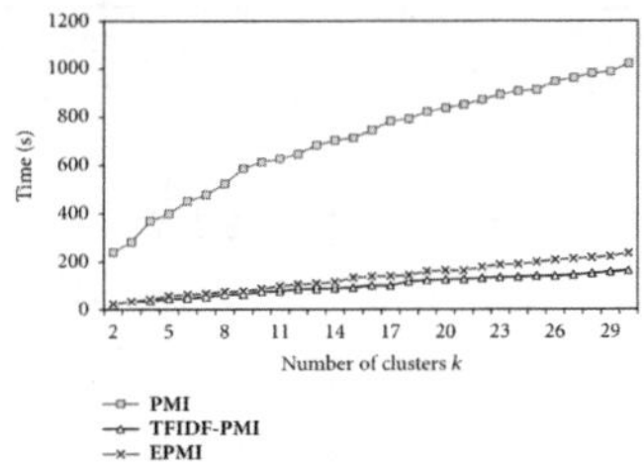

Figure 2. Time required for clustering in sentiment matrix built using three methods. The three different lines represent three different sentiment matrices.

Selection of K. The sentiment dimensions of the domain-specific lexicon is k. Now, we analyze the influence of different k values on the classification performance. Figure 3 shows the performance of Only k(EPMI) with the change in for the English product reviews. When k is 2, Only k(EPMI) shows the best performance for the books and DVD domains. For the kitchen and electronics domains, a larger k improves the classification performance of Only k(EPMI). The appropriate value of k for the domain-specific lexicon is different for different fields. We select the value of k through a fivefold cross-validation on the training set in our experiments.

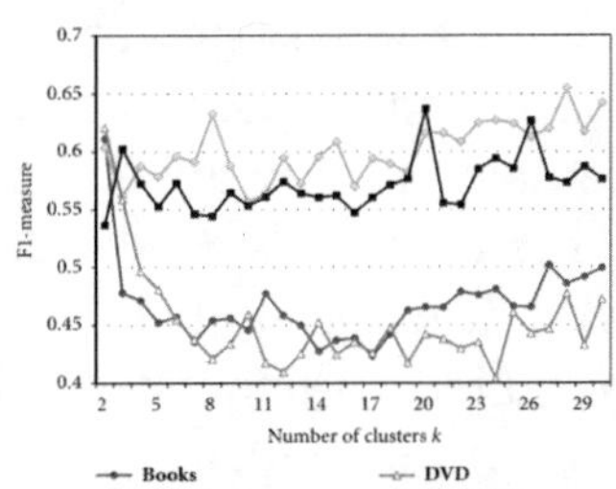

Figure 3. Performance of Only k(EPMI) with change in k.

However, we find that the performance of Only k(EPMI) is worse than that of Only 3 in the books and DVD domains (Table 5). We believe that this is because k=2 is not a good choice for Only k(EPMI) for performing sentiment classification tasks. To prove this point, we look at the performance results of Only k(k=2) for all English product reviews (Table 7).

Table 7. Performance results of Only k (EPMI). k is selected using two different methods.

	Selection of *k*	Books	Kitchen	DVD	Electronics
Only *k*	*k* = 2	61.1	60.3	62.1	53.6
	Cross-validation	61.6	64.9	62.7	63.2

Table 7 indicates that the performance of Only k(EPMI) is not good when k is fixed at 2. In our domain-specific lexicon, low sentiment dimensions such as k=2 is not good for DS. k has a substantial influence on our domain-specific lexicon for sentiment classification tasks. Therefore, it is necessary to select the k value by cross-validation.

NB versus SVM. For obtaining all the above results, we have chosen NB as the classifier. However, classification algorithms influence the classification performance.

Therefore, we choose another popular classification algorithm SVM as the classifier for the method with the best performance among each type of methods. The results are listed in Table 8, where ↑ indicates an improvement in performance compared to that when NB is used and ↓ indicates a deterioration in performance. SVM performs better than NB when using DUTIR+3 for Chinese reviews and when using BOW for the books and DVD domains.

In contrast, NB yields better performance when using the other approaches. Sentiment classification is perhaps one of the domains that have clear feature dependence, and hence, NB often performs unexpectedly well [41]. Although the domain-specific lexicon performs better with both NB and SVM, different types of models of text classification are probably required for documents with different properties. Hence, further empirical and theoretical study is required to understand the relationship between sentiment classification tasks and classification models.

Table 8. F1-measure classification results for shopping domain reviews (SVM).

Methods	Chinese			English			
	Hotel	Cloth	Fruit	Books	Kitchen	DVD	Electronics
No lexicon							
BOW	73.5↓	76.1↓	82.1↓	75.8↑	79.4	78.0↑	77.2
General lexicon							
DUTIR+3	79.5↑	82.1↑	82.5↑	-	-	-	-
SentiWordNet+3	-	-	-	74.1↓	76.2↓	74.9↓	76.3↓
Domain-specific lexicon							
DS+*k*	82.3↓	84.2↓	86.8↓	79.1	80.9↓	79.2↓	78.3↓

Lexicon Coverage. Finally, we discuss the classification performance in terms of the coverage (V), usage (U), and average (T). The results for the test set are listed in Tables 9 and 10. In both the Chinese and English domains, the average of BOW is relatively high. For Chinese product reviews, both the coverage and usage of DUTIR are the worst because DUTIR is a general lexicon that contains only few words that often appear in shopping reviews. The coverage of SentiWordNet is considerably higher than that of DUTIR. This partly explains why the performance of SentiWordNet is better than that of DUTIR for sentiment classification tasks. The better performance is also probably because SentiWordNet contains more words related to mobile shopping reviews than DUTIR. The coverage of SentiWordNet is higher than that of the domain-specific lexicon for English product reviews, whereas the usage of SentiWordNet is considerably low than that of DS. The very low usage of lexicons may impact their performance and waste the computing resources of mobile devices. The average of DS is considerably higher than that of the general lexicon for both Chinese and English product reviews. This result reflects the advantage of our domain-specific lexicon for mobile shopping reviews in another way.

Table 9. Coverage, usage, and average of lexicons for Chinese reviews.

	BOW			DUTIR			DS		
	V	*U*	*T*	*V*	*U*	*T*	*V*	*U*	*T*
Hotel	71.0	34.1	46.1	7.7	2.5	3.8	24.5	39.6	30.2
Cloth	73.4	36.9	79.1	8.2	2.7	4.1	29.0	40.2	33.7
Fruit	75.0	37.5	50.0	8.0	3.3	4.0	28.9	39.9	31.9

Table 10. Coverage, usage, and average of lexicons for English reviews.

	BOW			SentiWordNet			DS		
	V	*U*	*T*	*V*	*U*	*T*	*V*	*U*	*T*
Books	62.3	24.1	34.7	51.6	5.2	9.4	37.9	32.5	34.9
Kitchen	67.1	28.2	39.7	54.8	2.7	5.1	42.8	39.5	41.1
DVD	60.3	24.2	34.5	46.6	5.0	9.0	34.2	33.2	33.6
Electronics	63.3	25.9	36.7	49.6	2.8	5.2	38.5	35.1	36.7

CONCLUSIONS

The analysis of the sentiment of users' product reviews largely depends on the quality of sentiment lexicons. This paper presents a sentiment lexicon construction approach for mobile shopping. In this approach, a sentiment matrix that considers the relationship between sentiment words and product features is built. The sentiment words are clustered based on the distance between them in the matrix space. One characteristic of our lexicon is that the sentiment words are clustered into several categories rather than into binary or other fixed categories. In other words, the sentiment dimension of the words in our lexicon is flexible. In addition, the product features are filtered based on the idea of TFIDF. Moreover, the EPMI algorithm is proposed, which is more appropriate for the mobile review domain. The experimental results show that our sentiment lexicons outperform the benchmarks with statistically significant differences in terms of sentiment classification tasks, thus proving the effectiveness of the proposed approach.

DATA AVAILABILITY

The datasets generated and analyzed during the current study are available from the corresponding author on reasonable request.

CONFLICTS OF INTEREST

The author declares that there are no conflicts of interest regarding the publication of this paper.

ACKNOWLEDGMENTS

The work described in this paper was partially supported by the National Key R&D Program of China (Grant no. 2018YFC0407901), partially supported by the National Natural Science Foundation of China under Grants no. 61370091 and no. 61602149, partially supported by the Fundamental Research Funds for the Central Universities under Grant no. 2016B01714, and partially supported by the Priority Academic Program Development of Jiangsu Higher Education Institutions. Lau's work is supported by grants from the Research Grants Council of the Hong Kong SAR (Projects CityU 11502115 and CityU 11525716) and the NSFC Basic Research Program (Project 71671155).

REFERENCES

1. A. Montoyo, P. Martínez-Barco, and A. Balahur, "Subjectivity and sentiment analysis: An overview of the current state of the area and envisaged developments," Decision Support Systems, vol. 53, no. 4, pp. 675–679, 2012.
2. B. Pang, L. Lee, and S. Vaithyanathan, "Thumbs up?: sentiment classification using machine learning techniques," in Proceedings of the ACL-02 Conference on Empirical Methods in Natural Language Processing—Volume 10 (EMNLP '02), pp. 79–86, Association for Computational Linguistics, Stroudsburg, Pa, USA, July 2002.
3. P. D. Turney, "Thumbs up or thumbs down?" in Proceedings of the 40th Annual Meeting on Association for Computational Linguistics, pp. 417–424, Philadelphia, Pennsylvania, July 2002.
4. A. Ortigosa, J. M. Martín, and R. M. Carro, "Sentiment analysis in Facebook and its application to e-learning," Computers in Human Behavior, vol. 31, no. 1, pp. 527–541, 2014.
5. B. Liu, "Sentiment analysis and opinion mining," Morgan & Claypool, 2012.
6. M. Hu and B. Liu, "Mining and summarizing customer reviews," in Proceedings of the 10th ACM SIGKDD International Conference on Knowledge Discovery and Data Mining (KDD '04), pp. 168–177, August 2004.
7. Y.-J. Tai and H.-Y. Kao, "Automatic domain-specific sentiment lexicon generation with label propagation," in Proceedings of the International Conference on Information Integration and Web-Based Applications Services, pp. 53–62, 2013.
8. D. Maynard and A. Funk, "Automatic detection of political opinions in tweets," in Proceedings of the 1st Workshop on Making Sense of Microposts 2011: Big Things Come in Small Packages, MSM 2011 - Co-located with the 8th Extended Semantic Web Conference, ESWC 2011, pp. 81–92, Greece, May 2011.
9. Z. Zhang, Q. Ye, Z. Zhang, and Y. Li, "Sentiment classification of internet restaurant reviews written in cantonese," Expert Systems with Applications, vol. 38, no. 6, pp. 7674–7682, 2011.
10. X. Li, J. Cao, and Z. Pan, "Market impact analysis via deep learned architectures," Neural Computing and Applications, pp. 1–12, 2018.
11. F. Enríquez, J. A. Troyano, and T. López-Solaz, "An approach to the

use of word embeddings in an opinion classification task," Expert Systems with Applications, vol. 66, pp. 1–6, 2016.

12. Z. Hailong, G. Wenyan, and J. Bo, "Machine learning and lexicon based methods for sentiment classification: A survey," in Proceedings of the 11th Web Information System and Application Conference, WISA 2014, pp. 262–265, China, September 2014.
13. T. Nasukawa and J. Yi, "Sentiment analysis: Capturing favorability using natural language processing," in Proceedings of the 2nd International Conference on Knowledge Capture, K-CAP 2003, pp. 70–77, USA, October 2003.
14. G. Qiu, X. He, F. Zhang, Y. Shi, J. Bu, and C. Chen, "DASA: Dissatisfaction-oriented Advertising based on Sentiment Analysis," Expert Systems with Applications, vol. 37, no. 9, pp. 6182–6191, 2010.
15. S. Jadav, B. Tanawal, and H. Guadani, "Sentiment analysis: a review," International Journal of Advance Engineering and Research Development, vol. 4, pp. 957–962, 2017.
16. V. Sindhwani and P. Melville, "Document-word co-regularization for semi-supervised sentiment analysis," in Proceedings of the 8th IEEE International Conference on Data Mining, ICDM 2008, pp. 1025–1030, Italy, December 2008.
17. X. Li, H. Xie, L. Chen, J. Wang, and X. Deng, "News impact on stock price return via sentiment analysis," Knowledge-Based Systems, vol. 69, no. 1, pp. 14–23, 2014.
18. G. Badaro, R. Baly, R. Akel et al., "A Light Lexicon-based Mobile Application for Sentiment Mining of Arabic Tweets," in Proceedings of the Second Workshop on Arabic Natural Language Processing, pp. 18–25, Beijing, China, July 2015.
19. J. Kamps, M. Marx, R. J. Mokken, and M. De Rijke, "Using WordNet to measure semantic orientations of adjectives," in Proceedings of the 4th International Conference on Language Resources and Evaluation, LREC 2004, pp. 1115–1118, Portugal, May 2004.
20. W. Medhat, A. Hassan, and H. Korashy, "Sentiment analysis algorithms and applications: a survey," Ain Shams Engineering Journal, vol. 5, no. 4, pp. 1093–1113, 2014.
21. V. Hatzivassiloglou and K. R. McKeown, "Predicting the semantic orientation of adjectives," in Proceedings of the 35th Annual Meeting of

the Association for Computational Linguistics and Eighth Conference of the European Chapter of the Association for Computational Linguistics (ACL '97), pp. 174–181, 1997.

22. P. D. Turney and M. L. Littman, "Measuring praise and criticism: inference of semantic orientation from association," ACM Transactions on Information and System Security, vol. 21, no. 4, pp. 315–346, 2003.
23. A. Yang, J. Lin, Y. Zhou, and J. Chen, "Research on building a Chinese sentiment lexicon based on SO-PMI," Applied Mechanics and Materials, vol. 263-266, no. 1, pp. 1688–1693, 2013.
24. P. Ekman, "An Argument for Basic Emotions," Cognition & Emotion, vol. 6, no. 3-4, pp. 169–200, 1992.
25. V. L. Rubin, J. M. Stanton, and E. D. Liddy, Discerning Emotions in Texts, Stanford University, 2004.
26. A. Tellegen, D. Watson, and L. A. Clark, "On the dimensional and hierarchical structure of affect," Psychological Science, vol. 10, no. 4, pp. 297–303, 1999.
27. E. Cambria, S. Poria, A. Gelbukh, and M. Thelwall, "Sentiment Analysis Is a Big Suitcase," IEEE Intelligent Systems, vol. 32, no. 6, pp. 74–80, 2017.
28. E. Fast, B. Chen, and M. S. Bernstein, "Empath: Understanding topic signals in large-scale text," in Proceedings of the 34th Annual Conference on Human Factors in Computing Systems, CHI 2016, pp. 4647–4657, USA, May 2016.
29. H. Zhang, Z. Yu, M. Xu, and Y. Shi, "Feature-level sentiment analysis for Chinese product reviews," in Proceedings of the 3rd International Conference on Computer Research and Development (ICCRD), pp. 135–140, Shanghai, China, March 2011.
30. M. Gilad, "Experiments with mood classification in blog posts," ACM Transactions on Multimedia Computing Communications and Applications, 2005.
31. F. Benamara, C. Cesarano, A. Picariello, D. Reforgiato, and V. S. Subrahmanian, "Sentiment analysis: Adjectives and adverbs are better than adjectives alone," in Proceedings of the 2007 International Conference on Weblogs and Social Media, ICWSM 2007, USA, March 2007.
32. Y. Lu, X. Kong, X. Quan, W. Liu, and Y. Xu, "Exploring the Sentiment Strength of User Reviews," in Web-Age Information Management, vol.

6184 of Lecture Notes in Computer Science, pp. 471–482, Springer, Berlin, Germany, 2010.

33. T. Wilson, P. Hoffmann, S. Somasundaran et al., "OpinionFinder," in Proceedings of the HLT/EMNLP, pp. 34-35, Vancouver, British Columbia, Canada, October 2005.
34. C. Hou, F. Nie, D. Yi, and D. Tao, "Discriminative embedded clustering: a framework for grouping high-dimensional data," IEEE Transactions on Neural Networks and Learning Systems, vol. 26, no. 6, pp. 1287–1299, 2015.
35. J. Blitzer, M. Dredze, and F. Pereira, "Biographies, bollywood, boom-boxes and blenders: domain adaptation for sentiment classification," in Proceedings of the 45th Annual Meeting of the Association for Computational Linguistics (ACL '07), pp. 440–447, June 2007.
36. T. Mikolov, I. Sutskever, K. Chen, G. Corrado, and J. Dean, "Distributed representations of words and phrases and their compositionality," in Proceedings of the 27th Annual Conference on Neural Information Processing Systems (NIPS '13), pp. 3111–3119, December 2013.
37. F. Pedregosa, G. Varoquaux, and A. Gramfort, "Scikit-learn: machine learning in Python," Journal of Machine Learning Research, vol. 12, pp. 2825–2830, 2011.
38. D. Zhang, H. Xu, Z. Su, and Y. Xu, "Chinese comments sentiment classification based on word2vec and SVMperf," Expert Systems with Applications, vol. 42, no. 4, pp. 1857–1863, 2015.
39. H. Lin, L. Xu, H. Ren et al., "Constructing the affective lexicon ontology," Journal of The China Society for Science and Technical Information, vol. 27, pp. 180–185, 2008.
40. A. Edgar, R. Sidarta, S. Mariano, and F. S. Diego, "Comparative study of LSA vs Word2vec embeddings in small corpora: a case study in dreams database," in ASAI Simposio Argentino de Inteligencia Artificial, 2016.
41. P. Domingos and M. Pazzani, "Beyond independence: Conditions for the optimality of the simple bayesian classifier," Machine Learning, vol. 29, pp. 103–130, 1996.

CHAPTER

15

Using Sentence-Level Neural Network Models for Multiple-Choice Reading Comprehension Tasks

Yuanlong Wang[1], Ru Li[1,2], Hu Zhang,[1] Hongyan Tan,[1] and Qinghua Chai[3]

[1]School of Computer and Information Technology, Shanxi University, Taiyuan 030006, China

[2]Key Laboratory of Computation Intelligence and Chinese Information Processing of Ministry of Education, Shanxi University, Taiyuan 030006, China

[3]School of Foreign Languages, Shanxi University, Taiyuan 030006, China

ABSTRACT

Comprehending unstructured text is a challenging task for machines because

Citation: Yuanlong Wang, Ru Li, Hu Zhang, Hongyan Tan, and Qinghua Chai, "Using Sentence-Level Neural Network Models for Multiple-Choice Reading Comprehension Tasks", Journal on Wireless Communications and Mobile Computing, Volume 2018, Article 2678976, 8 pages, https://doi.org/10.1155/2018/2678976.

it involves understanding texts and answering questions. In this paper, we study the multiple-choice task for reading comprehension based on MC Test datasets and Chinese reading comprehension datasets, among which Chinese reading comprehension datasets which are built by ourselves. Observing the above-mentioned training sets, we find that "sentence comprehension" is more important than "word comprehension" in multiple-choice task, and therefore we propose sentence-level neural network models. Our model firstly uses LSTM network and a composition model to learn compositional vector representation for sentences and then trains a sentence-level attention model for obtaining the sentence-level attention between the sentence embedding in documents and the optional sentences embedding by dot product. Finally, a consensus attention is gained by merging individual attention with the merging function. Experimental results show that our model outperforms various state-of-the-art baselines significantly for both the multiple-choice reading comprehension datasets.

INTRODUCTION

Reading comprehension is the ability of reading texts, understanding their meanings, and answering questions. When machines are required to comprehend texts, they need to understand unstructured text and do reasoning based on the text [1–3]. It is a major task in the field of natural language processing and machine learning.

Recently, machine reading comprehension (MC) is increasingly drawing attention and several large reading comprehension datasets have also been released. For the several released datasets, the task is getting more and more difficult (from CNN/Daily Mail datasets to SQuAD and then to TriviaQA) as system performance has rapidly improved with each new released datasets.

The CNN/Daily Mail datasets [4] is a cloze-style reading comprehension task, which aims to comprehend a given document and then to answer questions based on the given document, and the answer to each question is a single word inside of the document. The SQuAD [5] is a question-answering reading comprehension task, which further constrains answers often including nonentities and being much longer phrases to be a continuous subspan of the document. Clearly, the question-answering task is more difficult than the cloze-style task.

The TriviaQA [6] is also a question-answering reading comprehension task, but the task in TriviaQA is more difficult than the task in SQuAD because answers in TriviaQA are independent of the evidence and belong to a diverse set of types.

Different from the above, the task based on the MCTest datasets [3] is a multiple-choice reading comprehension, each example of which consists of one document and four associated questions and each question gives four candidate answers and only one answer is correct among them. In this paper, we focus on such problem of answering multiple-choice questions in documents, and, at the same time, we also release a Chinese reading comprehension dataset for such multiple-choice task. To our knowledge, the dataset is the first Chinese reading comprehension dataset of this kind and is even more complex than MCTest datasets. The example of such dataset consists of one document and one associated question which gives five candidate answers. The specific details of this dataset are in Section 2. Frankly, the multiple-choice reading comprehension task remains quite challenging. For one thing, answers in the form of an optional sentence usually do not appear in the document; for another, finding the correct answer of the given question requires reasoning across multiple sentences. Hence, sentence comprehension is more important than word comprehension in the task of the multiple-choice reading comprehension.

To carry out the task of sentence comprehension, we propose a sentence-level attention model primarily inspired by the attention model for the Cloze-style reading comprehension [7, 8]. However, unlike the Cloze-style attention model, answers to multiple-choice questions are optional sentences. Karl et al. [9] train an encoder-decoder model to encode a sentence into a fixed length vector and subsequently decode both the following sentences. They also demonstrate that the low-dimensional vector embeddings are useful for other tasks. Pichotta et al. [10] present a sentence-level LSTM language model for script inference.

The results show that the model is useful for predicting missing information in text. Similar to the above model, we also present a sentence representation model which uses LSTM network to learn vector representation for sentences. Moreover, we use sentence composition model to represent sentence vector because the model can express hierarchical sentences from words to phrases, and to sentences.

In order to retain more information about two kinds of sentences representation model, we employ connection method to compose the final sentence vector. Then, we train a sentence attention model between optional sentences and sentences in the document. The machine is able to learn the relationships between the document and optional sentences by the attention-based neural network. Experimental results show that our approach can effectively improve the performance of the task of multiple-choice reading comprehension. In the following text, Chinese reading comprehension datasets, related work, details of our model, and experiments will be described, and, afterwards, our experiments will be analyzed.

CHINESE READING COMPREHENSION DATASETS

In this paper, we focus on the multiple-choice reading comprehension task. Similar to the MCTest datasets, each example consists of one document and one associated questions. And each question gives five candidate answers. However, the dataset is more complex than MCTest datasets, and it is a literary reading comprehension dataset from test materials of final exam in senior high school. Box 1 shows an example of Chinese reading comprehension datasets.

Document:
"Ruins" is a derogatory term that it is irrelevant to cultural and aesthetic in many Chinese mind, and interpretation of the word "ruins" is only a "city and village are changed into desolate places by destruction or natural disasters" in the "Modern Chinese Dictionary"; There is no fault for the interpretation, but it is not enough if it is measured by world knowledge. In Europe, the meaning of "ruins" has been enriched and expanded since modern times. It has been endowed with the connotation of culture and aesthetics, and has become an academic concept. The of meaning of the "ruins" is changed from the Renaissance in Europe.

Question:
Please choice two incorrect options according to the content of the document:

Choice:
A. One of the purposes of this paper is to correct the misunderstanding of the term "ruins" in the modern Chinese dictionary.
B. The Great Wall Ruins have condensed the vicissitudes of time in China and it have a "perception of the intoxicated" as the Acropolis ruins.
C. Remains of the ruins often reveals the extraordinary wisdom and great efforts of the predecessors, which bring to the future generations with the shock and resonance of the soul.
D. Awareness of the ruins is related to the aesthetic consciousness of countrymen, but also it is conducive to the popularity of the "repair the old as the old".
E. This paper not only contains historical interest, but also infiltrated the concern of reality, and express the author's desire to enhance the cultural quality of the nation.

Box 1. Example for the multiple-choice reading comprehension for literature (the original data is in Chinese, we translate this sample in English for clarity).

For the dataset, the description of questions is basically fixed, as in the following: "Question". Therefore, the role of question is ignored in the Chinese reading comprehension task. The goal of the task is to understand the individual document and to select the most consistent options with the meaning of the document. Thus the Chinese reading comprehension can be described as a triple:

$$\langle D, C, A \rangle \quad (1)$$

where D is the document, C denotes the choice, and A is a set in which each element is marked as 0 or 1 according to the document meaning (if the option is consistent with the document meaning, it is labeled as 1; otherwise it is labeled as 0). The A can be described as the following:

Question: "Please choose two incorrect options according to the content of the document: "

Answer: C E

A(Answer label): (1 1 0 1 0)

In the training stage, we choose a 769-literary-reading-comprehension dataset which is collected from test materials of final exam in senior high school. In the testing stage, the dataset includes three parts: 13 Beijing college entrance examination papers (BCEETest), 12 simulation materials (SBCEETest1) which is provided by iFLYTEK company, and 52 test materials of final exam in Beijing senior high school (SBCEETest2). All of datasets are collected by the Chinese information processing group of Shanxi University. The statistics of training and testing data are shown in Table 1.

Table 1. Statistics of multiple-choice reading comprehension datasets: train and three tests.

	Documents	Sentences	options
Train	769	28235	3845
BCEETest	13	548	65
SBCEETest1	12	517	60
SBCEETest2	52	2056	260

RELATED WORK

Machine comprehension is currently a hot topic within the machine learning community. In this section we will focus on the best-performing models applied to MCTest and CNN/Daily Mail according to two kinds of reading comprehension tasks.

Multiple-Choice Reading Comprehension

Existing models are mostly based on manually engineered features for MCTest [11–13]. These engineered feature models are extremely effective. However, this research often requires significant effort on the auxiliary tools to extract the feature and its capacity for generalization is limited.

Yin et al.[14] proposed a hierarchical attention-based convolutional neural network for multiple-choice reading comprehension task. The model considers multiple levels of granularity, from word to sentence level and then from sentence to snippet level. This model performs poorly on MCTest. A possible reason that can explain this is that the dataset is sparse. However, neural model can address the extracted features problem, so it appeals to increasing interest in multiple-choice reading comprehension task. For sequence data, the recurrent neural network often is used. So we propose a recurrent neural network model for the multiple-choice reading comprehension. Our model uses the bidirectional LSTM to get contextual representations of the sentence.

Cloze-Style Reading Comprehension

Hermann et al. [4] published the CNN/Daily Mail news corpus, where the content is formed by news articles and its summarization. Also, Cui et al. [7] released HFL-RC PD&CFT for Chinese reading comprehension datasets, which includes People Daily news datasets and Children 's Fairy tale datasets. On these datasets, many neural network models have been proposed for the Cloze-style reading comprehension tasks. Hermann et al. [4] proposed the attentive and impatient readers. The attentive reader uses bidirectional document and query encoders to compute an attention and the impatient reader computes attention over the document after reading every word of the query. Chen et al. [1] proposed a new neural network architecture for the Cloze-style reading comprehension. In contrast to the attentive reader, the attention weights of the model are computed with a bilinear term instead of simple dot product. Kadlec et al. [15] proposed the Attention Sum Reader, which uses attention to directly pick the answer from the context. The model uses attention as pointer over discrete tokens in the context document and then directly sums the word attention across all the occurrences. Cui et al. [7] presented the consensus attention-based neural network, namely, Consensus Attention Sum Reader, and released Chinese reading comprehension datasets. The model computes an attention to every time slice of query and makes a consensus attention among different steps. Cui et al. [8] also proposed the attention-over-attention neural network, namely, Attention-over-Attention Reader. The model presents an attention mechanism that places another attention over the primary attention, to indicate the "importance" of each attention. Dhingra et al.[16] proposed the gated-attention readers for text comprehension. The model integrates a multihop architecture with an attention mechanism which is based on multiplicative interactions between the query embedding and the intermediate states of a recurrent neural network document reader.

To summarize, all of them are attention-based RNN models which have been shown to be extremely effective for the word-level task. At each time-step, these models take a word as input, update a hidden state vector, and predict the answer. In this paper, we propose sentence-level attention model for the multiple-choice reading comprehension. Our work is primarily inspired by the attention model for the Cloze-style reading comprehension.

SENTENCE-LEVEL NEURAL NETWORK READER

In this section, we will introduce our sentence-level neural network models for the multiple-choice reading comprehension task, namely, Sentence-Level Attention Reader. Our model is primarily motivated by that of Cui et al. [7], which aims to directly estimate the answer of optional sentence from the sentence-level attention instead of calculating the answer of entity from the word-level attention. The level structure of our model is shown in Figure 1. Firstly, the document is divided into several sentences $D = \{s_1, s_2, \ldots s_n\}$ and the sentence embedding is computed by embedding layer. Secondly, we use the bidirectional LSTM to get contextual representations of the sentence, in which the representation of each sentence is formed by concatenating the forward and backward hidden states. Thirdly, the sentence-level attention is computed by a dot product between the sentence embedding in the document and the optional embedding. Finally, the individual attention is merged to a consensus attention by the merging function. The following will give a formal description of our proposed model.

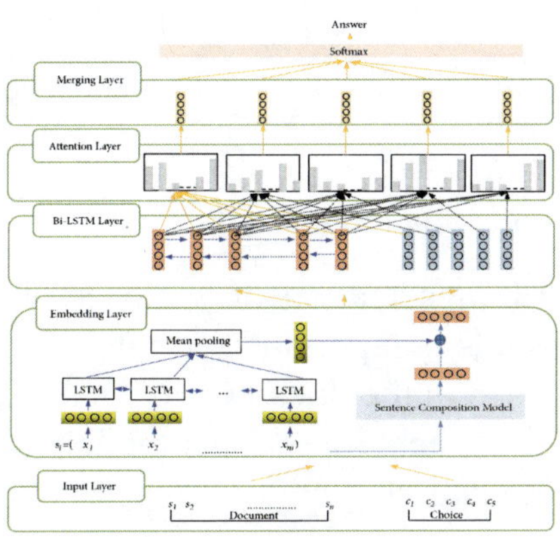

Figure 1. Sentence-level attention neural network. The network includes 5 layers: input layer, embedding layer, Bi-LSTM layer, attention layer, and merging layer.

Sentence Representation

The input of our model is the sentences in the document and options, and each sentence consists of word sequence. The sentence is translated into sentence embedding by embedding layer, which is composed of LSTM sentence model and sentence composition model[17] as illustrated in the embedding layer of Figure 1. The LSTM sentence model is a single bi-LSTM layer followed by an average pooling layer. The bi-LSTM layer is used to get the contextual representations of words and the average pooling layer is used to merge word vectors into sentence vectors. On the other hand, we used the sentence composition model to compose sentence vector. The sentence vector is combined by the trained neural network model, which is trained by the triple consisting of single words and phrases vector (as triple(w_1, w_2, p)). The sentence composition model is illustrated in Figure 2. We denote p_i as the final sentence vector. In order to retain more information about two kinds of sentences› representation model, we employ a multilayer neural network to compose the final sentence vector, $p_i(sp_1, sp_2) = sp_1{}^T M\, sp_2$, where sp_1 is the sentence vector for LSTM sentence model, sp_2 is the sentence vector for sentence composition model, and M is a parameter matrix.

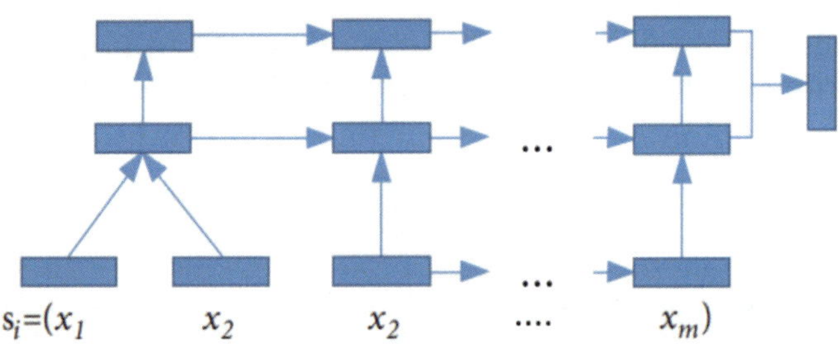

Figure 2. Sentence composition model.

In addition to the representation of sentences mentioned above, the context of sentence is also important for inferring the answer. So the embedding of the sentence in the document is inputted into bi-LSTM layer to get their contextual representations. In our model, the bidirectional LSTM is used as RNN implementation.

$$\overrightarrow{h_i} = LSTM\left(\overrightarrow{h_{i-1}}, p_i\right), \quad i = 1, 2, \ldots m \tag{2}$$

$$\overleftarrow{h_i} = LSTM\left(\overleftarrow{h_{i+1}}, p_i\right), \quad i = m, m-1, \ldots 1 \tag{3}$$

$$h_i = concat\left(\overrightarrow{h_i}, \overleftarrow{h_i}\right) \tag{4}$$

Finally, we take h_i to represent the contextual representations of sentences. $h_{c\text{-}s} \in R^d$ denote the sentence embedding of the option, where d denotes the number of options.

Sentence-Level Attention

In attention layer, we directly use a dot product of h_i and h_{c_s} to compute the "importance" of each sentence in the document for each option. And we use the softmax function to get a probability distribution. For each sentence in the document, "attention" is computed as follows.

$$\alpha(t) = softmax\left(h_i(t) \bullet h_{c\_s}\right) \tag{5}$$

where variable α(t) is the attention weight a tth sentence in document.

In merging layer, the consensus attention is calculated by a merging function as follows.

$$s \propto \begin{cases} \sum_{t=1}^{m} \alpha(t), & if\ mode = sum; \\ \frac{1}{m}\sum_{t=1}^{m} \alpha(t), & if\ mode = avg; \\ \max_{t=1\ldots m} \alpha(t), & if\ mode = max; \\ \frac{1}{n}\sum_{t=1}^{n} \alpha(t), & if\ mode = max + avg, \end{cases} \tag{6}$$

where n is the top number of the attention weight and n<m.

Output Layer

Finally, the answer is estimated by the softmax function.

$$a_i = soft\ \max\left(W_a * s_i\right), \quad i = 1 \ldots 5 \tag{7}$$

where W_a indicate the weight matrix in the softmax layer and a_i is a probability distribution of the answer. The prediction of answer labels (such as "1 1 0 1 0") is gotten by the probability. Figure 1 shows the proposed neural network architecture.

EXPERIMENTS

In this section we evaluate our model on the MCTest and our Chinese reading comprehension datasets. We find that although the model is simple, it achieves state-of-the-art performance on these datasets.

Experimental Details

We use stochastic gradient descent with AdaDelta update rule [18], which only uses the first-order information to adaptively update learning rate over time and has minimal computational overhead. To train model, we minimize the negative log-likelihood as the objective function. The batch size is set to 5 and the number of iterations is set to 25.

For word vectors we use Google's publicly available embedding [19], whose training dataset is 70 thousand literary papers. The dimension of word embedding is set to 200. While we are implementing the sentence-level attention reader, it is easy to overfit the training data. Thus, we adopt dropout method [20] for regularization purpose and handling overfitting problems. The dropout rate is 0.1 on Chinese reading comprehension datasets and 0.01 on MCTest datasets, respectively. Implementation of our model is done with theano [21].

The answer is predicted according to whether the option is consistent with the document meaning for multiple-choice task, so we only evaluate our system performance in terms of precision (P= right_options/sum_options).

Results on MCTest Dataset

To verify the effectiveness of our proposed model, we test firstly our model on public datasets. Table 2 presents the performance of feature engineering and neural methods on the MCTest test set. The first four rows represent feature engineering methods and the last four rows are neural methods. As we can see the feature engineering methods outperform the neural methods significantly. One possible reason is that the neural methods suffered from the relative lack of training data. So we are going to analyze the related feature and add it to our neural network model in future work.

Table 2. Experimental results for MCTest.

Method	MC160 Test	MC500 Test
Richardson et al.(2013)+RTE	0.691	0.633
Sachan et al.(2015)	-	0.678
Wang et al.(2015)	0.753	0.699
Trischler et al.(2016)	0.746	0.710
Attentive Reader	0.463	0.419
Neural Reasoner	0.476	0.456
HABCNN-TE	0.631	0.529
Sentence-Level Attention Reader (mode:max+avg)	0.664	0.673

For neural methods, the attentive reader [4] is implemented at word representation level and it is a deep model with thousands of parameters, so it performs poorly on MCTest. The neural reasoner [22] has multiple reasoning layers and all temporary reasoning affects the final answer representation. The HABCNN-TE [14] is convolutional architecture network. It can cut down on the parameter count, but the context representation can not be presented enough. Our method addresses the problems of the above methods. Firstly, the recurrent architecture network also cuts down on the parameter count and it can present the context representation at sentence level. Then, we use the max+avg method to reduce the impact of all snippets. Experimental results also demonstrate that our method performs better than the other three neural methods.

Results on Chinese Reading Comprehension Datasets

We have set four baselines for Chinese reading comprehension datasets. One is the HABCNN-TE method which is the most optimal method on MCTest datasets and the other three are as follows.

(i) The first baseline is inspired by Cui et al. [7]. We use the consensus attention-based neural network (called CAS Reader) for word of document and option. The model computes the attention of each document word directly, in respect to each option word at time t. The final consensus attention of option is computed by a merging function.

(ii) The second baseline uses a sliding window and matches a bag of words constructed from the document and the option, respectively (called Match Reader). This baseline is inspired from Zhang et al. [23].

(iii) The third baseline is the sentence similarity measure model (called SM Reader). The similarity is presented by the cosine similarity between the document sentence and the option sentence. The sentence representation is taken from Tai et al. [24]. The experimental results are given in Table 3.

Table 3. Comparison of different reader model on three testing datasets.

Method	BCEETest	SBCEETestl	SBCEETest2
HABCNN-TE	0.428	0.442	0.438
Match Reader	0.461	0.452	0.455
SM Reader	0.495	0.491	0.499
CAS Reader	0.513	0.503	0.516
Sentence-Level Attention Reader (mode:max+avg)	0.581	0.535	0.578

The results on three test sets show that our sentence-level attention reader gives competitive results among various state-of-the-art baselines. We can observe that the accuracy in BCEETest outperforms the other test set. A possible reason can be that the college entrance examination is more standardized than that of the simulation. Also, we have noticed that the performance of the sentence-level model is better than the word-level model. For example, in BCEETest set, the SM Reader (sentence-level) outperforms the Match Reader (word-level) by 3.4% and The Sentence-Level Attention Reader (sentence-level) outperforms the CAS Reader (word-level) by 4.9% in precision, respectively.

In experimenting we find out that the number of related sentences with the option is very important. So we also evaluate different merging functions as CAS Reader. The results are shown in Table 4. From the results, we can see that the avg and sum methods outperform the max method. A possible reason can be that the max method is equivalent to one sentence of document instead of the original document and a lot of information is lost. However, doing it achieves the best performance in which all sentences in document are used in the model. In order to measure it, we also use the max+avg method as the merging function. The "max" denotes the top N sentences and the "avg" denotes the average of top N sentences. In comparison with the avg method, the accuracy of the max+avg method increased by around 2% on three datasets. And this result is consistent with error analysis in Section 5.5. We suspect that some sentences interfere with the final answer as negative factor. Figure 3 shows the experiment about top N. We select randomly 5 options to do the experiment from the 13 Beijing college entrance examination papers (BCEETest). As we can see, the attention will not continue to increase in around 10. So N is set to 10 in our model. As shown in Box 2. The bold word denotes the most related sentences with the choice c_i; the italic word has a little relation with the choice c_i; the "......" is not relation.

Table 4. Results of different merging function.

	BCEETest	SBCEETest1	SBCEETest2
Mode:avg	0.562	0.513	0.550
Mode:sum	0.554	0.503	0.531
Mode:max	0.492	0.496	0.442
Mode:max+avg	0.581	0.535	0.578

"Ruins" is a derogatory term that it is irrelevant to cultural and aesthetic in many Chinese mind, and interpretation of the word "ruins" is only a "city and village are changed into desolate places by destruction or natural disasters" in the "Modern Chinese Dictionary"; There is no fault for the interpretation, but it is not enough if it is measured by world knowledge. *In Europe, the meaning of "ruins" has been enriched and expanded since modern times. It has been endowed with the connotation of culture and aesthetics, and has become an academic concept.......*

C_i="One of the purposes of this paper is to correct the misunderstanding of the term "ruins" in the modern Chinese dictionary."

Box 2. Example of related sentences with the choice.

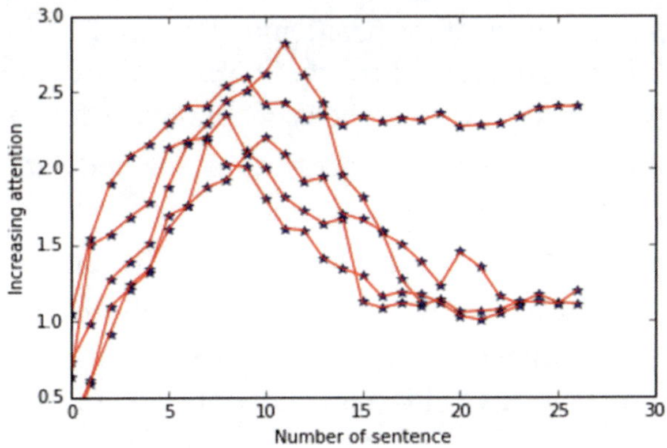

Figure 3. Experiment about the top N.

Sentence Representation Model Analysis

In this paper, we use two models for the sentence representation, which are LSTM sentence model and sentence composition model [17]. Therefore, we have tested the contribution of the two models to the final model, respectively. The results are shown in Table 5.

Table 5. Results of two sentence representation models.

	BCEETest	SBCEETest1	SBCEETest2
LSTM sentence model	0.518	0.495	0.489
Sentence composition model	0.483	0.506	0.522
Fusion model	0.581	0.535	0.578

The results on three test sets show that the precision of the fusion model is better than that of any single model. Therefore, we use the fusion model in sentence-level attention neural network.

Error Analysis

To better evaluate the proposed approach, we perform a qualitative analysis of its errors. Two major errors are revealed by our analysis, as discussed below.

(i) The positioning feature word (such as "The second paragraph…") often appears in the options. To further analyze the locating property of our model, we also examine the dependence of accuracy on the positioning feature word. And all sentences are replaced by related sentences of the positioning feature word in document. The accuracy has increased by about 3% on these three datasets. The positioning feature word we use is shown as follows.

[The end of paper; The second paragraph; The end paragraph; The end of paper; The first paragraph]

According to the above description, we will consider adding more features, such as location features, into our model in future work.

(ii) Our model may make mistakes when the option is expressed with emotion (such as "This paper not only contains historical interest, but also infiltrated the concern of reality and express the author's desire to enhance the cultural quality of the nation."). It is very difficult to calculate the attention between the option emotion and the document emotion. To handle such case correctly, our model will consider the emotion feature in future work. We have about more than 500 emotion feature words, like "thought provoking", "directly express one' s mind", and so forth.

CONCLUSION

In this paper, we introduce a sentence-level neural network model to handle the multiple-choice Chinese reading comprehension problems. The experimental results show that our model gives a state-of-the-art accuracy on all the evaluated datasets. We also use the max+avg method as the merging function and the accuracy of the max+avg method increased by about 2%. Furthermore, we analyze the positioning feature word and find that the accuracy increased by about 3%.

The future work will be carried out in the following aspects. First, we would like to extend our Chinese reading comprehension datasets and release it. Second, we are going to analyze the emotion feature and add it to our neural network model.

DATA AVAILABILITY

The Chinese reading comprehension data used to support the findings of this study are available from the corresponding author upon request.

CONFLICTS OF INTEREST

The authors declare that they have no conflicts of interest.

ACKNOWLEDGMENTS

This work was supported by the National Natural Science Foundation of China (nos. 61772324, 61673248), the Shanxi Natural Science Foundation of China (no. 201601D102030), and Program for Fostering Talents of Shanxi Province Joint Postgraduate Training Base (nos. 2017JD05, 2018JD01).

REFERENCES

1. D. Chen, J. Bolton, and C. D. Manning, "A thorough examination of the CNN/daily mail reading comprehension task," in Proceedings of the 54th Annual Meeting of the Association for Computational Linguistics, ACL 2016, pp. 2358–2367, August 2016.
2. Y. Z. Liu, S. M. Sun, and L. Y. X. Kand Ruobing, "Knowledge representation learning: a review," Journal of Computer Research and Development, vol. 53, no. 2, pp. 247–261, 2016.
3. R. Matthew, J. C. Christopher, and R. Erin, "MCTest: a challenge dataset for the open-domain machine comprehension of text," in Proceedings of the 2013 on Empirical Methods in Natural Language Processing, pp. 193–203, 2013.
4. H. Felix, B. Antoine, C. Sumit, and W. Jason, "The goldilocks principle: reading children s books with explicit memory representations," 2015, https://arxiv.org/abs/1511.02301.
5. R. Pranav, Z. Jian, L. Konstantin, and L. Percy, "SQuAD: 100,000+ Questions for machine comprehension of text," in Proceedings of the 2016 Conference on Empirical Methods in Natural Language Processing, pp. 2383–2392, 2016.
6. J. Mandar, C. Eunsol, SW. Daniel, and Z. Luke, "TriviaQA: a large scale distantly supervised challenge dataset for reading comprehension," in Proceeding of the 55th Annual Meeting of the Association for Computational Linguistics, pp. 1601–1611, 2017.
7. Y. M. Cui, T. Liu, and Z. P. Chen, "Consensus attention- based neural networks for Chinese reading comprehension," 2016, https://arxiv.org/help/prep.
8. Y. Cui, Z. Chen, S. Wei, S. Wang, T. Liu, and G. Hu, "Attention-over-attention neural networks for reading comprehension," in Proceedings of the 55th Annual Meeting of the Association for Computational Linguistics, pp. 593–602, 2017.
9. M. H. Karl, K. Tomas, G. Edward et al., "Teaching machines to read and comprehend," In Advances in Neural Information Processing Systems, pp. 1684–1692, 2015.
10. J. M. Karl PRaymond, "Using sentence-level LSTM language models for script inference," in Proceeding of the 54th Annual Meeting of the Association for Computational Linguistics, pp. 279–289, 2016.
11. S. Mrinmaya, D. Avinava, P. X. Eric, and R. Matthew, "Learning answer-

entailing structures for machine comprehension," in In Proceeding of the 53th Annual Meeting of the Association for Computational Linguistics, pp. 239–249, 2015.

12. H. Wang, B. Mohit, G. Kevin, and A. M. David, "Machine comprehension with syntax, frames, and semantics," in Proceedings of the 53th Annual Meeting of the Association for Computational Linguistics, pp. 700–706, 2015.
13. T. Adam, Z. Ye, and Y. Xingdi, "A parallel-hierarchical model for machine comprehension on sparse," in Proceedings of the 54th Annual Meeting of the Association for Computational Linguistics, pp. 432–441, 2016.
14. W. Yin, S. Ebert, and H. Schütze, "Attention-Based Convolutional Neural Network for Machine Comprehension," in Proceedings of the Workshop on Human-Computer Question Answering, pp. 15–21, San Diego, California, June 2016.
15. K. Rudolf, S. Martin, B. Ondrej, and K. Jan, "Text understanding with the attention sum reader network," 2016, https://arxiv.org/abs/1603.01547.
16. D. Bhuwan, H. Liu X, and L. Yang Z, "Gated-attention readers for text comprehension," in Proceeding of the 55th Annual Meeting of the Association for Computational Linguistics, pp. 1832–1846, 2017.
17. Y. L. Wang, "Sentence composition model for reading comprehension," Journal of Computer Application, vol. 37, no. 6, pp. 1741–1746, 2017.
18. D. Z. Matthew, "Adadelta: an adaptive learning rate method," 2012, https://arxiv.org/abs/1212.5701.
19. M. Tomas, C. Kai, C. Greg, and D. Jeffrey, "Efficient estimation of word representations in vector space," in Proceedings of the In Proceedings of workshop at ICLR, pp. 1–12, 2013.
20. S. Nitish, E. H. Geoffrey, K. Alex, S. Ilya, and S. Ruslan, "Dropout, a simple way to prevent neural networks from overfitting," Journal of Machine Learning Research, vol. 15, no. 1, pp. 1929–1958, 2014.
21. Theano Development Team, "Theano: a python framework for fast computation of mathematical expressions," 2016, https://arxiv.org/abs/1605.02688.
22. P. Baolin, L. Zhengdong, L. Hang, and W. Kanfai, "Toward neural network-based reasoning," 2015, https://arxiv.org/abs/1508.05508.

23. Zhang Z. C., Z. Yu, and T. Liu, "Answer sentence extraction of reading comprehension based on shallow sematic tree kernel," Journal of Chinese Information Processing, vol. 22, no. 1, pp. 80–86, 2008.

24. T. Kaisheng, S. Richard, and D. M. Christopher, "Improved semantic representations from tree-structured long short-term memory networks," in Proceedings of the 53th Annual Meeting of the Association for Computational Linguistics, pp. 1556–1566, 2015.

CHAPTER 16

A Bibliometric Review of Natural Language Processing Empowered Mobile Computing

Xieling Chen,[1] Ruoyao Ding,[2] Kai Xu,[3] Shan Wang,[4] Tianyong Hao,[5] and Yi Zhou[6]

[1]College of Economics, Jinan University, Guangzhou, China

[2]School of Information Science and Technology, Guangdong University of Foreign Studies, Guangzhou, China

[3]School of Computer Science and Technology, Guangdong University of Technology, Guangzhou, China

[4]Department of Chinese Language and Literature, University of Macau, Macau SAR, China

[5]School of Computer, South China Normal University, Guangzhou, China

[6]Zhongshan School of Medicine, Sun Yat-sen University, Guangzhou, China

Citation: Xieling Chen, Ruoyao Ding, Kai Xu, Shan Wang, Tianyong Hao, and Yi Zhou, "A Bibliometric Review of Natural Language Processing Empowered Mobile Computing", Journal on Wireless Communications and Mobile Computing, Volume 2018, Article ID 1827074, 21 pages, https://doi.org/10.1155/2018/1827074.

ABSTRACT

Natural Language Processing (NLP) empowered mobile computing is the use of NLP techniques in the context of mobile environment. Research in this field has drawn much attention given the continually increasing number of publications in the last five years. This study presents the status and development trend of the research field through an objective, systematic, and comprehensive review of relevant publications available from Web of Science. Analysis techniques including a descriptive statistics method, a geographic visualization method, a social network analysis method, a latent dirichlet allocation method, and an affinity propagation clustering method are used. We quantitatively analyze the publications in terms of statistical characteristics, geographical distribution, cooperation relationship, and topic discovery and distribution. This systematic analysis of the field illustrates the publications evolution over time and identifies current research interests and potential directions for future research. Our work can potentially assist researchers in keeping abreast of the research status. It can also help monitoring new scientific and technological development in the research field.

INTRODUCTION

With the development of mobile devices as well as the advances in wireless communication technologies, mobile computing is becoming a significantly important paradigm in today's world of networked computing systems [1]. Mobile computing enables a computer to be used normally while in the state of movement. Based on perceived situational information in personal and ubiquitous environments, mobile computing provides services automatically. With the rapid growth in use of mobile devices, far-reaching and diverse information is being produced rapidly and distributed instantly in digitized format [2]. A large amount of valuable information existing in unstructured texts are of great need of processing, such as web pages, short messages, Twitter/WeChat messages, etc. Natural Language Processing (NLP) focuses on the interactions between computers and natural language texts. NLP is capable of providing a computer program with the ability to process and understand unstructured texts. By automatically analyzing the meaning of user content to take appropriate actions, NLP can make applications smarter in the mobile environment.

NLP empowered mobile computing research field has attracted more and more interests from scientific community, witnessing 12 publications in 2000 to 55 publications in 2016 from Web of Science (WoS). Some representative examples are as follows. Chen et al. [3] applied the technique of multitask learning using deep neural networks to Mandarin-English code-mixing recognition. Three schemes of the auxiliary tasks were proposed to introduce the language information to networks and to improve the prediction of language switching for the primary task of senone classification. The proposed schemes enhanced the recognition on both languages and reduced the relative overall error rates by 4.4% on average when dealing with real-world Mandarin-English corpus in mobile voice search. Ilayaraja et al. [4] presented a weighted association rule mining prefetching technique to determine the secondary service item, with the consideration of access frequency of services, semantic distance among the successive query request, and spatial distance between service instances and user context (e.g., position, service type, and query request time). Wong et al. [5] analyzed the students' vocabulary usage using a corpus analysis tool to identify and unpack the contextual conditions in which a mobile- and cloud-assisted Chinese language learning environment promoted key learning outcomes. Räsänen and Saarinen [6] proposed a method based on sparse hyperdimensional coding of sequence structures for sequence prediction. Their experiments suggested that the method was capable of capturing the relevant variable-order structure from the sequences. A NLP based tool MOTTE was developed by Puppala et al. [7] for extracting and structuring data in pathology reports automatically to support clinical solution applications. With an aim of screening information on human immunodeficiency virus/acquired immune deficiency syndrome, Adesina et al. [8] designed a monolingual short message services based system for the retrieval of frequently asked questions.

Bibliometric analysis is defined as the use of statistical methods on evaluating scholarly publications from an objective and quantitative perspective within a certain field [9]. Benefits of bibliometric analysis include (1) organizing information in a specific thematic field [10], (2) evaluating scientific developments in knowledge of a specific subject and assessing the scientific quality [11], (3) determining the impact of research funding, (4) comparing research performance across different affiliations and document changes in the research workforce, and (5) identifying emerging areas of research focus and predicting future research success [12]. As for researchers, especially newcomers, bibliometric analysis can assist them in (1) better selecting potential research topics, (2) demonstrating the values and impacts of their relevant works, (3) recognizing appropriate academic researchers to seek research collaboration, and (4) keeping abreast of new research status and new technological changes [13].

Bibliometric analysis has been widely applied to various fields for the measurement of quality and productivity of academic output and has demonstrated excellent effectiveness from long-term practice. Relevant researches mainly focused on revealing publication statistical characteristics, exploring the collaboration relationship, and uncovering research themes and their evolution. Some examples are as follows. Geng et al. [14] conducted a bibliometric survey of the research field of residential energy and greenhouse gas emissions for the purpose of uncovering research status. In their work, citation analysis was used to assess the influence of journals, countries, and authors, while network analysis was performed to evaluate the relationships among countries, authors, and keywords. Based on 117,340 obesity-related research publications indexed in Scopus database published from 1993–2012, Khan et al. [15] reported research trends and collaboration patterns in the field. Roig-Tierno et al. [16] conducted a bibliometric analysis on research publications with the application of qualitative comparative analysis (QCA). Their study revealed the differences in quantitative terms of the three variants of QCA. Albort-Morant and Ribeiro-Soriano [17] focused on the research development of business incubators. They sorted 445 publications from WoS according to bibliographic indicators such as research area and year of publication. Their study revealed the lack of publications on business incubators and highlighted the fragmented nature of research themes. Merigó and Yang [18] aimed at identifying relevant researches and the newest trends in field of operation research and management science. The analysis involved some influential journals, two hundred most cited publications, and productive and influential authors. Zhang et al. [19] quantitatively and qualitatively evaluated carbon tax related literature from 1989 to 2014 using bibliometric analysis. Their study demonstrated that the USA was the leading country and the Vrije University Amsterdam and Massachusetts Institute of Technology and Stanford University were the most productive affiliations in the research field. Randhawa et al. [20] conducted a systematic review of publications on open innovation (OI) research area using bibliometrics, cocitation analysis, and text mining. Three distinct areas within OI research were identified, i.e., firm-centric aspects of OI, management of OI networks, and role of users and communities in OI. In order to discover the worldwide trends in the research field of drying brick/tile, Yataganbaba and Kurtbaş [21] analyzed relevant patents in terms of, e.g., publication number, authorship and ownership, and international collaboration patterns. Merigó et al. [10]

explored the research development trends in fuzzy sciences. Similar works have also been conducted in other fields, e.g., natural language processing [22], neuroimaging [23], and diabetes [24].

To the best of our knowledge, there is no scientific review of NLP empowered mobile computing research field currently. Thus, in this study, we conduct a bibliometric analysis on publications retrieved from WoS during the years 2000–2016 to explore the research status of the research field. The main objective is to address the following issues: (1) investigating publication statistical characteristics and publication collaborations, (2) exploring publication geographical distributions, (3) visualizing scientific collaboration relationships, and (4) reveling current hot research topic themes and research topic changes.

The rest of the paper is organized as follows. Section 2 introduces methods and materials. Bibliometric analysis results on retrieved research publications are reported in Section 3. Findings and discussion are shown in Section 4 while Section 5 summarizes the work.

METHODS AND MATERIALS

Five different methods are applied to analyze research publications in the NLP empowered mobile computing field retrieved from WoS. The details of the methods are described in Section 2.1 and the publication data is introduced in Section 2.2.

Methods

Descriptive Statistics Method

Descriptive statistics are brief descriptive coefficients that summarize a collection of information, which can be either a representation of the entire population or a sample. Descriptive statistics are commonly used as measures of central tendency and measures of variability. Measures of central tendency usually include mean, median, and mode, while measures of variability generally contain standard deviation, minimum and maximum variables, kurtosis, and skewness. These two measures use graphs, tables, and general discussions to simply describe data. This simplifies large amounts of data in a sensible way by presenting quantitative descriptions in a manageable form to help users understand the meaning of the data being analyzed.

Inthisstudy,descriptivestatisticsmethodwasappliedtoacquirecharacteristics of the retrieved publications, including publication distribution by year, most influential publications, productive journals, authors, affiliations, and countries/regions, as well as co-authors, coaffiliation, and cocountry/region publication distribution and topic distribution by year.

Geographic Visualization Method

Geographic visualization or Geovisualization is a set of tools and techniques supporting the analysis of geospatial or spatial data, emphasizing knowledge construction over knowledge storage or information transmission. By combining technologies, e.g., image processing, simulation, and virtual reality, computers can help present information in a way that patterns can be found. Geovisualization can be applied to all the stages of problem-solving in geographical analysis, from development of initial hypotheses to knowledge discovery, analysis, presentation, and evaluation. According to Tobler's First Law of Geography [25], everything is related to everything else, but near things are more related than distant things. Through Geovisualization, we can use location as the key index variable and get related information which is previously unfound. Locations or extents in the earth space–time may be recorded as dates/times of occurrence. Longitude, latitude, and elevation are represented as X, Y, and Z coordinates, respectively.

In this study, we applied geographic visualization analysis to explore geographical distributions of publications in country/region level.

Social Network Analysis Method

Social network analysis is a process of investigating social structures using networks and graph theory [26]. It focuses on relationship structures, ranging from casual acquaintance to close bonds. Network structures are characterized in terms of nodes (items, individuals, or things within the network) with the edges or links (relationships or interactions) connecting the nodes. Researches using social network analysis have been undertaken in different areas, e.g., collaboration graphs [27], social media networks [28], and disease transmission [29].

These networks are often visualized through sociograms in which nodes are represented as points and edges are represented as lines. The social network analysis can help identify the individuals, teams, and units who play central roles, leverage peer support, and strengthen the efficiency and effectiveness of existing channels [30].

In this study, we applied social network analysis to explore the cooperation relationships for specific countries/regions, affiliations, and authors in the NLP empowered mobile computing research field. The cooperation among countries/regions, affiliations, and authors was visualized using interactive force directed networks. In the networks, nodes represented specific countries/regions, affiliations or authors, and lines indicated cooperation. The size of nodes represented publication numbers of a specific country, affiliation, or author. The width of lines reflected cooperation frequencies between two countries/regions, affiliations, or authors. The color indicated specific continent of a country/region, or specific country/region of an affiliation or author. Users could explore the cooperation relationships for specific countries/regions, affiliations, or authors by dynamically dragging the nodes.

Latent Dirichlet Allocation Method

Latent Dirichlet allocation (LDA), proposed by Blei [31], is a generative probabilistic model. The basic idea is that documents are represented as random mixtures over latent topics, where each topic is characterized by a distribution over words, and topics are assumed to be uncorrelated.

LDA formally defines the following terms:

(1) A word is defined as an item from a vocabulary indexed by {1, ..., }.

(2) A document is a sequence of words denoted by d=(w_1, ... w_n).

(3) A corpus is a collection of documents denoted by D=(d_1, ...d_m).

LDA assumes the following generation process:

(1) The term distribution β which contains the probability of a word occurring in a given topic is determined by β ~ Dirichlet(δ).

(2) The proportions θ of the topic distribution for a document d are determined by θ ~ Dirichlet(α).

(3) For each word w_i in the document d, a topic is chosen by the distribution z_i~ Multinomial (θ) and a word is chosen from a multinomial probability distribution conditioned on the topic $z_i : p(w_i \mid z_i, \beta)$.

As for variational expectation-maximization (VEM) estimation, the log-likelihood for one document d∈D is given by

$$\ell(\alpha, \beta) = \log(p(d \mid \alpha, \beta))$$

$$= \log \int \left\{ \sum_{z} \left[\prod_{i=1}^{N} p(w_i \mid z_i, \beta)\, p(z_i \mid \theta) \right] \right\} \cdot p(\theta \mid \alpha)\, d\theta \quad (1)$$

Gibbs sampling defines a Markov chain in the space of possible variable assignments such that the stationary distribution of the Markov chain is the joint distribution over variables. Thus, it is a Markov Chain Monte Carlo method [32]. Its aim is to construct a Markov chain converging to the target probability distribution in the high dimensional model and then the sample distribution closest to the target probability distribution will be extracted. The log-likelihood for Gibbs sampling can be obtained through

$$\log(p(d \mid z)) = k \log\left(\frac{\Gamma(V\delta)}{\Gamma(\delta)^V}\right) + \sum_{K=1}^{k} \left\{ \left[\sum_{j=1}^{V} \log\left(\Gamma\left(n_K^{(j)} + \delta\right)\right) \right] - \log\left(\Gamma\left(n_K^{(\cdot)} + V\delta\right)\right) \right\}. \quad (2)$$

The perplexity, as shown in (3), is often used to evaluate the models on held-out data and is equivalent to the geometric mean per-word likelihood. The less the perplexity is, the better the model is.

$$\text{perplexity}(d) = \exp\left\{ -\frac{\log(p(d))}{\sum_{d=1}^{D} \sum_{j=1}^{V} n^{(jd)}} \right\} \quad (3)$$

In (4), $n^{(jd)}$ denotes how often the jth term occurs in the dth document. If the model is fitted through Gibbs sampling, the likelihood can be determined for the perplexity using

$$\log(p(d)) = \sum_{d=1}^{D} \sum_{j=1}^{V} n^{(jd)} \log\left[\sum_{K=1}^{k} \theta_K^{(d)} \beta_K^{(j)} \right] \quad (4)$$

Additionally, estimation using Gibbs sampling requires specification of values for the parameters of the prior distributions.

In this study, topic discovery and distribution were analyzed using LDA models with the following steps:

(1) We assigned the weights of segmented author keywords and Keywords Plus, publication title, and abstract as 0.4, 0.4 and 0.2, respectively, as determined in our former experiment [13].

(2) Term Frequency-Inverse Document Frequencies (TF-IDF) were used to filter out unimportant terms. As one of the most popular term-weighting schemes, TF-IDF increases proportionally to the number of times a term appears in a publication but is often offset by the frequency of the term in the whole collection of publications. We calculated the TF-IDF values of all terms to sort the terms. By manually examining these ranked terms, we defined a threshold as 0.1 empirically. Only the terms with a TF-IDF value greater than the threshold were kept for further analysis.

(3) Through sampling, 16 different topic numbers were set to c(2:10,15,20,40,50,80,150,250). For each topic number, 10-fold cross-validation was used to evaluate model performance. Specifically, dataset was split into 10 test datasets to conduct multiple runs. Perplexity criteria were used to select optimal topic number. α for Gibbs sampling was initialized as the mean value of α values for model fitting using VEM with the optimal topic number.

(4) With an initialized α and the optimal topic number, we adopted Gibbs sampling and VEM method to estimate the LDA model.

(5) By matching the topics detected by VEM and Gibbs sampling based on Hellinger distance, the best matches with the smallest distance could be identified. Hellinger distance is calculated as (5), in which P and Q denote two probability measures.

$$H^2(P,Q) = \frac{1}{2}\int\left(\sqrt{dP} - \sqrt{dQ}\right)^2 \quad (5)$$

Affinity Propagation Clustering Method

Affinity Propagation (AP) algorithm was proposed by Frey and Dueck [33]. It is a technique for data clustering based on message passing. AP does not require the predefined number of clusters. It identifies cluster centers, or exemplars as representative members of clusters. Initially, all nodes are considered as exemplars. "Preference" is used to reflect how likely one node is chosen as an exemplar. If no prior knowledge is available, all nodes will be assigned the same preference value. AP has been shown to be more efficient and effective in cluster identification than traditional clustering methods, e.g., k-means [34].

AP algorithm takes s(i,j) as function of similarity to reflect the fitness of the data point j being the exemplar of data point i. The aim of AP is to maximize the similarity s(i,j) between every data point i and its chosen exemplar j. Each node i also has a self-similarity s(i,i) . Individual data points initialized with a larger self-similarity are more likely to become exemplars. All data points are equally likely to be exemplars when they are initialized with the same constant self-similarity. The number of clusters produced will be increased and decreased accordingly with this common self-similarity input.

There are two types of messages contained in this technique. The responsibility r(i,j) is directed from i to candidate exemplar j. It indicates how well suited j is to be i's exemplar, taking into consideration competing potential exemplars. The availability a(i,j) is sent from candidate exemplar j back to i. It indicates j's desire to be an exemplar for i based on supporting feedback from other data points. Both the self-responsibility r(i,i) and the self-availability a(i,i) can reflect accumulated evidence that i is an exemplar. The update formulas for responsibility and availability are as follows:

$$r(i,j) \longleftarrow s(i,j) - \max_{j' \text{s.t. } j' \neq j} \left\{ a(i,j') + s(i,j') \right\}$$

$$\underset{i \neq j}{a(i,j)} \longleftarrow \min \left\{ 0, r(i,j) + \sum_{\forall i' \notin \{i,j\}} \max \left\{ 0, r(i',j \right\} \right\}$$

$$a(j,j) \longleftarrow \sum_{i' \text{s.t. } i' \neq j} \max \left\{ 0, r(i',j) \right\}. \tag{6}$$

Responsibility and availability of message updates are $m_{\text{new}} = \lambda m_{\text{old}} + (1 - \lambda) m_{\text{new}}$, where λ is a weighting factor between 0 and 1. In AP, the clustering is complete when the messages converge. Also, AP algorithm is able to determine when a specific data point has converged to cluster head status in its given cluster. A point becomes the cluster head when its self-responsibility plus self-availability becomes positive. Upon convergence, each node 's cluster head can be calculated using

$$CH_i = \arg\max_j \left\{ a(i,j) + r(i,j) \right\} \tag{7}$$

In our study, with the basis of term-topic posterior probability matrix, we applied AP clustering method for the cluster analysis of the topics identified by the LDA method.

Materials

Web of Science, as the most authoritative citation database, was used as the data source for retrieving research publications in the NLP empowered mobile computing field. First of all, a list of keywords related to the "natural language processing" and "mobile computing" was determined by a domain expert. With "Science Citation Index Expanded" and "Social Sciences Citation Index" as indexes, publications used in this study were identified using the specific query in Table 1. 716 publications in "article" type during years 2000–2016 were obtained. Citations counted to September 8th, 2017 were considered for each publication.

Table 1. The query used to retrieve research publications in the NLP empowered mobile computing field from WoS.

TS=(("natural language processing" OR "NLP" OR "semantic analysis" OR "bag of words" OR "word sense disambiguation" OR "named entity recognition" OR "NER" OR "sentiment analysis" OR "information extraction" "tokenization" OR "stemming" OR "lemmatization" OR "corpus" OR "stop words" OR "parts-of-speech" OR "language modeling" OR "n-grams" OR "syntactic analysis" OR "information retrieval" OR "language model") AND ("mobile computing" OR "mobile" OR "smart device" OR "smartphone" OR "cellphone" OR "telephony device" OR "Cellular network" OR "Android" OR "iOS" OR "phone"))

The raw data of the 716 publications were downloaded as plain text. Key elements including title, author, journal, publication date, subject category, language, funding, author keywords, Keywords Plus, abstract, and author address, as well as number of citations, pages, and references, were extracted.

In order to ensure they were closely related to the research field, manual verification was conducted by a domain expert on each publication. 471 publications were identified as relevant for analysis eventually. Further, corresponding affiliations and countries/regions were identified out from author address information. Key terms were extracted from author keywords, Keywords Plus, title, and abstract.

The statistical characteristics of the publications are shown as Table 2. The average page number of the publications is 15.66 and the average reference number of the publications is 33.29.

There are 48 subject categories included, where the top 3 categories are computer science (38.76%), engineering (16.27%), and telecommunications (10.98%).

Table 2. The statistical characteristics of the 471 publications.

Characteristics	Statistics
Total #pub.	471
#pub. with author keywords or Keywords Plus	412
#unique publication sources	287
#unique countries (or regions)/first countries (or regions)	60; 52
#unique affiliations/first affiliations	544; 345
#unique authors/first authors/last authors	1,408; 451; 441
Average #citations	10.42
Average #countries (or regions) in one pub.	1.25
Average #affiliations in one pub.	1.64
Average #authors in one pub.	3.27
Average #funds in one pub.	0.73
Average #pages in one pub.	15.66
Average #references in one pub.	33.29
Average #author keywords or Keywords Plus	6.81
Average #words/characters in title	10.57; 80.13
Average #words/characters in abstract	186.40; 1,265.58
Language distribution	English (98.73%); Estonian (0.42%); French (0.42%); Spanish (0.21%); Afrikaans (0.21%)
Subject category distribution (Top 10)	Computer Science (38.76%); Engineering (16.27%); Telecommunications (10.98%); Acoustics (5.82%); Information Science & Library Science (2.78%); Linguistics (2.51%); Psychology (2.12%); Operations Research & Management Science (1.85%); Business & Economics (1.32%); Communication (1.32%)
Top 10 terms in author keywords and Keywords Plus	Mobile (30.36%); Information (22.08%); Retrieval (16.77%); Recognition (16.56%); System (14.86%); Speech (14.01%); Model (12.10%); Network (12.10%); Language (11.04%); Analysis (9.98%)
Top 10 terms in titles	Mobile (34.18%); Information (17.83%); System (12.53%); Retrieval (12.10%); Recognition (10.62%); Speech (8.70%); Network (8.28%); Model (7.86%); Language (7.22%); Environment (6.37%)
Top 10 terms in abstracts	Mobile (66.67%); Information (56.90%); Paper (55.41%); System (48.20%); Result (46.07%); Data (38.00%); User (38.00%); Model (37.37%); Device (32.70%); Retrieval (31.42%)

The distribution characteristics of the 471 publications are shown in Figure 1. Figure 1(a) shows the distributions of the numbers of countries/regions, affiliations, authors, and funds. Figure 1(b) shows the distributions of the numbers of keywords, pages, and references. The distribution of the number of title characters is shown in Figure 1(c). In Figure 1(d) the right bottom illustrates the distribution of the number of abstract characters.

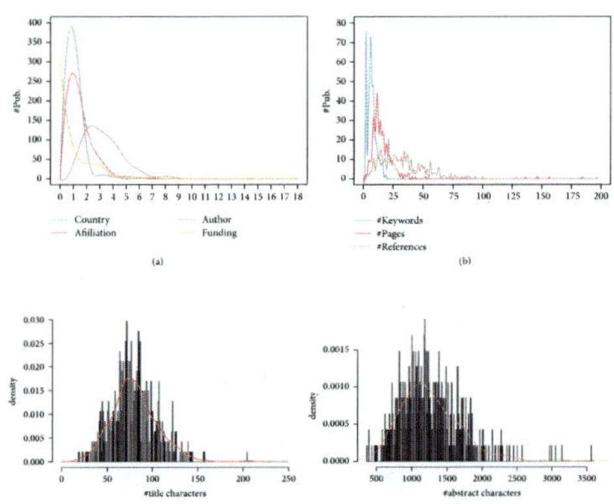

Figure 1. Distribution characteristics of the 471 publications.

RESULTS

Publication with Year

The total publications, total citations, average number of citations per publication, and the number of annual citations are demonstrated in Figure 2. The results show that the research in the NLP empowered mobile computing field exhibits an overall upward trend in fluctuation (from 12 publications in 2000 to 55 publications in 2016). The publication number presents a stable increasing trend since 2010. Based on the data for years 2010–2016, we developed a regression model by setting the independent variables as time/1000 and (time/1000)^2. The estimated regression model is calculated as $y = 6.7143 * 10^3 - 1.34777 * 10^4 x$. The adjusted goodness-of-fit $\overline{R^2}$ of the model is 0.9468. With the regression model, publication number in 2017 is predicted as 65, while the actual number of publications on WoS in 2017 is 66. The trend of citations does not keep step with publication number, and extreme values appear in 2002 as 431, 2007 as 503, and 2010 as 490. The average number of citations per publication is calculated as total citations/ total publications. It shows an overall downward trend in fluctuation from 21.92 in 2000 to 2.53 in 2016. We eliminated the influence of duration since first publication using the formula: the number of annual citations (C/Y) = total citations/(2016 + 1-publishing year). The number of annual citations increases in fluctuation from 15.47 in 2000 to 139 in 2016.

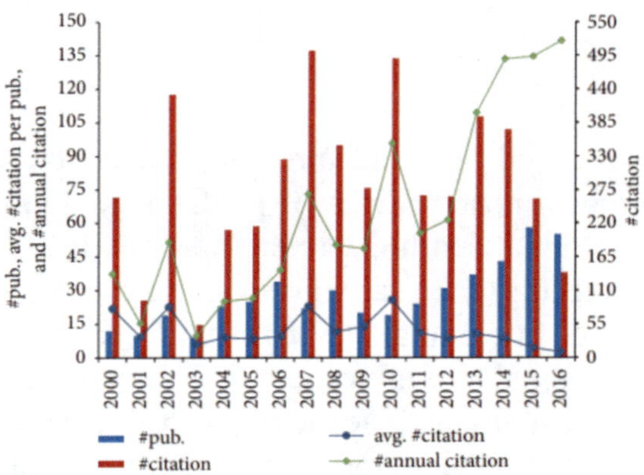

Figure 2. The statistics of the 417 publications (the light blue bars indicate total publications and the red bars indicate total citations. The dark blue line indicates average citations per publication and the green line indicates annual citations).

Productive Journals

The top 11 contributing journals in the research field are presented in Table 3. These journals contribute about 21% of the total publications and 29.20% of the total citations. The most productive 3 are IEEE/ACM Transactions on Audio Speech and Language Processing (25 publications, 447 citations, 17.88 ACP, and 11 -index), Speech Communication (11 publications, 179 citations, 16.27ACP, 6 H-index), and Computer Speech and Language (10 publications, 93 citations, 9.30 ACP, 6 H-index). Expert Systems with Applications has the highest ACP of 40.00. We found that 32 of the 100 most influential publications are published in the 11 journals. According to subject category of these 11 journals, computer science possesses the widest influence in the research field.

Table 3. Top 11 contributing journals in the NLP empowered mobile computing research field.

Rank	Journals	SC	TP	% *P*	TC	ACP	*H*	≥10	T100
1	IEEE/ACM Transactions on Audio Speech and Language Processing	A; E	25	5.31	447	17.88	11	12	11
2	Speech Communication	A; CS	11	2.34	179	16.27	6	6	5
3	Computer Speech and Language	CS	10	2.12	93	9.30	6	5	3
4	Expert Systems with Applications	CS; E; OR&MS	8	1.70	320	40.00	8	7	5
4	IEEE Transactions on Consumer Electronics	E; T	8	1.70	44	5.50	5	1	0
6	Mobile Information Systems	CS; T	7	1.49	95	13.57	3	2	2
6	Multimedia Tools and Applications	CS; E	7	1.49	71	10.14	3	1	1
6	Personal and Ubiquitous Computing	CS; T	7	1.49	67	9.57	4	3	1
9	Information Sciences	CS	6	1.27	85	14.17	5	3	3
10	EURASIP Journal on Wireless Communications and Networking	E; T	5	1.06	22	4.40	2	1	1
10	IEICE Transactions on Information and Systems	CS	5	1.06	11	2.20	2	0	0

Notice. Journal *IEEE Transactions on Audio Speech and Language Processing changed name as IEEE/ACM Transactions on Audio, Speech, and Language Processing* in 2013, and journal *IEEE Transactions on Speech and Audio Processing* ceased publication in 2005, and the current retitled publication is *IEEE/ACM Transactions on Audio, Speech, and Language Processing*. Therefore, publications from these 2 journals were combined as published by *IEEE/ACM Transactions on Audio, Speech, and Language Processing*; *Abbreviations*. SC: subject categories only with NLP empowered mobile computing research (A: acoustics; E: engineering; CS: computer science; OR&MS: operations research and management science; T: telecommunications); TP: total publications; % *P*: percentage of the publications; TC: total citations; ACP: average number of citations per publication, calculated as TC/TP; *H*: *H*-index; ≥10: number of publications with citations ≥10; T100: number of publications in the top 100 most influential publications.

In order to better measure the overall scientific importance of these 11 journals, 5 assessment indicators acquired from Scientific Journal Rankings were used, including Impact Factor (IF), SCImago Journal Rank (SJR), 5-Year IF, Source Normalized Impact per Paper (SNIP), and CiteScore. IF is a measure for reflecting the yearly average number of citations to recent publications published in a journal. It is the primary and widely used indicator on assessing one journal's significance. SJR is a measure of scientific influence of scholarly journals. It accounts for both the number of citations received by a journal and the importance or prestige of the journals where such citations come from. 5-Year IF is calculated by dividing the number of citations to the journal in a given year by the number of publications published in that journal in the previous five years. SNIP is defined as the ratio of the journal's citation count per publication and the citation potential in its subject field. CiteScore index, launched by Elsevier in December 2016, is calculated as the ratio of total citations received in a given year by all publications published in a given journal in three previous years and the number of publications published in the journal in three previous years.

Therefore, the 11 productive journals were compared by using their IF, SJR, 5-Year IF, SNIP, and CiteScore for year 2016, as shown in Figure 3. As for IF, SJR, and CiteScore, the top 3 are Information Sciences (IF 4.832, SJR

1.91, and CiteScore 5.37), Expert Systems with Applications (IF 3.928, SJR 1.433, and CiteScore 4.7), and IEEE/ACM Transactions on Audio Speech and Language Processing (IF 2.491, SJR 0.813, and CiteScore 3.5). As for 5-Year IF, the top 3 are Information Sciences (5-Year IF 4.731), Expert Systems with Applications (5-Year IF 3.526), and Personal and Ubiquitous Computing (5-Year IF 2.512). As for SNIP score, the top 3 are IEEE/ACM Transactions on Audio Speech and Language Processing (SNIP 3.143), Information Sciences (SNIP 2.537), and Expert Systems with Applications (SNIP 2.492).

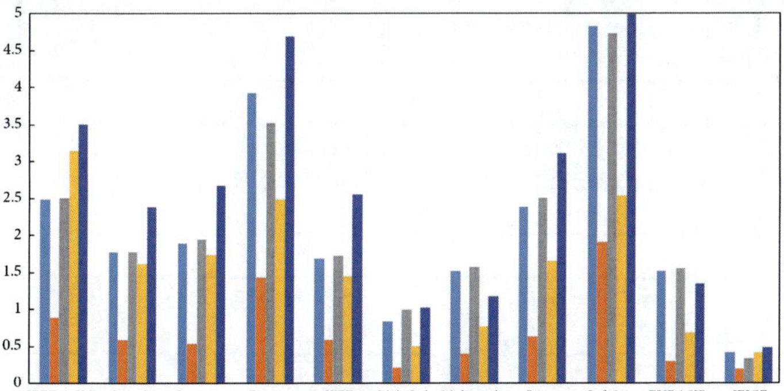

	IEEE-ACM Trans. Audio Speech Lang.	Speech Commun.	Comput. Speech Lang.	Expert Syst. Appl.	IEEE Trans. Consum. Electron.	Mob. Inf. Syst.	Multimed. Tools Appl.	Pers. Ubiquitous Comput.	Inf. Sci.	EURASIP J. Wirel. Commun.	IEICE Trans. Inf. Syst.
IF	2.491	1.768	1.9	3.928	1.694	0.849	1.53	2.395	4.832	1.529	0.411
SJR	0.813	0.593	0.536	1.433	0.587	0.219	0.396	0.648	1.91	0.304	0.191
5-Year IF	2.501	1.769	1.938	3.526	1.725	1	1.572	2.512	4.731	1.558	0.332
SNIP	3.143	1.628	1.75	2.492	1.447	0.509	0.775	1.651	2.537	0.698	0.419
CiteScore	3.5	2.38	2.67	4.7	2.56	1.03	1.19	3.12	5.37	1.36	0.49

Figure 3. Comparisons of IF, SJR, 5-Year IF, SNIP, and CiteScore for the top 11 productive journals for year 2016.

Most Influential Publications

The number of citations reflects the popularity and influence of a publication in the scientific community [10]. Thus, we used the total citations as a measurement of influence. There are 69 and 129 publications with the number of citations ≥20 and ≥10. Top 15 most influential publications are listed in Table 4. The publication by Miao et al. [35] in 2010 (376 citations) is the most influential one, followed by [36] published by MacKenzie and Soukoreff in 2002 (172 citations) and [37] by Strayer and Drews in 2007 (148 citations). We further consider the number of annual citations of the 15 publications. The top 3 publications measured by this indicator are [38] by Cao et al. published in 2015 (C/Y=56), [35] by Miao et al. in 2010 (C/

Y=53.71), and [39] by Mostafa in 2013 (C/Y=22). These 3 publications rank 14th, 1st, and 6th, respectively, according to total citations.

Table 4. Top 15 most influential publications in the NLP empowered mobile computing research field.

Rank	Title	Author/s	Year	TC	C/Y
1	Energy-Efficient Link Adaptation in Frequency-Selective Channels	Miao G. W., et al.	2010	376	53.71
2	Text Entry for Mobile Computing: Models and Methods, Theory and Practice	MacKenzie I. S.; Soukoreff R. W.	2002	172	11.47
3	Cell-Phone-Induced Driver Distraction	Strayer D. L.; Drews F. A.	2007	148	14.80
4	A Vector Space Modeling Approach to Spoken Language Identification	Li H. Z., et al.	2007	116	11.60
5	Context-Aware System for Proactive Personalized Service Based on Context History	Hong J. Y., et al.	2009	91	11.38
6	More than Words: Social Networks' Text Mining for Consumer Brand Sentiments	Mostafa M. M.	2013	88	22.00
7	The Effect of Mobility-Induced Location Errors on Geographic Routing in Mobile Ad Hoc and Sensor Networks: Analysis and Improvement Using Mobility Prediction	Son, D. J., et al.	2004	77	5.92
8	A Personalized Tourist Trip Design Algorithm for Mobile Tourist Guides	Souffriau W., et al.	2008	76	8.44

9	D'Agents: Applications and Performance of a Mobile-Agent System	Gray R. S., et al.	2002	73	4.87
10	Optical Encryption and QR Codes: Secure and Noise-Free Information Retrieval	Barrera J. F., et al.	2013	64	16.00
11	Text-Dependent Speaker Verification: Classifiers, Databases and RSR2015	Larcher A., et al.	2014	60	20.00
12	A Location-Aware Recommender System for Mobile Shopping Environments	Yang W. S., et al.	2008	59	6.56
12	An Application of Reinforcement Learning to Dialogue Strategy Selection in a Spoken Dialogue System for Email	Walker M. A.	2000	59	3.47
14	Landmark Recognition with Compact BoW Histogram and Ensemble ELM	Cao J. W., et al.	2016	56	56.00
14	Mobile-Agent Coordination Models for Internet Applications	Cabri G., et al.	2000	56	3.29

Abbreviations. *TC: total number of citations during 2000 and 2016; C/Y: the number of annual citations.*

Productive Authors and Affiliations

From the 471 publications, there are 1,408 authors. 451 of them are first authors and 441 are last authors. 20 authors have 3 or more publications, and 98 authors have 2 or more publications. 20 most productive authors are listed in Table 5. According to the result, the most productive authors are Chen, Tao from Singapore (4 publications supported by 4 funds, 108 citations, 27 ACP, and 4 H-index) and Mizzaro, Stefano from Italy (4 publications, 45 citations, 11.25 ACP, and 3 H-index). Chen, Tao is listed as first author of 3 publications and all the 3 publications appear in top 100 most influential publications. Mizzaro, Stefano cooperates with others in all his 4 publications and 1 publication appears in the top 100. As for the ranking based on citation number, the top 3 productive authors are Lee, Chin-Hui from the USA (173 citations and 57.67 ACP), Chen, Tao from Singapore (108 citations and 27 ACP), and Xie, Xing from China (51 citations and 17 ACP). Ranking based on the ACP indicator yields the same result. Kim, Harksoo from South Korea achieves the most funding supports, i.e., 7 for his 3 publications.

Table 5. The most productive authors in the NLP empowered mobile computing research field.

Rank	Name	Country	TP	TC	ACP	*H*	T100	*F*	FP	LP	CP
1	*Chen, Tao*	SG	4	108	27.00	4	3	4	3	0	4
1	*Mizzaro, Stefano*	IT	4	45	11.25	3	1	0	0	0	4
2	*Baek, Jin-Wook*	KR	3	27	9.00	3	1	0	1	0	3
2	*Bertino, Elisa*	USA	3	40	13.33	3	1	3	0	2	3
2	*Cacciapuoti, Angela Sara*	IT	3	18	6.00	2	1	4	3	0	3
2	*Caleffi, Marcello*	IT	3	18	6.00	2	1	4	0	2	3
2	*Christodoulakis, Stavros*	GR	3	9	3.00	1	0	0	0	3	3
2	*Crestani, F*	UK	3	37	12.33	2	1	0	0	3	3
2	*Jung, Jason J*	KR	3	4	1.33	1	0	2	0	2	3
2	*Karanastasi, Anastasia*	GR	3	9	3.00	1	0	0	1	0	3
2	*Kazasis, Fotis G*	GR	3	9	3.00	1	0	0	0	0	3
2	*Kim, Harksoo*	KR	3	4	1.33	1	0	7	0	2	3
2	*Lee, Chin-Hui*	USA	3	173	57.67	3	3	4	1	2	2
2	*Liu, Jia*	CN	3	3	1.00	1	0	6	0	1	3
2	*Muneyasu, Mitsuji*	JP	3	4	1.33	2	0	2	1	2	3
2	*Pierre, Samuel*	CA	3	38	12.67	2	1	0	0	0	3
2	*Seide, Frank*	CN	3	48	16.00	2	2	0	0	0	2
2	*Xie, Xing*	CN	3	51	17.00	3	2	3	1	0	3
2	*Yan, Yonghong*	CN	3	9	3.00	2	0	3	0	3	3
2	*Yeom, Heon Y*	KR	3	27	9.00	3	1	0	0	3	3

Abbreviations. CA: Canada; USA: the USA; UK: England; CN: China; KR: South Korea; GR: Greece; IT: Italy; JP: Japan; SG: Singapore; TP: total publications; TC: total citations; ACP: average number of citations per publication: *H*: *H*-index; T100: number of publications in the top 100 highly cited publications; *F*: number of publications with funding; FP: number of publications as first author; LP: number of publications as last author; CP: number of collaborated publications.

544 affiliations from 60 countries/regions have publications in the NLP empowered mobile computing research field. Table 6 lists 15 most productive affiliations. Among them, 5 are from the USA, 3 from China, 2 from Taiwan, 1 from India, 1 from Italy, 1 from South Korea, 1 from Singapore, and 1 from England. The top 4 most productive affiliations a Nanyang Technological University from Singapore (8 publications, 87 citations, 10.88 ACP, and 5 H-index), Tsinghua University from China (8 publications, 42 citations, 5.25 ACP, and 4 H-index), Microsoft Research Asia from China (7 publications, 115 citations, 16.43 ACP, and 5 H-index), and National Taiwan University from Taiwan (7 publications, 83 citations, 11.86 ACP, and 5 H-index). Nanyang Technological University cooperates with others in 5 publications and serves as first affiliation in 4 of them. 3 of these 5 publications appear in the list of top 100 most influential publications. Tsinghua University cooperates with others in 4 publications and serves as first affiliation in all 8 publications. These 8 publications are supported by 21 funds. As for the ranking based on the total citations, the top 3 are Georgia Institute of Technology from the USA (550 citations and 110 ACP), Microsoft Research Asia from China (115 citations and 16.43 ACP), and National Cheng Kung University from Taiwan (62 citations and 12.4 ACP). Ranking based on the ACP indicator yields the same result.

Table 6. The most productive affiliations in the NLP empowered mobile computing research field.

Rank	Name	Country	TP	TC	ACP	*H*	T100	*F*	FP	CP
1	*Nanyang Technological University*	SG	8	87	10.88	5	3	1	4	5
1	*Tsinghua University*	CN	8	42	5.25	4	1	21	8	4
3	*Microsoft Research Asia*	CN	7	115	16.43	5	4	3	3	6
3	*National Taiwan University*	TW	7	83	11.86	5	3	3	5	4
5	*Georgia Institute of Technology*	USA	5	550	110.00	4	4	6	2	4
5	*Massachusetts Institute of Technology*	USA	5	10	2.00	2	0	9	4	4
5	*National Cheng Kung University*	TW	5	62	12.40	3	2	6	4	1
5	*Purdue University*	USA	5	47	9.40	4	1	4	1	5
9	*Indian Institute of Technology*	IN	4	35	8.75	3	1	3	4	1
9	*Microsoft Corporation*	USA	4	28	7.00	3	1	1	4	2
9	*The Pennsylvania State University*	USA	4	26	6.50	3	0	8	2	2
9	*Seoul National University*	KR	4	31	7.75	4	1	5	4	0
9	*University of Strathclyde*	UK	4	43	10.75	2	1	0	4	0
9	*University of Udine*	IT	4	45	11.25	3	1	0	1	3
9	*Zhejiang University*	CN	4	43	10.75	2	1	5	3	3

Abbreviations. USA: the USA; UK: England; CN: China; SG: Singapore; TW: Taiwan; IN: India; KR: South Korea; IT: Italy; TP: total publications; TC: total citations; ACP: average number of citations per publication; *H*: *H*-index; T100: number of publications in the top 100 highly cited publications; *F*: number of publications with funding; FP: number of publications as first affiliation; CP: number of collaborated publications.

Geographical Distribution

The 471 publications are from 60 countries/regions. The number of publications affiliated with 1 country/region range [61, 150), 3 countries/regions range[37,61) and 5 range [11,17). Table 7 shows top 15 most productive countries/regions in the field. Figure 4 illustrates geographical distributions of the publications.

The top 4 countries are the USA (105 publications, 1,795 citations, 17.1 ACP, and 22 H-index), China (61 publications, 372 citations, 6.1 ACP, and 10 H-index), England (44 publications, 418 citations, 9.5 ACP, and 12 H-index), and South Korea (41 publications, 281 citations, 6.85 ACP, and 8 H-index). Among the 105 publications from the USA, 32 appear in the list of top 100 most influential publications. It is noted that publications from Singapore have the highest ACP, which indicates the high quality of the publications. As for most of the top 15 productive countries/regions, the international collaboration rates are around 30%, except for Greece with 0 and Australia with 61.11%. The USA is the closest collaborator for 9 of the 15 countries/regions. The ACP of internationally collaborated publications is much higher than that of noninternationally collaborated publications for countries/regions like China, Japan, Italy, France, Spain, and Singapore. This potentially indicates that international collaboration can improve the quality of their publications.

Table 7. The most productive countries/regions in the NLP empowered mobile computing research field.

Rank	Country	TP	TC	ACP	*H*	T100	FP (%)	Single-country/region		International collaboration	
								ACP	TP (%)	ACP	TFC (*n*)
1	USA	105	1,795	17.10	22	32	77.14	20.78	60.00	11.57	CN (12)
2	CN	61	372	6.10	10	10	91.80	4.17	57.38	9.04	USA (12)
3	UK	44	418	9.50	12	11	61.36	11.68	63.64	5.69	IE/CH (2)
4	KR	41	281	6.85	8	6	92.68	7.03	85.37	5.83	CN/USA (3)
5	TW	37	399	10.78	11	11	94.59	11.07	81.08	9.57	USA (4)
6	JP	24	77	3.21	3	1	79.17	1.44	75.00	8.50	CN (3)
7	IT	21	299	14.24	10	9	80.95	13.19	76.19	17.60	USA (3)
8	AU	18	218	12.11	7	7	61.11	18.00	38.89	8.36	USA (5)
8	CA	18	313	17.39	9	4	88.89	20.38	72.22	9.60	N/A
10	FR	17	157	9.24	6	5	64.71	4.45	64.71	18.00	CN/USA (2)
10	GR	17	38	2.24	3	0	100.00	2.24	100.00	0.00	N/A
10	ES	17	124	7.29	7	2	88.24	6.43	82.35	11.33	USA (2)
13	SG	16	355	22.19	9	7	75.00	14.90	62.50	34.33	USA (2)
14	HK SAR	15	98	6.53	6	2	53.33	9.17	40.00	4.78	CN/USA (4)
15	DE	14	114	8.14	5	3	85.71	8.11	64.29	8.20	CN (12)

Abbreviations. USA: America; UK: England; CN: China; SG: Singapore; TW: Taiwan; KR: South Korea; IT: Italy; JP: Japan; AU: Australia; CA: Canada; FR: France; GR: Greece; ES: Spain; HK SAR: Hong Kong SAR; DE: Germany; IE: Ireland; CH: Switzerland; TP: total publications; TC: total citations; ACP: average number of citations per publication; *H*: *H*-index; T100: number of publications in the top 100 highly cited publications; FP (%): percentage of publications as first affiliation; TFC (*n*): number of cooperation times with the closest collaborator, where $n \geq 2$.

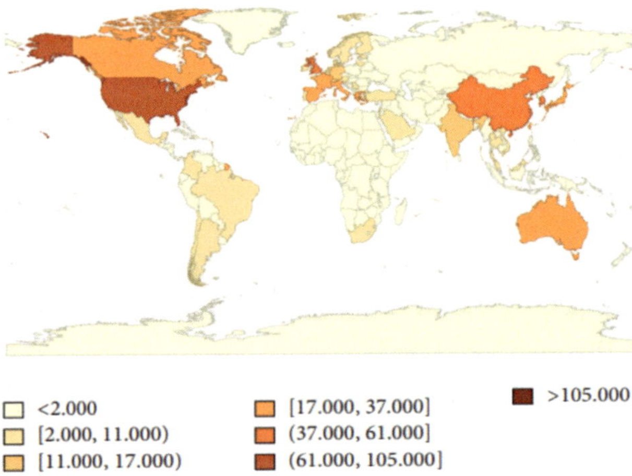

Figure 4. Geographical distributions of the NLP empowered mobile computing research publications.

Since the publications are mainly distributed in the USA, China, England, and South Korea, we further explored the annual publication distributions for these 4 countries, as shown in Figure 5. The number of publications for the USA and China is on the whole presenting upward trend in fluctuation. As for the USA, the number increases from 2 in 2000 to 9 in 2007 but dwindles to 2 in 2010. After that, the upward trend becomes more significant. The situation for China is quite like that for the USA after 2010, witnessing the great mass upsurge on the NLP empowered mobile computing research in these two countries since 2010. As for England and South Korea, the number of publications does not increase much in fluctuation with years going on.

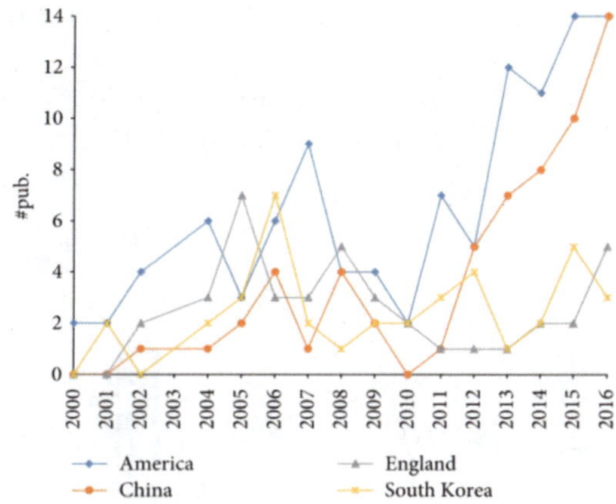

Figure 5. Publication distributions by year for the top 4 countries/regions.

Cooperation Relationship

Figure 6 shows the trends of the international collaborative and the percentage of international collaborative publications. We found that the international collaborative publications increase during the years 2000–2016. The percentage of international collaborations increases from 8.33% in 2000 to 32.73% in 2016. This indicates that international collaborations in the NLP empowered mobile computing research field have become increasingly important.

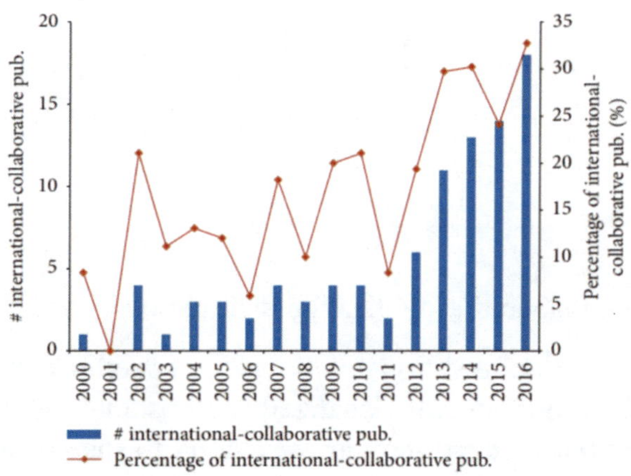

Figure 6. International collaborative publication distribution by year.

Figures 7 and 8 present the institutional level of cooperation and the author level of cooperation, respectively. The cooperation between different institutions is becoming more and more frequent. The percentage of institution-collaborative publication increases from 16.67% in 2000 to 58.18% in 2016. More than 90% of the publications are multiauthored since 2011. It is worth noticing that the percentage reaches up to 100% in 2015.

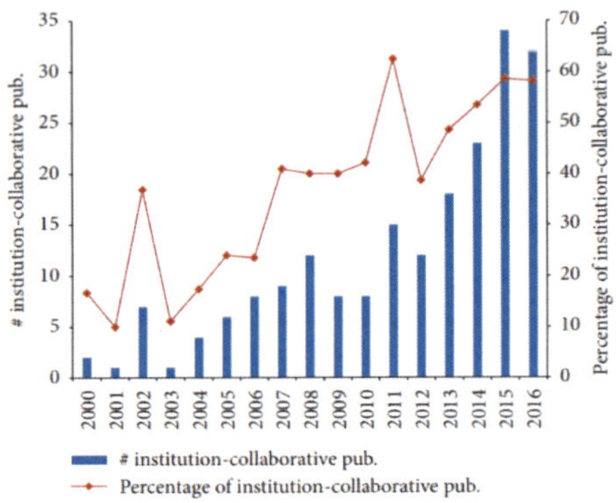

Figure 7. Institution-collaborative publication distribution by year.

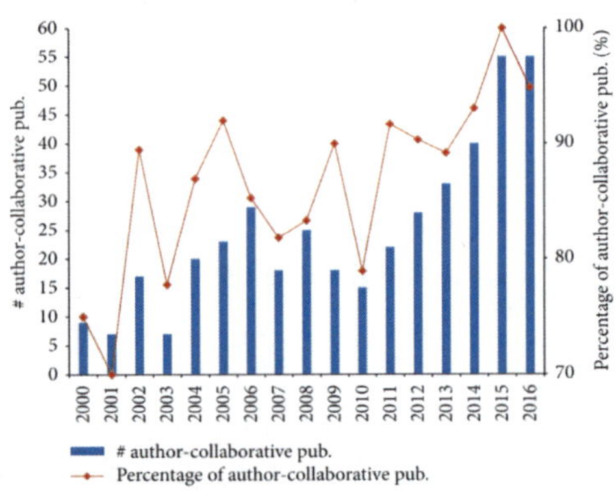

Figure 8. Author-collaborative publication distribution by year.

Furthermore, the cooperation relations for specific countries/regions, affiliations, and authors were visualized with social network analysis. A cooperation network for 48 countries/regions is shown in Figure 9. 17 of them come from Asia (represented as orange nodes), 3 from North America (represented as blue nodes), 22 from Europe (represented as green nodes), 3 from Africa (represented as purple nodes), 2 from South America (represented as brown nodes), and 1 from Oceania (represented as red node). There are 141 affiliations with the number of publications ≥ 2, and there exists cooperation among 91 of them. Figure 10 shows a cooperation network of the 91 affiliations. 23 of the 91 affiliations are from the USA and 14 from China. As for cooperation of author level, there are 98 authors with publication count ≥ 2. among them, 65 authors involve in cooperation. We created a cooperation network of the 65 authors, as shown in Figure 11.

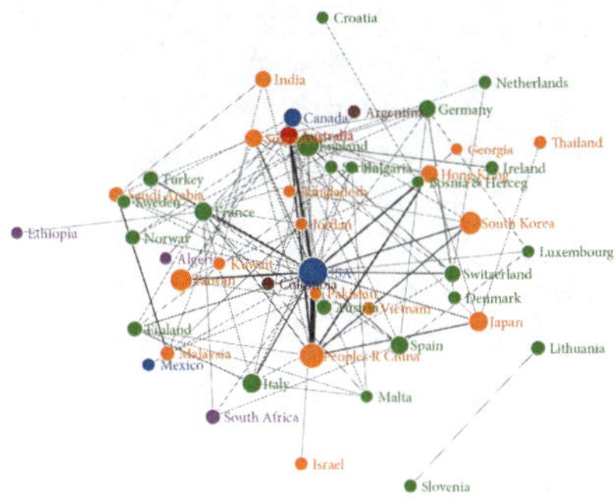

Figure 9. Cooperation network of 48 countries/regions (node colors represent different continents, e.g., orange for Asia, blue for North America, green for Europe, red for Oceania, purple for Africa, and brown for South America). The network can be accessed via the link (http://www.zhukun.org/haoty/resources.asp?id=NLPEMC_cocountry).

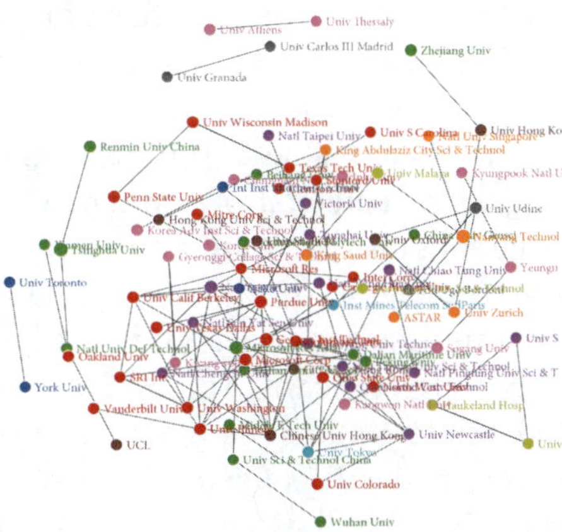

Figure 10. Cooperation network of 91 affiliations (node colors represent different countries/regions, e.g., red for the USA, pink for South Korea, and purple for Australia). The network can be accessed via the link (http://www.zhukun.org/haoty/resources.asp?id=NLPEMC_coaffiliation).

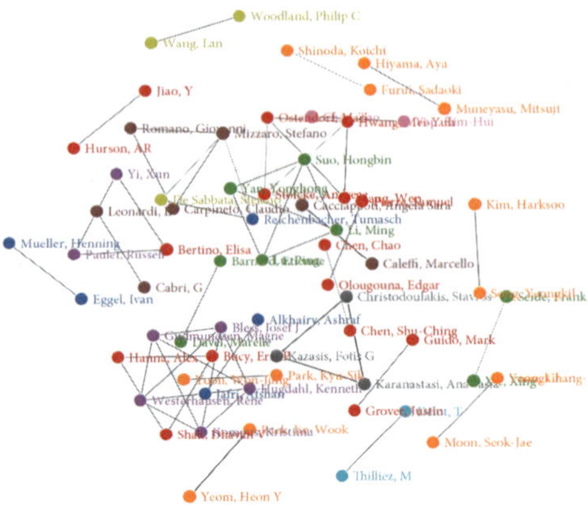

Figure 11. Cooperation network of 65 authors (node colors represent different countries/regions, e.g., range for South Korea, red for the USA, purple for Australia, green for China, and brown for Italy). The network can be accessed via the link (http://www.zhukun.org/haoty/resources.asp?id=NLPEMC_coauthor).

Topic Discovery and Distribution

By setting TF-IDF value threshold as 0.1, the terms were ranked by frequency. Table 8 lists top 20 most frequent terms, in which the top 5 terms are "Agent" (369), "Image" (215), "Sentiment" (128), "Dialogue" (83), and "Health" (81). Figure 12 presents the perplexities of models fitted by using Gibbs sampling with different numbers of topics. The result suggests that the optimal topic number is between 40 and 80. Hence, we set the topic number as 40. The α was set to the mean value 0.01101332 in the cross-validation fitted using VEM. Using the parameters, we estimated the LDA model using Gibbs sampling. By semantics analysis of representative terms in each topic, as well as reviewing text intention of the corresponding publications, we assigned potential theme to each topic. The order of topics are determined based on Hellinger distance. Specifically, Topic 36 is the best matching topic and Topic 11 ranks 2nd, while Topic 37 is the worse matching one. Due to space limitation, Table 9 only displays the top 10 best matching topics with the most frequent terms. Each publication was assigned to the most likely topic with the highest posterior probability. Integrating topic proportions for all the publications, we obtained a topic distribution. The 4 most frequent research topics are Topic 36 (6.38%), Topic 4 (4.26%), Topic 11 (3.83%), and Topic 17 (3.83%), while the 4 least frequent research topics are Topic 26 (1.49%), Topic 23 (1.28%), Topic 10 (1.06%), and Topic 20 (1.06%).

Table 8. Top 20 most frequent terms.

Rank	Stemmed terms	Occurrence number		
		Total	2000–2008	2009–2016
1	Agent	369	250	119
2	Image	215	70	145
3	Sentiment	128	0	128
4	Dialogue	83	49	34
5	Health	81	2	79
6	Music	76	27	49
7	Radio	74	10	64
8	Unit	74	51	23
9	Adaptation	70	40	30
10	Relevance	69	29	40
11	Geographic	66	37	29
12	Short Messages	66	9	57
13	Protocol	65	20	45
14	Chinese	64	29	35
15	Medical	60	16	44
16	Recommendation	60	4	56
17	Clustering	54	20	34
18	Privacy	54	9	45
19	Ad hoc	53	9	44
20	Traffic	52	17	35

Table 9. Top 15 most frequent terms for the top 10 best matching topics.

Topic	Potential theme	Top high frequency terms
36	Mobile agent computing	Agent; Coordination; Java; Migration; Protocol; Mobile-agent; Failure; Itinerary; Filtering; Turkish; Attack; Commerce; Context-aware; Truncation; Crash

11	Mobile agent computing	Agent; Planning; Ontology; Cloud; Multi-agent; Net; Interoperability; Neural; Peer-to-Peer; Broadband; Instruction; Complementarity; Natural Language; Traffic; Grounding
32	Mobile privacy and security	Privacy; Private; Secure; Location-Based Services; Encryption; Points of Interest; Protection; Approximate; Attack; Path; Privacy-preserving; Streaming; Password; Protocol; Cryptosystem
1	Image and syllable events	Image; Particular Allophones; Re-ranking; Composite Phoneme; Simple Phonemes; Syllable; Thing; iPad; On-Premise Signs; Spreading; Bow; Modern Orthography; Arabic; Content-based; Descriptor
4	Mobile social media computing	Sentiment; Opinion; Twitter; Tweet; Customer; Suggestion; Emojis; Emotion; Micro-blog; Protest; Brand; Suggestive; Microblog; Orientation; Box
8	Mobile radio	Radio; Phone-in; Localization; Australian; Formulation; Island; Reporting; Talkback; Involvement; Caller; Dialogic; Stance; Backlinking; Cloud; French
5	Mobile location computing	Geographic; Relevance; Seeking; Innovation; Subspace; Tourism; Birthright; Firm; Flier; Sensing; TILES (Temporal, Identity, Location, Environmental and Social); Cross-space; Location-aware; Personalized; Reposting
40	Context-aware computing	Dialogue; Context-aware; Estonian; Clarification; Array; Problematic; Reformulation; Verbose; Email; Mobile Information Services enabled by Mobile Publishing; Non-understanding; Publishing; Agent; Directive; Reinforcement
10	Second screen response	Gesture; Debate; PreFrontal Cortex; Adult; Presidential; Walking; Facial; Twitter; Educational; Gait; Political; Touch; Biometrics; Blink; Cortex
35	Language learning and modeling	Chinese; Information Retrieval; Peer-to-Peer; Conditional Random Field; Update; Apprentice; Affordances; Disyllabic; Website; Workplace; Self-study; Skip-chain; Descriptive; Mobile Peer-to-Peer; Multilingual

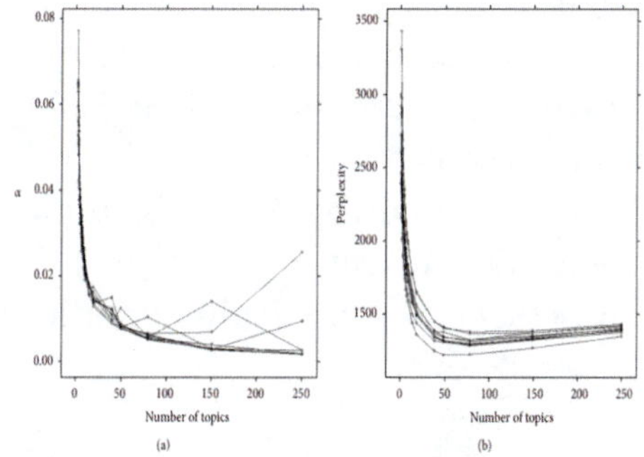

Figure 12. (a) Estimated α value for the models fitted using VEM. (b) Perplexities of the test data for the models fitted by using Gibbs sampling. Each line corresponded to one of the folds in the 10-fold cross-validation.

We used the AP clustering analysis to perform the cluster analysis of the 40 topics. One way for measuring topic similarity is based on term-level similarity with the hypothesis that topics may contain the same terms. The clustering result based on term-topic posterior probability matrix is shown in Figure 13, where the 40 topics are categorized into 8 groups.

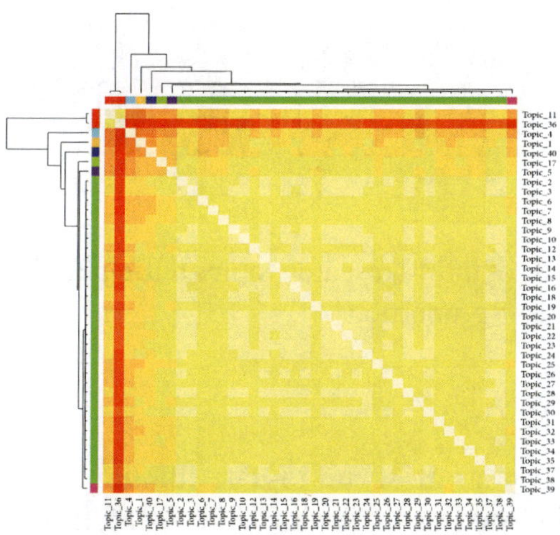

Figure 13. The visualized result of hierarchical clustering based on term-topic posterior probability matrix.

Identifying emerging research topics can provide valuable insights into the development of the research field. Likewise, identification of fading research topics can also help understand the hot spots evolution [40]. We then explored the annual publication proportions of the 40 research topics, as shown in Figure 14. We used Mann–Kendall test [41], a nonparametric trend test, to examine whether increasing or decreasing trends are existing in the 40 topics. Test results show that 12 topics, including Topic 1, Topic 4, Topic 7, Topic 10, Topic 14, Topic 18, Topic 20, Topic 26, Topic 29, Topic 32, Topic 33, and Topic 39, present a statistically significant increasing trend. While Topic 36 presents a statistically significant decreasing trend, both at the two-sided p=0.05 levels.

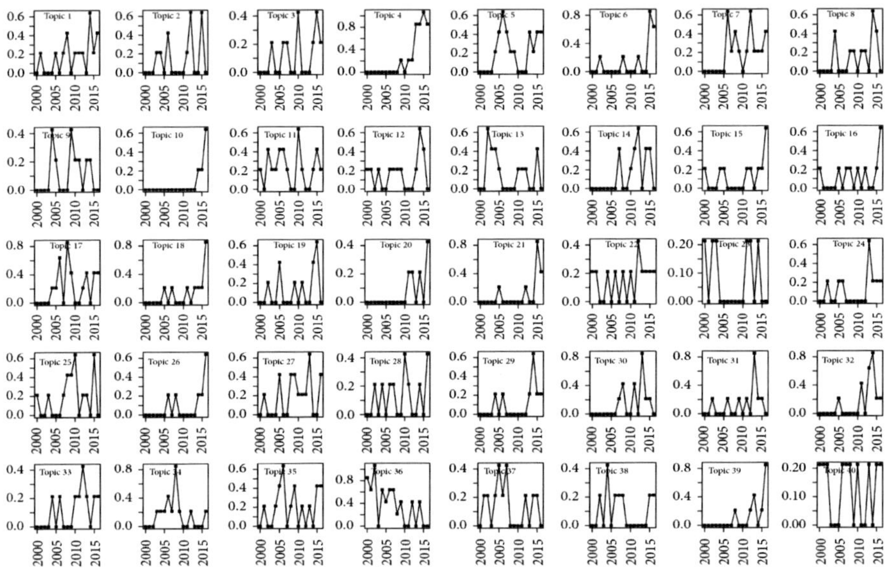

Figure 14. The trends of the 40 research topics during 2000–2016 (x-coordinate as year, y-coordinate as proportion %).

DISCUSSIONS

This study provides a most up-to-date bibliometric analysis on the publications in WoS during the years 2000–2016 in the NLP empowered mobile computing research field. Some interesting findings are discussed below.

The annual number of the publication distribution shows a significant growth trend, from 12 publications in 2000 to 55 publications in 2016. This indicates a growing interest in the research field.

The literature characteristics analysis shows that the 417 publications are widely dispersed throughout 287 journals. 11 most productive journals together contribute about 21% of the total publications. The top 3 are IEEE/ACM Transactions on Audio Speech and Language Processing, Speech Communication, and Computer Speech and Language. Computer science is the most shared subject among these 11 journals. Journal Information Sciences possesses the highest IF, SJR, 5-Year IF, and CiteScore, except for the SNIP score in year 2016.

Top 3 most influential publications are: [35] by Miao et al. published in 2010, [36] by MacKenzie and Soukoreff published in 2002, and [37] by Strayer and Drews published in 2007.

There are 1,408 authors and 544 affiliations involved in the publications. Most authors (79.18%) have only 1 publication, and 4.25% of the authors have 3 or more publications. The most productive authors are Chen, Tao from Singapore and Mizzaro, Stefano from Italy. In addition, most affiliations (70.06%) have 1 publication. 11.89% of the affiliations have 3 or more publications. The most productive affiliations are Nanyang Technological University from Singapore and Tsinghua University from China. Lee, Chin-Hui from USA with 57.67 ACP ranks 1st among top 20 productive authors, and Georgia Institute of Technology from USA with 110 ACP ranks 1st among 15 most productive affiliations.

Through geographic visualization analysis, 60 countries/regions have participated in the publications. The top 15 productive countries/regions are developed countries/regions, except for China. As the top 2, the USA and China have shown a significant growth in the numbers of scientific publications since 2010. These numbers are predicted to continue to increase in the coming years. This partially reflects the need of the development of NLP techniques in solving mobile computing issues.

Scientific collaboration analysis shows that there are significant growth of international collaborations, institution-collaborations as well as author-collaborations. Through social network analysis, we found that researchers tend to collaborate with others within the same country or area, with institutions under similar administration, or with a neighboring country or area. However, some research institutions might have separate administration arrangements from their associated universities or hospitals and a researcher might be affiliated with multiple institutions. The co-authors might actually work together but are affiliated with different institutions. Therefore, it is worth noticing that institution-wise collaboration might not be the actual collaboration among institutions.

Most topics identified using LDA method are recognizable, as they are related to major issues in the research field. Due to space constraints, here we only provide interpretations of some representative topics.

Topic 36 and Topic 11 contain words such as "Agent", "Mobile-agent", "Multi-agent", "Itinerary", "Migration", "Protocol", and "Truncation". Thus, Topic 36 and Topic 11 pertain to mobile agent computing. As an emerging and exciting paradigm for mobile computing applications [42], mobile agent can not only support mobile computers and disconnected operations but also provide an efficient, convenient and robust programming paradigm for implementing distributed applications. The use of mobile agent can bring about significant benefits, e.g., reduction of network traffic, overcoming network latency, and seamless system integration. Therefore, mobile agent is well adapted to the domain of mobile computing.

Topic 32 discusses events about mobile privacy and security. Words in this topic include "Privacy", "Private", "Secure", "Encryption", "Privacy-preserving", "Password", and "Cryptosystem". As pointed out by Mollah et al. [43], security and privacy challenges are introduced with the development of mobile cloud computing which aims at relieving challenges of the resource constrained mobile devices in mobile computing area. Studies centering on mobile privacy can be found. For example, Xi et al. [44] applied Private Information Retrieval techniques in finding the shortest path between an origin and a destination in location privacy issues without the risk of disclosing their privacy.

Topic 1 discusses mobile computing on image and syllable events. It includes words such as "Image", "Syllable", "Re-ranking", "Content-based", "Composite Phoneme", "Simple Phonemes", and "Modern Orthography". Image search in mobile device is quite worthy of challenge [45]. Many researchers are seeking ways to solve this problem. For example, Cai et al. [46] presented a new geometric reranking algorithm specific for small vocabulary in aforementioned scenarios based on Bag-of-Words model for image retrieval. Mobile computing on syllable events is another focus. A representative work is by Eddington and Elzinga [47]. They conducted a quantitative analysis on the phonetic context of word-internal flapping with great attention paid to stress placement, following phone, and syllabification.

Topic 4 mainly focuses on mobile social media event. Words like "Twitter", "Sentiment", "Tweet", "Emojis", "Micro-blog", "Opinion", "Public", and "Emotion" can be found within this topic. With the rapid development of social network, information spreading and evolution is facilitated with popularity of the environment of wireless communication, especially social media platform on mobile terminals [48]. Researchers are gradually paying attention to this area. For example, based on 100 million collected messages from Twitter, Wang et al. [49] presented a hybrid model for sentimental entity.

Based on topic distributions, we found that mobile agent computing, mobile social media computing, and sound related event computing are 3 highest-frequent research themes. From Figure 14 as well as Mann–Kendall test results, we found that some research themes present a statistically significant increasing trend, e.g., image and syllable related events, mobile social media computing, and healthy related events, while researches on mobile agent computing presents a statistically significant decreasing trend.

In the thematic analysis, the optimal number of topics was selected as 40 by a statistical measure of model fitting the data. However, mechanical reliance on statistical measures might lead to the selection of a less meaningful topic model [50]. Hence, we manually checked the robustness of the results by confirming identified topics using a qualitative assessment with the basis of prior knowledge. For each topic, we checked the semantic coherence of its high-frequency terms and examined the contents of publication with a high proportion of this topic.

Through the AP clustering analysis on the 40-topics, 8 clusters were identified, i.e., mobile agent computing, mobile social media computing, image and syllable related events, context-aware computing, sound related events, mobile location computing, healthy related events, and other events. The results of AP clustering analysis are on the whole sensible and easy-to-understand. However, we still found that the 8 categories vary a lot in topic numbers. One possible reason is the choice of clustering method. We then adopted hierarchical clustering method with category number setting to 8. The result was similar with AP clustering. Another possible reason is the sample size since the number of the relevant publications in WoS is limited.

This study is the first to thoroughly explore research status of the NLP empowered mobile computing research field in the statistical perspective. The study provides a comprehensive overview and an intellectual structure of the field from 2000 to 2016. The findings can potentially help researchers especially newcomers systematically understand the development of the field, learn the most influential journals, recognize potentially academic collaborators, and trace research hotspots.

For future work, there are several directions. First, more comprehensive data is expected to be included. Though WoS is a widely applied repository for bibliometric analysis due to its high authority, some relevant conference proceedings have not been indexed yet in WoS. Second, we intend to employ different data clustering methods and compare clustering results for deeper cluster analyzing.

CONCLUSIONS

We conducted a bibliometric analysis on natural language processing empowered mobile computing research publications from Web of Science published during years 2000–2016. The literature characteristics were uncovered using a descriptive statistics method. Geographical publication distribution was explored using a geographic visualization method. By applying a social network analysis method, cooperation relationships among countries/regions, affiliations, and authors were displayed. Finally, topic discovery and distribution were presented using a LDA method and an AP clustering method. We believe the analysis can help researchers comprehend the collaboration patterns and distribution of scholarly resources and research hot spots in the research field more systematically.

DISCLOSURE

Tianyong Hao and Yi Zhou are the corresponding authors.

Conflicts of Interest

The authors declare that they have no conflicts of interest.

ACKNOWLEDGMENTS

The work was substantially supported by the grant from National Natural Science Foundation of China (no. 61772146), the Innovative School Project in Higher Education of Guangdong Province (No. YQ2015062), Science and Technology Program of Guangzhou (no. 201604016136), and Major Project of Frontier and Key Technical Innovation of Guangdong Province (no. 2014B010118003).

REFERENCES

1. G. Deepak and B. S. Pradeep, "Challenging issues and limitations of mobile computing," vol. 3, pp. 177–181, 2012.View at: Google Scholar
2. K.-Y. Chung, J. Yoo, and K. J. Kim, "Recent trends on mobile computing and future networks," Personal and Ubiquitous Computing, vol. 18, no. 3, pp. 489–491, 2014.
3. M. Chen, J. Pan, Q. Zhao, and Y. Yan, "Multi-task learning in deep neural networks for Mandarin-english code-mixing speech recognition," IEICE Transaction on Information and Systems, vol. E99D, no. 10, pp. 2554–2557, 2016.
4. N. Ilayaraja, F. Mary Magdalene Jane, M. Safar, and R. Nadarajan, "WARM Based Data Pre-fetching and Cache Replacement Strategies for Location Dependent Information System in Wireless Environment," Wireless Personal Communications, vol. 90, no. 4, pp. 1811–1842, 2016.
5. L.-H. Wong, R. B. King, C. S. Chai, and M. Liu, "Seamlessly learning Chinese: contextual meaning making and vocabulary growth in a seamless Chinese as a second language learning environment," Instructional Science, vol. 44, no. 5, pp. 399–422, 2016.
6. O. J. Räsänen and J. P. Saarinen, "Sequence prediction with sparse distributed hyperdimensional coding applied to the analysis of mobile phone use patterns," IEEE Transactions on Neural Networks and Learning Systems, vol. 27, no. 9, pp. 1878–1889, 2016.
7. M. Puppala, T. He, S. Chen et al., "METEOR: An Enterprise Health Informatics Environment to Support Evidence-Based Medicine," IEEE Transactions on Biomedical Engineering, vol. 62, no. 12, pp. 2776–2786, 2015.
8. A. O. Adesina, K. K. Agbele, A. P. Abidoye, and H. O. Nyongesa, "Text messaging and retrieval techniques for a mobile health information system," Journal of Information Science, vol. 40, no. 6, pp. 736–748, 2014.
9. W.-T. Chiu and Y.-S. Ho, "Bibliometric analysis of tsunami research," Scientometrics, vol. 73, no. 1, pp. 3–17, 2007.
10. J. M. Merigó, A. M. Gil-Lafuente, and R. R. Yager, "An overview of fuzzy research with bibliometric indicators," Applied Soft Computing, vol. 27, pp. 420–433, 2015.
11. D. Bouyssou and T. Marchant, "Ranking scientists and departments

in a consistent manner," Journal of the Association for Information Science and Technology, vol. 62, no. 9, pp. 1761–1769, 2011.

12. A. Mazloumian, "Predicting Scholars' Scientific Impact," PLoS ONE, vol. 7, no. 11, Article ID e49246, 2012.
13. X. Chen, H. Xie, F. Wang, Z. Liu, J. Xu, and T. Hao, "Natural Language Processing in Medical Research: A Bibliometric Analysis," BMC Medical Informatics and Decision Making, vol. 18, supplement 1, no. 14, 2018.View at: Google Scholar
14. Y. Geng, W. Chen, Z. Liu et al., "A bibliometric review: Energy consumption and greenhouse gas emissions in the residential sector," Journal of Cleaner Production, vol. 159, pp. 301–316, 2017.
15. A. Khan, N. Choudhury, S. Uddin, L. Hossain, and L. A. Baur, "Longitudinal trends in global obesity research and collaboration: A review using bibliometric metadata," Obesity Reviews, vol. 17, no. 4, pp. 377–385, 2016.
16. N. Roig-Tierno, T. F. Gonzalez-Cruz, and J. Llopis-Martinez, "An overview of qualitative comparative analysis: A bibliometric analysis," Journal of Innovation Knowledge, vol. 2, no. 1, pp. 15–23, 2017.
17. G. Albort-Morant and D. Ribeiro-Soriano, "A bibliometric analysis of international impact of business incubators," Journal of Business Research, vol. 69, no. 5, pp. 1775–1779, 2016.
18. J. M. Merigó and J.-B. Yang, "A bibliometric analysis of operations research and management science," OMEGA - The International Journal of Management Science, vol. 73, pp. 37–48, 2017.
19. K. Zhang, Q. Wang, Q.-M. Liang, and H. Chen, "A bibliometric analysis of research on carbon tax from 1989 to 2014," Renewable & Sustainable Energy Reviews, vol. 58, pp. 297–310, 2016.
20. K. Randhawa, R. Wilden, and J. Hohberger, "A Bibliometric Review of Open Innovation: Setting a Research Agenda," Journal of Product Innovation Management, vol. 33, no. 6, pp. 750–772, 2016.
21. A. Yataganbaba and I. Kurtbaş, "A scientific approach with bibliometric analysis related to brick and tile drying: A review," Renewable & Sustainable Energy Reviews, vol. 59, pp. 206–224, 2016.
22. X. Chen, B. Chen, C. Zhang, and T. Hao, "Discovering the Recent Research in Natural Language Processing Field Based on a Statistical Approach," in Emerging Technologies for Education, vol. 10676

of Lecture Notes in Computer Science, pp. 507–517, Springer International Publishing, Cham, 2017.

23. H. J. Kim, D. Y. Yoon, E. S. Kim, K. Lee, J. S. Bae, and J.-H. Lee, "The 100 most-cited articles in neuroimaging: A bibliometric analysis," Results in Physics, vol. 139, pp. 149–156, 2016.
24. X. Chen, H. Weng, and T. Hao, "A Data-Driven Approach for Discovering the Recent Research Status of Diabetes in China," Lecture Notes in Computer Science (including subseries Lecture Notes in Artificial Intelligence and Lecture Notes in Bioinformatics): Preface, vol. 10594, pp. 89–101, 2017.
25. W. R. Tobler, "A computer movie simulating urban growth in the detroit region," Economic Geography, vol. 46, supplement 1, pp. 234–240, 1970.
26. E. Otte and R. Rousseau, "Social network analysis: a powerful strategy, also for the information sciences," Journal of Information Science, vol. 28, no. 6, pp. 441–453, 2002.
27. D. R. Radev, M. T. Joseph, B. Gibson, and P. Muthukrishnan, "A bibliometric and network analysis of the field of computational linguistics," Journal of the Association for Information Science and Technology, vol. 67, no. 3, pp. 683–706, 2016.
28. M. Grandjean, "A social network analysis of Twitter: Mapping the digital humanities community," Cogent Arts and Humanities, vol. 3, no. 1, Article ID 1171458, 2016.
29. M. Salathé, M. Kazandjieva, J. W. Lee, P. Levis, M. W. Feldman, and J. H. Jones, "A high-resolution human contact network for infectious disease transmission," Proceedings of the National Acadamy of Sciences of the United States of America, vol. 107, no. 51, pp. 22020–22025, 2010.
30. J. Scott, "Social network analysis," Sage, 2017.View at: Google Scholar
31. D. M. Blei, A. Y. Ng, and M. I. Jordan, "Latent Dirichlet allocation," Journal of Machine Learning Research, vol. 3, no. 4-5, pp. 993–1022, 2003.View at: Google Scholar
32. J. R. Finkel, T. Grenager, and C. Manning, "Incorporating non-local information into information extraction systems by Gibbs sampling," in Proceedings of the the 43rd Annual Meeting, pp. 363–370, Ann Arbor, Michigan, June 2005.
33. B. J. Frey and D. Dueck, "Clustering by passing messages between

data points," American Association for the Advancement of Science: Science, vol. 315, no. 5814, pp. 972–976, 2007.

34. A. F. El-Samak and W. Ashour, "Optimization of Traveling Salesman Problem Using Affinity Propagation Clustering and Genetic Algorithm," Journal of Artificial Intelligence and Soft Computing Research, vol. 5, no. 4, 2015.
35. G. Miao, N. Himayat, and G. Y. Li, "Energy-efficient link adaptation in frequency-selective channels," IEEE Transactions on Communications, vol. 58, no. 2, pp. 545–554, 2010.
36. I. S. MacKenzie and R. W. Soukoreff, "Text entry for mobile computing: Models and methods, theory and practice," Human–Computer Interaction, vol. 17, no. 2-3, pp. 147–198, 2002.
37. D. L. Strayer and F. A. Drews, "Cell-phone-induced driver distraction," Current Directions in Psychological Science, vol. 16, no. 3, pp. 128–131, 2007.
38. J. Cao, T. Chen, and J. Fan, "Landmark recognition with compact BoW histogram and ensemble ELM," Multimedia Tools and Applications, 2015.
39. M. M. Mostafa, "More than words: social networks' text mining for consumer brand sentiments," Expert Systems with Applications, vol. 40, no. 10, pp. 4241–4251, 2013.
40. H. Jiang, M. Qiang, and P. Lin, "A topic modeling based bibliometric exploration of hydropower research," Renewable & Sustainable Energy Reviews, vol. 57, pp. 226–237, 2016.
41. H. B. Mann, "Nonparametric tests against trend," Econometrica, vol. 13, pp. 245–259, 1945.
42. D. B. Lange and M. Oshima, "Seven Good Reasons for Mobile Agents," Communications of the ACM, vol. 42, no. 3, pp. 88-89, 1999.
43. M. B. Mollah, M. A. K. Azad, and A. Vasilakos, "Security and privacy challenges in mobile cloud computing: Survey and way ahead," Journal of Network and Computer Applications, vol. 84, pp. 38–54, 2017.
44. Y. Xi, L. Schwiebert, and W. Shi, "Privacy preserving shortest path routing with an application to navigation," Pervasive and Mobile Computing, vol. 13, pp. 142–149, 2014.
45. T. Yan, V. Kumar, and D. Ganesan, "CrowdSearch: exploiting crowds for accurate real-time image search on mobile phones," in Proceedings of the 8th International Conference on Mobile Systems, Applications,

and Services (MobiSys '10), pp. 77–90, ACM, San Francisco, Calif, USA, June 2010.

46. Y. Cai, S. Li, Y. Cheng, and R. Ji, "Local consistent hierarchical Hough Match for image re-ranking," Journal of Visual Communication and Image Representation, vol. 37, pp. 32–39, 2016.
47. D. Eddington and D. Elzinga, "The phonetic context of american english flapping: Quantitative evidence," Language and Speech, vol. 51, no. 3, pp. 245–266, 2008.
48. X. Wang, H. Zhang, S. Yuan, J. Wang, and Y. Zhou, "Sentiment processing of social media information from both wireless and wired network," EURASIP Journal on Wireless Communications and Networking, vol. 2016, no. 1, article no. 164, 2016.
49. Z. Wang, X. Cui, L. Gao, Q. Yin, L. Ke, and S. Zhang, "A hybrid model of sentimental entity recognition on mobile social media," EURASIP Journal on Wireless Communications and Networking, vol. 2016, no. 1, article no. 253, 2016.
50. K. E. C. Levy and M. Franklin, "Driving Regulation: Using Topic Models to Examine Political Contention in the U.S. Trucking Industry," Social Science Computer Review, vol. 32, no. 2, pp. 182–194, 2014.

CHAPTER

17

A Mobile-Based Question-Answering and Early Warning System for Assisting Diabetes Management

Wenxiu Xie,[1] Ruoyao Ding,[1] Jun Yan,[2] and Yingying Qu[3]

[1]School of Information Science and Technology, Guangdong University of Foreign Studies, Guangzhou, China

[2]AI Lab, Yidu Cloud (Beijing) Technology Co. Ltd., Beijing, China

[3]School of Business, Guangdong University of Foreign Studies, Guangzhou, China

ABSTRACT

With increasing demand for preventive management of chronic diseases in real time by using the Internet, interest in developing a convenient device on health management and monitoring has intensified. Unlike other chronic

Citation: Wenxiu Xie, Ruoyao Ding, Jun Yan, and Yingying Qu, "A Mobile-Based Question-Answering and Early Warning System for Assisting Diabetes Management", Journal on Wireless Communications and Mobile Computing, Volume 2018, Article ID 9163160, 14 pages, https://doi.org/10.1155/2018/9163160.

diseases, diabetes particularly type 2 is a lifelong chronic disease and usually requires daily health management by patients themselves. This study is to develop a mobile-based diabetes question-answering (Q&A) and early warning system named Dia-AID, assisting diabetes patients and populations at high risk. The Dia-AID system consists of three modules: a large-scale multilanguage diabetes frequently asked question repository, a multimode fusion Q&A framework, and a health data management module. A list of services including risk assessment and health early warning is provided to users for health condition monitoring. Using the diabetes frequently asked question repository as data, experiments are conducted on answer ranking and answer selection aspects. Results show that two essential methods in the system outperform baseline methods on both aspects.

INTRODUCTION

With the increasing attention of ubiquitous healthcare (U-healthcare) services and the developing of information technology, there has been a great need for preventive management of chronic diseases and management of individual health conditions [1]. Diabetes mellitus, a.k.a. diabetes, as one of the most representative chronic diseases, has become a serious global public health issue and the most challenging health problem in the 21st century [2–4]. The statistics of the number of diabetes patients 20-79 years of age in the past 18 years are shown in Figure 1, according to the latest global estimation from the International Diabetes Federation (IDF) and the Research2guidance report (http://www.research2guidance.com). Compared to 151 million in 2000, there is nearly a threefold increase in the number of adults living with diabetes mellitus. Moreover, the number is expected to increase from 425 million in 2017 to 629 million in 2045, which means that one out of 11 adults will suffer from diabetes [5]. In addition, as reported by the World Health Organization (WHO), diabetes was the direct cause of 1.6 million deaths in 2015. However, nearly 50% of diabetes patients are undiagnosed and remain unaware of their conditions. Among the patient population, the majority of diabetes cases are type 2 diabetes mellitus (T2DM) [6]. Unlike type 1 diabetes mellitus which remains unpreventable with current knowledge, 80% of type 2 diabetes mellitus can be prevented by keeping moderate blood sugar and lifestyle [7]. People with diabetes type 2 frequently need counseling on healthy diet and regular physical activity to reduce the risk of complication [8]. Thus, diabetes management is a crucial and necessary procedure for diabetes patients or people at a high diabetes risk [9–11].

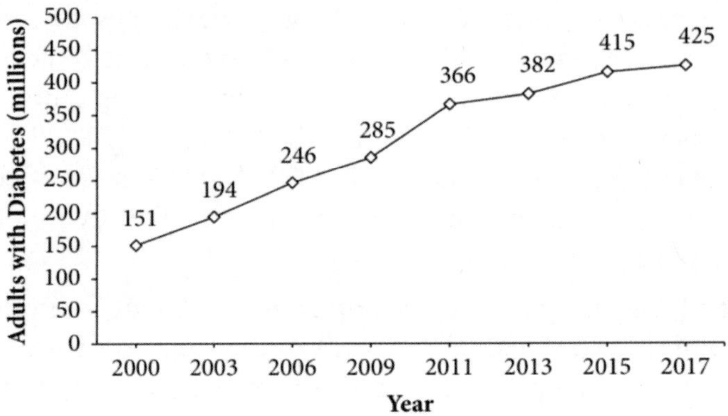

Figure 1. Total number of adults with diabetes (20-79 years old) around the world during 2000 to 2017.

Recently, the focus of healthcare is shifting from treatment to prevention and early diagnosis of disease [12]. Fox et al. [13] addressed that 31% of US smartphone owners used their phones to search for medical information online, 30% of Internet users consulted online reviews of rankings of healthcare services or treatments, and 26% of Internet users read other people's experiences about health or medical issues. By 2015, nearly 500 million smartphone users used mobile health applications especially for diet and disease management [7]. Later, Krebs et al. [14] showed that 58.23% (934/1604) of mobile phone users downloaded a health-related mobile app and used it at least once per day. As a convenient platform for checking users' health status on a real-time basis, mobile applications have been developed from information provision to lifestyle-oriented smart health management. Moreover, existing research presented that continuous real-time consulting and monitoring supported by smartphones is applicable for improving efficiency of diabetes self-management [7, 15–17]. Therefore, developing a mobile-based system for diabetes patients to assist in their health management is of great importance.

Many studies have shown that current medical search engines, e.g., PubMed, Medical Subject Headings (MeSH), and Unified Medical Language System (UMLS), are often unable to serve users with clinically relevant answers in a timely manner and thus fail to satisfy patients' counseling need [18, 19]. Hersh et al. [20] found that a healthcare professional took more than 30 minutes on average to seek an answer utilizing information retrieval systems. The process needs about 2 minutes on average to obtain an answer even for experienced doctors [21]. Instead, based on natural language processing techniques, question answering (Q&A) aims to provide users with direct, precise answers to their questions, and thus it is more preferred. Hence, there is an increasing demand to develop convenient and effective question-answering systems for the medical domain [21–24]. Moreover, there is a particularly growing demand of Q&A systems for effectively and efficiently assisting diabetes patients to better utilize ever-accumulating expert knowledge [1, 7, 15].

To that end, this study aims to develop a mobile-based question-answering and early warning system, called Dia-AID. The system consists of 3 modules: a large-scale multilanguage diabetes FAQ repository, a multimode fusion Q&A framework, and a health data management module with early warning function. The repository captures diabetes questions with expert-defined answers and stores the question-answer knowledge in an interpretable and extendible form. The framework contains three different Q&A resolution strategies: knowledge-based Q&A, FAQ-based Q&A, and web-based Q&A. The health data management module containing early warning provides a convenient counseling service on a smart health platform to assist diabetes patients in monitoring their health conditions.

The contributions of this work include the following: (1) a large-scale multilanguage diabetes FAQ repository is built with a consistent representation format; (2) a novel multimode fusion Q&A framework that integrates three modes of Q&A technologies is proposed to fulfill diabetes information seeking need; (3) a health data management module containing early warning function is developed to monitor patient health status.

The rest of this paper is organized as follows. Section 2 introduces related work in biomedical question answering. Section 3 describes the mobile-based question-answering and early warning system Dia-AID in detail. Section 4 presents the experiment results of our methods based on the FAQ data repository. Section 5 addresses the conclusions.

RELATED WORK

The aim of question answering is to provide precise answers instead of relevant documents from unstructured data sources to inquirers. The research of open domain question answering (Q&A) started from the prompt and instantiated work in the Text Retrieval Conference (TREC) evaluation campaign [25]. Recently, with the increasing demand of domain-specific applications, a growing interest has shifted from open domain Q&A to restricted domain Q&A [26, 27]. Molla et al. [28] addressed that restricted domain Q&A targeting domain-specific information was expected to achieve effective and reliable performance in real-world applications. Further, as claimed by Mishra et al. [29], restricted domain Q&A could fulfill the specialized information requirements of domain experts, therefore improving the satisfaction of users. Similarly, Yu et al. [30] and Rinaldi et al. [31] noted that restricted domain Q&A, such as biomedical domain [24, 32], could exploit domain-specific knowledge resources for deeper text analysis, as well as taking advantage of domain-specific typology formatting conventions to improve the answer extraction performance.

In light of Athenikos et al.'s research [27], medical domain question answering was facing the challenge of highly complex domain-specific terminology and lexical and ontological resources. Also emphasized by Abacha et al. [33], the key process was to translate the semantic relations expressed in questions into a machine-readable representation to analyze the natural language questions deeply and efficiently. They presented a complete question analysis approach including medical entity recognition, semantic relation extraction, and automatic translation to SPARQL queries. Result presented that 60% of the questions were correctly translated to SPARQL queries via the proposed method. Later, Anca [34] proposed the GFMed for dealing with the same problem and the challenge of querying a large number of Linked Data from various domains. GFMed was a Q&A system for biomedical interlinked data aiming to fill the gap between end users and formal languages by introducing a grammatical framework to translate biomedical information in natural language to the corresponding SPARQL language. The experimental results demonstrated that the proposed methodology for building Controlled Nature Language for querying Linked Data was valid. Abacha et al. [35] proposed an approach for "Answer Search" based on semantic search and query relaxation to resolve the problem of automatic Q&A in medical domain. They defined question focuses as medical entities that were the most closely linked to answers to improve the overall performance of question answering. Terol et al. [36] claimed a general Q&A system that was capable of working over any restricted domain. Taking medical domain as an example application, their system answered medical questions according to a generic question taxonomy and gained 94.4% overall precision on the task.

During question-answering process, question representation is an essential step in question analysis and answer retrieval. Zhang et al. [37]

proposed a system based on multilayer self-organizing map, providing an efficient solution to the organization problem of structured data of electronic books. A tree-structured representation was proposed to formulate the rich features of an e-book author. Their experiment results corroborated that the proposed models based on the tree-structured representation outperformed content-based models. Later in their further research, an efficient learning framework Tree2Vector for transforming tree-structured data into vectorial representations was proposed [38]. By utilizing Tree2Vector framework to map tree-structured book data into vectorial space, their continued experiments further presented that the mapped vectorial space could explore term spatial distributions over a book rather than the traditional document modeling methods [39].

A recent trend among medical Q&A systems was to incorporate the organized medical information throughout Q&A process in order to utilize the information for efficient health management in various areas such as U-healthcare [40, 41]. Jung et al. [42] developed a decision supporting method mainly for pain management for chronic disease patients based on frequent pattern tree mining. The proposed method aimed to reduce time and expenses for pain decision-making of patients who were frequently exposed to pain. Chung et al. [12] presented a knowledge-based health service by leveraging a hybrid wireless fidelity peer-to-peer architecture. The service was proposed to provide patients with efficient and economical healthcare through correct measurement of various biosignals, so that users could easily predict and manage both health and disease. Han et al. [43] introduced a U-health service system THE_MUSS, focusing on achieving reusability and resolvability, to provide stress and weight management services.

In subsequent medical Q&A developments, diabetes mellitus, as one of the top three major worldwide causes of death from noncommunicable diseases, has prompted numerous researches investigating the prevention, prevalence, and mortality of diabetes mellitus [15, 44–53]. There is a great demand for a Q&A system that can effectively and efficiently provide health consulting services and assist people in monitoring and managing their individual health conditions. Jung et al. [7] explored a mobile healthcare application for providing self-diabetes management to patients. By interoperating with Electronic Medical Record (EMR), the healthcare application provided services such as weight management, cardio-cerebrovascular risk evaluation, and exercise management. Waki et al. [54] developed a real-time interactive system DialBetics to achieve diabetes self-management, particularly HbA1c management. By an evaluation strategy, the system helped patients improve their HbA1c significantly by monitoring health data compared with continuing self-care regimen patients. More recently, Yoo et al. [1] proposed a Personal Health Record- (PHR-) based diabetes index service model through a mobile device, offering users a management information service for preventing diabetes. Users were able to check their health conditions on a real-time basis and receive information about desirable health behaviors and dietary habits related to diabetes.

Yet, the existing diabetes management applications provided general information search and management, while ignoring counseling services, which were crucial for managing the health condition of diabetes patients. Besides, as claimed by Mishra et al. [29], the cons of restricted domain Q&A included the limited repository of domain-specific questions. To overcome these difficulties, we built a LMD-FAQ repository to provide users with concise and accurate answers by physicians or experts from debates related professional websites. Moreover, we aim to leverage the LMD-FAQ repository to provide counseling services of diet, medication, and symptoms for diabetes patients. In addition, based on our previous work [55], by analyzing global clinical trials of 190 countries provided by the National Institutes of Health (NIH), we discovered 6 representative health characteristics that were closely related to diabetes mellitus to better manage users' health conditions. The six representative health characteristics were Body Mass Index (BMI), Glucose, Systolic Hypertension, Diastolic Hypertension, HbA1c, and creatinine. Further, we defined several early warning intervals of health characteristics by referring to the existing international medical standards for health management and risk warning.

METHODS AND MATERIALS

The architecture of our mobile-based diabetes question-answering and early warning system Dia-AID is shown in Figure 2. It consists of 3 modules: a large-scale multilanguage diabetes FAQ repository (LMD-FAQ repository), a novel multimode fusion question-answering framework (MMF-QA), and a diabetes data management module with early warning (DM-EW). The LMD-FAQ repository contains a large number of diabetes question-answer pairs acquired from mainstream diabetes-related professional websites. The MMF-QA framework integrates three strategies: knowledge-based Q&A, FAQ-based Q&A, and web-based Q&A. The DM-EW module records patients' health data and monitors their health conditions in real time. Six representative health characteristics that are closely related to diabetes mellitus, that is, BMI, glucose, systolic hypertension, diastolic hypertension, HbA1c, and creatinine, are applied. In case of a rapid characteristic change or a predication of deterioration, the module will automatically warn patients and provide them with dietary guidelines.

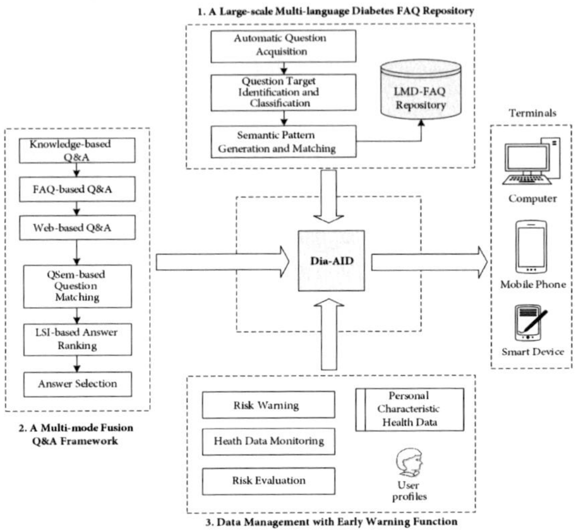

Figure 2. The architecture of the diabetes question-answering and early warning system, Dia-AID.

The Large-Scale Multilanguage Diabetes FAQ Repository

Frequently Asked Questions (FAQs) provide specific answers to the questions that are frequently asked when users browse specific websites. For example, the website Health China (http://health.china.com) allows users to ask questions in free text and those who are experts in the field answer the questions freely. These questions with professional answers are collected and organized as FAQ data. The FAQ data can dramatically benefit question answering by reusing the accumulated professional knowledge. In this paper, we develop a method to automatically construct a large-scale multilanguage diabetes FAQ (LMD-FAQ) repository through identifying FAQ data from professional diabetes websites.

As illustrated in Figure 2, our method includes four steps: (1) The first step is automatic question acquisition. We first analyze the page structures of specific websites to identify diabetes questions. The websites, elaborately selected by domain experts, include Diabetes Clinical Guidelines (Chinese Medical Association Diabetes Branch), professional diabetes websites

(International Diabetes Union, the American Diabetes Association, etc.), diabetes professional information websites (CDC Health Channel), and diabetes interactive question-answering websites (Yahoo! Knowledge). The questions and associated answers are then extracted using regular expression matching with the page codes. (2) The second step is question target identification and classification. Based on our previous work [56, 57], an automated answer type identification and classification method is applied to extract the target and intent of questions by utilizing both syntactic and semantic analysis.

Considering that syntactic structures vary according to the ways questions are asked, four typical situations are identified and analyzed with each of them having a specific processing strategy. During the process, question target features are extracted via a principle-based syntactic parser and then expanded with their hypernymy features and semantic labels. Finally, the expanded features are sent to a trained classifier to predict corresponding answer types. (3) The third step is semantic pattern generation and matching. Semantic pattern is utilized to index the questions with answers in a more structured and semantic way. With question target and answer type extracted by the second step, the questions are represented by a structural semantic pattern, which consists of five components: the question target, question type, concept, event, and constraint. An entropy-based method proposed in previous work [58] is applied for automated semantic pattern generation. Figure 3 shows the visualization of example FAQ data in the LMD-FAQ repository.

Figure 3. The visualization of example FAQ data in the LMD-FAQ repository.

Based on the above procedure, the method extracts FAQ data from professional websites, formats them using a consistent representation, and indexes them with semantic patterns for fast retrieval. Through the automatic process and the human review on the indexed data, the FAQ repository can be incrementally maintained. Currently, the LMD-FAQ repository comprises 19,317 English frequently asked QA pairs and 6,041 Chinese QA pairs. The repository provides our Q&A system with fundamental data support for answering commonly posted questions.

The Multimode Fusion Question-Answering Framework

The multimode fusion question-answering framework (MMF-QA) integrates three Q&A models: knowledge-based Q&A, FAQ-based Q&A, and web-based Q&A. The overall framework is shown in Figure 4. The procedure of the models is described as follows.

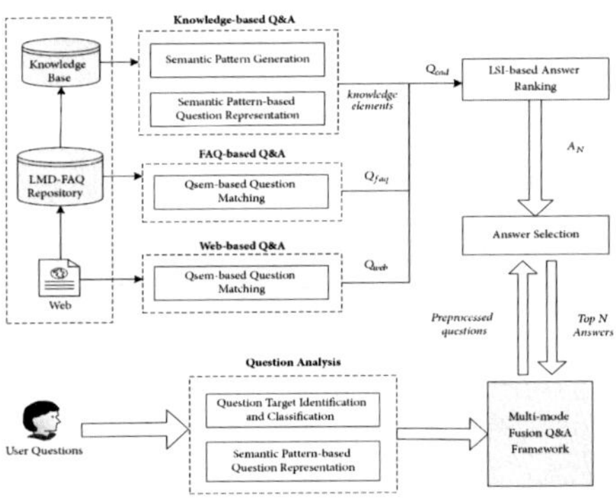

Figure 4. The multimode fusion Q&A framework, MMF-QA.

The knowledge-based Q&A model relies on a diabetes knowledge base to generate concise answers for posted questions. For a new given question, the model analyzes the structure and keywords of the question and then generates a corresponding semantic pattern. Thus, the question is transformed from natural language to a structural semantic representation that captures semantic information such as question target, question type, concept, event, and constraint The question then is further represented as a tuple: ([Concept_1], Relation, [Concept_2]), in which "Concept_1" and "Concept_2" are used to label meaningful entities. The represented question is used for answer extraction from knowledge base. For instance, "What's the symptoms of diabetes?" is represented as ([symptoms], Rel: of, [diabetes]).

Therefore, the knowledge-based Q&A process mainly maps entities and their relations to formally represented tuples, which are further used to match knowledge base to retrieve accurately matched knowledge elements as answers.

The FAQ-based Q&A model computes matching scores between a given question and questions in the FAQ repository. The questions with matching scores larger than a specific threshold are kept as candidates. The candidate questions then are ranked and the top k questions with the highest scores are returned. The model consists of three main steps: Qsem-based question matching, LSI-based answer ranking, and answer selection. As claimed by [59], a major challenge of FAQ-based Q&A is to match questions to corresponding question-answer pairs. Here, we apply a QSem-based question matching framework, proposed in one of our previous works [60], to support answering FAQs through reusing accumulated QA data. The framework considers both question word types and semantic pattern according to their functionalities in question matching. The question word types include question target word, user-oriented word, and irrelevant word. These three word types are semantically labeled by a predefined ontology to enrich the semantic representation of questions. For each word type, different similarity strategies are applied to calculate the similarity, as described in [60]. The similarity calculations for question target and user-oriented word type between question q_i and a FAQ candidate faq_j are shown in (1), (2), and (3), respectively.

$$Simi_{QT}\left(q_i, faq_j\right) = \frac{2 \times \left|q_i\left(QTW \longrightarrow L^*\right) \cap faq_j\left(QTW \longrightarrow L^*\right)\right|}{\left|q_i\left(QTW \longrightarrow L^*\right)\right| + \left|faq_j\left(QTW \longrightarrow L^*\right)\right|} \quad (1)$$

$$SMatch\left(w_m, w_n\right) = \begin{cases} 0, & \left|\left(w_m \cup w_m \longrightarrow S\left(w_m\right)\right) \cap \left(w_n \cup w_n \longrightarrow S\left(w_n\right)\right)\right| = 0 \\ 1, & \left|\left(w_m \cup w_m \longrightarrow S\left(w_m\right)\right) \cap \left(w_n \cup w_n \longrightarrow S\left(w_n\right)\right)\right| \geq 1 \end{cases} \quad (2) \quad (2)$$

$$Simi_{UO}\left(q_i, faq_j\right) = \frac{2 \times \sum SMatch\left(q_i\left(UOW\right), faq_j\left(UOW\right)\right)}{\left|q_i\left(UOW\right)\right| + \left|faq_j\left(UOW\right)\right|} \quad (3)$$

In the equations, $Simi_{QT}$ denotes the similarity score of QT word type between a given new question q_i and an existing FAQ question faq_j. L^* denotes the set of semantic labels corresponding to target words of the question. $q_i(QTW \rightarrow L^*)$ and $faq_j(QTW \rightarrow L^*)$ represent the semantic labels of QT words in q_i and faq_j through semantic labeling, respectively.

$w_m \cup w_m \rightarrow S(w_m)$ denotes synonymy words expansion of word w_m. SMatch denotes the synonymy-based word matching of two words w_m and w_n. $w_m \cup w_m \rightarrow S(w_m)$ is the synonymy extension of word w_m by adding synonymy word collection $S(w_m)$. By integrating the previous three parts of matching, the overall matching score $Simi_{SC}(q_i, faq_j)$ of the two questions q_i and faq_j through balancing the similarity of each part is calculated as shown in

$$MatchSC\left(q_i, faq_j\right) = \alpha \times Simi_{QT} + \beta \times Simi_{UO} + (1 - \alpha - \beta) \times Simi_{SP} \tag{4}$$

After question matching, top k FAQs with the highest matching scores are selected as candidates set Q_{faq}. Meanwhile, the web-based Q&A model uses a similar strategy to compute the matching scores to web question collections. It extracts k answers from websites via the standard question answering techniques. Similarly, the web-based Q&A returns a candidate question-answer set Q_{web}. Q_{web} and Q_{faq} are merged as the final answer candidates Q_{cad} for answer ranking and answer selection.

We propose a LSI-based answer ranking method to re-rank the questions in Q_{cad}. The ranking method consists of three steps: feature extraction, Latent Semantic Indexing (LSI) similarity calculation, and ranking. The extracted features of Chinese questions are bag-of-words (BOWs) and Character, while the features for English questions are bagof-words feature only. The LSI approach takes advantage of implicit higher-order semantic structure and matches words in queries with words in documents [61]. Here we treat each candidate answer as a short document and detect the most relevant answers via the LSI-based method. After that, the candidate answers are re-ranked based on the similarity values and the top N answers as candidate list A_N are returned

Finally, there is an answer selection process. The selection of a candidate answer as correct or incorrect can be treated as a binary classification task. The question and corresponding top N candidate answers in list A_N are transformed to N QA pairs. We propose an answer selection approach via a Logistic Regression (LR) classifier, which includes four steps: feature extraction, parameter tuning, model training, and answer selecting. Using the features similar to the LSI-based approach, QA pairs are randomly selected from the LMD-FAQ repository as training data. The QA pairs with correct answers are labeled as "1", and "0" otherwise. We then tune the parameter

"*C*" (inverse of regularization strength) to avoid over fitting/under fitting issue. After parameter optimization, the best parameter is applied in the LR classifier, which then is applied to select the best N candidate answers, where the top 1 is the best answer and the remaining *N-1* answers in list A_N are relevant answers. Figure 5 shows the screen snapshots of the knowledge-based Q&A, FAQ-based Q&A, and web-based Q&A modes.

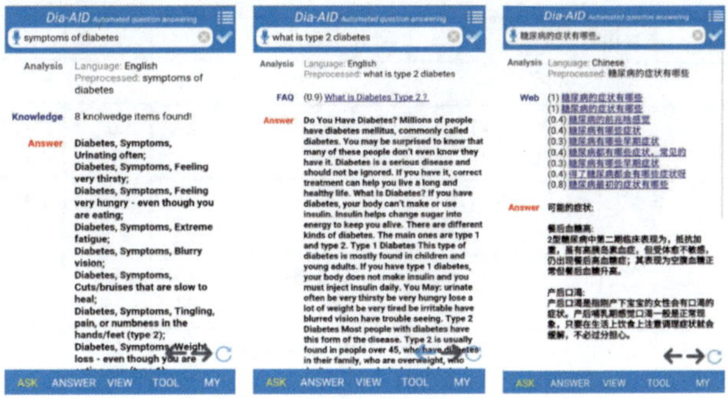

Figure 5. The screen snapshots of the mobile-based system for providing diabetes information services using the three Q&A models.

Diabetes Data Management with Early Warning

Since diabetes patients and people at high risk usually need long-term health management, we develop a real-time data management module incorporating early warning to achieve patient health self-management.

In the data management module, users are required to register their basic information. After that, the users can log in to report their recent health data related to six main characteristics: HbA1c, BMI, glucose, systolic hypertension (hypertension_S), diastolic hypertension (hypertension_D), and creatinine. The health data then are stored in server side securely.

With the historical health data, the module calculates and monitors the health status in real time. For each of the characteristics, we set an alarm value according to literature review on IDF documents and reports. Once the health data has a dramatic change or the characteristics are close to their corresponding alarm value ranges, the system will automatically deliver a warning message to the users about the situation. To evaluate the usability of the system, a 2-month randomized study is designed. Thirty people volunteered as internal test users to monitor their health condition via the Dia-AID system. During the test, users measure and report the data of the six characteristics by themselves. Based on each new data report, the system calculates the existing data and newly submitted data to make a summarization of the health condition in real time. Table 1 shows the reported health data records by a user *Cecil.*

Table 1. The reported health data records of the user *Cecil.*

Characteristic	Value	Time	Characteristic	Value	Time
HBA1C	7.5	2017-11-01 10:22:03	HBA1C	9.0	2017-11-04 19:15:18
GLUCOSE	12.0	2017-11-01 10:22:03	BMI	22.0	2017-11-04 19:15:18
BMI	22.1	2017-11-01 10:22:03	GLUCOSE	15.0	2017-11-04 19:15:18
HYPERTENSION_S	111.0	2017-11-01 10:22:03	HYPERTENSION_S	113.0	2017-11-04 19:15:18
HYPERTENSION_D	82.0	2017-11-01 10:22:03	HYPERTENSION_D	84.0	2017-11-04 19:15:18
CREATININE	1.18	2017-11-01 10:22:03	CREATININE	1.24	2017-11-04 19:15:18
HBA1C	6.0	2017-11-02 18:24:39	HBA1C	9.0	2017-11-05 18:10:25
BMI	22.0	2017-11-02 18:24:39	BMI	24.0	2017-11-05 18:10:25
GLUCOSE	10.0	2017-11-02 18:24:39	GLUCOSE	15.0	2017-11-05 18:10:25
HYPERTENSION_S	110.0	2017-11-02 18:24:39	HYPERTENSION_S	113.0	2017-11-05 18:10:25
HYPERTENSION_D	80.0	2017-11-02 18:24:39	HYPERTENSION_D	84.0	2017-11-05 18:10:25
CREATININE	1.2	2017-11-02 18:24:39	CREATININE	1.24	2017-11-05 18:10:25
HBA1C	7.8	2017-11-03 18:30:28	HBA1C	10.0	2017-11-06 19:21:13
BMI	21.9	2017-11-03 18:30:28	BMI	24.0	2017-11-06 19:21:13
GLUCOSE	12.0	2017-11-03 18:30:28	GLUCOSE	18.0	2017-11-06 19:21:13
HYPERTENSION_S	111.0	2017-11-03 18:30:28	HYPERTENSION_S	115.0	2017-11-06 19:21:13
HYPERTENSION_D	82.0	2017-11-03 18:30:28	HYPERTENSION_D	86.0	2017-11-06 19:21:13
CREATININE	1.2	2017-11-03 18:30:28	CREATININE	1.15	2017-11-06 19:21:13

The system records all the reported health data and generates data change curves automatically. For example, Figure 6 shows the trend curve of *Cecil*'s diastolic hypertension in the last 7 days. When the current newly submitted health data is within safe range and there is no dramatic change compared with last report, the system shows the user with the health status messages, e.g., "Your health status is good" in green color. Once the system identifies current user data exceeding alarm range (either too high or too low) according to the current change trend, the system will evaluate how long it takes to reach the alarm value. The system will evaluate how long it will take to reach the alarm value. If the period is too short, the system will automatically warn the current user. For example, the system warns the user *Cecil* that diastolic hypertension is too high and will be in a danger range after 2 days if the user does not have any control on it. Through the health data management incorporating early warning, users can review their health status and take actions to reduce the risk of diabetes according to the warning messages.

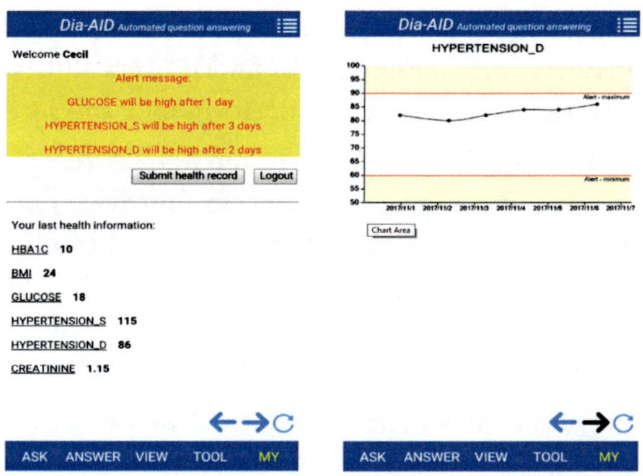

Figure 6. The health data management with early warning function and health record visualization by time for the user *Cecil*.

RESULTS

Datasets

Since there is no available diabetes FAQ dataset for evaluation, the evaluations of the proposed LSI-based answer ranking approach and answer selection method were based on the constructed LMD-FAQ repository. To test the LSI-based answer ranking approach, we randomly selected 500, 750,1000,1250,1500, and 1750 Chinese question-answer tuples (question, <answer-set>) from the repository, respectively, as six subdatasets of **Evaluation dataset-A**. For each question-answer tuple, it contains one question and an answer set which consists of one correct answer and nine incorrect answers randomly generated from the rest of the repository. Thus, each question contains 10 candidate answers for ranking. For answer selection evaluation, we suppose each question has k candidate answers; i.e., for each question, *k-1* incorrect answers are randomly generated as negative samples. In this paper, *k* is set to 5 and 10. For the setting *k*=5, 6000 QA pairs are randomly generated as **Training dataset-B1**, and 2500 QA pairs are randomly generated as **Testing dataset-C1**. For the setting *k*=10, 8000 QA pairs are randomly generated as **Training dataset-B2**, and 5000 QA pairs are randomly generated as **Testing dataset-C2**.

Evaluation Metrics

The evaluation metrics include Mean Reciprocal Rank (MRR), Accuracy@N of the returned answers, precision, recall, and F1 measure, all of which are commonly used metrics to evaluate the performance of Q&A systems.

(i) MRR: Mean Reciprocal Rank of the first correct answer, as shown in (5) (i.e., 1 if a correct answer was retrieved at rank 1, 0.5 if a correct answer was retrieved at rank 2, and so on. *Q* is the test set and |Q| denotes the number of questions in *Q*. $rank_i$ represents the position of the first correct answer in answer ranking candidates to a test question Q_i).

(ii) Accuracy@N: proportion of correct answers in top N returned answers by the system, as shown in (6) ($C_i(N) = 1$ if there is at least one correct answer in top N candidates; otherwise, it is 0).

(iii) Precision for any of the categories is the number of true positives (TP) (i.e., the number of questions correctly labeled as belonging to the positive categories) that are divided by the total number of questions labeled as belonging to the positive categories, as shown in (7). False positive (FP) is the number of questions that the system incorrectly labeled.

(iv) Recall is defined as the number of true positives divided by the total number of questions that actually belong to positive categories (i.e., the sum of true positive and false negative), as shown in (8).

(v) F1-measure considers both the precision and the recall to compute a balanced score, as shown in (9).

$$MRR = \frac{1}{|Q|}\sum_{i=1}^{|Q|}\frac{1}{rank_i} \quad (5)$$

$$Accuracy@N = \frac{1}{|Q|}\sum_{i=1}^{|Q|}C_i(N) \quad (6)$$

$$Precision = \frac{TP}{TP + FP} \quad (7)$$

$$Recall = \frac{TP}{TP + FN} \quad (8)$$

$$F1 = \frac{2 * Precision * Recall}{Precision + Recall} \quad (9)$$

Results

To validate the proposed LSI-based answer ranking method, we conduct the following two experiments. The first experiment is to verify the effectiveness of the LSI-based answer ranking method by comparing to five baselines. We adopt Doc2Vec, Latent Dirichlet Allocation (LDA), Locality Sensitive Hashing (LSH), docsim, and Synonyms [62] as baselines. We randomly select 500 questions and measure the performance in MRR and Accuracy@*N* (Acc@*N*, N=1, 2, 3, 4, 5). Compared with the baselines, our method achieves the best performance in all evaluation metrics, as shown in Table 2. For MRR, our method improves by 17.80% compared to LSH which has the best performance among baselines. For Acc@1, LSH also obtains the best performance as 0.6733 among baselines. Our method outperformed LSH with an improvement of 23.52%. In addition, our method ranks 94.99% of the correct answers in the top five of candidate answers. The improvements of MRR and Acc@1 prove that the proposed method can potentially promote the positions of correct answers.

Table 2. Evaluation results compared to baselines.

	MRR	Acc@1	Acc@2	Acc@3	Acc@4	Acc@5
Doc2Vec	0.2811	0.0721	0.1923	0.2905	0.3967	0.5250
LDA	0.5536	0.3326	0.5811	0.7294	0.8016	0.8597
Synonyms	0.6082	0.4108	0.6332	0.7454	0.8376	0.8877
docsim	0.7233	0.6312	0.7074	0.7515	0.7895	0.8336
LSH	0.7517	0.6733	0.7394	0.7835	0.8056	0.8276
Our Method	**0.8855**	**0.8317**	**0.8918**	**0.9259**	**0.9459**	**0.9499**

To assess the stability of the proposed method, the second experiment is conducted by comparing to the same five baselines with the measures of MRR and Acc@1. The used dataset is Evaluation dataset-A. Figure 7 illustrates the experiment results measured in MRR, while Figure 8 shows the results measured in Acc@1. From the result, our method achieves stable performance over all different sizes of the question sets. This result is promising since our method ranks most of the correct answers in the top of the candidate answer list. Moreover, compared to the baselines, our method gains the best performance measured in Acc@1 on all the question sets. From the results, even with the increasing number of questions, nearly 85% of correct answers are ranked in the top of the candidate answer list.

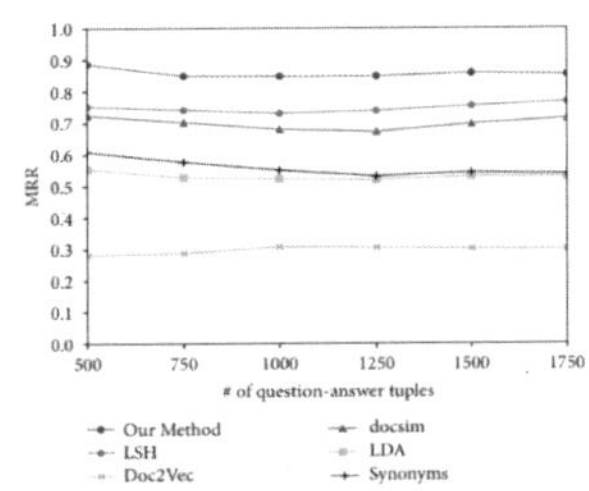

Figure 7. The performance comparison between the proposed method and baselines with the increasing number of question-answer tuples using the MRR measure.

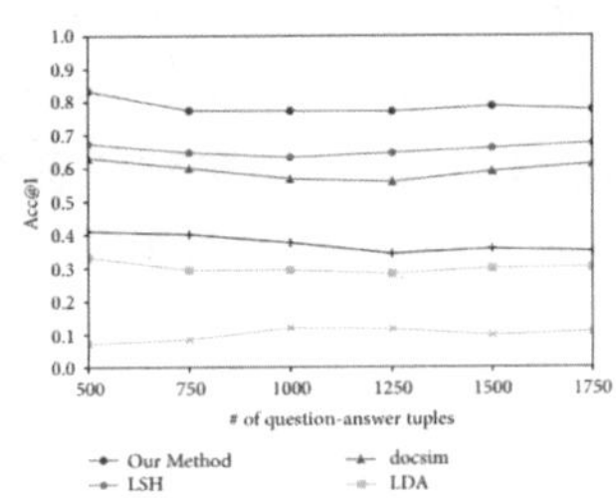

Figure 8. The performance comparison between the proposed method and baselines with the increasing number of question-answer tuples using the Acc@1 measure.

Since our answer selection approach uses a binary classifier, we assess the method by evaluating the effectiveness of answer classification. During the evaluation, three experiments are designed: the first is to train optimized parameters, the second aims to assess the stability of classification, and the third aims to evaluate the effectiveness by comparing with baseline methods. The datasets used for evaluation are from the constructed LMD-FAQ repository and the evaluation metrics are precision, recall, F1, and accuracy.

To avoid the overfitting/underfitting problem, we tune the parameter "*C*" (inverse of regularization strength) for the LR classifier as described above. 12,651 QA pairs are randomly selected from the LMD-FAQ repository as the dataset. The dataset then is randomly shuffled into two subgroups as training (70%) and testing (30%). We use *k*-fold cross-validation to assess the model performance. Figure 9 demonstrates the validation curve, where training accuracy represents the results on testing dataset and validation accuracy denotes the 10-fold cross-validation results. From the results, the method gains the best performance when "*C*" is equal to 1, which is the best parameter applied in the following two experiments.

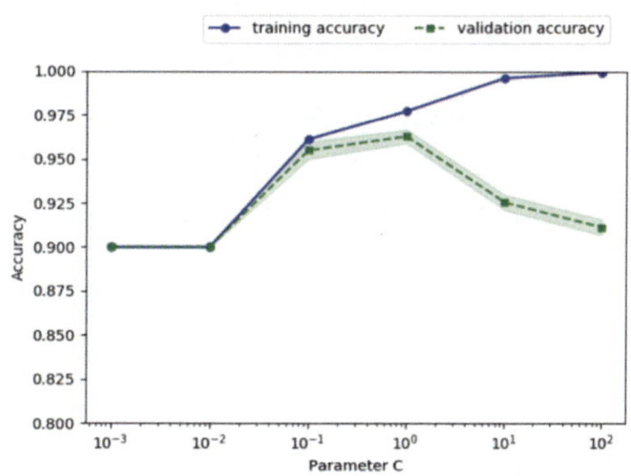

Figure 9. The validation curve of parameter "*C*" using different values.

The stability of the proposed method is tested with different sizes of training data and different k values. By setting *k*=5, the Training dataset-B1 is randomly divided into 5 training subsets containing 2000, 3000, 4000, 5000, and 6000 question-answer pairs, respectively. Similarly, by setting *k*=10, the Training dataset B2 is randomly divided into 5 training subsets with 4000, 5000, 6000, 7000, and 8000 question-answer pairs. The datasets C1 and C2 are used as testing datasets independently. The results are measured in accuracy (Acc), precision, recall, and F1-measure (F1). As shown in Figure 10, our method receives a stable performance on all evaluation metrics with *k*=5. When the size of training dataset is larger than 3000, the performance on all metrics increases. The experiment results indicate that our method is not affected much by training dataset size. As illustrated in Figure 11, the performance measured in accuracy remains stable on all sizes of training datasets. With the increasing of training dataset size, the performance measured in F1 increases. Comparing the performance on the two dataset settings, our method yields a better performance when k equals 10, which indicates that the proposed method remains stable even with more incorrect answers in candidate answer lists.

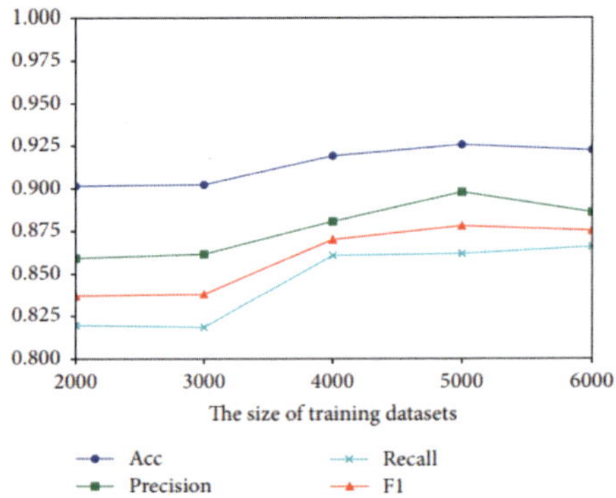

Figure 10. The performance with the increasing size of training datasets when *k*=5.

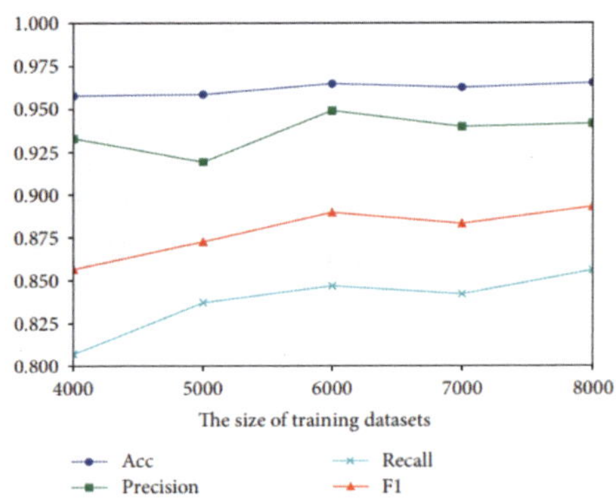

Figure 11. The performance with the increasing size of training datasets when *k*=10.

We further compare our method with five commonly used classification methods: Support Vector Machine (SVM), Perceptron (PPN), Random Forest (RF), Gaussian Naive Bayes (GaussianNB), and k-Nearest Neighbor (KNN). The datasets used are the Training dataset-B1 and Training dataset-B2 and the corresponding Testing dataset-C1 and Testing dataset-C2. The evaluation metrics are accuracy, precision, recall, and F1. Table 3 shows the comparison results using different dataset settings. By setting *k*=5, an accuracy of 0.9222, a precision of 0.8859, a recall of 0.8657, and an F1 of 0.8753 are achieved as the best performance compared to five baseline methods. By setting *k*=10, our method also obtains the highest performance on all evaluation metrics compared to the baselines. Particularly, the higher precision and F1 are more preferable since our expectation is the return of more correct answers to users to improve user satisfaction.

Table 3. The comparison of our answer selection method with baseline methods using different *k* settings.

Setting	Methods	Accuracy	Precision	Recall	F1
k=5	KNN	0.8052	0.6820	0.5679	0.5746
	GaussianNB	0.7383	0.6980	0.8026	0.6956
	RF	0.8301	0.7339	0.7097	0.7203
	SVM	0.8373	0.7513	0.8029	0.7706
	PPN	0.8842	0.8129	0.8540	0.8305
	Our method	**0.9222**	**0.8859**	**0.8657**	**0.8753**
k=10	KNN	0.9032	0.8076	0.5258	0.5247
	RF	0.9106	0.7523	0.7277	0.7391
	GaussianNB	0.8956	0.7197	0.7737	0.7422
	SVM	0.9154	0.7642	0.8399	0.7951
	PPN	0.9271	0.7897	**0.8633**	0.8206
	Our method	**0.9651**	**0.9415**	0.8559	**0.8929**

CONCLUSIONS

Aimed at assisting diabetes patients or populations at high risk of diabetes to have long-term health management, this paper designed and developed a mobile-based question-answering and early warning system, Dia-AID. The system assists users in providing diabetes information and monitoring their health status through diabetes question answering, risk assessment, and health record management.

We evaluated two essential models in our system and compared them with five baseline methods on various metrics. The results showed that our methods achieved the best performance compared with the baseline methods.

Data Availability

The diabetes data is not made publicly available.

Conflicts of Interest

There are no conflicts of interest in this paper.

Acknowledgments

The work was substantially supported by a grant from the National Natural Science Foundation of China (no. 61772146), the Science and Technology Plan of Guangzhou (no. 201804010296), the Innovative School Project in Higher Education of Guangdong Province (no. YQ2015062), and Scientific Research Innovation Team in Department of Education of Guangdong Province (no. 2017KCXTD013).

REFERENCES

1. H. Yoo and K. Chung, "PHR Based Diabetes Index Service Model Using Life Behavior Analysis," Wireless Personal Communications, vol. 93, no. 1, pp. 161–174, 2017.
2. P. Zimmet, K. G. M. M. Alberti, and J. Shaw, "Global and societal implications of the diabetes epidemic," Nature, vol. 414, no. 6865, pp. 782–787, 2001.
3. F. Aguiree and A. Brown, "IDF Diabetes Atlas," in IDF Diabetes Atlas - sixth Edition, International Diabetes Federation, Belgium, 2013.
4. P. Z. Zimmet, D. J. Magliano, W. H. Herman, and J. E. Shaw, "Diabetes: a 21st century challenge," The Lancet Diabetes & Endocrinology, vol. 2, no. 1, pp. 56–64, 2014.
5. J. G. Melton, IDF Diabetes Atlas, 8th edition, 2017.
6. G. Roglic, "WHO Global report on diabetes: a summary," International Journal of Noncommunicable Diseases, vol. 1, no. 1, pp. 3–8, 2016.
7. E.-Y. Jung, J. Kim, K.-Y. Chung, and D. K. Park, "Mobile healthcare application with EMR interoperability for diabetes patients," Cluster Computing, vol. 17, no. 3, pp. 871–880, 2014.
8. World Health Organization, "Global Report on Diabetes," Isbn, vol. 978, article 88, 2016.
9. J. Beck, D. A. Greenwood, L. Blanton et al., "2017 National Standards for Diabetes Self-Management Education and Support," Diabetes Care, article dci170025, 2017.
10. A. D. American Diabetes Association, "4. Lifestyle Management," Diabetes Care, vol. 40, no. Suppl. 1, pp. S33–S43, 2017.
11. Diabetes Prevention Program Research Group, "10-year follow-up of diabetes incidence and weight loss in the Diabetes Prevention Program Outcomes Study," The Lancet, vol. 374, no. 9702, pp. 1677–1686, 2009.
12. K. Chung, J.-C. Kim, and R. C. Park, "Knowledge-based health service considering user convenience using hybrid Wi-Fi P2P," Information Technology and Management, vol. 17, no. 1, pp. 67–80, 2016.
13. Susannah Fox and Maeve Duggan, "Health Online 2013 | Pew Research Center," National survey by the Pew Research Center's Internet and American Life Project, 2013. http://www.pewinternet.org/2013/01/15/health-online-2013/.

14. P. Krebs and D. T. Duncan, "Health app use among US mobile phone owners: a national survey," JMIR mHealth and uHealth, vol. 3, no. 4, article e101, 2015.
15. S. Chavez, D. Fedele, Y. Guo et al., "Mobile apps for the management of diabetes," Diabetes Care, vol. 40, no. 10, pp. e145–e146, 2017.
16. K. Waki, H. Fujita, Y. Uchimura et al., "DialBetics: Smartphone-based self-management for type 2 diabetes patients," Journal of Diabetes Science and Technology, vol. 6, no. 4, pp. 983–985, 2012.
17. P. P. Committee and A. Classification, "Standards of medical care in diabetes—2010," Diabetes Care, vol. 33, no. S1, pp. S11–S61, 2010.
18. D. Demner-Fushman and J. Lin, "Answer extraction, semantic clustering, and extractive summarization for clinical question answering," in Proceedings of the 21st International Conference on Computational Linguistics and 44th Annual Meeting of the Association for Computational Linguistics, COLING/ACL 2006, pp. 841–848, July 2006.
19. S. Schulz, M. Honeck, and U. Hahn, "Biomedical text retrieval in languages with a complex morphology," in Proceedings of the meeting of the association for computational linguistics, vol. 3, pp. 61–68, July 2002.
20. W. R. Hersh, M. Katherine Crabtree, D. H. Hickam et al., "Factors associated with success in searching MEDLINE and applying evidence to answer clinical questions," Journal of the American Medical Informatics Association , vol. 9, no. 3, pp. 283–293, 2002.
21. J. W. Ely, J. A. Osheroff, M. H. Ebell et al., "Analysis of questions asked by family doctors regarding patient care," BMJ, vol. 319, no. 7206, pp. 358–361, 1999.
22. J. W. Ely, "Obstacles to answering doctors' questions about patient care with evidence: qualitative study," BMJ, vol. 324, no. 7339, pp. 710–710.
23. G. R. Bergus, C. S. Randall, S. D. Sinift, and D. M. Rosenthal, "Does the structure of clinical questions affect the outcome of curbside consultations with specialty colleagues?" Archives of Family Medicine, vol. 9, no. 6, pp. 541–547, 2000.
24. P. Sondhi, P. Raj, V. V. Kumar, and A. Mittal, "Question processing and clustering in INDOC: A biomedical question answering system," Eurasip Journal on Bioinformatics and Systems Biology, vol.

2007, 2007.

25. E. M. Voorhees, “The TREC question answering track,” Natural Language Engineering, vol. 7, no. 4, pp. 361–378, 2001.
26. T. Hao, W. Xie, C. Chen, and Y. Shen, “Systematic comparison of question target classification taxonomies towards question answering,” Communications in Computer and Information Science, vol. 568, pp. 131–143, 2015.
27. S. J. Athenikos and H. Han, “Biomedical question answering: A survey,” Computer Methods and Programs in Biomedicine, vol. 99, no. 1, pp. 1–24, 2010.
28. D. Mollá and J. L. Vicedo, “Question answering in restricted domains: An overview,” Computational Linguistics, vol. 33, no. 1, pp. 41–61, 2007.
29. A. Mishra and S. K. Jain, “A survey on question answering systems with classification,” Journal of King Saud University - Computer and Information Sciences, vol. 28, no. 3, pp. 345–361, 2016.
30. H. Yu and C. Sable, “Being Erlang Shen: Identifying Answerable Questions,” in Proceedings of the Nineteenth International Joint Conference on Artificial Intelligence on Knowledge and Reasoning for Answering Questions, 2005.
31. F. Rinaldi, J. Dowdall, G. Schneider, and A. Persidis, “Answering questions in the genomics domain,” in Proceedings of the ACL 2004 Workshop on Question Answering in Restricted Domains, pp. 46–53, 2004.
32. A. M. Cohen, J. Yang, S. Fisher, B. Roark, and W. R. Hersh, “The OHSU Biomedical Question Answering System Framework,” in Proceedings of the Sixteenth Text Retrieval Conference, 2007.
33. A. B. Abacha and P. Zweigenbaum, “Medical question answering: Translating medical questions into SPARQL queries,” in Proceedings of the 2nd ACM SIGHIT International Health Informatics Symposium, IHI’12, pp. 41–50, January 2012.
34. A. Marginean, “Question answering over biomedical linked data with Grammatical Framework,” Journal of Web Semantics: Science, Services and Agents on the World Wide Web, vol. 8, no. 4, pp. 565–580, 2017.
35. A. Ben Abacha and P. Zweigenbaum, “MEANS: A medical question-answering system combining NLP techniques and semantic Web

technologies," Information Processing & Management, vol. 51, no. 5, pp. 570–594, 2015.

36. R. M. Terol, P. Martínez-Barco, and M. Palomar, "A knowledge based method for the medical question answering problem," Computers in Biology and Medicine, vol. 37, no. 10, pp. 1511–1521, 2007.
37. H. Zhang, T. W. S. Chow, and Q. M. J. Wu, "Organizing Books and Authors by Multilayer SOM," IEEE Transactions on Neural Networks and Learning Systems, vol. 27, no. 12, pp. 2537–2550, 2016.
38. H. Zhang, S. Wang, X. Xu, T. W. Chow, and Q. M. Wu, "Tree2Vector: Learning a Vectorial Representation for Tree-Structured Data," IEEE Transactions on Neural Networks and Learning Systems, pp. 1–15, 2018.
39. H. Zhang, S. Wang, Z. Mingbo, X. Xu, and Y. Ye, "Locality Reconstruction Models for Book Representation," IEEE Transactions on Knowledge and Data Engineering, 2018.
40. K.-Y. Chung, J. Yoo, and K. J. Kim, "Recent trends on mobile computing and future networks," Personal and Ubiquitous Computing, vol. 18, no. 3, pp. 489–491, 2014.
41. S.-K. Kang, K.-Y. Chung, and J.-H. Lee, "Development of head detection and tracking systems for visual surveillance," Personal and Ubiquitous Computing, vol. 18, no. 3, pp. 515–522, 2014.
42. H. Jung, K.-Y. Chung, and Y.-H. Lee, "Decision supporting method for chronic disease patients based on mining frequent pattern tree," Multimedia Tools and Applications, vol. 74, no. 20, pp. 8979–8991, 2015.
43. D. Han, M. Lee, and S. Park, "THE-MUSS: Mobile u-health service system," Computer Methods and Programs in Biomedicine, vol. 97, no. 2, pp. 178–188, 2010.
44. S. Wild, G. Roglic, A. Green, R. Sicree, and H. King, "Global prevalence of diabetes: estimates for the year 2000 and projections for 2030," Diabetes Care, vol. 27, no. 5, pp. 1047–1053, 2004.
45. M. E. Cox and D. Edelman, "Tests for screening and diagnosis of type 2 diabetes," Clinical Diabetes, vol. 27, no. 4, pp. 132–138, 2009.
46. G. Danaei, M. M. Finucane, Y. Lu et al., "National, regional, and global trends in fasting plasma glucose and diabetes prevalence since 1980: systematic analysis of health examination surveys and epidemiological studies with 370 country-years and 2·7 million participants," The

Lancet, vol. 378, no. 9785, pp. 31–40, 2011.

47. R. A. Bailey, Y. Wang, V. Zhu, and M. F. Rupnow, "Chronic kidney disease in US adults with type 2 diabetes: an updated national estimate of prevalence based on kidney disease: improving Global Outcomes (KDIGO) staging," BMC Research Notes, vol. 7, article 415, 2014.
48. P.-J. Lin, D. M. Kent, A. Winn, J. T. Cohen, and P. J. Neumann, "Multiple chronic conditions in type 2 diabetes mellitus: prevalence and consequences," The American Journal of Managed Care, vol. 21, no. 1, pp. e23–e34, 2015.
49. M. L. Tracey, M. Gilmartin, K. O'Neill et al., "Epidemiology of diabetes and complications among adults in the Republic of Ireland 1998–2015: a systematic review and meta-analysis," BMC Public Health, vol. 16, article 132, no. 1, 2016.
50. L. Yang, J. Shao, Y. Bian et al., "Prevalence of type 2 diabetes mellitus among inland residents in China (2000–2014): A meta-analysis," Journal of Diabetes Investigation, vol. 7, no. 6, pp. 845–852, 2016.
51. K. Iglay, H. Hannachi, P. J. Howie et al., "Prevalence and co-prevalence of comorbidities among patients with type 2 diabetes mellitus," Current Medical Research and Opinion, vol. 32, no. 7, pp. 1243–1252, 2016.
52. P. Zimmet, K. G. Alberti, D. J. Magliano, and P. H. Bennett, "Diabetes mellitus statistics on prevalence and mortality: Facts and fallacies," Nature Reviews Endocrinology, vol. 12, no. 10, pp. 616–622, 2016.
53. I. Dedov, M. Shestakova, M. M. Benedetti, D. Simon, I. Pakhomov, and G. Galstyan, "Prevalence of type 2 diabetes mellitus (T2DM) in the adult Russian population (NATION study)," Diabetes Research and Clinical Practice, vol. 115, pp. 90–95, 2016.
54. K. Waki, H. Fujita, Y. Uchimura et al., "DialBetics: A novel smartphone-based self-management support system for type 2 diabetes patients," Journal of Diabetes Science and Technology, vol. 8, no. 2, pp. 209–215, 2014.
55. T. Hao, H. Liu, and C. Weng, "Valx: A system for extracting and structuring numeric lab test comparison statements from text," Methods of Information in Medicine, vol. 55, no. 3, pp. 266–275, 2016.
56. T. Hao, W. Xie, and F. Xu, "A wordnet expansion-based approach for question targets identification and classification," Lecture Notes

in Computer Science (including subseries Lecture Notes in Artificial Intelligence and Lecture Notes in Bioinformatics): Preface, vol. 9427, pp. 333–344, 2015.

57. T. Hao, W. Xie, Q. Wu, H. Weng, and Y. Qu, "Leveraging question target word features through semantic relation expansion for answer type classification," Knowledge-Based Systems, vol. 133, pp. 43–52, 2017.
58. T. Hao, D. Hu, L. Wenyin, and Q. Zeng, "Semantic patterns for user-interactive question answering," Concurrency and Computation: Practice and Experience, vol. 20, no. 7, pp. 783–799, 2008.
59. Z. M. Juan, "An effective similarity measurement for FAQ question answering system," in Proceedings of the International Conference on Electrical and Control Engineering, ICECE 2010, pp. 4638–4641, June 2010.
60. T. Hao and Y. Qu, "QSem: A novel question representation framework for question matching over accumulated question-answer data," Journal of Information Science, vol. 42, no. 5, pp. 583–596, 2016.
61. S. Deerwester, S. T. Dumais, G. W. Furnas, T. K. Landauer, and R. Harshman, "Indexing by latent semantic analysis," Journal of the Association for Information Science and Technology, vol. 41, no. 6, pp. 391–407, 1990.
62. H. L. Wang and H. Y. Xi, "Chinese synonyms toolkit," 2018, https://github.com/huyingxi/Synonyms.

CHAPTER

18

Research on New English Mobile Teaching Mode under the Impact of Mobile Internet Age

Dan Xu

Faculty of International Studies, Henan Normal University, Xinxiang, China

ABSTRACT

The rapid development of mobile technology has provided a new opportunity for the reform of English listening and speaking teaching mode. Mobile technology enables learners to use mobile devices to learn anywhere, anytime. Mobile technology assists language learning with unparalleled advantages in extending learning time and space, enriching learning interactions, and improving learning efficiency. This paper introduces the concept and characteristics of mobile learning and smartphones, the theoretical basis of

Citation: Xu, D. (2019), "Research on New English Mobile Teaching Mode under the Impact of Mobile Internet Age".Open Journal of Social Sciences, vol. 7, pp. 109-117. doi:10.4236/jss.2019.75008.

mobile learning and related technical support, through the feasibility analysis of mobile phone-based mobile learning in supporting English teaching. At the same time, a new English teaching mode under the background of mobile internet is summarized and designed. It provides a realistic basis for the design of mobile learning teaching mode with smartphone as the terminal, which adds practical application cases for mobile learning theory, solves the problem of lack of contextual interaction in traditional English teaching, and limitations of learning time and place.

Keywords: Mobile Network, Big Data, English Mobile Teaching, Mobile Learning

INTRODUCTION

Currently, mobile technology has led to a new learning style of mobile learning. Mobile learning has changed the way people learn, from formal learning to informal learning, providing a new form of lifelong learning. Today, there are a variety of terminal types that support mobile learning, such as electronic dictionaries, PDAs, notebooks, and mobile phones. The mobile phone has high holding rate and strong integration, and has the unparalleled advantages of other learning devices. In particular, it's light and easy to provide good hardware support for mobile learning. People use mobile phones to learn, get information, and promote personal development. In recent years, more and more researchers have proved that mobile learning is effective [1] [2] [3] . With the coming era of 5G network, mobile learning brings more broad prospects and hopes to education. The rapid development of mobile technology has provided a new opportunity for the reform of English listening and speaking teaching mode. Mobile technology enables learners to use mobile devices to learn anywhere, anytime. Mobile technology assists language learning with unparalleled advantages in expanding learning time and space, enriching learning interactions, and improving learning efficiency [4] .

OVERVIEW OF MOBILE LEARNING

Mobile terminal equipment has its particularity, and the mobile learning method also shows its complexity. Therefore, the development of mobile-based English mobile learning software is inseparable from the support of relevant theories. The following will analyze the relevant theoretical basis and enlightenment from four aspects: informal learning theory, mixed learning theory, activity learning theory and constructivism theory [5] .

Informal Learning

"Formal study" mainly refers to academic education in schools and continuing education after participating in work. "Informal learning" refers to the time and place of informal learning, which conveys and infiltrates knowledge through non-teaching social interactions, self-initiated, self-regulating, self-responsible learning by learners. Informal learning, as opposed to formal learning, is also called implicit learning [6] . In view of the obvious characteristics of informal communication, such as communication, students should learn from outside the classroom. In addition to mobile-based mobile learning methods, in order to improve the enthusiasm and participation of students in communication, they should be given Provide an environment that is easy to communicate. In this environment, knowledge and sharing can be achieved through communication and communication between students and students, between students and teachers, and between students and experts. That is to say, learners break the tradition of personally creating knowledge meanings before, and establish a new model of learners to jointly create knowledge meaning, which is one of the most prominent features of mobile-based mobile learning.

Mixed Learning Theory

Combining the advantages of modern E-Learning with the traditional way of learning is mixed learning. Students are the main body of learning, and teachers inspire, guide and supervise this learning in a timely manner. Therefore, students' enthusiasm, initiative and creativity also play an equally important role. In order to achieve good learning outcomes, it is necessary to combine the two to make them mutually influence and complement each other.

The current hybrid learning method is increasingly required to be combined with previous traditional methods, driven by equal network technologies. To be precise: it is to combine the creation, proactive and other characteristics of the students as the main body of learning with the inspiration, guidance and supervision of the teachers, and to achieve the best learning objectives through the complementarity of the two. The root cause, the specific requirements for solving and satisfying different problems in different ways is the essence of mixed learning, and it also needs to satisfy the different information and media delivery teaching methods to obtain the maximum return with the least effort.

Activity Learning Theory

Learning in practice is the basic concept of activity learning theory, that is, learning is a practical activity in which learners can solve a problem by mutual help, mutual learning, discussion and sharing under the leadership of experts. In addition, the theory of activity learning also points out that the process of learning is not the dissemination and acceptance of knowledge, but a purposeful and proactive practice, and a purposeful and actionable thinking activity. Because thinking and action exist in complementarity and interdependence, learning this action and conscious ideology are complementary and interdependent. Activity learning theory takes the problem as one of the main factors affecting the learning effect of the activity, emphasizing the important role of the problem in the activity learning. The theory holds that only those who are closely related to the life of the learner can bring the learner into the "recent development zone". The problem is that it is possible to stimulate the learner's interest in learning, so that the learner can actively find a solution to the problem and ultimately acquire knowledge [7] .

Constructivist Learning Theory

Mobile learning takes constructivist learning as its main underlying theory. The point is that students must be proactive in acquiring knowledge and creating their own knowledge structures, rather than accepting what the teacher transmits. Therefore, the student's learning process is an independent, active learning and personal behavior of creating knowledge, rather than a passive acceptance process. In addition, the external information has no specific meaning, and the realization of its meaning is based on the students' learning experience of new and old knowledge, and is formed by the role of both.

From this point of view, students are the main body of learning, to mobilize the enthusiasm of the main body of learning, so that they are actively learning to be the focus of the entire teaching activities [8] . The main body of constructivism is the teacher, and the central point is the student. In the process of students constructing the meaning of knowledge, the teacher plays a great role in promoting, and the students are the builders of the meaning of knowledge. Therefore, the process of student learning is not to inculcate knowledge and information, and the teacher's teaching process is not to spread and instill knowledge [9] .

NEW ENGLISH TEACHING MODE UNDER THE BACKGROUND OF MOBILE INTERNET

This chapter will elaborate on the new English teaching mode proposed in this paper from the design of teaching mode, the implementation steps of teaching mode and the formative evaluation of teaching mode.

The Design of New English Teaching Mode

"Mobile English Supported College English Mixed Listening and Speaking Teaching Mode" is a mixed teaching model based on the interaction between extracurricular self-learning and in-class interactive learning. Simply put, this model can be divided into three stages: pre-class preparation, in-class practice and after-school exploration, to achieve the following five dimensions [10] :

1) A mix of formal learning methods and extracurricular informal learning methods.

This model extends some links of oral learning to extracurricular activities to make up for the lack of limited teaching time in oral class. Students learn foreign cultural knowledge related to oral learning content through extracurricular informal learning, and improve accuracy and fluency through repeated listening and oral practice after class. Extracurricular informal learning is a useful supplement to formal learning in the class. Students can not only prepare well before class, but also carry out higher level learning after class [11] .

2) A mix of instructor-led teaching and student-autonomous learning in class.

In the formal learning phase of the class, it is necessary to learn the language knowledge related to listening and speaking skills. In the early part of the classroom teaching time, the teacher teaches language knowledge, including vocabulary, grammar, pronunciation, intonation and so on. In addition to the foreign cultural knowledge that the students have contacted before class, the content of the listening and speaking of this lesson will be explained in detail. In the latter part of the classroom teaching time, students learn independently through group interaction and exercise listening and speaking skills in interaction. According to the actual needs of the learning content, the teacher flexibly arranges the teaching and learning methods of the classroom.

3) A mixture of teacher dominance and student subjectivity in classroom teaching.

In the classroom teaching stage, both the teacher's leading role and the student's cognitive subject role should be fully reflected. Whether it is the language knowledge teaching in the previous paragraph or the language skills training in the latter stage, the teacher is the identity of the instructor and organizer. Through the scaffolding teaching strategy, the students are gradually guided from the learning of language knowledge to the acquisition of language skills, and help students. Master the learning strategy. As a cognitive subject, students should fully participate in the classroom learning, abandon the passive acceptance of the state of knowledge under the traditional teaching mode, and carry out meaningful learning in the interaction. As mentioned in the social and cultural theory mentioned above, "participation" itself is a kind of learning, which is the process of students actively constructing.

4) A mixture of traditional and new media in the process of teaching and learning.

The teaching media in the mixed teaching mode has diversified characteristics. Teachers and students choose appropriate media to learn according to their actual needs, such as voice room, audio-visual materials, multimedia computer, computer network, mobile phone, laptop computer, learning machine and other media types, so as to realize the mixing of traditional media and new media.

5) A mixture of English language knowledge and English listening and speaking skills in teaching content.

This model breaks the drawbacks of traditional classroom emphasizing knowledge over skills, realizing that both language knowledge and listening and speaking skills are equally important. Full language knowledge learning is a necessary condition for the development of listening and speaking skills. In turn, the improvement of listening and speaking skills can promote students' deeper understanding of language knowledge, foster the habit and sense of thinking in English in listening and speaking, and improve their reading and writing abilities [12] [13] [14] .

Implementation Steps of the New English Teaching Model

The proposed new English teaching model is implemented in three steps:

1) Pre-class preparation stage: teachers create situations to stimulate students' interest in learning.

Make full use of the convenience of mobile learning, so that students can frequently access the information related to the content of the classroom to prepare for the pre-study, to lay the foundation for teachers in the classroom learning stage and students to actively learn.

2) In-class learning phase: students learn language and language skills by experiencing situations.

In the classroom teaching, we should break the traditional single teaching method, and through the integration of multimedia technology and mobile technology and English listening and speaking courses, change the presentation method, teaching method and learning interaction mode of teaching content, and rely on powerful information technology cognitive tools. And a wealth of learning resources to promote students' ability to solve complex problems in the real context and improve the overall quality, thereby improving the effectiveness of the English classroom. At the right time, teachers instruct students to use self-study and self-study on mobile devices such as English learning machines, mobile phones and audio players. When they need feedback, they can use mobile phone text messages to grasp the effect of classroom real-time teaching, and adjust teaching in time. Students can also use your mobile phone to check the information when appropriate. Throughout the classroom teaching stage, teachers should adopt a scaffolding teaching strategy, gradually transition from the lecturer to the mentors, monitors and other identities, and transfer the subjective rights of the classroom learning to the students, so that the students can experience the language and positive thinking in the context. Learn meaningfully. At this stage, there are both transfer-receiving and student-dependent learning, as well as providing conditions for cooperative learning among students.

3) Post-class expansion: students interpret the situation and improve their communication skills.

Through organized learning in the classroom, students have already had a certain degree of cognition and exercise in the language knowledge of this unit, and have a more thorough understanding of language knowledge in light of the cultural background.

In the classroom teaching, the teacher also trained the listening strategies and oral strategies for the students' difficulties in listening and speaking. It can be said that after the class preparation and classroom learning, the students have basically formed a cognition of the unit content, and improved the accuracy of the hearing and the proficiency of the spoken language. But this is not the end of learning content. The purpose of language learning is to use it in language clearing. Therefore, after the class, the teacher designs the task situation, arranges the communication tasks that need to be completed cooperatively, enables the students to use the language in life, explores in the cooperation, and gradually improves the language communication ability in the deductive situation.

Formative Evaluation of New English Teaching Model

The evaluation of English courses should be based on the objectives and requirements of the curriculum standards to implement effective monitoring of the entire process and results. In college English listening and speaking, evaluation should effectively stimulate students' enthusiasm for learning, so that they can experience progress and success in the process of oral English learning, build self-confidence, adjust learning strategies, and promote the comprehensive development of comprehensive language. At the same time, the evaluation should enable teachers to obtain feedback on teaching, reflect on and adjust their teaching behavior, and continuously improve the level of education and teaching. The evaluation should also enable schools to keep abreast of the implementation of curriculum standards, improve teaching management, and promote the continuous improvement and development of English courses. Effectively developing formative evaluation has three major advantages, which can motivate students to learn continuously; it can help students reflect and regulate the learning process, learn how to learn; provide teachers with feedback information for teachers to reflect and adjust teaching behavior [15] .

THE DEVELOPMENT TREND OF MOBILE LEARNING IN FUTURE EDUCATION

In the modern society, the rapid development of science and technology is our focus. In the past, the use of paper to learn is no longer able to adapt to today's social development. At present, various jobs have basically realized digital office, and school education has also introduced the teaching information equipment such as multimedia intelligent voice system, but the current teaching mode still relies on the traditional teacher-led teaching form, which has not been realized. a breakthrough in the true sense. The emergence of the concept of mobile learning has broken the inherent thinking of teaching. The characteristic of mobile learning is that it can not only adapt to the traditional teaching mode, but also make good use of its own characteristics combined with advanced technology to complement the traditional teaching mode. At the same time, the emergence of mobile learning has subverted the learner's previous learning style and inherent learning thinking. At present, educational researchers continue to pay attention to this learning style, and mobile learning has become a hot topic in the field of education [16] .The emergence of mobile learning is very good to cater to the problems that arise in today's society. People need to continue learning when they leave the school, and the quality of teaching in some educational institutions cannot be guaranteed. Mobile learning can connect all the learning resources of these teaching resources. To form a shared resource that spans time and space, which is a good complement to the current teaching system. Moreover, this flexible mobile learning method enables learners to choose their own learning content learning time and place, etc., and enhances the development direction of personalized learning mode. One of the advantages of mobile learning is the ability to disseminate learning knowledge as a foundational tool using a variety of modern, portable, portable devices. Nowadays, with the widespread popularity of smartphones in China, the advantages of convenient carrying and versatility have become the most suitable terminal equipment for mobile learning, and the related technical support of smart phones is constantly improving. It is believed that with the realization of wireless network technology and the continuous improvement of production technology innovation by various manufacturers, the functions of smart phones will be more perfect, and mobile learning based on smart phones will usher in a promising future [17] [18] .

CONCLUSION

This paper starts with the concept and characteristics of mobile learning, through the feasibility analysis of mobile phone-based mobile learning in supporting English teaching, and concludes a new English teaching mode under the background of mobile internet. It provides a realistic basis for the design of mobile learning teaching mode with smart phone as the terminal, which adds practical application cases for mobile learning theory, solves the problem of lack of contextual interaction in traditional English teaching, and limitations of learning time and place. At the same time, it discusses and prospects the application and development of mobile learning in various fields in the future. Mobile learning is still a new form of learning, and learning with a smartphone is a new learning. At present, the teaching mode of mobile learning is still in the initial exploration period, and there is no mature teaching mode. The teaching mode of specific subjects needs to be summarized and explored in future practice.

Conflicts of Interest

The author declares no conflicts of interest regarding the publication of this paper.

REFERENCES

1. Philip,T.M.(2017)LearningwithMobileTechnologies.Communications of the ACM, 60, 34-36. https://doi.org/10.1145/2976735
2. Tesoriero, R., Gallud, J.A. and Lozano, M. (2014) Enhancing Visitors' Experience in Art Museums Using Mobile Technologies. Information Systems Frontiers, 16, 303-327. https://doi.org/10.1007/s10796-012-9345-1
3. Mosalanejad, L., Najafipour, S. and Dastpak, M. (2013) Is the Mobile Based Learning Can Be Effective in Academic Learning? A Study to Check If Mobile-Based Learning Is Desirable in Presenting Educational Workshops. Turkish Online Journal of Distance Education, 14, 155-163.
4. Jung, H.J. (2015) Fostering an English Teaching Environment: Factors Influencing English as a Foreign Language Teachers' Adoption of Mobile Learning. Informatics in Education, 14, 219-241. https://doi.org/10.15388/infedu.2015.13
5. Shuang, H., Dennen, V.P. and Li, M. (2017) Influential Factors for Mobile Learning Acceptance among Chinese Users. Educational Technology Research & Development, 65, 101-123. https://doi.org/10.1007/s11423-016-9465-2
6. Callanan, M., Cervantes, C. and Loomis, M. (2011) Informal Learning. Wiley Interdisciplinary Reviews Cognitive Science, 2, 646-655. https://doi.org/10.1002/wcs.143
7. Arnseth, H.C. (2008) Activity Theory and Situated Learning Theory: Contrasting Views of Educational Practice. Pedagogy Culture & Society, 16, 289-302.https://doi.org/10.1080/14681360802346663
8. Kocadere, S.A. and Ozgen, D. (2012) Assessment of Basic Design Course in Terms of Constructivist Learning Theory. Procedia—Social and Behavioral Sciences, 51, 115-119. https://doi.org/10.1016/j.sbspro.2012.08.128
9. Oz, H. (2015) An Investigation of Preservice English Teachers' Perceptions of Mobile Assisted Language Learning. English Language Teaching, 8, 22-34.https://doi.org/10.5539/elt.v8n2p22
10. Zhong, S., Yao, X., You, J., et al. (2018) Detecting the Correlation between Mobile Learning Behavior and Personal Characteristics among Elementary School Students. Interactive Learning Environments, 26, 1023-1038.https://doi.org/10.1080/10494820.2018.1428633

11. Jones, S.K. (2015) An Exploration of Band Students' Experiences with Informal Learning. Bulletin of the Council for Research in Music Education, No. 206, 61-79.https://doi.org/10.5406/bulcouresmusedu.206.0061
12. Damelang, A. and Kloß, G. (2013) Poverty and the Social Participation of Young People—An Analysis of Poverty-Related Withdrawal Mechanisms. Journal for Labour Market Research, 46, 321-333. https://doi.org/10.1007/s12651-013-0148-8
13. Tayebinik, M. and Puteh, M. (2012) Mobile Learning to Support Teaching English as a Second Language. Social Science Electronic Publishing, 3, 56-62.
14. Che, P.C., Lin, H.Y., Jang, H.C., et al. (2011) A Study of English Mobile Learning Applications at National Chengchi University. International Journal of Distance Education Technologies, 7, 38-60.
15. Liu, M., Navarrete, C., Maradiegue, E., et al. (2014) Mobile Learning and English Language Learners: A Case Study of Using iPod Touch as a Teaching and Learning Tool. Journal of Interactive Learning Research, 25, 373-403.
16. 16. Paledi, V.N. and Alexander, P.M. (2017) Actor-Network Theory to Depict Context Sensitive M-Learning Readiness in Higher Education. Electronic Journal of Information Systems in Developing Countries, 83, 1-26. https://doi.org/10.1002/j.1681-4835.2017.tb00619.x
17. Campbell, K., Taylor, V. and Douglas, S. (2017) Effectiveness of Online Cancer Education for Nurses and Allied Health Professionals; a Systematic Review Using Kirkpatrick Evaluation Framework. Journal of Cancer Education, 34, 339-356.https://doi.org/10.1007/s13187-017-1308-2
18. Peters, M.A., Jandric, P. and Hayes, S. (2018) The Curious Promise of Educationalising Technological Unemployment: What Can Places of Learning Really Do about the Future of Work? Educational Philosophy & Theory, 51, 242-254.

INDEX

A

Academic education 417
Acquisition 232, 233, 236, 242, 243, 245
Activity learning theory 416, 418
Aestheticism 280
Affinity propagation clustering method 350
Analytic schema 85, 89, 107, 114
Application dependent 3, 5, 6, 7, 10
Application domain 4, 7, 15
Arithmetic operation 207, 209, 216, 220
Arithmetic series 290
Artificial intelligence 52
Attention-based neural network 333, 336, 341
Authenticity 232, 244
Automatic caption 286, 287
Automatic Grammar Checker 286
Automatic lexicon 305
Axioms 205, 214

B

Backtracking 292
Benchmarking 251, 261, 264
Bert Model 69
Bibliometric analysis 351, 352, 353, 381
Big data 19, 20, 44
Binary classification 66, 73
Bipolar dimensions 308
Body Mass Index (BMI) 393
Brainstorming 214
Business incubator 352, 382
Business process management 118

C

Calibration 296
Capitalism 20, 45, 49
Chronic diseases 387, 388
Cinematic narrative technique 281
Cloze-style 333, 336, 337
Cloze-style reading comprehension 333, 336, 337
Cluster analysis 278, 281, 282
Coefficient 27, 28, 44
Cognitive effort 212
Cognitive load theory 29
Cognitive skill 242, 245
Coherence constraint (CC) 12
Coherence rule (CR) 12
Comma separated value (CSV) 251
Common high-frequency 277
Communication medium 211
Communication system 119
Communicative competences 232
Composite attribute 5, 6, 7, 8, 9, 10, 12
Computational agents 163, 164, 167, 178
Computational Context Modeling Diagram 161, 165, 182
Computational efficiency 312
Computational power 67
Computational vector 280
Computer aided language learning 286
Computer department 15
Computer language 288
Computer scientists 85
Conceptualization 52, 53
Connectivity 287
Constructivism 416, 418
Constructivism theory 416
Constructor 56
Context adaptation 164, 168, 169, 170, 172, 173, 174, 176, 177, 178, 179
Context-aware application 168
Context-awareness 160, 179
Context Management Service 161
Context Modeling Profile 162
Contextual representation 336, 337, 338, 339
Convolutional architecture network 341
Convolutional neural network (CNN) 275
Cosine distance 317
Creative language 64, 65, 75
Cultural quality 344

D

Database conceptual model 53
Database extraction process 254
Database requester 7
Database value 256
Data management 388, 390, 393, 399, 401
Data Mining 250
Data modeling 278
Dataset 332, 333, 334, 335, 336, 339, 340, 341, 342, 344
Decoding symbol 204
Deductive system 205
Deep Belief Network (DBN) 274
Deep Learning 274, 283, 284
Deep learning techniques 258, 264
Descriptive Adjectives 231, 244, 245
Descriptive statistics 353
Desktop configuration 260
Detractors 211
Diabetes Clinical Guidelines 394

Diabetes mellitus 388, 392, 393, 394, 413
Diachronic manner 204
Diastolic hypertension 394, 399, 401
Dictionary construction 287
Dimensionality 277
Dimensional Vector Model 280, 281
Dissemination 418
Distributed Representation 277, 278
Document structuring 22
Domain database 11
Dynamic agent 167

E

Electronic dictionaries 7
Electronic Medical Record (EMR) 392
Emoji Predication 66, 73, 75
Emojis 66, 77, 78, 79
Emotional polarity 308, 316
Empirical languages 94
English listening 415, 416, 420, 421, 422
Enthusiasm 417, 418, 422
Episodic coordination 188, 190, 193
Episodic linguistic model 186, 187, 196

F

Feminine-nature 237, 238
Field synchronicity 204
Flexibility 314, 316
Formal conceptualization 52
Formal learning 416, 417, 419
Frequently Asked Questions (FAQs) 394

G

Gender-number-nature 233
Generalization 335
Geographical distribution 350
Geographic coordinates 172, 176, 177
Geographic visualization 350, 354, 377, 380
Google Assistant 250
Google Directions 172, 182
Grammar file 254
Grammar formalism 292
Grammar themes 231, 232, 237, 242, 244, 245
Grammatical component 236
Grammatical Context 232
Grammatical framework 391
Grammatical rule 189, 190
Grammatical structure 232, 233
Graphic symbols 66

H

Hash table 289
Healthcare 388, 389, 392, 409
Healthcare industry 117, 118, 119, 122, 152
Healthcare information systems 118
Healthcare interoperable systems 118
Health consulting service 392
Health management 387, 388, 389, 392, 393, 399, 407
Health Services Specification Project (HSSP) 118, 127
Heterogeneous data 52
Hierarchical clustering method 274, 278
Hierarchical Message Description's (HMD) 123

High-frequency 273, 274, 277, 278, 279
Human experience 239
Human immunodeficiency 351
Human-software relationship 159
Hybrid learning method 417
Hybrid sentiment 318, 319
Hyperdimensional coding 351, 381
Hyperintensionality 85
Hypermedia 51
Hyperparameter 70
Hypertext 51

I

Individual level 191
Information and Communication Theory 186
Information management 20
Inheritance relationship 5, 8, 11, 12
Interface software 118
International Diabetes Federation (IDF) 388
Interoperability 117, 118, 119, 120, 121, 122, 123, 124, 125, 127, 129, 130, 131, 134, 136, 152, 153
Irony Detection 64, 65, 66, 71, 72, 73, 75, 77, 80

J

Java profiler 261
Java Theorem Prover (JTP) 58
Java Virtual Machine 260, 261, 262

K

Knowledge Base 58, 61
Knowledge representation 53, 54

L

Language encompassing 185
Language skill 286
Language switching 351
Latent semantic 276
Learning-based model 65, 75
Learning-Language-Retention 232, 233
Learning process 242
Lexical component 242
Lexical gap 277
Lexicalization 22, 24
Lexicon 5, 6, 7, 13, 14, 15
Life science 191
Linguistic analysis 9
Linguistic context 90
Linguistic grammar 187, 190
Linguistic implementation 211
Linguistic-outline-analysis 231
Linguistic processes 186, 187, 188, 189, 190
Linguistic situation 204, 208, 212, 218, 219, 220, 221, 222, 223, 224
Linguistic-speaking 233
Linguistic standard 239
Link navigation 51
Literary connection 211
Logical analysis 83, 89, 90, 92, 99
Logical strata 91
Logistic curve 296

M

Machine reading comprehension (MC) 332
Machine translation 185, 186, 187, 189, 190, 196, 197
Macrostructure 28, 35, 36, 43, 44
Manifestations 84

Mass communication 20
Mathematical component 203, 205
Mathematical diagonal 206
Mathematical language 84
Mathematical pattern 205
Mathematical rule 206
Mathematical structure 204, 211
Measurement scale 294
Measurement Theory 293, 295
Meeting alert application 169, 171, 173, 174, 175
Memory association 189, 190
Merging function 332, 337, 339, 341, 342, 344
Microstructure 28, 44
Mixed learning theory 416
Mobile-based mobile learning 417
Mobile computing 350, 353, 355, 359, 360, 362, 364, 366, 367, 368, 369, 376, 377, 378, 379, 380, 381, 384
Mobile environment 350
Mobile internet 416, 423
Mobile learning theory 416, 423
Mobile shopping 304, 305, 306, 308, 309, 310, 311, 312, 314, 315, 316, 318, 325, 326
Mobile technology 415, 416
Mobile terminal equipment 416
Modality coordination 188
Modernism 281
Multiple-choice task 332, 333, 340
Musketeers 238
Mutual information algorithm 304

N

Native-language 232, 233, 234, 236, 244
Natural language 3, 4, 5, 6, 7, 8, 273, 274, 275, 276
Natural language deep learning process 274
Natural Language Generation systems (NLGs) 19
Natural Language Query 249, 270
Natural science 191, 192, 193
Networked computing system 350
Neural network 64, 65, 71, 75
Neuroscience 186, 198, 199
Newton algorithm 290
Next Sentence Prediction (NSP) 68
Nominal groups (NG) 3
Notation 84, 95, 103, 108

O

Object Management Group (OMG) 118, 156
Object Oriented Data Base 4
Online product 305, 318
Ontology 51, 52, 53, 54, 56, 58, 59, 60
Open innovation (OI) 352
Open software application 287
Open-source software 318
Organizational level 191

P

Pain management 392
Parameter matrix 338
Partial function 89, 98
Participating systems 72, 74
Part of Speech (POS) 251, 259
Patient administration 118, 120, 124, 129, 130
Pattern tree mining 392
Personal Health Record- (PHR-) 393
Personal philosophy 281

Phoenix 56, 57, 58
Physical science 191
Point wise mutual information (PMI) 305
Polarity contrast 67, 74
Pragmatic connection 211
Preventive management 387, 388
Primitive sentiment matrix 311, 312
Probability 292, 293, 294, 296, 297
Probability distribution 339
Problem-solving 354
Procedural memory 188, 189, 190
Programming language 85
Programming project 288
Program snippet 288
Promising technology 160
Proposed system 254, 260, 265
Public office 87

Q

Quantifier 84, 95, 101, 103, 105, 113

R

Rapid development 415, 416, 422
Reading comprehension 332
Realism 274, 280
Recent development zone 418
Reference Information Model (RIM) 120
Reference relationships 5, 6, 11
Referential expressions 22, 25
Refined Message Information Model (RMIM) 123
Relational database (RDB) 4
Research development 352, 353
Residential energy 352
Reticular dopaminergic system 188
Rhetoric 83
Robust knowledge 308
Romanticism 280
Russell's quantificational theory 87

S

Seamless communication 118
Search Engine Optimization (SEO) 26
Search Engine Results Page (SERP) 26
Second Language Acquisition (SLA) 231, 245
Self-regulating 417
Semantic analysis 3, 5
Semantic structures 20, 21, 36, 43
Semantic value 4, 5, 7, 10, 12
Semantic Web 52, 59, 61, 62, 118, 124, 127, 129, 130, 137, 154, 155
Semi-automatic generation 15
Sentence embedding 332, 337, 338, 339
Sentence-level attention 332, 333, 337, 340, 342, 343
Sentiment analysis 304, 327, 328, 329
Sentiment lexicon 304, 305, 306, 307, 308, 318, 319, 320, 321, 326, 327, 329
Sentiment matrix 311, 313, 315
Sequence prediction 351
Serialization 163, 176, 177
Service Functional Models (SFM) 120
Service Oriented Architecture (SOA) 118
Singularizer 95, 106
Smartphone 303, 304
Snippet 97

Social interactions 417
Social media 63, 64, 65, 66, 75, 76
Social network analysis 350, 354, 355, 370, 377, 380, 383
Socio- semantic coherence 21, 44
Softmax function 339
Software 159, 160, 161, 162, 164, 165, 168, 170, 171, 173, 177, 178, 179, 181, 183
Software agents 52
Software designer 165, 177
Software excellence 261
Spanish grammar 231, 232, 239, 241, 242, 244
Spanish language communication 231, 232, 237, 238, 239, 243, 245
Special Interest Group 120
Statistical translation 186, 187, 190, 193, 194, 196, 197
Stochastic gradient descent 340
Structural semantic pattern 395
Structured data query language 250
Structured Query Language (SQL) 250
Support vector machine (SVM) 306
Surface realization 22, 26
Surface structure 205, 206, 210
Sustainability 26
Syntactic 204, 207, 211, 216, 225
Syntactic translation 60

T

Technical support 416, 423
Temporal character 186, 192
Term frequency–inverse document frequency (TFIDF) 306
Text mining 352, 384
Text Retrieval Conference (TREC) 390
Tokenization 68
Training data 64, 65, 67, 75
Translation machine 189, 190
Transmitting system 118, 126
Transparent Intensional Logic (TIL) 85
Trivialization 91, 93, 95
Twitter processor 68
Typographical adjustment 22

U

Unified Medical Language System (UMLS) 389

V

Vector representation 309, 319, 332, 333
Vector Space model 275
Visual Machine 262
Vocabulary 51, 52, 53, 57, 60

W

Warning system 388, 390, 393, 394, 407
Web applications 160, 161, 163, 165, 167, 177, 178, 179
Web content 51
Web of Science (WoS) 351
Web Ontologies Language 54
Web page 26
Web Service Business Process Execution Language 162, 184
Web Service Description Language 160
Web Service Modeling Framework (WSMF) 121, 134
Web Service Modeling Ontology (WSMO) 121

Web services 160, 162, 163, 164, 167, 168, 170, 171, 172, 176, 177, 178, 179, 183
Wireless communication technology 350
Word Episodic Symbolization 186
Word normalization 68
Word representation level 341
Word segmentation 68
Word vector dimension 274, 279
World Health Organization (WHO) 388
World Wide Web Consortium (W3C) 54

Z

Zoological 186, 191, 192, 196

Printed in the United States
By Bookmasters